Psychosocial Stress

TRENDS IN THEORY AND RESEARCH

Psychosocial Stress

TRENDS IN THEORY AND RESEARCH

EDITED BY

Howard B. Kaplan

Department of Psychiatry
Baylor College of Medicine
Texas Medical Center
Houston, Texas

1983

ACADEMIC PRESS
A Subsidiary of Harcourt Brace Jovanovich, Publishers
New York   London
Paris   San Diego   San Francisco   São Paulo   Sydney   Tokyo   Toronto

ACADEMIC PRESS, INC.
111 Fifth Avenue, New York, New York 10003

United Kingdom Edition published by
ACADEMIC PRESS, INC. (LONDON) LTD.
24/28 Oval Road, London NW1 7DX

Library of Congress Cataloging in Publication Data

Psychosocial stress.

Includes index.
1. Stress (Psychology)--Addresses, essays, lectures.
2. Stress (Psychology)--Social aspects--Addresses,
essays, lectures. I. Kaplan, Howard B. [DNLM:
1. Stress. 2. Stress, Psychological 3. Life change
events. WM 172 P9746]
BF575.S75P84 1983   158   83-9969
ISBN 0-12-397560-3

PRINTED IN THE UNITED STATES OF AMERICA

83 84 85 86   9 8 7 6 5 4 3 2 1

To Diane Susan, Samuel Charles, and Rachel Esther,
who reflect or help me to attain all that I value,
and who only occasionally are a source of
psychosocial stress

Contents

PART TWO

Toward a Theoretical Synthesis

PART THREE

Methodological Issues

6. *Methodological Issues in the Study of Psychosocial Stress*

RONALD C. KESSLER

Contributors

Numbers in parentheses indicate the pages on which the authors' contributions begin.

Howard B. Kaplan (195), Department of Psychiatry, Baylor College of Medicine, Texas Medical Center, Houston, Texas 77030

Ronald C. Kessler (267), Department of Sociology, University of Michigan, Ann Arbor, Michigan 48109

Elizabeth G. Menaghan (157), Department of Sociology, The Ohio State University, Columbus, Ohio 43210

Leonard I. Pearlin (3), Human Development and Aging Program, University of California, San Francisco, California 94143

Peggy A. Thoits (33), Department of Sociology, Princeton University, Princeton, New Jersey 08544

R. Jay Turner (105), Health Care Research Unit, The University of Western Ontario, London, Ontario N6A 5B8, Canada

Preface

Research into the psychosocial basis of psychological distress has a long history in the behavioral sciences, but even a cursory examination of the pertinent literature reveals that the research focuses on a limited number of areas. The ultimate sources of psychological distress are most frequently found in both ongoing interpersonal relationships and discrete life events. The literature also suggests that the distressful effects of interpersonal role strains are mitigated by individuals' self-protective mechanisms and interpersonal support networks. Finally, the literature also reveals that research is limited by the analytic techniques available and by the absence of a general theoretical framework that would serve both to guide the analyses and to provide a basis for integrating new research findings.

With these considerations in mind, I enthusiastically accepted the invitation to organize and chair a session for the Mental Health Research Committee of the International Sociological Association at the 10th World Congress of Sociology meeting in Mexico City in August of 1982. The session was to be devoted to trends in theory and research on psychosocial stress. In planning the session I judged that what was most needed at the moment was a summary of our understanding of the psychosocial bases of psychological distress and its correlates, an illumination of important but unresolved issues, suggestions for new directions of research, an examination of the analytic techniques that might facilitate such research, and an integrating theoretical framework that might structure our perception of discrete research findings.

Four scholars associated with particular aspects of research on psychosocial stress were invited to present papers that were to be revised and expanded into contributions to the present volume. These four presentations as well as my own concluding remarks constitute the basis for five of the chapters comprising this volume. One other contribution (that dealing with coping mechanisms) was later invited to improve the coverage and cohesiveness of the volume.

The volume is divided into three parts. Part I (Chapters 1–4) considers four of the themes that dominate research on psychosocial stress. In Chapter 1, Leonard I. Pearlin examines the variety of strains experienced in the context of ordinary social roles. He notes particularly those generated by noxious or unduly demanding role requirements and those associated with interpersonal conflicts, role conflict, role captivity, and the loss, addition, or restructuring of roles. Pearlin argues that the stress-inducing nature of role strains results from their adverse effects upon two components of the self—mastery and self-esteem. When the self is threatened and injured, the person becomes vulnerable to stress. In Chapter 2, Peggy A. Thoits presents generalizations regarding the strength and nature of the associations between life events and psychological status. She draws theoretical implications from her conclusion that the association between events and psychological disturbance is due primarily to major, time-clustered, undesirable events. Like Pearlin, Thoits speculates that psychological symptoms may result from the self-relevant meanings that events have for people. The relevant meanings are lowered self-esteem and loss of self-control. In Chapter 3, R. Jay Turner provides impressive documentation, from his own work as well as the work of others, for the conclusion that emotionally supportive relationships have important implications for physical and psychological health. Like Thoits, however, Turner recognizes that the modest magnitudes of the observed relationships require consideration of the factors that combine with environmental features to produce different perceptions of social support. In agreement with the observations of the foregoing contributors, Turner suggests that the availability and perception of social support are conditioned by prior experiences and by the attitudes toward the self and the world that are the products of those experiences. In Chapter 4, Elizabeth G. Menaghan reviews the literature dealing with the determinants of various coping efforts that are more or less effective in modifying the relationship between chronic role problems and life events, on the one hand, and life stress and associated outcomes, on the other. In examining influences upon the effectiveness of coping efforts, three criteria of efficacy are proposed: reduction in emotional distress, reduction in problems, and (continuing a theme from the preceeding chapters) the maintenance of a sense of self as worthwhile and potent. In closing the discussion Menaghan offers a thoughtful agenda for future research in this area.

In Part II the treatments of the literature presented in Chapters 1–4 are considered in the context of an inclusive theoretical framework. In Chapter 5, Howard B. Kaplan presents a model centering upon mutual influences among the person's need–value system, self-disvaluing circumstances, and perceptual processes. Psychological distress and its correlates are viewed as direct outcomes of subjectively perceived self-disvaluing circumstances. This conceptual framework is presented as a device for integrating the existing body of research findings with those that may derive from future research efforts, whose promise is suggested by this model.

The successful conduct of such research depends upon the resolution of a number of strategic methodological issues. In Part III the more salient of these issues are discussed. Ronald C. Kessler (Chapter 6) describes the advantages and disadvantages of four nonexperimental research designs (normal population surveys, case-only studies, prospective case-control studies, and retrospective case-control studies). Each is considered in relation to three research problems: documenting a causal impact of strain, describing the course of adjustment to crisis, and analyzing predictors of adjustment. Criteria for choosing among the designs are presented, and the most appropriate analytical strategies for various combinations of design and research question are described.

The value of this attempt to reflect the state of the art in research on psychosocial stress with regard to substance, theory, and method is demonstrated by the extent to which it highlights lacunae in our knowledge and points to new and promising directions for the construction and empirical testing of these theories by scholars intent on understanding social and social-psychological influences upon psychological distress and its correlates.

The preparation of this volume was facilitated by theoretical formulations and empirical analyses accomplished in the course of research supported by Research Grant DA 02497 from the National Institute on Drug Abuse. I am grateful to Academic Press for constant support of this project and earlier work.

PART I

Dominant Themes in Research on Psychosocial Stress

1

Role Strains and Personal Stress

LEONARD I. PEARLIN

INTRODUCTION

In this chapter I attempt to specify and extend the notion of role strain as a potential source of personal stress. However, my interest in looking at role strain and in identifying its varieties is motivated to a considerable extent by concerns that reach beyond the conceptual boundaries of roles.

I am generally concerned, first, that researchers are not giving a deserved effort to the exploration of the social origins of stress. Looking at the total balance of work going on, one is struck by the rather limited and routine investigations of the causes of stress as compared to the active and imaginative current research into social supports and, to a lesser extent, coping. I am not at all critical of the attention presently being given these mediators of stress; on the contrary, I applaud it. What I find worrisome is that we may be directing inordinate energies toward finding the conditions that prevent or buffer stress without being commensurately energetic about learning how stress arises in the first place. If we are to achieve a reliable understanding of how the

impact of stressful conditions is mediated, we need also to identify and
to understand how they originate. Indeed, much the same can be said
with regard to the manifestations of stress. That is, if we are to understand both the origins and mediators of stress, we need also to direct
our research toward the identification of the ways in which stress can
be expressed and reflected in the functioning, feelings, and behavior of
people. As I have previously argued (Pearlin et al., 1981), the advance-
ment of our knowledge about any one of the three conceptual domains
of stress—its origins, mediators, and manifestations—depends to some
substantial degree on our knowledge of the others, for the recognition
and understanding of each depends on its relationship to the others.

In asserting that there should be more attention to the origins of
stress, I do not mean to suggest that this issue is ignored in research; on
the contrary, the sources of stress have come under frequent scrutiny.
However, the search for causes has been predominantly confined to life
events, not to the more structured and durable social and economic
antecedents of stress. By looking closely at social roles in this chapter,
therefore, I hope in some small measure to correct another imbalance
that currently exists in stress research—that created by the preoccupation with life events as precursors of stress. I would not deny what is
obvious, that life events can and do cause stress. However, I do assert
that change qua change has been overrated as an antecedent of stress.
This is becoming evident in a growing literature pointing to the quality
of the event as the determinant of whether or not it will result in stress,
not the occurrence of the event per se (Dohrenwend and Pearlin, 1982;
Gersten et al., 1974; Mueller et al., 1977; Ross and Mirowsky, 1979;
Vinokur and Selzer, 1975).

I would also suggest that even when events result in stress, they do so
together with the more structured aspects of social roles. There is some
indication that the failure simply to reestablish homeostasis does not
explain the stressful effects of certain life events. Instead, evidence
from our own work (Pearlin and Lieberman, 1979; Pearlin et al., 1981)
and that of Brown and Harris (1978) shows that events can create stress
by adversely altering or intensifying the more enduring aspects of key
social roles. The altered circumstances of roles with which people have
to contend in their daily lives, in turn, are highly productive of stress.
Because life events may exert their effects directly through their influence on roles does not mean that we need not pay attention to events. It
does mean, however, that when we consider life events as antecedents
of stress, we might profitably do so in conjunction with a consideration
of roles. Focusing on roles as sources of stress, then, should bring the

part played by life events in the stress process into a more balanced and interesting perspective.

To the sociological stress researcher, there are additional reasons why roles are fertile areas of study. Probably the most compelling reason is that they are generally potent sources of stress. They are potent, I believe, because people usually attach considerable importance to role activities. Most roles are within such institutions as family, occupation, economy, and education; and because such institutions function for the maintenance of societies, people typically are socialized to invest themselves in their institutional roles. Thus, when people encounter problems within these kinds of contexts, they are likely to react with deep concern, for difficulties experienced in vitally important areas are not easily treated with indifference. By definition, stresses linked to institutional roles cannot be anything but important, both to the lives of individuals and to the structure and functioning of social systems.

Roles are also attractive to the stress researcher because they represent areas on which an array of social forces converge, with the result that they reflect properties of the broader contexts in which they are located. The study of how people are affected by their jobs, for example, can also inform us of the consequences of different organizational arrangements, of the function of occupation as a source of social status, or of the values and goals engendered by occupational experience. Roles are thus excellent vantage points from which, if we turn in one direction, we observe aspects of broader social organization and, if we turn in the other, we observe the behavior of individuals.

Finally, to the extent that as sociologists we are interested in ordinary people representative of major population groups rather than in exotic and extraordinary individuals, and to the extent that we are concerned with repeated and patterned behavior and experience rather than ephemeral, once-in-a-lifetime episodes, attention to social roles and the strains experienced within them serves us well. Clearly, it is around daily and enduring roles such as breadwinning and work or marriage and parenthood that much of our lives are structured through time. It is here that researchers are most likely to find the seedbeds of stress among large collectivities. I certainly do not wish to challenge the importance of stresses whose roots are outside social roles; there are many threatening conditions that may have little or nothing to do with roles but which are, nevertheless, real and powerful antecedents of stress. However, if stress is to be understood as a product of identifiable social conditions shared by large numbers of people and not simply as the result of randomly occurring circumstances that by chance touch the lives of some of us, then the study of social roles is the inseparable companion of the study of personal stress.

THE INTELLECTUAL PAST OF PRESENT INTEREST IN ROLES

Clearly, there is no shortage of reasons why social roles must be prominently reckoned with by researchers seriously concerned with the etiology of stress. Some of these reasons, furthermore, can be recognized in the intellectual history of current stress research. Some of the earliest contributors to present-day research were not at all concerned with or even cognizant of personal stress. Past generations of sociologists, at least as far back as Durkheim, were concerned with the effects of broad conditions of social organization and malintegration on modes of behavior and on personality formation (Pearlin, 1982a). It is, however, a short step from these conceptual orientations to those that point more directly to the connections between the roles people play in the institutions of society and the emotional and physical stress they experience. Established theory is especially useful in helping to identify strains and stresses tied to individuals' continuing participation in structured social contexts and has essentially no conceptual part in the more current absorption in life events and their consequences. Given this fact, the fascination with life events is all the more puzzling.

Of course, this fascination has not entirely been at the expense of research into structured experiences, such as those confronted within social roles. On the contrary, much recent research has actively continued to be influenced by the perspectives of earlier decades. This is particularly true in the case of studies that have looked at occupational stress and the structure of the workplace. I shall not attempt to review the large body of research into the stressful effects of different types of work and of work settings. Two outstanding recent conceptual and substantive overviews are available, however (Kahn et al., 1982; Levi et al., 1982). An impressive array of occupational conditions thought to be associated with various indicators of stress is assembled in these reviews. Included among the organizational aspects of the workplace are such conditions as role ambiguity, role conflict, and the organization of systems of reward and authority. With regard to the job itself, other factors identified as stressful include shift work, underload and overload, hazards, and so on. Together, the studies examining numerous aspects of occupational life indicate that work and its organization can constitute one of the structured, continuing sources of stress.

Over the past 3 decades, family roles have also been closely examined in relation to personal stress, resulting again in a literature too voluminous to review here. As in the case of occupation, however, there are comprehensive and critical overviews available (e.g., Croog, 1970; McCubbin et al., 1982). Unlike occupation, however, the family has multiple dimensions in the stress process. It is, first, a major reservoir of problems and tribulations. Numerous facets of marital relations, parent–child encounters, and the transitional points along the family life cycle have been viewed as fertile ground out of which stress can grow. Second, quite distinct from its functions as a source of stress, it is also likely to be an arena in which problems generated elsewhere are transplanted. Third, the family domain is frequently the place where the wounds that people incur outside are most likely to be healed. The family is truly many things to its members: It is commonly an active and rich source of pain, it is sensitively reflective of problems whose roots are outside its boundaries, and it is commonly where people turn to find relief from pain. In the stress process, it has a uniquely pivotal position.

There is a history of occupational and family research, then, that has succeeded in focusing attention on the relationship between the properties of important institutionalized roles and personal stress. A great deal remains to be done. Thus, all too frequently the connections between role and stress are assumed rather than empirically demonstrated. When they are put to empirical test, our assumptions, even those that have the ring of validity, are often found to be incorrect. The understanding of the stressful effects of roles will be advanced, I believe, by considering both the objective features of roles and the ways they are subjectively experienced. We know that stress springs from experience, but we don't always know clearly what the objective bases of the experience may be. Clearly, in accounting for personal stress, future research needs to combine its interest in the objective properties of roles with its interest in subjective experience. This is an important issue, one that I shall raise again later.

THE CONCEPT OF ROLE STRAIN: SPECIFICATION AND EXTENSIONS

Much of the remainder of this chapter is concerned with various dimensions and nuances of role strain. The notion of role strain has been with us for some time (Goode, 1960; Heiss, 1981; Marks, 1977), although—as with most concepts—it has undergone modification in meaning and usage. As I employ the concept, it refers simply to the hardships, challenges, and conflicts or other problems that people come to experience as they engage over time in normal social roles. These strains, in turn, stand as potentially powerful antecedents of stress and its emotional and physical manifestations.

The range and variety of strains that individuals can experience are impressive. The configurations of circumstances that underlie and give rise to the strains are both numerous and complex, and they may arise within one or more of the multiple roles in which individuals typically engage. Furthermore, the strains a person experiences may arise not only directly, but also indirectly through the difficulties that other people encounter. The indirect exposure results from the fact that roles are embedded in role sets (Merton, 1957), that is, clusters of related roles within which interaction between the role-occupants takes place. A role set for a university professor would involve departmental peers, various echelons of administrators, supporting staff, students, colleagues on committees, and sometimes such mysterious characters as computer specialists or statistical consultants. Clearly, problems that arise at any locus in the role set may result in problems elsewhere. Some of the strains that I describe later are best understood within the context of role sets.

The role strains that I identify in this chapter are quite varied with regard to our empirical knowledge about them. Some of the strains have been examined quite closely, both in my studies and those of other researchers; some have not been directly investigated but are the serendipitious or suggested by-products of investigations; finally, there are role strains about which it is only possible to speculate at this time. My discussion identifies and is organized around six types of role strains: (1) those involving problems between the individual and the nature of the tasks she or he is expected to perform; (2) interpersonal problems within role sets; (3) intrapersonal problems resulting from participation in multiple role sets; (4) role captivity; (5) the gain and loss of roles; and (6) the restructuring and change of roles within role sets. A discussion of each type follows.

Role Tasks and Role Strains

The first type of role strain I discuss is in some respects the simplest, for it concerns only the relationship of the individual to the tasks that must be performed and the nonsocial environment in which the tasks are set. Some of the earliest interest in social stress was anchored in the sheer burdens and physical demands imposed by a person's roles, particularly in the occupational area. As I noted earlier, matters such as shift work, role overload, noise, dirt, dangers, and other noxious elements of the work environment and of the work itself have traditionally been the objects of study by stress researchers. Sometimes entire occupations known to be hazardous or exceptionally difficult are studied. Air controllers, for example, represent an occupational group that has been intensively examined (Rose *et al.*, 1978).

It is my general impression that the nature of the task is less important to on-the-job strain—or, for that matter, to the strains of homemakers—than one might suppose from the emphases given this type of problem. Role overload is a good case in point. We find in our data evidence that overload is likely to occur, when it is present at all, at opposite ends of the occupational spectrum, that is, among highly placed white-collar workers and among the least-skilled manual workers. However, it is related to indicators of stress only among workers at the lower end of the spectrum, suggesting that an overload of work is experienced as a strain primarily where the work is not self-generated but is imposed by others. Curiously, too, we find that noxious and hazardous physical conditions are not particularly associated with emotional stress.

Although the economic rewards of labor are not strictly speaking part of the tasks of occupational role, they are importantly intertwined with such tasks. Both the absolute level of income derived from occupation and unfavorable changes in this level are by themselves crucial conditions of stress (Brenner, 1973). In addition, many workers evaluate their incomes not absolutely, but in relation to what they feel they put into their work. Thus, the strain experienced will vary closely with the magnitude of the discrepancy seen between the level of difficulty and devotion demanded by the tasks that are performed and the level of the material rewards that are received. There is some indication that strains arise among homemakers around similar issues of equity, the issues in this case involving disparities between the care, skill, and effort put into the household tasks and the recognition and appreciation for the effort given to the homemakers by other family members.

I am suggesting that the nature of role tasks may not be enough to account for the strains that people experience in dealing with these tasks. Their subjective evaluations of the tasks, their sense of whether they are receiving fair and just rewards for their efforts, and whether or not they have regulatory control over tasks all combine with the objec--

tive properties of the role demands in determining whether or not strain will result. In the next section I return in greater detail to the combination of objective and subjective factors.

Interpersonal Conflicts

Because roles are usually embedded in role sets, the potential for conflict among those sharing the role set is considerable. Indeed, many of the frustrations and problems of people have been traced directly and proximately to their encounters and confrontations with others sharing the same role sets. This is perhaps nowhere more clear than in marriage. There are, of course, a number of ways in which the behavioral styles of wives and husbands can collide, leaving one or both with enduring discordant elements in their lives. From what I have observed, one of the more common elements of discord—and one of the more stressful—involves a breakdown in reciprocity. By reciprocity and its failure, I mean the sense of inequity people have about their marriages. In reviewing their own marriages, people see themselves in marital relations where, to a greater or lesser degree, they invest more than their partner in the relationship, they work harder, attach greater importance to the relationship, and are more considerate of their partners than they think their partners are of them. In this appraisal process, people experience themselves as contributing more to the marriage than their spouses, but without the benefits being correspondingly greater. As in people's evaluations of their occupational efforts and occupational rewards, it is a dimension of strain within marriage whose main feature is the conviction that the relationship is laced with unfairness and exploitation.

A second marital strain occurs when people judge that their spouses do not either recognize or accept the quintessential elements of their selves. In other words, people do not find reflected in their spouses' eyes the prized images they possess of themselves. There is thus a failure to have the self authenticated by an important other, which results in the feeling of being a stranger to the marriage partner.

A third strain rooted in the interpersonal exchanges of marriage concerns the failure to have the rather routine expectations of marriage fulfilled. I refer here to such ordinary, though essential, logistical tasks as housekeeping and wage earning. In these circumstances, strain is experienced when one of the partners to the marriage sees his or her mate as failing to satisfy expectations concerning the performance of household maintenance tasks. Although considerable attention has been paid in the research literature to the fulfillment of expectations, our data indicate that it is not among the more powerful precursors of stress.

A final marital strain concerns affection and its expression. Its nature need not be belabored; the strain exists when people feel they are not receiving from their mates affectionate attention, or when sexual relations are experienced as unsatisfactory. As with other marital strains, the inability to experience intimate exchange leaves people experiencing an important relationship as incomplete or misdirected. Understandably, it is clearly associated with indicators of emotional distress.

Let us turn from marital strains to those that, although still within the family domain, involve very different sets of interpersonal relations— those of parents and children. The relationships between parents and children have been the center of intense interest for many decades. The characteristic mark of this interest is its concern with the effect that parents have on the development of children. However, the effect children have on their parents' functioning and development has been largely ignored (Bell, 1968). For those of us primarily concerned with the social stresses experienced by adult members of the society, the impact of children on the lives of their parents is of utmost concern.

It is not a simple matter to identify this impact, partly because the influences that children exert over their parents change considerably over the life course. The newborn, for example, imposes strains on its parents very different from those presented by the adolescent or young adult. We have discovered, for example, that the concerns of parents of school-aged children center on problems in general comportment, misbehavior in school, the failure to achieve acceptable grades, the acquisition of friends of undesired quality, inability to get along with other children, disrespectfulness displayed toward their parents, disregard of the status that parenthood symbolizes, and, finally, unwillingness to share the logistical burdens of the household.

Among parents of older children—beginning when children are approximately 15 or 16 years old and continuing into adulthood—these kinds of concerns tend to be pushed aside by other types of problems. In the adolescent and adult phases of child rearing, parents are judging whether their children's behavior is aligned with their long-range goals and aspirations. When parents evaluate their children as being on a trajectory that deviates from cherished goals, there is likely to be considerable strain, even if the children are independent adults. Parents don't easily become accustomed to what they consider to be their children's failures. In a similar vein, parents cannot easily accept what they regard as children's straying from important moral precepts. A loss of interest in religion, the excessive consumption of alcohol, the use of illegal drugs, and an indifference to such virtues as hard work are the kinds of behaviors that parents monitor closely and to which they can be deeply reactive when they judge their adolescent and adult children as wanting. Finally, among those parents whose children have been launched from the nest, a breakdown in contact and communication can itself be a source of strain. The strains of parenthood, then, certainly do not end when children reach a particular age; parental strains have a persistency that can extend across the entire life cycle.

It should be pointed out that our search for family strains has been directed to individual experience. We have been concerned with the problems and dilemmas that some individuals confront in their marriages and, as a separate course of strains, the uncertainties and disappointments that individuals occasionally have in their roles as parents. However, in contrast to the identification of role strains in the lives of individual family members, it is possible to think of strains that beset the entire family system and its sets of interrelated roles. Indeed, some of the earliest inquiries into stress focused on the family as the unit of analysis (Burr, 1973; Hill, 1949) rather than exclusively on the individual. Thus, one may ask not only how marital and parental problems are experienced by individuals, but also how these affect such dimensions of family functioning as its cohesiveness, levels of interaction, or stability. There is a good deal to support this perspective in considering interpersonal conflict, for it is reasonable to suppose that one relationship in the family is unlikely to escape completely the spin-offs from enduring conflicts in another family relationship. Individual actions in the family combine to form a system qualitatively different from the sum total of its individual constituents.

Focusing still on interpersonal strains, I turn now to a consideration of those that can arise in the occupational sphere. The general interest of researchers in occupation as a source of stress is certainly understandable. In terms of sheer time, much of our lives may be invested in our work; it is a major determinant of the status we are accorded by others; it is a major determinant of the esteem we accord ourselves; and, for most people, economic resources are derived entirely from work. As I noted earlier, previous research has helped to stimulate awareness of a number of issues, such as role ambiguity, conflicts within roles resulting from incompatible demands placed on the individual, occupational hazards, and role overload. In general, however, empirical research has not given merited attention to interpersonal conflicts that can arise on the job.

An aspect of occupational life that is coming into recognition as an important source of stress and that we have had the opportunity to observe (Pearlin and Lieberman, 1979) concerns the relationships formed around authority. The aspect of authority that is a particularly potent antecedent of stress is its capacity to induce depersonalization among workers. Depersonalization essentially stems from a failure of superordinates to give appropriate recognition to individual workers, to acknowledge their contributions, and to be able to differentiate among the qualities that different workers bring to the job. Basically, depersonalization is the sense of facelessness that arises when workers feel authorities and supervisory personnel do not distinguish them positively from other workers. Subordinates are left to feel they are part of a large collectivity whose members are regarded as interchangeable or that some workers in the system are the recipients of undue recognition while the value of one's own contributions is unnoticed or demeaned. Work and authority relations thus fail to advance or to validate the investment of self in work.

The strains that grow out of interpersonal encounters in marriage, parenthood, and occupation cannot inform us, of course, about the interpersonal problems and conflicts experienced by the nonmarried, the childless, the homemakers, the unemployed, and the retired. These latter groups are a substantial portion of the population and also represent those who are at special risk for exposure to stressful conditions. In fact, we have sought to identify some of the strains of those who do not fall within the major institutional roles, specifically the homemakers, the retired, and the nonmarried. I shall not review in detail the many interpersonal strains found in each of these roles and statuses. Briefly, for the homemaker they can involve such experiences as loneliness and boredom, and the absence of appreciation and respect from others; for the retired, the disuse of skills and talents; and for the nonmarried, the absence of intimacy, sexual relations, and expressive exchange, and the constriction of social activities.

I have suggested at various points that to form a complete picture of the nature of role strains we cannot look at the role alone but also must take into systematic account the subjective dispositions individuals bring with them to their roles. It is not always possible to predict if a role will be onerous solely on the basis of the conditions that can be observed within the role. Whether or not these conditions are experienced as innocuous or as hardships frequently depends on how individuals' subjective values and aspirations combine with the conditions. This is an important issue underlying interpersonal role strains, and it deserves further discussion.

The threats and conflicts that are experienced within roles may grow directly out of the difficulties, hardships, interpersonal frustrations, or insults to personal identity that are built into the role. Or, as they frequently do, they may result from conditions that by themselves appear to be relatively neutral or benign, but that are noneless experienced as conflictful because they move against the grain of things we prize and hold dear. Whether or not the structure and substance of interpersonal relations result in stress often depends on how they fit with what people are looking for and consider to be desirable. Thus, the same set of objective conditions may affect people very differently, depending on the congeniality or incompatibility between the conditions they face and their values.

One example of this can be drawn from a study of powerlessness (alienation) among workers in a mental hospital (Pearlin, 1962). Bureaucratized occupational settings are very well suited to investigations of the effects of structural arrangements, because the relations between people, at least those that are formal, are often clearly prescribed in such settings. In this study I was concerned with whether alienation among workers varied according to whether the supervisors to whom they were primarily responsible were structurally distant or proximate. Thus, one's significant supervisor could be located at the next hierarchical level, the second level removed, the third, and so on. I had supposed that positional distance between subordinates and significant superordinates inhibits the exchange of influence, thus making authority more unilateral and preemptory—conditions that are conducive to powerlessness and alienation. However, I found only a small association between these positional relationships and the level of alienation among subordinates. But this picture becomes dramatically expanded when certain values are taken into account.

Concretely, I was able to observe the part played by obeisance to authority. Obeisance, as measured in this study, refers to people's tendency to endow their superordinates with rights, wisdom, privileges, and honors that they would not accord to themselves, their peers, or those they view as status inferiors. Among workers expressing a high level of obeisance, alienation was entirely unrelated to their position relative to that of their superiors. Workers rejecting obeisance, in contrast, were quite likely to be alienated when their superordinates were not hierarchically adjoining. Thus, in the one group structural separation does not produce alienation because it is entirely consistent with the valuation of status distance; in the other group, separation violates conceptions of appropriate relations between superordinates and subordinates and, consequently, produces alienation.

Another illustration of the merging of interpersonal role relations and values can be drawn from marriage (Pearlin, 1975b). The equality or inequality of the status characteristics of marital partners has been of historic interest to researchers concerned with the stability and stress of marriage (e.g., Burgess and Wallin, 1943). There was some evidence, not very powerful, that when the partners are drawn from different status backgrounds, the marriage is more buffeted by stress and more vulnerable to disappointments. Again, when values are interposed on the status relations of the spouses, the story becomes more complicated but also more interesting.

Briefly, it is possible to classify individuals according to whether their spouses come from lower-status backgrounds (as judged by the occupation of their fathers), whether they are of equal status, or whether their spouses are of higher status. In the first instance, one has "married down" and is hypogamous, and in the last, one has "married up" and is hypergamous. Basically, if this aspect of the marital structure is observed alone, it bears no relationship to marital strains and stresses. When values and aspirations indicative of status striving are introduced, however, several important relationships emerge. Status strivers—those who place great store on achievement, prestige acquisition, and economic mobility—react to status inequality very differently from those not holding these values. First, among people who have married down and who are also status strivers, marriage is likely to be marked by the absence of reciprocity, little affective exchange, less disposition to turn to the spouse during times of crisis, and—not surprisingly—more emotional distress. It is apparent that to those who are oriented upward, a lower-status spouse can come to stand as a bitter and resented symbol of failure, not meriting affection or consideration. By contrast, hypogamous people who place little or no value on status striving have marital relations undistinguished from those of people of equal status. We see here, then, that the *same structural arrangement* in marriage, hypogamy, can produce different levels of strain when combined with *different values*. The same example can be used to show also how the *same values* can lead to different consequences when combined with *different structural conditions*. Thus, the very status values that stimulated marital strains in hypogamy have the opposite outcomes under conditions of hypergamy. We see this in the fact that the status-striving individual who has married up is likely to have a much more benign marriage than that of the striver who has married down and, for that matter, a more tranquil one than that of spouses of equal status. Unlike the hypogamous striver whose spouse is a reminder of unfulfilled wishes, the hypergamous striver may see his or her marriage as a badge of success and a sign of dreams come true.

We are able to see in these illustrations that people exposed to the same structural conditions of work and family roles do not necessarily experience these conditions in the same way. Whether or not such conditions come to be felt as role strain depends both on the objective attributes of the roles and the values that are brought to the roles—the things that are thought to be good, desirable, and worth striving after. In a real sense, values help shape the meaning of structured conditions; they determine whether the conditions violate what is decent or proper, whether they are shrugged off with indifference, or whether they are applauded. Thus, I can underscore what I earlier stated: The strains people experience as they fulfill their various roles do not always depend fully on the objective circumstances people encounter in their roles. They depend also on whether these circumstances are seen as an affront to cherished values or as a support of them.

The future researcher who fixes his or her attention on social roles as a source of stress has a double challenge. It is imperative that we be able to recognize the structural features of roles and of role sets that have the capacity to produce strains in their incumbents. This is difficult enough by itself, but it is not sufficient. We must also ask how the structural arrangements come to be experienced as strains, and in answering this query we will surely be led to a consideration of people's hopes and priorities, their dreams and their commitments. These kinds of dispositions determine whether the role is threatening or reassuring, defeating or reinforcing. The sociological student of stress needs to be oriented to structure and, in addition, has to understand the meaning of structure for people engaged in it.

Multiple Roles and Intrapersonal Conflict

Interpersonal conflict involves multiple individuals within a single role set; I am now concerned with conflict within the individual resulting from his or her participation in multiple role sets. Conflict and strain may be embedded in an uncongeniality between elements of the several different roles in which people typically engage. The expectations and demands of one role may collide with those of another, presumably leaving the incumbent in a state of confusion and cross-pressures. How, after all, can the church deacon who is bent on destroying a business competitor avoid the pain of the apparent dilemmas and contradictions in his or her religious participation and occupational activities? These kinds of seeming conflicts represent potential sources of strain, but they may be less serious than they appear to be. It cannot be assumed that when there is discontinuity among the elements of different roles played by the same individual, conflict must inexorably follow. This is so first because multiple roles are usually segregated from one another in time and space. Typically, for example, we are not engaged in our business at the same time we are acting as deacons in our churches. The family is the sphere where the segregation of roles is most tenuous, for our actions as marital partners may go on in close, often blurred, spatial and temporal proximity to our actions as parents. Indeed, our behavior in one of these roles can certainly affect our behavior and its effects in the other role. The general point, however, is that the segregation of roles facilitates the psychological separation of the conflicting expectations they may encompass.

There is a second mechanism that prevents apparent role conflict from becoming experienced conflict. To understand this mechanism we must see that conflict is most likely to result when we are pulled simultaneously by incompatible forces that are of equal importance to us. When one role is of much more vital concern to us than the other, then the incongruities between them are less apt to become internalized conflict. We are merely able to shrug off the claims of the less important role and respond to the call of the more important. This provides the key to one coping response to role conflict: the management of role priorities (Pearlin and Schooler, 1978). When the roles in conflict are initially of similar importance, people may find that they are able to relegate one of them to a position of relative unimportance. In this manner, elements of roles that are objectively discontinuous are not experienced as inner conflict.

Although logical conflict does not always translate into personal conflict, people are not always able to escape conflict entirely or even to minimize it substantially. We have observed a situation where, for many people, conflict is not escapable, involving wives and mothers who are employed outside the household. These are people who traditionally have been viewed as vulnerable to conflicts between work and family roles. Aside from the problems that women encounter on the job, they are undoubtedly more exposed than men to conflicts between demands of the job, on one hand, and demands of their housework, their marital roles, and their parental roles on the other. As could be expected, our data indicate that the more the job is in conflict with these familial roles, the more likely women are to be depressed (Pearlin, 1975a).

However, there are interesting variations in these relationships, which can be explicated by looking at the working women who also have children at home. First, the conflict between occupational and maternal roles is greatest among those women who are most invested in their work. These are the women, for example, who do not agree that "As soon as I leave work, I put it out of my mind" or that "The most important thing about my job is that it provides me the things I need in life." The women who disavow such sentiments are more often in middle-class occupations. Among middle-class women, therefore, there is a conflict between work and family roles that results from a competing involvement in both roles. By contrast, when there is role conflict between work and home among working-class women, it is more likely to stem from conditions of home than investment in career. Specifically, the two roles are particularly apt to conflict when the working mother has preschoolers at home. I presume that this is less problematic in middle-class families because alternative child-care provisions are more available. The main lessons to be learned from these comparisons are, first, that role conflict is most apt to lead to psychological conflict when the roles are of similar importance or equally unrelinquishable and, second, that the source of conflict between two roles can vary with social class and with the structure of role sets. Clearly, where there are conflicts between two or more roles, the nature of the conflicts might vary among role players having different social and economic characteristics. Once again, we see that it is not enough to examine the roles; if we are to understand role strain we need also to examine the dispositions people bring to the roles.

Aside from psychological conflicts stemming from incompatible demands and expectations, the multiplicity of roles may create strain through a quite different avenue: the contagion of role strains, where the strains that arise in one role bring about strainful conditions in other roles. Do difficult conditions on the job, for example, contribute to marital conflict, or vice versa? Our own data suggest some contagion of strain across role sets, but the magnitude of correlations between the strains felt in different roles is at best modest. The modesty of the correlations is surprising if we think of behavior as primarily guided by underlying personality dispositions, for this perspective emphasizes the continuities in actions and affect as we move from one role to another. From a structural point of view, however, contagion would be limited by the temporal and spatial segregation of roles, by the fact that the norms that guide behavior vary from one role to another, and by the fact that the people with whom we interact are different for our different roles. Clearly, these differentiations do not mean that our institutionalized roles are unrelated to one another. It is fair to state, however, that at this time little is known about the permeability of strains and stresses across role boundaries.

Role Captivity

I have so far considered the strains that can result from three types of role conditions: (1) the attempt to satisfy difficult role demands and tasks, (2) interpersonal conflict between people within a role set, and (3) intrapersonal conflict stemming from an uncongeniality between elements of one's roles in different role sets. These are conditions that by themselves and in conjunction with select values and aspirations are capable of producing frustration, confusion, and threat in those exposed to them. I turn now to still a different type of role conflict, this one reflected in situations where we are bound to one role while wishing to play another. I refer to this situation as role captivity. The essential feature of role captivity is not that the conditions of the role are difficult or conflictful; it is that the role is unwanted, regardless of the conditions it presents.

Role captivity, in this sense, is a phenomenon affecting many people engaged in a variety of roles. It describes, for example, people who are retired but would prefer to work, as well as those who are employed but would prefer to be able to afford retirement. It includes, too, those who are parents of dependent children and wish they were not, along with those who are childless but wish they were parents. The essential character of role captivity, whenever it occurs, is that it entails an inescapable obligation to be and do one thing at the very time the individual wants to be and do something different. This conflict generates stress.

My interest in and attention to role captivity is largely attributable to some of the research into sex roles (Pearlin, 1975a). It has been recognized for many years that women, more than men, are susceptible to certain symptoms of psychological distress, depression in particular. There have been many efforts to explain these differences, most of them quite speculative. One explanation has posited that women are more likely than men to have limited and fixed roles (Gove and Tudor, 1973). Unlike men who have both family roles and an outside job to which they can turn, women often have but the family and household, leaving them no escape route when the going is tough. The restriction of range and choice of roles, it has been presumed, is what underlies women's greater disposition to symptomatology indicative of stress. If this were so, it could be expected that women who had employment outside the household would more closely resemble men than homemaking women in the symptoms they report. However, this is not the case: Our data show that women with outside employment are not different from homemakers in level of psychological distress (Pearlin, 1975a). Thus it is apparent that the sheer number and range of roles played by women, at least to the extent that they could be observed in our study, do not affect their psychological distress. However, although whether women are homemakers or outside workers is by itself unimportant to their psychological well-being, the consistency of what they *do* with what they *want* to do did surface as an important issue.

I state this partly on the basis of answers to a question addressed to homemakers that asked (Pearlin, 1975a): "If you had your choice, would you like to be working [outside the home] full-time, working part-time, or not working at all?" There is a progressive relationship between homemakers' responses to this query and their levels of depression. That is, those who would like to work full time in preference to being a homemaker express most emotional despair, those not preferring any outside work express least, and those wanting part-time employment are between the two extremes. This relationship between role captivity and depression is not limited to homemakers. The same question asked of retirees produced the same relationship. The crux of this distress is not necessarily that people find being a homemaker or a retiree onerous; it is being these things while wanting to be something else that constitutes the strain. And, as our data suggest, the strainful nature of role captivity increases as the discrepancy between the being and the wanting increases. This is a source of strain that is worth looking at under any circumstances; in times of constricting opportunity structures, it becomes even more worthy of consideration.

The Loss and Gain of Roles

The various kinds of role strains I have described are each relatively durable. We usually cannot quickly change the noxious conditions we may face in our roles or readily reconstruct the relationships with others who are participants in our role sets; it is difficult to escape from the dilemmas and contradictions of our multiple roles, and it is typically not a simple matter to cross over from the roles to which we are bound to those that we prefer. Inherent in the very notion of role strain, consequently, is tenacity and persistence.

However, this feature of role strain should not lead us to assume that people simply remain immersed and immobile in the mire of their problems, static and unchanging. On the contrary, we might profitably look at role strains from a developmental perspective—how people change over time as a consequence of the strains they experience. Partly, people change as a result of their own efforts to cope with their strains, something about which we are just beginning to learn. Partly, too, we change as a result of the effects of strains on self-concept, something about which I have more to say later. We don't know a great deal about the developmental effects of role strains, obviously; but we know enough now to be certain that these strains, despite their persistence, do not encase people in a static state through time.

Furthermore, the roles that we play at one stage of our lives may not necessarily be the same as at another stage. It is remarkable how frequently people may yield old roles and statuses and acquire new ones across the life span. The gaining of roles is especially evident in early adulthood, when people for the first time are involved in the tasks of beginning their own nuclear families and getting an economic and occupational foothold (Pearlin and Lieberman, 1979). At a later segment of the life span, by contrast, loss of certain roles is more likely to be in evidence. Despite these modal differences, loss and gain can occur at any age. In recent years, these role transitions, or "passages," have come under close scrutiny as potential sources of stress.

Unfortunately, as interest in transitions grew so did confusion about them and their relevance to stress (Pearlin, 1982b). In particular, there is a fairly substantial body of research that regards these transitions as life events and views events, in turn, as benchmarks of stress in the lives of people. Underlying this view is the implicit assumption that any life change is capable of arousing stress. From this position, what is important about change as a source of stress is the magnitude of the readjustment it imposes on people, not its quality or direction. Thus, a sought-after change might be as stressful as one that people have sought to avoid. The major shortcoming of the assumption that any change is stressful in proportion to its magnitude is simply that it is not empirically correct. Current research is showing consistently that stress-related events are distinguished by their undesired and involuntary qualities. Life events are important to stress not generally but selectively. This fact, in turn, is directly relevant to the loss and acquisition of roles as sources of strain.

Concretely, it is important to distinguish whether loss and gain are part of the scheduled progression of the individual through the family and occupational life cycle, or if they are eruptive, nonscheduled occurrences. There is no evidence that scheduled role transitions, those built into the life cycle, are particularly stressful (Pearlin, 1980a). I am not saying that these transitions are unimportant. Marriage, having children, seeing adult children leave home, retirement—these kinds of losses and gains are not merely passing events, they are forces that profoundly restructure the lives of people. They quite possibly affect life style, social isolation and integration, goals and aspirations, self-image, values and ideologies, and so on. But with limited exceptions, such as the death of a spouse, they are not stressful.

As I have discussed elsewhere (Pearlin, 1980b), I believe they are not stressful for the very reason that they are scheduled. This means that far in advance of entering into a scheduled role we are at least partially presocialized to understand what will be expected of us and what we can expect of others in that role. We are also likely to understand clearly that some of these expectations, such as those attendant on being a parent, will change at different stages of life. Finally, even before entrance into certain roles (e.g., occupation), we know that we eventually have to give them up. Because socialization may take place long before our entrance into or exit from the roles, our preparation for scheduled transitions may not always be synchronized with the actual conditions with which we have to deal. Then we are left to our own coping devices in place of the normative expectations to which we were earlier socialized. Although there may be slippage between antic- ipatory socialization for later roles and the actual conditions of the roles, the early and long preparation for scheduled transitions mini- mizes what might otherwise be their stressful impact.

Not so the nonscheduled role changes. Shifts in roles and statuses, particularly those involving loss, that are not tied to life-cycle move- ment are capable of evoking considerable distress. Death of a child, involuntary loss of job, "premature" death of a spouse, and divorce are among the nonscheduled transitions that can place people under sub- stantial stress. Even when events of this sort do not take us by surprise, they still may carry a painful blow. Partly, perhaps, this results from the absence of anticipatory socialization. No matter how far in advance we have forewarnings of divorce, for example, we are not trained for it in the same way we are trained for marriage. Similarly, we are not socialized to being chronically ill, although there is a sick role; we are not prepared early in our lives to be young widows or widowers; we are never made ready to survive our children; and so on.

Differences in the nature and degree of anticipatory role socializa- tion, however, cannot fully explain the differences in the stressful ef- fects of scheduled and nonscheduled losses and gains. Although lack of prior preparation may account for some of the greater negative effects of the unscheduled disruptions over scheduled transitions, there are other reasons that we have been able to identify. We have learned that the relationship of this type of event to stress is largely indirect (Pearlin et al., 1981). Contrary to the assumptions often made of undesired events, they do not necessarily lead to stress simply because they are events or even because they are undesired events. Instead, events of this order often have the capacity to bring about deleterious alterations in the more persistent circumstances of roles with which people have to grapple on a daily basis. Thus, in an intensive examination that took involuntary job loss as an example of this process, we demonstrated, first, that job loss contributed to economic strains; these strains, in turn, lead to diminished self-concepts, and the strains, together with their effects on the self, are what largely account for the stress.

Therefore, the gains and losses of roles, whether scheduled or un-scheduled, do not automatically generate stress simply because they involve life changes. Rather, their connection to stress is largely indi-rect. They first act as levers for creating durable strains in economic, family, or other roles, and these strains stimulate stress. The loss of role, therefore, causes stress by restructuring important areas of experi-ence; of course, the unscheduled losses are most likely to precipitate such restructuring. Clearly, we need to examine role transitions and disruptions as sources of stress; just as clearly, the pathways from these events to stress are circuitous and complex.

Role Restructuring

A concomitant of the gains and losses of roles that I have been de-scribing is the entrance into and exit from role sets. A role, of course, is part of a larger constellation of interacting roles, so the occupant of one role is automatically embedded in a network of interrelated roles. Hand in hand with the acquisition and relinquishment of roles, conse-quently, is the engagement with and disengagement from larger role sets. Being married and having children, for example, represent the creation of new role sets no less than the gaining of new roles. Being divorced, retired, or widowed, on the other hand, involves both role loss and the disintegration of role sets. Understandably, the strains one may experience in role entrance can result both from having to master a new role and the new role set; correspondingly, when one exits from a role, one has to learn how to live both without the role and the role set that went with it.

Not all role change involves a change in role set, however. There are many situations in which a role undergoes considerable restructuring within a role set whose occupants are stable. Although this kind of role change has not been singled out for study as a source of strains, there is reason to believe that it can pose difficulties more severe than those encountered in ordinary role transitions. This is particularly the case, first, when the restructuring comes about through the force of circumstances rather than from voluntary effort and, second, when there is a redistribution within the role set of status, privilege, or influence over the behavior of others. Essentially, then, I am calling attention to situations where it is necessary to adapt to shifts in the expectations, obligations, and governing norms among role-related people whose prior relationships were guided by significantly different constraints and imperatives. Although the literature does not yield systematic scrutiny of role restructuring, numerous examples can be found that will help clarify the nature of the phenomenon.

One illustration lies in the relationships between many elderly parents and their adult children. Strictly speaking, of course, the role set remains unaltered as children and parents age and as they move along the life course. That is, parents and children remain just that to each other, as long as they live. What changes is a broad set of behaviors, sentiments, concerns, and responsibilities: Many that formerly defined the role of parents may be gradually assumed by children, and those that were centered primarily in children's roles may be incorporated into the parental role. One investigation, for example, revealed a number of areas in which adult children feel obliged to take increased responsibility for their aging parents' welfare (Lieberman, 1978). These include such diverse areas as urging the parent to go to the doctor for hearing problems, taking over holiday dinner rituals, urging parents not to be idle, intervening in father–mother quarrels, discussing parents' financial problems, and cautioning against hard work.

What is potentially strainful in these exchanges is not simply that people are called upon to adapt to change per se; it is the nature of the change that makes it problematic. Those who were the providers of help, protection, and succor are now its recipients and those who received are now its donors; parents who in an earlier life stage controlled, directed, and guided their children's behavior are now subject to children's judgments about their well-being; patterns of autonomy and dependence now tend to be reversed. Changes of this order displace and come to substitute for relationships between parents and children that have a long and deeply implanted history. It is difficult to imagine that this kind of profound restructuring can take place without also upsetting valued elements of self-image that were nurtured in the past.

In the case of the elderly, physical infirmity and the inability to provide their own economic resources serve as levers for role restructuring. However, there are examples of restructuring that involve very different circumstances. One case that has been brought to my attention involves divorced parents and their young children (J. Wallerstein, personal communication, June, 1982). Briefly, divorce and family disruption can immobilize newly single parents; many household duties and functions normally performed by parents are simply left undone. Not unusually in these circumstances, young children will step into the breach and emerge as household managers, assuming responsibility for the logistical operations and decision making necessary for family maintenance. Reversal of roles can take place in a number of vital areas of family life. The children become engaged in the care and training of parents, and the parents come to rely on their children for many of their needs.

A second instance of which I have been told (R. Munoz, personal communication, June, 1982) involves still other circumstances—specifically, non-English-speaking households. The hardships experienced by people who do not have the use of the language hardly need elaboration. It is a bewildering, penalizing, and threatening state of affairs. When children in such households reach school age and begin to acquire a speaking and reading knowledge of the language, they are catapulated into a position of unusual importance. The children become their parents' liaison to the outside world, their translators and interpreters, negotiators, advisors, and guides. Children, in effect, gain possession of a needed resource—language—and this unusual circumstance, in turn, restructures family roles.

With these illustrations as background, it can now be understood more clearly why role changes that involve a change in role sets are less strainful than changes occurring within a stable set. One of the tasks with which an individual has to deal in role restructuring is overcoming the earlier modes of relating and behaving. And it is not only one's own attempt to cling to the past or get on with the present that is at issue; one must deal with and reconcile the whole set of responses that are set in motion by the restructuring, many of them probably in conflict with one another. It is for this reason that in formal organization a change in role is usually accompanied by a deliberate change in role set. The enlistee who is promoted to the officer ranks is given a command away from former comrades, the new Ph.D. (usually) leaves the university that awarded the degree, and so on. These illustrations point up that where there are changes in roles, adaptation to these changes is much easier in new role sets where there are no old expectations and established dispositions to be overcome. Whether one's new role has more status and privilege or less, adaptation is likely to be less strainful when it does not entail the restructuring of roles within a set made up of established actors. Movement out of the set helps to avoid considerable potential conflict.

There is a final anecdotal illustration I would like to describe that captures the difference between old and new role sets as contexts of changes. It concerns a physician who was stricken with a serious illness requiring intensive medical and nursing care over a period of many weeks. It initially seemed reasonable that as a patient he should go to the medical center in which he was a department head. He was well known, highly placed, and familiar with the excellent quality of the hospital's facilities and personnel. He could go there free of any doubt of the good treatment and special attention he would receive. The problem was that the other members of the role set could not easily shift to treating him as their patient rather than as their chief and as a person expertly informed of his own ailment. It was difficult for them to prescribe a regimen and to expect from him the same uncritical compliance they would expect from other patients. They tended to defer to his professional standing in the institution, although what he wanted and needed was the opportunity to sink into the sick role like other patients. But they continued to ask permission where they might have issued orders; they sought guidance where they might have made independent decisions. In short, the doctor was not allowed to make a complete exchange, imposing a seriously burdening strain on him. After a period of this, he reluctantly decided to move to another hospital where he immediately and gratefully was able to pass over to others responsibility for his care. In the familiar role set, all actors were inhibited from restructuring roles in a manner appropriate to the person's changed health status.

Although these few illustrations of role restructuring and exchange are not exhaustive, they help to identify one way in which our social roles can be significant sources of strain and stress in our lives. Restructuring may be an outgrowth of the life course, especially as it involves aged parents and adult children. It can also result from career dislocations, occupational mobility, or eruptive life crises. It can entail either loss or gain, be permanent or short-lived, and be especially likely to occur in a continuous role set. It is an overlooked source of stress about which there is little empirical information. Our limited knowledge of the phenomenon, however, should not be taken as a reflection of its importance as a potentially stressful condition.

ROLE STRAINS AND THE SELF

Role strains are not life threatening; they don't descend upon us with sudden force as some events do; they usually do not involve new or unknown demands; they typically don't create confrontations on which our entire futures depend. In general, they are not traumatic. How is it, then, that they are so productive of stress—often far in excess of that produced by life events? The answer, I believe, lies in the rather specific and potent relationship of life strains to certain components of the self, mastery and self-esteem in particular.

The sine qua non of role strains is their chronicity; simply, they tend to persist with dogged tenacity. They come about insidiously and they are slow to dissipate. The very fact that they maintain a relatively stable presence in the lives of people enhances their power to impinge on the ways that people come to think and feel about themselves. The process is slow and insidious, but it is real. Conditions that we live with over time, especially if they invoke aspects of our lives that are important to us, must make some imprint on our selves.

But what is the form and nature of the imprint? Here it is again useful to remind ourselves that by definition role strains represent conditions that people don't like; they are viewed as noxious and uncomfortable. Next, it can be recognized that the very persistence of strains stands as an indication to people of their impotence in avoiding, escaping, or diminishing the presence of strains in their lives. Role strains, then, are a lurking reminder to people of their own incapacity to alter the un-desired, unwanted conditions in which they are enmeshed. There are two aspects of self that become particularly vulnerable to injury by the persistence and intractability of role strain: mastery and self-esteem.

As I have specified and measured mastery in my work, it refers to the extent to which people feel that they are able to manage and control the forces that importantly affect their lives (Pearlin and Schooler, 1978). Quite clearly, adversity that becomes a fixture of life can come to impli-cate these dimensions of self.They symbolize, first, the inability to be master of one's own fate or to alter even those aspects of life that are particularly noxious. Second, to the extent that continued role strains are interpreted as personal failure, they can prompt a process of self-denigration. The results of our analysis have shown empirically that chronic strains have an erosive effect on mastery and self-esteem (Pearlin et al., 1981), and it is understandable that this should be the case. More eruptive, shorter-lived sources of stress, especially those that can be interpreted as arising out of chance circumstances, do not have the same negative effects on the self.

I return, then, to the earlier query: How is it that role strains are so fertile grounds for symptoms of stress? The answer is that they dimin-ish crucial aspects of the self and when this occurs, I submit, the indi-vidual becomes especially vulnerable to stress (Pearlin and Radabaugh,

1976). To a large extent, therefore, the effects of role strains on stress are indirect, working through the diminishment of self. The threatened and injured self, in turn, opens the inner doors to stress. Role strains directly implicate the self, threats to the self directly lead to stress and, in this manner, role strains indirectly result in stress. Damage to the self, then, is one of the key elements in the stress process.

Of course, the protection, preservation, and enhancement of mastery and self-esteem are inherently in the compelling interests of people. One does not suffer lightly threats to the self. Typically people strive to avoid or correct the circumstances that lie behind such threats. Some of these efforts represent coping behavior. Coping has at least three distinct functions: the avoidance or correction of situations seen as causing the stress, the modification of the meaning of the situation in a manner that neutralizes threats, and the management of stress symptoms so that they do not overwhelm the individual.

Many behavioral, perceptual, and cognitive devices, most of which are probably not yet recognized in our research, may serve one or more of these coping functions. These are treated in the chapter by Menaghan and I shall not review them here. I would like to emphasize, however, that the same set of coping actions can result both in positive and negative results, depending on where one looks for coping efficacy and whether short-run or long-run consequences are examined. The consumption of alcohol stands as one example of this point: The use of alcohol may produce some immediate relief of the symptoms of stress, but it contains at the same time its own seeds of life problems. In this context, I believe, it is useful to regard certain forms of deviance as representing an effort to cope with threats to the self. I shall explicate what I mean.

One of the coping practices I have been able to observe is the arrangement of roles in a way that devalues those that are a source of pain, and values more highly those that promise to be a source of reward. Essentially, selves are less at risk when threats are diverted to components of life that are of peripheral importance. This means, first,that people may demean the importance of roles in which they experience distress. Second—and this is where deviance becomes an issue—at the same time that they are devaluing the roles in which there is insult to the self, people may be seeking to create and move other more rewarding roles to positions of central importance. The roles that become prized under these conditions may be recognized and applauded by special subgroups but lack broad social approval.

These kinds of relationships have been empirically documented (e.g., Kaplan et al., 1982), of course. Deviance has been recognized as an effort to avoid self-denigration and to win self-esteem. To the extent that the loss of self-esteem is a consequence of chronic role strains, deviance becomes an issue within the framework of the stress process. The essential point is that as we attempt to identify the connections between role strains and psychological stress, we inevitably must encounter the self as one of the pivotal links. The damaged self can be an active precondition of emotional stress in the short run and, in the long run, it can be a condition contributing to socially deviant behavior.

CONCLUSIONS

One of the purposes of this chapter has been to provide some counterbalance to the recent tendency to look primarily at eventful change in searching for the precursors of stress. In contrast to eventful experience, the notion of role strains calls attention to those elements of experience that are structured through time. I do not want to argue that life changes are unimportant to stress, but regarding them as the exclusive or even principal precursors of stress is highly misleading. Furthermore, where change does prompt stress, it may be through the adverse effects of the change on the durable elements of people's roles. Roles, of course, are not carved in stone; roles change and so do the people within them, but usually slowly and insidiously. The important point is that we must move away from the rather uncritical and predominating attention to chance events when searching for the roots of stress.

What are the strains that people can experience in the context of their ordinary social roles? I have attempted to identify a variety of such experiences: (1) those generated by role tasks that cannot be satisfied or that are noxious, (2) conflicts with others sharing the same role sets, (3) conflicts between demands imposed by the multiple roles played by the same person, (4) being captive of an unwanted role, (5) the scheduled and unscheduled losses and gains of roles, and, finally, (6) the restructuring and exchange of roles within and between role sets.

It must be underscored that it can be misleading to assume that conflict, discontinuity, and change in roles are inevitably incorporated in the form of personal inner conflict and confusion. Whether or not the objective features of roles are transformed into role strains often depends on the dispositions people bring with them to their roles. The conditions that people experience in their roles, therefore, must be seen in conjunction with their values and aspirations in order to understand fully how conditions of roles become strainful antecedents of stress.

If there is a single issue to be drawn from this chapter, it is that there is no one source of stress more important than all others. In the experiences attached to roles I do not wish to imply that no other kinds of experience need to be considered; I do not want primarily to espouse one set of causes over another. It is my intention, rather, to bring the study of stress closer to the study of ordinary lives. To understand how stress comes about, we do not always have to reach out to the exotic, rare, or eventful. We need only to take a careful look at the structure of experience in the pursuit of everyday life.

REFERENCES

Bell, R. Q.
    1968   "A reinterpretation of the direction of effects in studies of socialization." Psychological Review 75:81–95.
Brenner, Harvey M.
    1973   Mental Illness and the Economy. Cambridge, Mass.: Harvard University Press.
Brown, George W., and Tirrel Harris
    1978   Social Origins of Depression. New York: The Free Press.
Burgess, E. W., and P. Wallin
    1943   "Homogamy and social characteristics." American Journal of Sociology 49:109–124.
Burr, Wesley
    1973   Theory Construction and the Sociology of the Family. New York: Wiley.
Croog, S. H.
    1970   "The family as a source of stress." Pp. 19–25 in Sol Levine and Norman A. Scotch (eds.), Social Stress. Chicago: Aldine.
Dohrenwend, B., and L. Pearlin
    1982   "Report on stress and life events." Pp. 55–80 in Glen R. Elliott and Carl Eisdorfer (eds.), Stress and Human Health. New York: Springer.
Gersten, J. C., T. S. Langner, J. G. Eisenberg, and L. Orzek
    1974   "Child behavior and life events: Undesirable change or change per se." Pp. 159–170 in Barbara S. Dohrenwend and Bruce P. Dohrenwend (eds.), Stressful Life Events: Their Nature and Effects. New York: Wiley.
Goode, W. J.
    1960   "A theory of role strain." American Sociological Review 25:483–496.
Gove, W., and J. Tudor
    1973   "Adult sex roles and mental illness." American Journal of Sociology 78:812–835.
Heiss, J.
    1981   "Social roles." Pp. 94–129 in Morris Rosenberg and Ralph H. Turner (eds.), Social Psychology. New York: Basic Books.
Hill, Reuben
    1949   Families under Stress. Westport, Conn.: Greenwood Press.

Kahn, R., K. Hein, J. House, S. Kasl, and A. McLean
  1982   "Report on stress in organizational settings." Pp. 81–117 in Glen R. Elliott
          and Carl Eisdorfer (eds.), Stress and Human Health. New York: Springer.
Kaplan, H. B., S. S. Martin, and C. Robbins
  1982   "Application of a general theory of deviant behavior: Self-derogation and
          adolescent drug use." Journal of Health and Social Behavior 23:274–
          294.
Levi, L., M. Frankenhaeuser, and B. Gardell
  1982   "Report on work stress related to social structures and processes." Pp.
          119–146 in Glen R. Elliott and Carl Eisdorfer (eds.), Stress and Human
          Health. New York: Springer.
Lieberman, G. L.
  1978   "Children of the elderly as natural helpers: Some demographic differ-
          ences." American Journal of Community Psychology 6:489–498.
Marks, S. R.
  1977   "Multiple roles and role strain: Some notes on human energy, time and
          commitment." American Sociological Review 42:921–936.
McCubbin, Hamilton I., A. Elizabeth Cauble, and Joan M. Patterson (eds.)
  1982   Family Stress, Coping, and Social Support. Springfield, Ill.: Thomas.
Merton, R. K.
  1957   "The role set: Problems in sociological theory." British Journal of Sociology
          8:106–120.
Mueller, D. P., D. W. Edwards, and R. M. Yarvis
  1977   "Stressful life events and psychiatric symptomatology: Change or un-
          desirability?" Journal of Health and Social Behavior 18:307–317.
Pearlin, L. I.
  1962   "Alienation from work: A study of nursing personnel." American So-
          ciological Review 27:314–326.
  1975a   "Sex roles and depression." Pp. 191–207 in Nancy Datan and Leon H.
          Ginsberg (eds.), Life-Span Developmental Psychology: Normative Life
          Crises. New York: Academic Press.
  1975b   "Status inequality and stress in marriage." American Sociological Review
          40:344–357.
  1980a   "The life cycle and life strains." Pp. 349–360 in Hubert M. Blalock, Jr. (ed.),
          Sociological Theory and Research. New York: The Free Press.
  1980b   "Life strains and psychological distress among adults." Pp. 174–192 in
          Neil J. Smelser and Erik H. Erikson (eds.), Themes of Work and Love in
          Adulthood. Cambridge: Harvard University Press.
  1982a   "The social contexts of stress." Pp. 367–379 In Leo Goldberger and Shlomo
          Breznitz (eds.), Handbook of Stress. New York: The Free Press.
  1982b   "Discontinuities in the study of aging." Pp. 55–74 in Tamara K. Hareven
          and Kathleen J. Adams (eds.), Aging and Life Course Transitions. New
          York: Guilford Press.
Pearlin, L. I., and M. A. Lieberman
  1979   "Social sources of emotional distress." Pp. 217–248 in Roberta Simmons
          (ed.), Research in Community and Mental Health. Volume 1. Greenwich,
          Conn.: JAI Press.
Pearlin, L. I., M. A. Lieberman, E. G. Menaghan, and J. T. Mullan
  1981   "The stress process." Journal of Health and Social Behavior 22:337–356.

Pearlin, L. I., and C. Radabaugh
    1976   "Economic strains and the coping functions of alcohol." American Journal
              of Sociology 82:652–663.
Pearlin, L. I., and C. Schooler
    1978   "The structure of coping." Journal of Health and Social Behavior 19:2–21.
Rose, Robert M., C. D. Jenkins, and M. W. Hurst
    1978   Air Traffic Controller Health Change Study. Boston: Boston University
              Press.
Ross, C., and J. Mirowsky II
    1979   "A comparison of life event weighting schemes: Change, undesirability and
              effect-proportional indices." Journal of Health and Social Behavior
              20:166–177.
Vinokur, A., and M. L. Selzer
    1975   "Desirable versus undesirable life events: Their relationship to stress and
              mental disease." Journal of Personality and Social Psychology 32:329–339.

2

Dimensions of Life Events That Influence Psychological Distress: An Evaluation and Synthesis of the Literature

PEGGY A. THOITS

INTRODUCTION

Research on the psychological effects of major life events has burgeoned in the past 20 years, especially since the publication and popularization of the Holmes–Rahe scale of life-change events (Holmes and Rahe, 1967). It is time to take stock of this literature, that is, to draw generalizations regarding the strength of the association between life events and psychological disturbance and to explore further the specific nature of this relationship. In particular, what types of life events influence psychological disturbance, and how do life events actually affect mental health directly, indirectly, and interactively? These, then, are the stock-taking purposes of this chapter. But before this effort at critical examination and synthesis is launched, a few terms require definition, and a brief background on the history and methods of life-events research is appropriate.

For the purposes of this chapter, *life events* or *life changes* are defined as objective experiences that disrupt or threaten to disrupt an individual's usual activities, causing a substantial readjustment in that individual's behavior (B. P. Dohrenwend and B. S. Dohrenwend, 1969:133; Holmes and Rahe, 1967). Examples of life events include marriage, divorce, graduation, and loss of job—changes that most persons experience in the natural life cycle—as well as more unusual or extreme experiences such as front-line combat, concentration-camp internment, and natural disaster. Readjustments in behavior due to these disruptions of everyday life are believed to result in disturbing physiological and psychological reactions; hence, the phrase *stressful life events* is often used in the empirical literature. The phrase *stressful life events* will be avoided in this chapter, however, as it is potentially misleading. The phrase implies that life events are identifiable by the responses they evoke (stressful life events are those that produce stress), a tautological error made by many early theorists in this field (Levine and Scotch, 1970; McGrath, 1970). The phrase suggests, too, that all events invariably produce stress reactions, an implication that this chapter will show to be untrue. Life events here are defined independently of stress responses, so that the degree to which life changes actually cause psychological reactions, and the particular types of changes that provoke particular types of reactions, may be examined.

Three dependent variables are of interest in this chapter: psychological distress, psychiatric disorder, and psychopathological behavior. *Psychological distress* is defined here as a general state of unpleasant arousal, indicated by self-reports of physiological and bodily changes (e.g., dizziness, shaking or sweating hands, trouble sleeping) and/or by changes in mood (poor spirits, depression, anxiety). *Psychiatric disorder* refers to impaired or totally disorganized cognitive, emotional, or behavioral functioning, usually indicated by various clinical diagnoses of neurosis or psychosis.[1] *Psychopathological behavior* refers to destructive actions against self or others that are thought to be indicative of psychiatric disorder, such as suicide attempts, assaultive violence, and drug or alcohol addiction. These latter behaviors, of course, are arguably not indicators of psychiatric disorder, but simply indicators of

---

[1]Although the most recent *Diagnostic and Statistical Manual of Mental Disorders* (American Psychiatric Association, 1980) no longer uses the category *neurosis*, most studies to be reviewed here were performed before this revision of the manual and thus do utilize classifications of neuroses described in earlier manuals (American Psychiatric Association, 1952, 1968).

socially unacceptable behavior. However, because psychological factors are implicated both theoretically and empirically in the genesis of such behaviors (Kaplan, 1980), these actions will be included as mental-health outcomes of interest. In short, this chapter is concerned with psychological disturbance, either as reported by individuals themselves (distress) or as defined and judged by clinicians (psychiatric disorder, psychopathological behavior). The scope of psychological outcomes of interest here is consistent with the definition of mental disorder in the most recent *Diagnostic and Statistical Manual of Mental Disorders* (American Psychiatric Association, 1980).

The Origins of Life-Events Research

The foundation for life-events research can be traced to W. B. Cannon (B. S. Dohrenwend and B. P. Dohrenwend, 1974; Mason 1975a). Cannon (1929) proposed and demonstrated with laboratory animals that emotion-provoking stimuli can produce the physiological and bodily alterations necessary for fight or flight (e.g., increased blood sugar and adrenalin, circulatory changes, more red corpuscles, rapid clotting). He also proposed that physical illness would result from "the persistent derangement of bodily functions . . . due to persistence of the stimuli which evoke the reactions" (1929:261). In support of this hypothesis Cannon cited clinical cases of pathology that appeared to follow directly severe emotional trauma in the lives of several patients. In brief, Cannon's research and observations suggested that traumatic events might produce physiological reactions that would, if not discharged or eliminated, generate illness.

This argument was adopted and modified somewhat by Adolf Meyer in the 1930s (B. S. Dohrenwend and B. P. Dohrenwend, 1974). Meyer (1951) trained physicians to utilize a life chart as a diagnostic tool. He suggested that life events might be important factors in the etiology of disease and that these events need not be major traumas to be pathogenic. That is, ordinary, normative changes in patients' lives, such as births, deaths, and job changes, might play a part in disease etiology.

Hans Selye's extensive laboratory experiments and theoretical writings on stress, beginning in the 1930s, contributed substantially to the viability of this hypothesis and stimulated a great deal of further research (Mason, 1975a, 1975b). Selye (1956) proposed and demonstrated that a variety of noxious agents or stressors—cold, heat, X rays, pain, forced exercise, and so on—elicited a single syndrome of physiological reactions, which he called the General Adaptation Syndrome

(GAS).[2] Further, this nonspecific syndrome—that is, this configuration of physiological changes in response to *any* stressor—had three stages: the alarm reaction, the stage of resistance, and the stage of exhaustion. Without adequate defenses against the stressor, diseases of adaptation might result.

Subsequent research has cast doubt on the nonspecificity of the response to noxious stimuli and, in fact, suggests that emotional arousal may have been the underlying factor responsible for the physiological reactions that Selye consistently observed (Mason, 1975b). However, Selye's theoretical generalizations, as well as those of Meyer, gave legitimacy and impetus to studies not only of reactions to physical stimuli but to studies of psychosocial stimuli as potential stressors as well. By 1950, life stresses (which include life events and chronic, ongoing difficulties in peoples' lives) were accepted as important factors in the etiology of disease, particularly psychosomatic disease (Wolff *et al.*, 1950). Since then, stress research has branched into two directions: Biologists, physiologists, and biochemists have focused on the physiological processes that intervene in, or explain, the relationship between psychosocial stimuli and particular disorders (Fröberg *et al.*, 1971; Jemmott and Locke, 1982); physicians, psychiatrists, epidemiologists, and sociologists have focused on the relationship between life events or chronic strains and various physical and psychological disorders. That physiological processes intervene in these relationships generally is assumed, rather than tested, by these researchers. This chapter reviews only this latter branch of research, with psychological outcome studies of particular concern.

Methods of Life-Events Research

Since World War II, the relationship between life events and psychological disturbance has been studied in three major ways. First, there have been studies of the psychiatric effects of particular events. During and after World War II, for example, soldiers' reactions to different degrees of combat (e.g., Grinker and Spiegal, 1945; Hastings, 1944; Star, 1949), civilians' responses to air raids (Bremer, 1951; Janis, 1951), and survivors' psychiatric adjustments after concentration-camp imprison-

---

[2]Selye posited a triad of physiological reactions: (1) adrenal cortical enlargement, (2) atrophy of the thymus and other lymhatic nodes, and (3) bleeding ulcers of the stomach and small intestines.

ment (Eitinger, 1964) were studied. Subsequently, the psychological impacts of other events have been investigated, for example, the effects of natural and man-made disasters (Barton, 1969; Gleser et al., 1981; Lifton, 1968; Lindemann, 1944; Tyhurst, 1951; White and Haas, 1975), residential relocation following slum clearance (Fried, 1963), job loss due to plant shutdowns (Cobb and Kasl, 1977; Gore, 1978), bereavement (Clayton et al., 1971, 1972; Lindemann, 1944; Parkes, 1972; Stein and Susser, 1970), rape (Burgess and Holmstrom, 1974, 1979; McCombie, 1975), terminal illness or major surgery (see reviews by Cohen and Lazarus, 1979; Silver and Wortman, 1980), graduate examinations (Mechanic, 1962), and even President Kennedy's assassination (Sheatsley and Feldman, 1964). Studies of the psychological effects of particular events generally have examined the correlation between degree of exposure to the event and the intensity of psychological reactions, or have examined subjects' reactions to an event over time, with psychiatric assessments made before, during, and after the event's occurrence. Designs that compare the psychological adjustment of persons who have experienced a particular event with matched controls who have not experienced the event have been comparatively rare (but see Cobb and Kasl, 1977; Sterling et al., 1977; Thoits, 1979; Thoits and Hannan, 1979). Without such comparisons, of course, it is difficult to assign causal effects of the event unambiguously.

The second approach to the study of the events–disorder relationship, the community survey, examines the psychological effects of multiple events in the lives of random samples of adults or children. This approach was enabled by the development of life-event scales, particularly the Holmes–Rahe Social Readjustment Rating Scale (SRRS) (Holmes and Rahe, 1967). A brief description of the development of this scale seems appropriate at this point.

Holmes, Rahe, and their colleagues combed thousands of U. S. Navy medical records for events associated with injury or the onset of illness. They derived a list of 43 events, which then were rated by convenience samples of judges for the amount of readjustment each event required. Compared to a standard life change, marriage, with a readjustment value set at 500, judges independently assigned ratings to other events using a scale ranging from 0 to infinity. Judges' ratings of each event were averaged and divided by 100 to form life-change unit (LCU) scores. The 43 events ranged in LCU weights from 100 for the death of a spouse to 11 for minor violations of the law (see Table 2.1).

The SRRS and other life-events scales developed subsequently by other researchers (Brown and Harris, 1978; Coddington, 1972; B. S.

TABLE 2.1

Social Readjustment Rating Scale[a]

Rank	Life event	Mean value
1	Death of spouse	100
2	Divorce	73
3	Marital separation	65
4	Jail term	63
5	Death of close family member	63
6	Personal injury or illness	53
7	Marriage	50
8	Fired at work	47
9	Marital reconciliation	45
10	Retirement	45
11	Change in health of family member	44
12	Pregnancy	40
13	Sex difficulties	39
14	Gain of new family member	39
15	Business readjustment	39
16	Change in financial state	38
17	Death of close friend	37
18	Change to different line of work	36
19	Change in number of arguments with spouse	35
20	Mortgage over $10,000	31
21	Foreclosure of mortgage or loan	30
22	Change in responsibilities at work	29
23	Son or daughter leaving home	29
24	Trouble with in-laws	29
25	Outstanding personal achievement	28
26	Wife begin or stop work	26
27	Begin or end school	26
28	Change in living conditions	25
29	Revision of personal habits	24
30	Trouble with boss	23
31	Change in work hours or conditions	20
32	Change in residence	20
33	Change in schools	20
34	Change in recreation	19
35	Change in church activities	19
36	Change in social activities	18
37	Mortgage or loan less than $10,000	17
38	Change in sleeping habits	16
39	Change in number of family get-togethers	15
40	Change in eating habits	15
41	Vacation	13
42	Christmas	12
43	Minor violations of the law	11

[a]From Holmes and Rahe, 1967:216, Table 3. Reprinted with permission from *Journal of Psychosomatic Research*, Pergamon Press, Ltd.

Dohrenwend *et al.*, 1978; Hough *et al.*, 1976; Paykel *et al.*, 1971) could be incorporated easily into large-scale surveys of community residents. Respondents typically are asked which of a list of life events they have experienced over a past specified time period (e.g., over the past 3 months, past year, past 4 years) and also respond to validated inventories of psychological distress, depression, or anxiety symptoms or to indices of psychopathological behaviors (Brown and Harris, 1978; Coates *et al.*, 1969, 1976; Coddington, 1972; B. S. Dohrenwend, 1973; Gersten *et al.*, 1974; Kaplan *et al.*, 1983; Markush and Favero, 1974; Myers *et al.*, 1971, 1972, 1974). Such community studies allow researchers to examine the cumulative impacts of various types of events, weighted or unweighted by their readjustment values, on respondents' current psychological well-being. Most of these studies are retrospective in design. That is, they explore the influence of past recalled events on current psychological state. Of course, such cross-sectional retrospective designs may incorporate biases. Preexisting psychological disturbance may influence the occurrence of certain events, such as divorce, loss of job, and criminal arrest (Hinkle, 1974). And respondents may recall an excess of events in order to explain their current distress (Brown, 1974). However, several of these studies are panel surveys. Such data permit researchers to disentangle the effects of past events on current psychological disturbance from the effects of prior disturbance on the recent occurrence of events. To date, few researchers have examined these mutual influences over time. (See Turner and Noh, 1982, for an exception.)

Finally, several studies have compared the number and types of life events experienced by psychiatric patients prior to hospitalization to those experienced by nonpatient control subjects. Patient versus nonpatient comparisons have been made for schizophrenia (e.g., Birley and Brown, 1970; Brown and Birley, 1968), depression and suicide attempts (e.g., Barrett, 1979; Brown and Harris, 1978; Paykel, 1974; Paykel *et al.*, 1969, 1975), adolescent affective disorders (e.g., Barrett, 1979), and undifferentiated disorders (e.g., Dekker and Webb, 1974). These studies allow the identification of events that might precipitate more serious psychiatric disorders. However, it is important to realize that selection into treatment occurs on the basis of a variety of factors unrelated to the severity of illness per se (Mechanic, 1974). Further, help seeking may be a direct consequence of the experience of life events themselves (Mechanic, 1974). Thus, the results of comparisons between hospitalized and nonhospitalized samples can be misleading without consideration of such selection factors.

The Basic Life-Events Finding—and a Problem

Despite the methodological drawbacks to each of these three research designs, strikingly consistent findings have emerged from studies using such research strategies over the past 30 years. Life events are significantly associated with increased psychological disturbance.[3] The more exposure to life events in a given period, the greater the distress symptomatology, the greater the likelihood of hospitalization for psychiatric disorder, and the greater the probability of psychopathological behavior. Although dozens of representative findings could be cited, only three will be described here.

Clayton and her colleagues (Clayton and Darvish, 1979; Clayton et al., 1968, 1971, 1972) examined the psychological impacts of bereavement on two randomly selected samples of white widows and widowers in St. Louis, Missouri (total $N = 149$). All bereaved individuals were interviewed 1 month and again 13 months after the death of their spouse. At 1 month, 89% of the bereaved reported one or more symptoms of depression (e.g., crying, sleep disturbance, low mood, loss of appetite; Clayton and Darvish, 1979). A depressive syndrome similar to clinical depression was exhibited by 42%. At 13 months, 48% still reported one or more depressive symptoms, and 16% retained a full depressive syndrome. Thus, it seems clear that a majority of people respond with psychological symptoms to this loss event and a substantial minority become seriously depressed immediately after the event. Although depressive symptoms generally subside with time, a few individuals remain seriously depressed. The experience of one major life event, then, may precipitate symptoms similar to psychiatric disorder, although such persons are more likely to have already been psychiatrically ill (Clayton and Darvish, 1979). It should be noted, however, that these findings are based on subsamples of the originally contacted groups; the initial refusal rates were 42% and 34% in the two studies. Thus, the results of these studies may be biased in some unknown way.

Myers and his co-workers (Myers et al., 1971, 1972, 1974) examined the relationship between the total number of life events experienced during a year and respondents' current levels of psychological distress, using panel data collected in a mental health agency catchment area in

[3]Life events are also significantly related to the occurrence of a variety of physical diseases and injuries. For reviews of the physical health effects of life events see Cohen (1975); Holmes and Masuda (1974); Jemmott and Locke (1982); Rahe (1974); Rahe and Arthur (1978); Theorell (1974).

New Haven. A random sample of 720 adults were interviewed twice, once in 1967 and again in 1969. At each interview, respondents were asked which of a list of 62 life events they or members of their families had experienced over the past year. The list of events included selected items from the SRRS, other items developed by Antonovsky and Kats (1967), and items developed by the researchers themselves. The psychological distress inventory was formulated by Macmillan (1957) and further modified by Gurin et al. (1960). It consisted of a list of 20 psychological and psychosomatic symptoms, rated on a four-point scale (e.g., "Are you ever bothered by nightmares or dreams that frighten or upset you?" with four possible responses—"Often," "Sometimes," "Hardly ever," "Never"). The items on the scale are summed; values range from 20 (high distress) to 80 (little or no distress). This scale, and others similar to it (Langner, 1962), have been shown to have criterion validity; that is, these scales discriminate significantly between known well and psychiatrically impaired individuals.[4]

At each time point, Myers and his colleagues found a significant association between the number of events experienced and the individual's psychological distress score. For example, the correlation between events and symptom scores was $-.34$ in 1967 (Myers et al., 1971). Furthermore, a net increase in the number of events over time was associated with an increase in distress symptoms. The authors concluded that these findings "demonstrate the importance of social and interpersonal forces frequently external to the individual in influencing psychological status. The sheer quantity of events alone seems to have a striking effect upon one's capacity to maintain a state of mental health" (Myers et al., 1972:404).

Brown and Birley (1968) compared the life changes experienced by 50 hospitalized schizophrenics to those experienced by 377 employed workers (a control sample). Events that occurred to patients in the 3 months prior to the established onset of symptoms were compared to events that occurred to controls in the 3 months prior to interview. Subjects were asked if they had experienced any of a list of events that was developed by the researchers on commonsense grounds. The list contained role changes, major health changes, residence changes, forecasts of change, valued goal fulfillments or disappointments, and other dramatic crisis events thought to have positive or negative emotional impacts on most individuals. Events to which subjects or their close

[4]The inadequacies of such scales are discussed later in the chapter; see section "Dependent Variable Measures."

relatives were exposed were counted. Dates of these events were also established. Events and event dates for schizophrenics were cross-checked by interviews with a relative.

Sixty percent of the patients had at least one event that was judged by the researchers to be independent or possibly independent of the psychiatric illness itself during the 3-week period before symptom onset. Only 19.5% of the controls experienced such events in the 3-week period prior to interview. Before those 3 weeks, patients and controls did not differ significantly in the number of experienced events. An average of 22.7% of the patients and 19.5% of the controls experienced one or more events in the earlier 3-week periods. Sociodemographic differences between patients and controls did not account for these main findings. Furthermore, because events before illness *onset* were examined, rather than events before hospital *admission*, the possible effect of events on treatment seeking did not bias these results (see Mechanic, 1974). Brown and Birley concluded that "there is reasonably sound evidence that environmental factors can precipitate a schizophrenic attack and that such events tend to cluster in the three weeks before onset" (1968:211).

The results of these and many other studies tend to confirm the basic relationship between life events and psychological disturbance. However, as Rabkin and Struening (1976) have pointed out, correlations between life change and psychological (or physical) disorder, although significant, have been disappointingly low. Correlations are usually under .30; they rarely exceed .40 (see Mueller *et al.*, 1977; Ross and Mirowsky, 1979). This means that events explain at most 9–16% of the variance in psychological outcomes. Given the theoretical importance attached by most researchers to life changes as an etiological factor (or set of factors), the weak explanatory power of events is an embarrassment. Why is the relationship such a modest one?

Several very different answers to this question have been suggested. They may be classified generally into three replies: (1) Methodological problems, particularly measurement problems, attenuate the actual strength of the relationship; (2) failure to specify the *types* of events that generate disturbance attenuates the relationship; and (3) individuals' utilization of efficacious coping responses and/or social support explains the modest relationship—that is, the correlation between events and disturbance is low because many individuals use distress-reducing coping resources. Because other chapters in this volume address the third category of answers in depth (see chapters by Turner and by Menaghan), this chapter explores the issues raised by the first two. It will be argued here that neither methodological issues nor lack of event specificity adequately accounts for the modest events–disturbance correlation. Rather, when methodological problems are corrected and when specific dimensions of events most highly associated with disturbance are identified, more complex relationships between events and disturbance are suggested. Failure to examine these more complex relationships has left us with very modest amounts of explained variance in psychological outcomes.

MEASUREMENT AND OTHER METHODOLOGICAL PROBLEMS

The life-events literature has been extensively criticized for its methodological inadequacies (Brown, 1974; Cleary, 1981; B. P. Dohrenwend, 1974, 1979; Hurst, 1979; Mechanic, 1974; Rabkin and Struening, 1976; Wershow and Reinhart, 1974). The most serious inadequacies concern the measurement of both the dependent and independent variables. The strength of the relationship between events and disturbance, it has been argued, might be increased if outcome criteria were refined and life-event checklists were improved (Rabkin and Struening, 1976). This section reviews problems with measuring the dependent and independent variables, in that order, and assesses the various impacts of these problems on the strength of the basic relationhip.

Dependent Variable Measures

Psychological outcomes are typically measured by clinical diagnosis (if patient to control comparisons are made), by treatment status (inpatient, outpatient, nonpatient), by short symptom inventories of distress, or by official records or self-reports of psychopathological behaviors. Each of these outcome measures has its drawbacks.

Diagnoses

Clinical diagnoses are notoriously unreliable, as is well known (Spitzer and Fleiss, 1974). Interrater and test–retest reliabilities rarely exceed .5 (except in studies that formulate explicit criteria for defining a "case;" e.g., Brown and Harris, 1978). Furthermore, classifications by general diagnosis (e.g., depression, schizophrenia) often lump together subjects with differentiable disorders (Wershow and Reinhart, 1974). Depression, for example, could be classified into endogenous and reactive types, or into even more refined categories (Barrett, 1979). Unreliable categorization and undifferentiated subtypes may lower correlations between life events and outcome states as well as obscure important variations in the relationship by specific types of disorder.

Treatment Status

Often researchers differentiate cases from controls on the basis of treatment status alone. That is, they compare the prior life experiences of inpatients or outpatients of a psychiatric agency to those of persons not in treatment. Again, failure to distinguish between types of disorder among patients may reduce the correlation between events and disorder. But the low association between events and disorder also may exist because patient versus nonpatient status is simply an inadequate indicator of the presence or absence of disturbance (Finlay-Jones, 1981). As pointed out earlier, patient status is likely to be an indicator, at least in part, of help-seeking behavior (Hudgens, 1974; Mechanic, 1974; Rabkin and, Struening, 1976). Help-seeking tendencies are differentially distributed by sex, ethnicity, social class, and other characteristics (Mechanic, 1974). Some persons with serious clinical symptoms do not seek treatment at all, whereas others with minor symptoms immediately contact a health or mental health agency. If help seeking is more an indicator of sociocultural characteristics or of the prior experience of stressors (Mechanic, 1974) and less an indicator of the presence or absence of disturbance per se, low associations between events and disorder might be expected from studies that compare treated to untreated samples.

Moreover, admission to treatment may be an inadequate indicator of symptom onset. Time of symptom onset, of course, is crucial for studies of etiological factors. Because initial onset is more difficult to determine for psychological than for physical disorders, many researchers simply utilize new admissions to treatment as a proxy for symptom onset. This practice may lead to misleading results. If onset occurs long before admission to treatment, then recent life events may be products of already-existing disturbance, rather than precipitants of it, as is usually assumed.

Symptom Inventories

Symptom inventories, used in community surveys, have different drawbacks. The most popular inventories of distress—the Health Opinion Survey (Macmillan, 1957), the Gurin Index (Gurin et al., 1960), and the Langner 22-Item Index (Langner, 1962)—consist of several psychological and psychosomatic symptom items, evaluated on an ordinal scale (e.g., "How often do you have trouble getting to sleep or staying asleep?"—"Often," "Sometimes," "Seldom," "Never"). These indexes have been shown to be valid by the known-groups technique; that is, scores on the indexes significantly discriminate psychiatric patients from nonpatients in the community (Leighton et al., 1963; Macmillan, 1957; Manis et al., 1963; Spiro et al., 1972; Tousignant et al., 1974). Further, each scale has a strong coefficient of internal consistency, indicating good reliability (Thoits, 1981). However, four problems limit the utility of these indexes (Crandell and Dohrenwend, 1967; B. P. Dohrenwend, 1966; Norland and Weirath, 1978; Seiler, 1973; Spiro et al., 1972; Tousignant et al., 1974).

First, as Norland and Weirath (1978) point out, the known-groups technique of validation may be suspect when hospitalized patients are used as a criterion group. A variety of nonpsychiatric factors determine presence in treatment, so a psychiatric condition actually may not differentiate patient and nonpatient samples, or nonpsychiatric factors may be confounded with this differentiation.

Second, the scales lack diagnostic specificity; that is, they serve primarily as indicators of generalized distress or anxiety rather than of specific disorders (Leighton et al., 1963; Myers et al., 1971; Schwartz et al., 1973; Seiler, 1973; Spiro et al., 1972; Tousignant et al., 1974). Lack of specificity, again, can obscure important variations in the events–disturbance relationship.

Third, the differential social desirability of many of the index items may bias responses, as may yea- or nay-saying response sets (B. P. Dohrenwend, 1966; B. P. Dohrenwend and B. S. Dohrenwend, 1969). Some evidence exists that items vary in perceived desirability by the race, ethnicity, and sex of respondents (B. P. Dohrenwend and B. S. Dohrenwend, 1969; Phillips and Clancy, 1970, 1972; Phillips and Segal, 1969). Although five studies (Clancy and Gove, 1974; Gove and Geerkin, 1977; Johnson and Meile, 1981; Meile and Gregg, 1973; Schuessler et al., 1978) have shown that these response biases have no consistent effects on the relationships between sociodemographic variables and symptom scores, others do indicate some bias (Carr and Krause, 1978; Canover and Climent, 1976). Thus, the possibility of response biases in symptom scores must not be ignored.

Finally, the indexes contain a physical health bias. That is, the preponderance of psychosomatic symptom items in these indexes makes it likely that physically ill respondents will obtain high scores, thus confounding the presence of physical illness with psychological distress (see Thoits, 1981, for an empirical illustration of this problem). In short, low correlations between life events and symptom scores may be due to the invalidity of the indexes, to the nonspecificity of the indexes, to reduced variation in the indexes from systematic response biases, to the confounding of physical with psychological disturbance, or to some combination of these effects. Although more recent symptom indices for particular diagnoses, such as the Centre for Epidemiology Depression Scale (CES-D scale) for depression (Radloff, 1977) and the Symptom Check List-90 (SCL-90) scale for a variety of specified neurotic disorders (Derogatis et al., 1973), cannot be critiqued for lack of diagnostic specificity, these scales are subject to other criticisms discussed here.

Psychopathological Behaviors

Measures of psychopathological behaviors can be even more heavily critiqued. First, there is considerable debate whether deviant behaviors are actually indicators of psychiatric disorder (B. P. Dohrenwend and B. S. Dohrenwend, 1976; Gove and Tudor, 1977; Scheff, 1966; Szasz, 1960). Thus, the validity of these indicators is in serious question. Second, because these behaviors are generally considered socially unacceptable, they tend to be underreported in both official records (for advantaged sociodemographic groups) and in self-report inventories (Douglas, 1967; Gibbs and Martin, 1964; Nettler, 1978). Underreporting, of course, introduces unknown biases in treatment data and in community studies. Consequently, studies with psychopathological behaviors as outcome variables must be viewed with considerable caution.[5]

Timing of Measurement

Finally, critical to the understanding of the relationship between life events and psychological disturbance is the timing of the measurement of psychological reactions. Very little is known about the length of the time lag between event occurrences and initial symptom formation. Even less is known about the time required for symptoms to abate. Consequently, if psychological measures are taken too soon or too late after event impacts have occurred, no relationship or a very modest relationship between events and symptoms will be found. The low correlation between events and disturbance reported in most studies may be due, in fact, to these timing problems. Typically, studies corre-

---

[5]See Scott (1970) for an additional review of the inadequacies of a variety of indicators of mental health and mental illness.

late the number of events over, say, a past year with subjects' current level of symptomatology or with some indicator of presumed presence or absence of disturbance (e.g., patient versus nonpatient status). The lag between events and subsequent measurement of disturbance could be considerable. Some research indicates that symptom onset is most likely to begin 3–4 weeks after a closely spaced cluster of events (Brown and Birley, 1968; Brown and Harris, 1978; Paykel, 1974, 1979), and other research reports higher correlations between events and disturbance when events are aggregated over short time periods rather than long (Grant et al., 1981); thus, many life-event studies may be underestimating the impact of life events on disturbance—enough time may have passed for symptom abatement to occur. Clearly, then, not only do measures of psychological distress or disorder require improvement, but closer attention must be paid in future research to the timing of such measurements relative to previous event experiences.

Life-Event Measures

The need for improved measures of the independent variable, life change, has received even more attention in recent critical literature. Of particular concern are issues of reliability, validity, content, contamination, and weighting. Each will be discussed in turn.

Reliability and Validity

Although at least 1000 publications have utilized the SRRS since its development (Holmes, 1979), remarkably few studies of the reliability and validity of the scale, or of others like it, have been made. Moreover, those estimates that have been made of reliability and validity have varied enormously. This variability is due in part to techniques used to assess reliability and validity and in part to differences in data-collection method.

To estimate reliability, researchers typically have (1) examined the distribution of recalled events over time, (2) computed test–retest correlations, or (3) estimated the internal consistency of life-event scales. To assess validity, researchers have utilized informants to verify the occurrence of events reported by respondents. The percentage agreement between the reports of respondents and informants, although thought to assess the actual occurrence of events, is really a form of interrater reliability. Results from each form of assessment will be examined in turn.

Examining the distribution of reported events over time gives the investigator some idea of the reliability of recall. If recall is accurate, no significant decline in the average number of events reported from recent to more remote months should be found. Uhlenhuth et al. (1977) found that respondents' reports of previous life events declined with time, falling off at a rate of about 5% per month over an 18-month period. Significantly more events were reported to have occurred in recent months than in remote months. "Fateful" events—events beyond the respondents' control—were even more likely to be forgotten with time, falling off at a rate of 9% per month. Similar findings were reported in an earlier study (Nelson et al., 1972). Uhlenhuth and his colleagues concluded that memory even for important events may be highly unreliable.

In contrast, three major, carefully conducted studies with community and patient respondents indicated no significant decline in recall over a year's time (Brown and Harris, 1978; Brown et al., 1973; Paykel et al., 1969). Moreover, rates of event occurrence did not differ significantly between patients and controls during more remote months. The inconsistent results of these five studies taken together may be accounted for, at least partially, by differences in data-collection methods. The Nelson et al. and Uhlenhuth et al. investigations relied on self-administered events questionnaires, whereas the Brown and the Paykel studies utilized interview data. The opportunity to probe respondents' replies in interviews may have elicited better recall of events over long periods of time (Brown and Harris, 1978). Furthermore, the use in interviews of standardized sets of questions that establish the meaning and scope of each event may enhance event recognition and recall (Brown and Harris, 1978).

Methods of data collection also may explain partially the differences in reliability obtained from test–retest, internal consistency, and inter-rater-agreement studies. Test–retest reliabilities and internal consistency estimates have been extremely varied in value, but on average have been low to moderate in size. Interrater-agreement studies have yielded somewhat higher reliabilities. The former typically have been based on self-administered questionnaire data, the latter almost exclusively on data from interviews (Neugebauer, 1981).

For example, test–retest correlations of the number of events reported to have occurred during a defined period have ranged from as low as .07 to as high as .90 (Horowitz et al., 1977; Jenkins et al., 1979; Neugebauer, 1981; Rahe, 1974; Sarason et al., 1978). The majority of these test–retest correlations appear to fall in the low-to-moderate range, between .30 and .60 (see Neugebauer, 1981). When the test–retest reliability for specific events is examined, more questions can be raised about reliability of recall. For example, although Horowitz et al. (1977) found a correlation of .82 between the number of events reported to have occurred in a defined period at a first and second assessment by questionnaire, only 60% of the events checked at the first assessment were rechecked by the respondent at the follow-up, 6 months later. Jenkins et al. (1979) report similar unreliabilities for specific items on life-event scales.

Estimates of internal consistency for life-event scales have been in the low-to-moderate range as well. Hurst, Jenkins, and Rose (1978) reported coefficient alphas for three different life-event scales, the Holmes–Rahe (Holmes and Rahe, 1967) Schedule of Recent Events, the Paykel et al. (1971) list, and their own list of 103 items. The alphas were .51, .41, and .53, respectively. Lei and Skinner (1980) report an alpha of .80 for the Holmes–Rahe scale, but their sample consisted of drug and alcohol patients only. Cleary (1980) has argued that, although alpha coefficients for life events scales typically exceed .40 in value, these estimates are inappropriate tests of scale reliability. Theoretically, life events should be independent of one another, so alpha coefficients should equal zero (Cleary, 1980). Values of .40 or greater simply indicate that life events are related to one another. On the other hand, if life-event scales are intended to measure an underlying factor, life change, then alpha coefficients are appropriate measures of internal consistency. Whether one agrees with Cleary's theoretical premise or not, internal consistency estimates add to the picture of high variability and, on average, of only moderate degrees of reliability in life-event measurement.

As noted earlier, test–retest and internal-consistency estimates generally have been based on questionnaire data. Interrater reliabilities, also considered validity estimates, generally have been obtained from personal interviews. These estimates of reliability tend to be somewhat higher (Neugebauer, 1981). Hudgens and his associates (Hudgens et al., 1970) report a 57% agreement between patient and informant accounts of events occurring to the patient over a 12-month period. Rahe et al. (1973) cite similar figures; patients' self-reports and the reports of their spouses "as if" they were the patient correlated .50 to .75. Brown and his colleagues (Brown et al., 1973) and Brown and Harris (1978) report agreements between subjects' accounts and those supplied by relatives of .79 or better. However, lower interrater reliabilities have been found, too; Schless and Mendels (1978) report interpair agreements of only .43. Horowitz et al. (1977) report agreements ranging from 46 to 76% on specific event items.

In sum, the reliability of life-event measures seems highly questionable when time distributions of events, test–retest correlations, and internal consistency coefficients are examined in studies based on questionnaire data. Single-event reliabilities in questionnaire studies may be particularly unstable. Brown and Harris (1978) suggest that the brief, single-item description of life events that are typical on event questionnaires may be responsible for these marked instabilities. Not only may such single-item indicators be differently interpreted across a variety of respondents (a serious validity problem), but the same respondents may interpret a single item differently from a first to a second assessment. The more subjective the item (e.g., "major change in income," "major change in social activities"), the more likely such interpretive variations may occur over time. Interview data based on more detailed, explicit, and probing sets of questions about events yield somewhat more reliable event measures. Recall remains fairly stable over time and interrater reliabilities (or validity estimates) tend to be moderate to strong. But event measurement in interviews is still far from perfect. Although in general reports of objective, important events tend to be more reliable than reports of subjective and minor events, regardless of data-collection method (Neugebauer, 1981), even major events requiring substantial amounts of readjustment are more than occasionally forgotten by respondents. In short, the reliability and validity of life-event measures are generally quite modest. These imperfections in measurement almost certainly have attenuated the correlations between events and psychological disturbance.

Content and Contamination

The content of life-event scales raises other serious problems. The first concerns event sampling. The SRRS does not exhaust the full universe of possible events. No checklist can, as B. S. Dohrenwend and her colleagues (B. S. Dohrenwend et al., 1978) reasonably point out. But the SRRS and other checklists typically omit certain universal human experiences (e.g., being the victim of a crime) and exclude other common but socially controversial events (e.g., marital infidelity, abortion, acknowledgment of one's homosexuality). "Nonevents"—events that are desired or anticipated but do not occur—have also been omitted (Gersten et al., 1974). The checklists selectively emphasize events of young adulthood (Rabkin and Struening, 1976), heavily underrepresent events that occur to women (Makosky, 1980), and omit events that are common in the lives of the poor, certain racial and ethnic groups, and particular occupational groups (Hurst, 1979; Rabkin and Struening, 1976). Omission of important events obviously may lower the correlation between life change and psychological disturbance. Moreover, biased lists of events may obscure important variations in the frequency and impacts of events among sociodemographic groups (see the section "Life-Event Processes: Theoretical Implications" for further discussion of this topic).

A second content problem concerns the number of undesirable, or negative, events relative to desirable events on these scales. The SRRS and most other checklists contain a preponderance of undesirable events. Other items are worded ambiguously ("major change in living conditions," "major change in financial state," etc.), thus obscuring the desirability or undesirability of the event. Because more recent research has attempted to identify whether change per se or the amount of undesirable change is most predictive of psychological disorder (an issue about which more will be said in a later section), the bias and the ambiguity in the SRRS and other scales have proved to be handicaps. The confounding of total amount of change with total undesirable change again may have lowered the correlation between events and disorder.

A third content problem concerns the types of events that are included. Many investigators acknowledge that their scales contain several distinct types of events: role transformations, environmental changes, impositions of pain, socially isolating and integrating changes, permanent and transitory events, voluntary and involuntary events. Few investigators have systematically selected specific types of events for investigation using a guiding theoretical rationale. Combining different types of events into a total change score again may have weakened the events–disorder relationship (an issue taken up in more detail in the next major section).

A related problem concerns the interrelationships among events. Not all events occur independently (Cleary, 1980; Pugh et al., 1971; Rahe et al., 1971; Ruch, 1977; Skinner and Lei, 1980b). For example, divorce may generate a series of other changes, such as a residential move, a drop in income, and changes in social or family activities. As Tausig notes, "This raises the possibility that we may increase artificially the reported frequency of events for certain respondents that would result in misclassifying them as having high numbers of life events. We might then fail to find a correlation between event frequency and illness because too many events are counted for some respondents" (1982:53). On the other hand, the closer the causal relationships between two or more events (for example, job loss and a significant drop in income), the more likely a respondent might be to report them as a single major event (job loss). This would result in an undercounting of events and thus would attenuate correlations.

A fourth extremely serious content problem is the inclusion of contaminated, or confounded, events. Several critics of life-events research (Brown, 1974; B. P. Dohrenwend, 1974; Hinkle, 1974; Hudgens, 1974; Lehman, 1978; Rabkin and Struening, 1976; Thoits, 1981) have argued that many items on checklists are either indications of or possible products of existing psychological disorder, rather than independent events that cause disorder. For example, on the SRRS, "change in eating habits," "change in sleeping habits," and "sexual difficulties" may be indicators of a psychosomatic disorder or depression rather than events that themselves generate disorder. Similarly, being fired, having trouble with boss or spouse, and divorce may be products of already-existing disturbance rather than antecedents of disturbance. Many, if not most, items on event checklists may be confounded with the very outcomes they are intended to predict. Hudgens states, "by my count, 29 of the 43 events on Holmes' [SRRS] (Holmes and Rahe, 1967) are events that are often the symptoms or consequences of illness. The same is true of 32 of 61 events on Paykel's (Paykel et al., 1971) long scale of events and 18 of 33 events on his short scale" (1974:131). Note that the inclusion of confounded events on checklists should *inflate* the correlation between number of events and psychological symptomatology. When confounded events are excluded for separate analysis, the events–disorder relationship may be much weaker than previously reported. For example, Tausig (1982) reports that the correlation of SRRS scores with depression drops from .252 to .207 (a significant decrease) when depression-related items are excluded from the SRRS. Similarly, I have shown (Thoits 1981) that when psychological distress is measured with an index containing many psychosomatic symptoms, the events–distress correlation is substantially reduced when health-related events are excluded from the events checklist. In other words, health events (illnesses, injuries) are strongly associated with somatic symptoms on the distress indices currently in use. This uninteresting and confounding association may account heavily for the overall relationship between events and psychological distress (*and* between events and physical illness) found in most community studies,[6] al-

---

[6]On the other hand, this finding may mean that health-related events are very important determinants of psychological disturbance. But until health-related events and other events are correlated with outcome measures that are *free* of health-related items, this conclusion cannot be confidently made. No study to date has examined such relation-

though other investigators (McFarlane *et al.*, 1980; Tausig, 1982) argue that these possibly contaminated events do not inflate the correlations as seriously as I claim.

Biased Recall

Events may be contaminated in other ways. Life-event studies typically rely on subjects' ability to recall events that have occurred over long periods of time (Hudgens, 1974; Hudgens *et al.*, 1970; Paykel, 1974). The reliability of recall over long periods is certainly questionable, as discussed earlier (see the section "Reliability and Validity"). It is also possible that recall is distorted or biased toward negative events, especially if subjects seek to explain a current disorder in terms of past events. Brown (1974) calls this the problem of "retrospective contamination" or "effort after meaning." Simple unreliable recall may lower the correlation of events with disorder. But to the extent that *biased* recall occurs, the correlation should be inflated, or more specifically, the correlation between negative events and disorder should be inflated.

Event Weighting

A final critique of life-event checklists focuses on the problem of weighting events. Recall that the SRRS weights each event by the mean readjustment rating given to it by panels of judges. Other methods of weighting events include asking subjects to rate subjectively the distress caused by experienced events (Vinokur and Selzer, 1975), deriving weights from multiple regression techniques (Ross and Mirowsky, 1979; Rubin *et al.*, 1971), using group mean ratings from the specific sample studied (Hurst, 1979), and simply weighting each experienced event by one (i.e., weighting them equally). The SRRS scores have been criticized first because the use of weights for nonspecific changes (e.g., "major change in working conditions") obscures the very different weights given by raters when the desirability of the change is taken into account (e.g., "major change for the worse in working conditions," "major change for the better in working conditions"). Undesirable changes are given much more readjustment weight than desirable changes (Hough *et al.*, 1976; Ross and Mirowsky, 1979). Second,

---

ships. However, McFarlane *et al.* (1980) report significant modest correlations of non-health-related events and psychological distress among individuals who have *not* experienced recent health changes, suggesting that possibly confounded health events are not totally responsible for the correlation between life events and psychological distress. Tausig (1982) reports similar data.

weightings may differ significantly between subjects who have experienced the event being rated and those who have not, although the evidence on this still is mixed (B. S. Dohrenwend et al., 1978; Horowitz et al., 1974, 1977; Hurst et al., 1978; Lundberg and Theorell, 1976; Paykel et al., 1971; Rosenberg and Dohrenwend, 1975; Ruch and Holmes, 1971). Third, insufficient attention has been given to cultural or ethnic variability in readjustment ratings and to differences in ratings by various sociodemographic groups. For example, Miller et al. (1974) have shown that rural Americans assign different weights to events than the urban raters employed by Holmes and Rahe. Several studies (Askenasy et al., 1977; Fairbank and Hough, 1981; Hough et al., 1976; Masuda and Holmes, 1978; Rosenberg and Dohrenwend, 1975) have shown that ethnic groups (e.g., blacks, Mexican–Americans) differ from whites in rating the stressfulness of events. There have also been indications that males and females rate certain events quite differently, with females tending to rate events as more stressful or requiring greater readjustment, although event experience may reduce such differences (Bradley, 1980; Horowitz et al., 1974, 1977; Lundberg and Theorell, 1976; Masuda and Holmes, 1978; Sarason et al., 1978). Adults under 30 years of age may perceive events differently from older adults, as well (Horowitz et al., 1974, 1977). These studies, taken together, suggest that the application of one set of weighting norms to subjects of different subcultures, ethnic groups, or sociodemographic groups may decrease the accuracy of prediction of disorder. The same criticism may apply to weights derived from multiple regression techniques or group mean ratings; weights will depend upon the experiential or cultural perceptions of the particular sample employed (Cleary, 1981).

A different criticism applies to the use of subjective weights supplied by the subjects under study. Several investigations have shown that psychiatric patients tend to rate events as more stressful than nonpatients (Grant et al., 1976; Lundberg and Theorell, 1976; Paykel et al., 1971; Schless et al., 1974; Theorell, 1974). As B. P. Dohrenwend points out, "it is incredible that some researchers have advocated scoring the magnitude of life events (the amount of readjustment, change, or upset involved) in terms of subjective ratings by the individuals whose stress experiences in relation to their psychopathology are being studied. . . . This procedure is virtually guaranteed to confound the relationship between stress and psychopathology" (1979:8). That is, in such studies (e.g., Sarason et al., 1978) the correlation found between life experiences and disturbance may be due primarily to the biased ratings of events made by disturbed individuals.

Although work continues to develop more representative and uncontaminated weights (e.g., B. S. Dohrenwend *et al.*, 1978), recent studies indicate that little predictive power is gained from the use of either objective or subjective weights (Gersten *et al.*, 1974; Grant *et al.*, 1978a; Lei and Skinner, 1980; McFarlane *et al.*, 1980; Mueller *et al.*, 1977; Ross and Mirowsky, 1979; Skinner and Lei, 1980a). Weighting all events equally (by one) results in virtually identical or higher correlations between the total number of life events and symptoms of disorder. (See the section "Major versus Minor Events" for further discussion of this issue.)

Causal Ordering

A recurring theme in this brief methodological review has been the difficulty of establishing a clear causal relationship between life events and psychological disturbance. Virtually all life-events researchers implicitly or explicitly adopt a social-causation approach (B. P. Dohrenwend and B. S. Dohrenwend, 1969). That is, all assume that life events somehow cause psychological disturbance, rather than vice versa. But due to inadequacies of research design and/or measurement, many of these studies—if not most—can be attacked from a social-selection framework. That is, it may plausibly be argued that psychological impairment precedes and precipitates the occurrence of major life changes in people's lives; damaged individuals are selected into a category of high life-change experience. Cross-sectional studies utilizing respondents' retrospective reports of life events are particularly open to this alternative interpretation, for a number of reasons detailed in this section (e.g., failure to establish dates of symptom onset relative to event dates, biased recall of events, scales that include events possibly confounded with psychiatric functioning, potentially biased subjective weightings of events). Interestingly, although panel data on life changes and psychological disturbance have been collected by some investigators (e.g., Grant *et al.*, 1981; Monroe, 1982; Myers *et al.*, 1971, 1974; Pearlin *et al.*, 1981; Turner and Noh, 1982), only one investigation (Turner and Noh, 1982) has attempted to disentangle the mutual influences of events and disturbance on each other over time. However, some researchers do control for prior disturbance scores when examining the effect of events on subsequent disturbance (e.g., Monroe, 1982; Pearlin *et al.*, 1981; Thoits, 1981). This procedure partially eliminates the bias in estimates due to contaminated events, but does not guarantee that unobserved variables, such as personality dispositions or social competence (Heller, 1979; Turner and Gartrell, 1978), may be responsible for a spurious correlation between events and psychiatric state. In sum, although the bulk of the evidence strongly suggests that life changes do, in fact, cause psychological impairment, the possibility of a reverse causal ordering exists. And this reverse causal effect, if not controlled, may inflate the correlations typically found.

Summary

The methodological criticisms raised by reviewers attempting to explain the disappointingly weak (but significant) association between events and disturbance have resulted in improved research strategies in recent years (Brown and Harris, 1978; Hurst, 1979). Life events lists have been expanded, ambiguously worded events have been specified with respect to their desirability, accurate recall of events has been independently verified and has been simplified by restricting events to those which are datable in onset, and contaminated events have been separately analyzed (Tausig, 1982). Dependent variable measures have been similarly improved, with diagnostic criteria specified, dates of symptom onset determined, and differentiable symptom patterns in psychological distress scales separately analyzed (Barrett, 1979; Brown and Harris, 1978). Interestingly, however, these improvements have not yielded substantial increases in the size of the correlations between number of events and disturbance in recent literature (Fontana et al., 1979; Hurst, 1979; McFarlane et al., 1980; Mueller et al., 1977; Tausig, 1982; Thoits, 1981). Nor have percentage differences between patients and controls who have experienced events become more dramatic (Barrett, 1979; Brown and Harris, 1978; Paykel, 1979). This may be due to two counter-balancing influences, although no direct evidence can be cited on this. On the one hand, measures of the independent and dependent variables have been improved, probably increasing the correlations between events and specific disturbances. On the other hand, contaminated events have been excluded, analyzed separately, or partially "purified" by controlling for prior disturbance, thus decreasing the correlation between events and disorder. In short, more recent evidence continues to indicate that the relationships between life changes and psychological outcomes are far from strong.

In their efforts to enhance the predictiveness of life events, researchers have increasingly turned their attention away from methodological issues and focused on the specific kinds of events that are associated with particular psychological outcomes. These efforts have yielded a wealth of useful findings that, although failing to increase correlations dramatically, have very interesting theoretical implications. We turn now to an examination of the qualities of events most strongly associated with various psychological disorders.

DIMENSIONS OF LIFE EVENTS MOST PREDICTIVE OF PSYCHOLOGICAL DISTURBANCE

Change versus Undesirability

Holmes, Rahe, and their co-workers initially postulated, and have continued to argue, that the crucial quality of life events that produces illness is change, or the total amount of readjustment required by events (Holmes, 1979; Holmes and Rahe, 1967; Masuda and Holmes, 1967; Rahe, 1974). The more life change individuals experience, regardless of the positive or negative aspects of change events, the more likely their coping or resistance resources will be overtaxed and illness will follow. On the other hand, implicit in studies of single events (e.g., combat, disasters, bereavement, rape) and explicit in other empirical and theoretical work (Brown and Birley, 1968; Brown and Harris, 1978; Hudgens, 1974; Paykel et al., 1971) is an alternative hypothesis. The more severe a single undesirable event, or the more undesirable events experienced, the more likely coping abilities will be overwhelmed and disorder will result. The crucial quality of life events in this formulation is believed to be their undesirability; such events threaten the physical survival or emotional well-being of the individual. Note that both formulations assume that individuals' defensive resources will be exceeded or depleted. They differ only with respect to the cause of that depletion: change per se or undesirable change.

At least 20 studies have examined the comparative ability of total amount of change and total undesirable change to predict psychological disturbance. Undesirable events were identified in several ways across these studies. Events were classified on the basis of researchers' or judges' evaluations of their cultural or social desirability, or on the basis of respondents' subjective ratings of each event on some ordinal scale (e.g., gain–loss, positive–negative, desirable–undesirable). All but three studies (B. S. Dohrenwend, 1973; Fontana et al., 1979; Husaini and Neff, 1980) find psychological disturbance to be more highly correlated with total undesirable change than total amount of change (Chiriboga, 1977; Dekker and Webb, 1974; Gersten et al., 1974; Grant et al., 1978b, 1981; Johnson and Sarason, 1978; Kaplan et al., 1983; McFarlane et al., 1980; Monroe, 1982; Mueller et al., 1977, 1978; Paykel, 1974, 1979; Ross and Mirowsky, 1979; Sarason et al., 1978;

Streiner et al., 1981; Tausig, 1982; Tennant and Andrews, 1978; Thoits, 1978; Vinokur and Selzer, 1975). This consistency is impressive, given that these studies employ a variety of samples, life-event scales, desirability classifications, event-weighting schemes, and measures of psychological outcome. Moreover, several of these studies demonstrate that the correlation between total amount of change and disturbance drops nearly to zero when the effects of undesirable events are partialled out (Mueller et al., 1977; Ross and Mirowsky, 1979; Tennant and Andrews, 1978; Vinokur and Selzer, 1975), although one study provides an exception (Husaini and Neff, 1980). Corroborative evidence comes from other studies indicating that readjustment and undesirability are highly correlated dimensions; correlations range from .60 to .89, indicating that there is considerable overlap in the two dimensions (Fontana et al., 1979; Gersten et al., 1974; Jenkins et al., 1979; Paykel et al., 1971; Ross and Mirowsky, 1979; Zeiss, 1980), although Tennant and Andrews (1976) report only a .44 correlation. In short, the relationship between total number of events (or total amount of change) and psychological disturbance found in a host of previous studies can almost certainly be attributed to the effects of undesirable events alone. As Ross and Mirowsky put it, "The correlation between absolute change and symptomatology is spurious, actually caused by undesirability" (1979:173).

Several studies have also compared the relative effects of total events and/or undesirable events to the effects of one or more of the following: desirable events, ambiguous events, and the balance of undesirable and desirable events (total undesirable minus total desirable events) (B. S. Dohrenwend, 1973; Fontana et al., 1972; Gersten et al., 1974; Johnson and Sarason, 1978; McFarlane et al., 1980; Mueller et al., 1977; Paykel, 1974; Ross and Mirowsky, 1979; Sarason et al., 1978; Tausig, 1982; Vinokur and Selzer, 1975). The results again are consistent. Desirable events (weighted or unweighted by their readjustment values) have either no association or a very weak positive and rarely significant association with disturbance. Only one study found a significant negative effect of desirable events on symptoms (Grant et al., 1981); this study utilized a 2-month reporting interval for past events. Positive changes, then, appear to add little or nothing to explained variance in disturbance.[7] Ambiguous events and the balance of undesirable and desirable events are weakly but significantly correlated with psychological outcomes. These associations are probably due to an embedded

---

[7]This finding has never been satisfactorily explained. See Thoits (1979) and Thoits and Hannan (1979) for additional discussions of this problem.

undesirability dimension, although no researcher has checked on this. Because ambiguous changes and the balance of positive and negative changes are much less predictive of psychological disturbance than undesirable change alone, little attention is now directed at such measures.

In short, the simple sum of undesirable events experienced by an individual over a given period is more strongly associated with patient status (e.g., Dekker and Webb, 1974; Fontana et al., 1972; Paykel, 1974), diagnoses of depression and schizophrenia (e.g., Jacobs and Myers, 1976; Paykel, 1974), symptoms of psychological distress (e.g., Gersten et al., 1974; McFarlane et al., 1980; Mueller et al., 1977; Ross and Mirowsky, 1979; Tausig, 1982; Vinokur and Selzer, 1975), and psychopathological behaviors (e.g., Gersten et al., 1974; Kaplan et al., 1983; Paykel, 1974) than the total number of events experienced, either in weighted or unweighted form. Undesirability, then, is a crucial dimension of events implicated in the etiology of psychological disturbance.

As an interesting contrast, I know of only three studies that compare the relative predictiveness of total change and undesirable change for *physical* health outcomes (Chiriboga, 1977; Cooley et al., 1979; Ensel and Tausig, 1982). These studies indicate that total amount of change best predicts physical health outcomes whereas undesirable change best predicts psychological outcomes (J. B. Jemmott, personal communication, November 15, 1982). These findings suggest that sheer amount of readjustment may exhaust individuals physically, leaving them vulnerable to disease or injury, whereas undesirable events may threaten individuals' self-esteem or sense of mastery and thus damage them psychologically. Some undesirable events may have dual impacts (e.g., death of spouse, loss of job). This observation may help explain the significant modest correlation between physical and mental health (B. P. Dohrenwend, 1979; Murphy and Brown, 1980; Vaillant 1979).

Other dimensions than change and undesirability have also been explored and found predictive. In particular, researchers have hypothesized that events over which individuals have no control and events that are unexpected or unanticipated may be more distress producing than controllable and anticipated occurrences.

Controllable versus Uncontrollable Events

Although they differ in some respects, three social psychological theories of helplessness postulate that the experience of undesirable,

uncontrollable events may result in harmful psychological consequences (Abramson *et al.*, 1978, and Seligman, 1975; Glass and Singer,
1972; Schmale, 1972). More specifically, each suggests that when aversive events (e.g., losses, failures to reach valued goals, outcomes that
are independent of efforts) are perceived to be uncontrollable, feelings
of helplessness and hopelessness will result. These feelings in turn
may generate psychological disturbance—in particular, depressive
symptoms. The basic relationships in these theories have been supported by extensive laboratory experiments and clinical research (Garber and Seligman, 1980; Glass and Singer, 1972; Schmale, 1972; Seligman, 1975). Interestingly, the combination of undesirability and
uncontrollability dimensions in experience implicitly has been assumed to be disturbing in the life-events literature on singular events
(e.g., combat, air raids, concentration-camp experience, disaster, rape,
terminal illness, death of spouse). This literature may be seen as supportive of helplessness theory to the extent that such events tend to
result in chronic disturbance (Silver and Wortman, 1980).

However, for the most part, life-events researchers (with the exception
of B. S. Dohrenwend, 1977; B. S. Dohrenwend and B. P. Dohrenwend,
1981) have been unaware of the helplessness literature. Consequently,
the majority of life-events studies that explore the relationships between
event controllability and disturbance have done so without regard to the
desirability of events. That is, helplessness theories point to the interaction, or joint occurrence, of two event qualities, undesirability and
uncontrollability. Life-event studies, on the other hand, explore the
effects of controllability alone (with a few exceptions, to be discussed
later).

Controllability has been assessed in two basic ways, by researchers' a
priori classifications of events as controllable or not (Brown and Birley,
1968; B. P. Dohrenwend, 1974) and by respondents' evaluations of the
controllability (or preventability) of events that they have experienced
(Husaini and Neff, 1980; McFarlane *et al.*, 1980). A priori classifications generally have subdivided events into those "independent of the
person's psychiatric state" and "not independent," based on the probability that the person was responsible for bringing about its occurrence.
The results of a variety of studies using such measures have been somewhat inconsistent. Several studies have found that uncontrollable
events are more strongly associated with psychological disturbance
than controllable events. These results were obtained for clinical depression (Fava *et al.*, 1981; Paykel, 1974, 1979), psychological distress
symptoms (B. S. Dohrenwend, 1973; Grant *et al.*, 1981; Husaini and
Neff, 1980, 1981; McFarlane *et al.*, 1980; Streiner *et al.*, 1981), depres-

sive symptoms (Grant et al., 1981; Husaini and Neff, 1980, 1981), and suicide attempts (Paykel, 1974, 1979). However, Brown and Birley (1968), Jacobs and Myers (1976), and Schwartz and Myers (1977a, 1977b) found controllable and uncontrollable events (events judged "posibly independent" and "independent" of psychiatric condition) to be equally implicated in the onset of schizophrenia. Similarly, B. P. and B. S. Dohrenwend (1969) and Myers et al. (1972) reported roughly comparable effects of controllable and uncontrollable events on psychological distress scores. Mueller et al. (1978) found that the incidence of events independent of the person's psychiatric condition did not differ significantly between first-admission patients in a community mental health center and nonpatient controls. And two studies (B. P. Dohrenwend, 1974; Fontana et al., 1972) found controllable events to be more common than uncontrollable events among psychiatric inpatients compared to controls, and among persons with high distress scores compared to those with low scores. Fontana et al. (1979) also found controllable events to be associated with alcohol abuse among psychiatric patients. These inconsistent results are not attributable to the method of measuring controllability (researcher versus subject evaluations). Rather, results seem to vary by the dependent variable measure. Uncontrollable events are consistently more strongly associated than controllable events with depressive outcomes (clinical depression, depressive symptoms, suicide attempts). When the dependent measure is of conditions less clearly linked with depression (psychological distress, schizophrenia, psychiatric status), inconsistent findings are obtained. Hence, with respect to depressive outcomes only, these studies are consistent with the helplessness literature.

Five studies examine the joint influence of desirability and controllability (Brown and Birley, 1968; B. P. Dohrenwend, 1974; Mueller et al., 1978; McFarlane et al., 1980; Streiner et al., 1981). Because none of these studies utilized measures of depressive outcomes, inconsistent findings were again obtained. Two studies found that the association between negative events and psychiatric outcome did not differ by the controllability of events (Brown and Birley, 1968; Mueller et al., 1978). One study found uncontrollable negative events to be more common among the unimpaired (i.e., among community residents compared to psychiatric patients, and among less distressed community residents compared to the more distressed; B. P. Dohrenwend, 1974). And two studies (McFarlane et al., 1980; Streiner et al., 1981) reported that undesirable events over which respondents believed they had no control correlated most strongly with psychological distress, regardless of whether they were anticipated or not (correlations ranged from .28

to .40, depending on the event weightings and subsamples examined).
Undesirable events over which respondents believed they did have
control were weakly and nonsignificantly correlated with distress and,
in general, both controlled and uncontrolled desirable events were unrelated to distress.[8] In short, the contradictory results of these five
studies preclude any firm conclusions regarding the interaction of desirability and controllability dimensions for nondepressive outcomes.
Unfortunately no studies have examined such interactions with respect
to depressive outcomes.

It is important to note that the controllability dimension alone does
not correlate more strongly with disturbance than the desirability dimension in any of the studies cited. Undesirable events are most closely associated with disturbance. Unfortunately, no study directly compares the correlations of undesirable, uncontrollable events with
disturbance to the total undesirable events correlations, so it is unknown whether the interaction of these two qualities better specifies
the events–disorder relationship. Certainly the helplessness literature
suggests this should be so, particularly for depressive outcomes. But
this possibility has yet to be tested.

B. S. Dohrenwend and Martin (1979) raised an important question
regarding the controllability dimension. Are individuals' perceptions
of control a function of the actual nature of the events they experience,
or are these perceptions a function of personality dispositions instead?
If personality dispositions (for example, fatalism, internal–external
locus of control, sense of mastery, Type A or B personality traits) determine these event interpretations, then the events–disturbance relationship may be spurious, due instead to this antecedent, unmeasured
variable.

Several studies partially refute this possibility. Johnson and Sarason
(1978) found that neither positive nor negative life changes were related to measures of depression and anxiety when only individuals with
internal locus-of-control orientations were examined; that is, individuals who believe that they have control over their lives were unaffected by experienced life changes. Negative changes were significantly related to depression and anxiety only for individuals with
external locus-of-control orientations (i.e., fatalistic attitudes). Johnson
and Sarason concluded "it is the individual who experiences high

---

[8]There was an exception to this generalization (McFarlane et al., 1980). Distress was
weakly but significantly increased by controllable positive events that were unexpected.
This is an odd finding on experiential grounds. How can a controllable positive event be
unanticipated? The authors gave no examples.

levels of change but feels he/she has no control over events who is most susceptible to the effects of life stress" (1978:207). These results do not show the events–disturbance relationship to be spurious, but do indicate that it may be conditional on beliefs regarding control. Lefcourt (1981) reported similar findings and concludes, as did Johnson and Sarason, that locus-of-control orientation serves as a moderator variable, rather than as an antecedent explanatory variable. Research by Wheaton (1980) also refuted the possibility of spuriousness. His tables show that a control for fatalism does not eliminate the significant relationship between life events and psychological distress. Relatedly, in a very clever analysis B. S. Dohrenwend and Martin (1979) demonstrated that perceptions of control over life events were not consistent within individuals over time but varied across situational contingencies. Thus, by implication, they too suggest that the events–disturbance relationship is nonspurious.

Despite these reassuring findings, it should be clear that the controllability issue is a complex one, deserving further attention. First, it appears that the degree to which individuals are responsible for an event's occurrence must be assessed objectively by researchers or judges, rather than subjectively by respondents. Perceptual tendencies, attributional styles, or personality dispositions may bias subjects' assessments, as may subjects' psychiatric states (Gong-Guy and Hammen, 1980). Also, the undesirability of the event itself may affect subjects' assessments of controllability (B. S. Dohrenwend, 1978; Fontana et al., 1979; Paykel, 1979). Second, the interaction of undesirability and uncontrollability needs further examination in life-events research, particularly for nondepressive outcomes. This interaction of event qualities may or may not be specific to depression, but it clearly may enhance the specificity and strength of the associations between events and certain psychological outcomes. Finally, the possibility that attributional dispositions interact with certain types of events (especially undesirable events) deserves further investigation; fatalistic attributions are one type of learned coping response which may have deleterious psychological consequences (Pearlin et al., 1981; Turner and Noh, 1981; Wheaton, 1980). But, one must hastily add, because these dispositions are learned, the effects of event histories on fatalistic attitudes also require examination. The interrelationships among events of certain types, fatalistic attributions, and psychological outcomes may be dynamic and complex. And whenever complexities in causality are involved, cross-sectional measures may be confounded or biased.

One comforting fact may be drawn from the studies examining controllability of events. Although the uncontrollable events–disturbance relationships were not consistently *stronger* than those for controllable events, in all but one of the studies cited here (Mueller *et al.*, 1978) uncontrollable events were significantly *associated* with disturbance. Why is this important? Uncontrollable events are generally those for which individuals were not responsible or could not have prevented. In short, these events are measures of change uncontaminated by the person's psychiatric condition (at least when such events are objectively assessed). The fact that uncontrollable or "independent" events are consistently associated with a variety of measures of psychological outcomes helps counter the criticism that the events–disorder relationship in cross-sectional studies may be a spurious function of preexisting psychological disturbance (Brown, 1974; Hinkle, 1974).

Related to issues of control are those of anticipation or predictability. This dimension of life events will now be examined.

Expected versus Unexpected Events

Glass and Singer (1972), in addition to positing the importance of controllability, argued and demonstrated that unpredictable noxious events (e.g., noise, electric shock) were more damaging than predictable ones. (See Miller, 1981, for a complete review of the theoretical and experimental literature on predictability.) This assumption once again has been implicit in many of the life-event studies of singular events (unexpected disasters, rape, bereavement among younger adults). However, few studies of multiple events have examined the role of anticipation, or expectedness, in event impacts. Those that have report a regular finding: Unexpected events tend to be more disturbing than expected ones.

The predictability or expectedness of events has been determined primarily by the self-reports of respondents (Fontana *et al.*, 1979; McFarlane *et al.*, 1980; Streiner *et al.*, 1981). However, some researchers have examined the differential impacts of "normative" and "nonnormative" events (Pearlin and Lieberman, 1979). Pearlin and Lieberman define normative events as "gains and losses or major alterations of roles that predictably occur in the course of the unfolding life-cycle . . . [with] expectedness and regularity" (1979:220). Nonnormative events, on the other hand, are crises that are common but "are not easily predictable by people because they are not built into their movement across the span of life" (1979:220).

The results of studies using these quite different operationalizations of expectedness are similar. Unexpected events (as indicated by self-report) tend to increase psychological distress (Fontana *et al.*, 1979; Husaini and Neff, 1980), and to be associated with clinical depression (Brown and Harris, 1978:116).[9] Nonnormative events (e.g., divorce, separation, job loss, illness or death of child) significantly increase symptoms of distress, whereas normative events (e.g., marriage, birth of child, retirement) tend to be weakly and nonsignificantly associated with distress (Pearlin and Lieberman, 1979). It is, of course, quite possible that these effects are due to the confounding of unpredictability with undesirability; there is considerable overlap in at least the objective classifications of events on these two dimensions. However, the results of McFarlane's study (McFarlane *et al.*, 1980; Streiner *et al.*, 1981) suggest that desirability may interact with controllability and anticipation in somewhat complex ways. They found undesirable, uncontrollable events to be equally distressing whether anticipated or not. But desirable, controllable events were significantly distressing only when unexpected. One might conservatively conclude from these few studies, then, that anticipation *may* be an important dimension of life events, but its effects have not been adequately assessed either independently of or in combination with other event characteristics.

Major versus Minor Events

There is some confusion in the life-events literature regarding whether event magnitudes make an etiological difference. This confusion stems from two sources, one theoretical, the other empirical.

Theoretically, the field has been dominated by the Holmes and Rahe (1967) proposition that the more change or readjustment required by one or more events, the greater the likelihood illness symptoms will appear and the more severe these symptoms will be. Although many studies have substantiated this hypothesis with respect to psychological disturbance (e.g., Markush and Favero, 1974; Mueller *et al.*, 1977; Myers *et al.*, 1974; Ross and Mirowsky, 1979), there has been growing recognition among researchers that the relationship between total amount of change and disturbance is spurious, due instead to the impacts of undesirable events only (see the section "Change versus Undesirability"). Furthermore, because undesirable events typically are

---

[9]It should be noted that Brown and Harris do not interpret their findings regarding prior "warning" of an event as etiologically relevant. However, they do report a statistically significant difference between depressed patients and control subjects with regard to such warnings. Only 5% of the patients but 19% of the controls reported event anticipation lasting for more than 6 months.

rated as requiring more readjustment (see Table 2.1 and the section "Event Weighting"), the effects of event magnitude have been attributed to the undesirability dimension as well. In short, recent evidence regarding the role of undesirability has tended to deemphasize the theoretical importance of event magnitudes as an etiological dimension.

This deemphasis has been encouraged by another set of empirical findings, noted in an earlier section on "Event Weighting." A majority of studies indicate that when compared to the effects of sheer number of events, particularly number of undesirable events, readjustment weightings add little or nothing to explained variance in psychological outcomes. These studies imply that event magnitudes make no difference; rather, degree of disturbance is simply a function of the cumulation of events, in particular, undesirable ones. This implication, however, flies in the face of our intuitions. Surely a divorce or death should have a greater psychological impact than having a minor traffic accident.

These nonintuitive findings, it turns out, have a simple explanation. They are quite likely due to a statistical artifact, well known in psychometric research (Lorimor et al., 1979). The correlation between a simple count of checked items and a sum of weighted items on an index is so high (.90 or better) that the two scoring systems become virtually identical. Thus, the implication that event magnitudes have little to add to explained variance should not be drawn from studies that compare the effects of number of events to number of weighted events. Such studies do not provide an informative test of the predictive utility of magnitude ratings. Rather, one must turn to studies that contrast directly the effects of major and minor events on psychological state.[10]

Interestingly, such studies have been few in number, probably due to the tremendous influence of the Holmes–Rahe weight-and-sum approach in the field. However, those studies that do contrast the influ-

[10]Shrout (1981) points out that researchers who wish to retain event weightings when summating events can reduce the correlation between weighted and unweighted sums by utilizing positive readjustment values for desirable events and negative values for undesirable events. Note, however, that this procedure violates the Holmes–Rahe (1967) proposition that event impacts are due to their change magnitude. By implication, negative weights are impossible (Shrout, 1981). For researchers who do not adhere to the Holmes–Rahe proposition, a different problem with positive and negative weights is involved. The use of positive and negative values implies that desirable events reduce or counterbalance the unpleasant effects of undesirable events. No supportive evidence for this implication has been found (see the section "Change versus Undesirability"); weighted balance scores may reduce substantially the correlation between events and disturbance (Gersten et al., 1974; Mueller et al., 1977).

ences of major and minor events generally confirm our intuitive notions regarding relative impacts. Perhaps the best example of these
relative effects is provided by Brown and Harris's (1978) study of the
origins of depression.

Brown and Harris partitioned events into "severe" and "nonsevere"
types. They defined severe events as experiences of long-term or moderate long-term threat to an individual (e.g., the discovery of a spouse's
infidelity). Nonsevere events were experiences that are threatening
only in the short term, usually less than a week (e.g., a child nearly hit
by a car). (It is important to note that the Holmes–Rahe [1967] conception of life-event magnitude differs in only one respect from Brown and
Harris's conception of event severity. Holmes and Rahe define major
events as those that require a substantial amount of readjustment over a
long period. Brown and Harris define severe events as those that are
threatening in the long term. The difference between the two conceptions rests on the undesirability of the event. Holmes and Rahe disregard undesirability, whereas Brown and Harris restrict attention to it.
But the two definitions concur that long-term impact is a crucial characteristic of a major event. The distinction between long-term and
short-term events becomes useful in a subsequent section on life event
processes.) Brown and Harris found severe events to be four times more
common among clinically depressed female patients than among normal women. The incidence of nonsevere events was unrelated to clinical state. Moreover, the number of severe events experienced by depressed patients, compared to normal women, increased dramatically
in the 3-week period before symptom onset, whereas the rate of nonsevere events for both groups remained stable and roughly equal over
time. These results clearly indicate that major undesirable events play
an important etiological role in depression, but minor events do not.
Other studies that directly compare the effects of major and minor
events also support this generalization (Fava et al., 1981; Paykel, 1974).

Interestingly, the contrast between major and minor events has been
made primarily by researchers dealing with depressive outcomes. The
generalization may not apply to all types of psychiatric outcomes. For
example, Jacobs and Myers (1976) found that the number of severe
events did not distinguish schizophrenic patients from community
control subjects. Rather, schizophrenics reported more moderate and
minor events than did controls. Rabkin (1980) has attributed these findings to the possible oversensitivity of schizophrenics to experiences
that ordinary persons find nonhazardous. That is, this finding may
reflect the influence of the disorder, rather than a veridical difference
in event experiences. But for psychological distress and for patholog-

ical behavioral outcomes, researchers who have controlled for the number of undesirable events and then examined the influence of the magnitude of readjustment required by those events find that event magnitudes significantly affect psychological disorder (Husaini and Neff, 1980; Kaplan et al., 1983).

In short, the conclusion by many researchers that event magnitudes are unrelated to psychological disorder is premature. This erroneous conclusion seems to have been a product of artifactual analytical procedures. When events are categorized into major and minor types and their effects on psychological outcomes are compared, or when magnitude effects are examined while the number of events are controlled, the etiological significance of this dimension of events is revealed. Needed in future research is additional confirmation of the role of event magnitude in the production of a variety of types of psychiatric disorder. Further confirmation will suggest a reasonable combination of the Holmes–Rahe hypothesis regarding change with more recent findings regarding the importance of undesirable events. The coping capacities of individuals may be overwhelmed by the experience of undesirable events that require a large amount of readjustment. Psychological disturbance may well be a product of the interaction, or joint occurrence, of these event dimensions in experience.

Additive, Curvilinear, and Interactive Effects of Events

Most researchers, especially those following the Holmes–Rahe tradition, assume that the effects of life events are additive. That is, they assume that three severe events are more likely to bring about disorder than two, and two more than one. It is often assumed that magnitude effects are additive as well. Two or more minor events should have the same cumulative impact as one severe event. These assumptions certainly seem to be supported by repeated reports in the literature of significant positive associations between various measures of psychological outcome and the number of life events experienced over time, in weighted and unweighted form. But interestingly, as Brown and Harris (1978) pointed out, these additivity assumptions rarely have been tested systematically. That is, the risks of disturbance across varying levels of life event exposure have not often been compared directly. Systematic comparisons might reveal an entirely different function than an additive one.

For example, it is rare for individuals in the general population to experience more than one or two life events, particularly undesirable life events, during a 6- to 12-month period (Brown and Harris, 1978; Myers et al., 1971; Paykel, 1974; Thoits, 1978). This observation suggests that event effects might be captured better by a dichotomous variable than a continuous variable, where 0 indicates that no events were experienced and 1 indicates that one or more events were experienced in a given time period. Additional events beyond one may not contribute significantly to explained variance in disturbance.

On the other hand, low numbers of life events may not affect the psychological well-being of an individual, but beyond some threshold number, additional events may adversely affect mental health. Such threshold effects, like dichotomous effects, may be obscured by the calculation of simple correlations between number of events and disturbance.

Even more complicated functions might be expected. There may be a curvilinear relationship between events and disturbance, in one of two possible directions. Physiological stress theorists (Fröberg et al., 1971; Levi, 1974) have suggested that both overstimulation and understimulation of an organism can produce stress reactions. If life changes are viewed as types of stimulation, then both very low and very high numbers of life events (or very low and very high cumulative event magnitudes) might be accompanied by high degrees of disturbance. On the other hand, experience with previous events might improve coping skills and thus subsequent life crises may be handled more effectively (Ruch et al., 1980). Thus, disturbance might at first increase, then decrease, as event experiences accumulate.

Alternatively, events may have interactive or multiplicative impacts in one of two possible directions. For example, a person who has experienced one event may react with even more distress to a second that follows soon after the first; to the person, life might appear to be rapidly spiraling out of control. This would produce a positive interaction between event occurrences; two or more events would result in more distress than would be expected from the simple sum of their singular effects. However, it is also possible that a negative event-interaction term might be found. With repeated exposure to undesirable events, the individual might become decreasingly reactive to them, as fatigue or resignation sets in.

Unfortunately, the full range of these speculations has never been tested, and the piecemeal evidence produced to date is inconclusive. Only Brown and Harris (1978), Miller and Ingham (1979), and Myers et al. (1971) have examined risks of disturbance at increasing levels of event exposure. Myers and his co-workers (Myers et al., 1971) divided a sample of community respondents into unimpaired, moderately impaired, and very impaired groups on the basis of their Gurin psychological symptom scores. Then they examined the percentage in each category who had experienced one or more events, two or more events, three or more events, and so on. They found that at each level of event experience, the percentage of very impaired exceeded the percentage of moderately impaired and unimpaired. For example, "nearly one-half of the very impaired report three or more events, whereas the percentages drop to 37 for the moderately impaired and only 17 for the unimpaired. Corresponding percentages for six or more events are 24, 10, and 4" (1971:152). In a subsequent analysis, Myers et al. (1972) showed that a net increase in the number of events experienced from a first interview to a second is associated with higher symptom scores and a net decrease in events over time with lower symptom scores. They concluded (implicitly) that the relationship between events and impairment is a linear or additive one. On closer examination however, their data reveal some curvilinearity or perhaps a threshold point in the relationship. The greatest percentage increase in the number of unimpaired occurs between the categories of one or more events and two or more events (see Table 2.2). At higher levels of event exposure the percentage change in the number of unimpaired drops off fairly rapidly. Similarly, in their longitudinal analysis a net increase or decrease of one event appears not to produce much change in symptomatology. Two or more events result in greater or lessened symptoms, respectively.

Brown and Harris (1978) reported somewhat similar findings, but certain flaws in their procedures render their conclusions uncertain. Brown and Harris contrasted the relative percentages of depressed patients and normal women who had experienced one, two, or three or more severe events in a previous 38-week period. They found that the risk of depression was significantly greater only for women with three or more events. However, this very modest support for a threshold effect (or for curvilinearity) is probably due to the manner in which Brown and Harris categorized events as severe. For example, for one woman the birth of a child was rated as severely threatening because she had separated from her husband a few months prior to the birth. Thus, their classifications of events already may have included some additivity; risk comparisons across numbers of events thus showed little apparent effect of event frequency. When Brown and Harris next counted all *related* events as one severe event, and contrasted risks across numbers of *unrelated* severe events, the evidence for additivity became somewhat stronger. The risk of depression became greater as the number of unrelated severe events increased. These results are still

TABLE 2.2

Cumulative Percentage of Number of Events Experienced by Respondents, Differing by Mental Status[a]

Number of events	Mental status (%)		
	Unimpaired	Moderately impaired	Very impaired
0 or more	100	100	100
1 or more	73	82	89
2 or more	39	58	65
3 or more	17	37	49
4 or more	11	24	37
5 or more	7	16	30
6 or more	4	10	24
7 or more	3	6	19
8 or more	1	4	14
9 or more	0	3	11
Total N	327	442	169

[a]From Myers et al., 1971:152. © 1971, The Williams & Wilkins Co., Baltimore.

fairly uninformative, however, as risk comparisons for women experiencing no events were not assessed.

Miller and Ingham (1979) surveyed a community sample using the Brown and Harris (1978) interview schedule to assess the number of undesirable events and ongoing difficulties experienced by respondents over a previous 3 months. They plotted the depression, irritability, dizziness, headache, anxiety, tiredness, and backache symptom scores of respondents at each level of "major stressors" (number of events and ongoing difficulties objectively rated as severely threatening). These symptom scores show a linearly increasing trend as the number of major stressors increases. However, for persons experiencing four or more major stressors, symptom levels tend to stabilize or fall off, suggesting some curvilinearity (a ∩-shaped curve) in the relationship between events and symptoms. Only depression scores continue to rise. Miller and Ingham discount this curvilinearity, arguing instead that most symptoms cease to increase because respondents at the highest levels of stress exposure were selected out of the sample by obtaining medical or psychiatric treatment.

Four researchers have tested explicitly for curvilinearity in the relationship between events and disturbance and obtained mixed results (Cooke, 1981; Cooke and Greene, 1981; Ruch et al., 1980; Wildman and

Johnson, 1977). Wildman and Johnson administered the SRRS and the Langner symptom index to a group of college students and to a small probability sample of adults in a Midwest city. They found significant curvilinear relationship (a U-shaped curve) between total LCU scores and psychological distress among the students, but a threshold effect among community respondents (a backwards-L-shaped function). Ruch and her colleagues reported a significant U-shaped curvilinear relationship between past LCU scores and the degree of emotional reaction displayed, during an initial interview at a sexual assault treatment center, by women who had been raped. However, Cooke (1981) and Cooke and Greene (1981) reported no significant effects when second- and third-order terms were included in a regression equation that predicted depression scores from undesirable life events that a community sample of women had experienced (weighted normatively by degree of upsettingness). Interestingly, Cooke and Greene reported that somatic symptoms in this sample were a product not of social exits or other miscellaneous events alone, but of the joint occurrence of these two types of events. Thus, although they found no curvilinearity in the relationship between total undesirable events and disturbance, they found a positive interaction of exits with other undesirable events for somatic complaints.

In sum, although the bulk of the evidence in the literature implies that life events are additive in their effects, to date no strong systematic evidence on this point is available. Some studies show threshold and curvilinear relationships, but no consistent patterns across studies can be discerned. This is probably due to inconsistencies across studies in the way life events are measured (total number of events, weighted or unweighted by magnitude; total undesirable events; total undesirable severe events; and total severe events plus severe difficulties). It seems clear that a closer examination of the functional forms of the relationships between number of events and disturbance and magnitude of events and disturbance are required. A better theoretical understanding of life-event processes might be obtained from further specification of the nature of these relationships. And, to the extent that threshold, curvilinear, or interactive effects are involved, higher correlations between events and disorder might be obtained from such specifications.

Time Clustering of Events

Consideration of multiple events raises another issue in the literature that has not been accorded the importance it deserves: the timing of events with respect to one another. It was noted earlier that some events are often related to, or even causal of, others. Divorce may force a residential relocation and the giving up of child custody, ill health can result in job loss, and job loss, almost by definition, will entail a major drop in income. Such related events tend to cluster within a relatively short period of time. Even unrelated events such as the death of a family member and a child leaving home for college may occur within a few days or weeks of one another. Most researchers have ignored the clustering in time of both related and unrelated events, preferring to count all events as separate, time-independent occurrences. Yet at the same time most researchers implicitly or explicitly assume that disruptive experiences are psychologically harmful because they overwhelm the coping resources of the individual. It seems likely that coping resources would be especially overtaxed when disruptive events follow fast upon one another, leaving little time for adjustment and recovery. Singular events, even severely threatening ones, if well spaced, should be less likely to overwhelm a person's coping capacities and result in disorder.

Given these processual implications, it is surprising that not much has been made of the finding that life events tend to cluster in the 3 to 4 weeks prior to onset of schizophrenic symptoms (Beck and Worthen, 1972; Brown and Birley, 1968), depressive symptoms (Brown and Harris, 1978; Paykel, 1974, 1979; Surtees and Ingham, 1980), and suicide attempts (Paykel, 1974, 1979). Other studies report longer intervals over which events are more frequent, usually 3–6 months before symptom onset or clinical relapse, but time-clustering impacts are still implied (Fontana et al., 1972; Jacobs and Myers, 1976; Paykel and Tanner, 1976; Rabkin, 1980; Tennant et al., 1981). Each of these studies compares patients' experiences over time to those of a control sample. Average weekly or monthly numbers of events remain fairly constant over time for controls, but increase significantly among patients several weeks before the established date of symptom onset. Although one might argue that biased recall of events, particularly negative events, could account for such patient–control differences (Jenkins et al., 1979), the majority of these studies employed informants to verify the occurrence and timing of patients' reported experiences. The results of these studies clearly imply that the simple number of events experienced over, say, a year's time should be much less predictive of disorder than the number of closely spaced events.

Additional supportive evidence for this time-clustering implication comes from a study by Surtees and Ingham (1980). These researchers computed measures of life events that included not only their degree of magnitude (severity of threat) but their time of occurrence. The impacts of events were assumed to dissipate at a constant rate over a period of 28 weeks. Surtees and Ingham hypothesized that residual effects from events that were not fully dissipated would summate with the impacts of subsequent events (assumed to decay at the same rate). The severity and timing of events occuring to clinically depressed patients over the 7 months prior to hospital discharge were examined. Residual adversity scores were computed at the end of this period and correlated with symptom level at discharge. The correlation of events with symptoms was improved substantially by the inclusion of residual event effects. For events judged independent of the patients' illness, the correlation of residual adversity with symptoms was .30, compared to a .18 correlation of simple number of events with symptoms. For the combination of illness-independent events and ongoing severe difficulties, residual adversity correlated .42 with symptoms, compared to a .26 simple correlation of events and difficulties with symptoms.

Taken together, these studies suggest strongly that the associations between events and disorder have been low in the majority of studies because most researchers have aggregated events over long periods of time, ignoring the time-clustering factor altogether. Attention to the timing of events relative to one another might well enhance the predictiveness of events for the onset and severity of disorder. Moreover, time-clustering issues have important theoretical, or processual, implications for the etiology of disorder. These implications will be taken up in some detail in a subsequent section, "Life-Event Processes: Theoretical Implications."

Factor-Analytic Dimensions of Events

Up to this point, we have examined the predictive utility of a variety of event qualities identified implicitly or explicitly by researchers as theoretically important (e.g., desirability, controllability, magnitude). That is, studies reviewed so far have categorized events on these theoretical dimensions. But some researchers have identified event dimensions empirically. Through the use of factor analysis, cluster analysis, and multidimensional scaling, several event dimensions have been found that have not been anticipated theoretically.

Generally speaking, factors derived from empirical procedures tend to tap spheres of life activities. For example, Rahe and his colleagues (Rahe et al., 1971; see also Pugh et al., 1971) report four clusters of items from an analysis of the Schedule of Recent Events: personal and social changes, work changes, marital changes, and disciplinary changes (jail, court-martial, etc.). Miller *et al.* (1974) find four factors, too: life-space changes (recreational and work events), personal life-style changes, relationship changes, and relationship terminations (primarily deaths). Skinner and Lei (1980b) report six factors: changes in personal and social activities, work changes, marital problems, residence changes, family changes, and school changes. Redfield and Stone (1979) find three factors: personal catastrophes (undesirable events), achievements (desirable events), and domestic changes (pregnancy, birth of a child, retirement). And Ruch (1977) reports three dimensions: magnitude of change, desirability of change, and area of life change (personal and interpersonal events versus financial and occupational events). It is notable that in each of these quite different analyses based on varying samples, life event scales, and analytic techniques, the area of life activity emerges as a significant factor or set of factors.

Interestingly, when events are categorized by sphere of activity, no particular sphere tends to distinguish patients from nonpatients consistently. That is, patients and respondents with higher impairment scores tend to report more events in the majority of spheres than nonpatients and respondents with lower impairment scores (Barrett, 1979; Myers *et al.*, 1971; Paykel, 1974; Rabkin, 1980; Schwartz and Myers, 1977a, 1977b; Skinner and Lei, 1980b). Although some researchers (Redfield and Stone, 1979; Skinner and Lei, 1980b) have argued that the use of factor scores may enhance the prediction of specific types of disorder, little evidence thus far suggests that such dimensions help distinguish either types or degrees of disturbance.

These factor-analytic studies indicate that life-event scales are not measuring what they were originally intended to measure, specifically the one underlying concept of degree of life change (Holmes and Rahe, 1967). Although the empirical factors do not correspond often to classifications of events made on theoretical grounds, the multidimensionality revealed is consonant with the growing recognition among researchers that life-event scales tap factors that are more complex than originally conceived. Degree of change per se is not distress producing. Rather, change *in combination* with other event qualities (e.g., undesirability, uncontrollability, time clustering) appears to produce distress.

The results of factor-analytic studies reveal, too, that certain life events are substantially intercorrelated, particularly within certain activity spheres. These intercorrelations may indicate response sets. That is, memories may be organized by area of activity. Recall of one family event may prompt memories of other events in the same domain. On the other hand, these factor-analytic results may indicate that life events in one sphere tend to generate other events in that same sphere. Marital difficulties, for example, may cause a sequence of separations, reconciliations, and child-related events, but leave occupational activities unaltered, at least initially. One might even expect events in the same domain to cluster closely in time and events in different domains to occur at greater intervals. The sequence and timing of events in different areas of activity might have implications for the genesis of disorder. For example, a cluster of events confined to one sphere of activities may be less disturbing than a cluster of occupational events followed somewhat later by a set of family events. But to date no researcher has explored the implications of domain clusters and/or domain sequences of events for the generation of disturbance.

In sum, factor-analytic studies reveal activity domains as an important dimension of events. This dimension has not yet enhanced the prediction of disturbance. But the implications of this empirical dimension for methodological problems of event recall and for theoretical issues of event sequencing and timing have not been examined fully.

Dimensions of Events Associated with Specific Disorders

One goal of life-events research has been to identify types of events most predictive of specific psychiatric disorders. Event specificity should yield important clues to the etiology of different disorders. But after two decades of research, this promise has remained unfulfilled for the most part. With the exception of depressive outcomes (discussed later), little event specificity can be discerned for psychological distress, neuroses, schizophrenia, or various types of psychopathological behaviors. That is, events associated with one type of outcome tend to be associated with others. As seen from this review, typically patients of all types and respondents exhibiting higher distress scores have experienced more major undesirable events than nonpatients or respondents with low scores (see the section "Change versus Undesirability," for example).

Although patient to nonpatient and high-impairment to low-impairment comparisons are informative, the presence or absence of event specificity can be more adequately assessed by directly comparing the experiences of patients with differing clinical conditions. The most common comparisons made have been between depressives and schizophrenics. Two excellent reviews of such studies are available (Lloyd, 1980b; Rabkin, 1980).

Rabkin concludes with respect to schizophrenia that "the weight of the evidence currently available suggests that schizophrenics do not report significantly more events preceding illness onset than do other psychiatric patients, nor are the events that they report of a singular nature or qualitatively unlike those reported by others" (1980:424). Schizophrenics, in fact, generally report fewer events than depressed patients (although more, of course, than normal respondents) (Lloyd, 1980b; Paykel, 1979; Rabkin, 1980). If severity of disorder were a simple function of the accumulation of stressors, then schizophrenics should exhibit substantially higher or at least equal event frequencies compared to depressives. Schizophrenics tend to experience similar types of events as depressives—undesirable events, social exits, and interpersonal difficulties—although at lesser frequencies (Paykel, 1979). These results strongly suggest that events are not sufficient, either quantitatively or qualitatively, to explain the onset of schizophrenic symptoms (Rabkin, 1980). Life events appear to trigger schizophrenia, rather than play a major formative role (Brown et al., 1973). That is, predispositional factors probably account for more of the variance in this outcome than do life events; events interact with predispositional factors rather than exert a main effect. Although some researchers have argued that this conclusion is premature and based upon insufficient evidence (B. P. Dohrenwend and Egri, 1981), no studies to date indicate a substantial causal influence of events in schizophrenia nor any evidence of event specificity.[11]

In contrast to schizophrenia, depressive outcomes do appear to depend somewhat on the types of events experienced. Depressives and suicide attempters report more life events than schizophrenics in general (Lloyd, 1980b; Paykel, 1979; Rabkin, 1980). "Certain events, such as those that are undesirable, markedly threatening, or that reflect the loss of a significant other, have emerged as particularly likely to precede a depressive disorder" (Lloyd, 1980b:547). In a related review, Finlay-Jones (1981) concurs with these conclusions, but adds a cautionary note: "None of the studies directly ruled out the possibility of a

[11]B. P. Dohrenwend and Egri (1981) assert that independent, uncontrollable events—experiences outside the control of the individual—are more common among schizophrenics than normal subjects and/or other clinical subjects. They base this assertion on a subset of studies that meet several ideal criteria of research design (Brown and Birley, 1968; Jacobs and Myers, 1976). But these studies do *not* show independent events to be more frequent among cases than controls.

personality variable producing a spurious association between life events and depression. . . . Yet the association between severe life events and the onset of depression remains when [those events that are brought about by some behavior of the respondent] are excluded" (1981:237). Interestingly, the implications of this last remark have not been capitalized upon by the majority of investigators. It suggests, and a variety of studies confirm (Barrett, 1979; Paykel, 1979; see also the section "Controllable versus Uncontrollable Events"), that the experience of uncontrollable events distinguishes depressives (and suicide attempters) from patients with other conditions. In sum, depressives and those prone to suicide appear to experience more events, particularly more undesirable, social-loss, and uncontrollable events, than schizophrenics, those with anxiety disorders, or those with higher distress scores (Barrett, 1979; see also the section "Controllable versus Uncontrollable Events").

Most investigators have concluded that life events play a direct causal role in the etiology of depression and that some event specificity is involved (Barrett, 1979; Brown and Harris, 1978; Brown et al., 1973; Finlay-Jones, 1981; Lloyd, 1980b; Paykel, 1979). But it is important to note that event specificity may not explain much variance in depressive outcomes. Paykel (1979) estimates that less than 10% of all subjects who experience a social exit (e.g., death or separation) will become depressed within a 6-month period. In terms of relative risk, an exit event increases the risk of depression 6.5 times that for persons not so exposed. For suicide attempts and schizophrenia, exits increase the risk by factors of 6.7 and 3.9, respectively. But when these specific-risk factors are compared to those for *any* event, little additional predictive value of exits is revealed. Any event in a previous 6 months raises the risks of depression, suicide attempts, and schizophrenia by 5.4, 6.3, and 3.0 times that of unexposed persons, respectively.

In sum, other than for depression and suicide attempts, little event specificity can be discerned from the literature. A variety of psychiatric disorders may follow from the experience of multiple, severe, undesirable events. Although social losses and uncontrollable events are more frequent among depressives and suicide attempters than among patients with other clinical symptoms, these specific types of events may not explain much variance in outcomes when compared to the variance explained by any event. Paykel concludes appropriately:

> It remains true that event experience is often not followed by psychiatric illness. The event is only responsible in part for the onset of clinical depression and must be regarded as interacting with a host of other factors in determining whether the outcome is an illness and which specific illness. It is not merely the event but the soil on which it falls. (1979:83)

Summary

This review of event dimensions was undertaken in an attempt to resolve a persistent and puzzling problem, the low association between events and disturbance almost universally reported in the literature. From this review it appears that certain dimensions may increase the association between events and disorder somewhat, most notably the dimensions of undesirability, uncontrollability, unpredictability, event magnitude, additivity, and time clustering. The most powerful of these dimensions appear to be undesirability, magnitude, and time clustering. (Uncontrollability is also an important quality but primarily with respect to depressive outcomes.) Although associations between events and disturbance are enhanced somewhat by attention to these particular event qualities, correlations (when reported) still remain modest, rarely exceeding .40 in value (Brown and Harris, 1978; McFarlane *et al.*, 1980; Mueller *et al.*, 1977; Paykel, 1979). Essentially, attention to event characteristics simply has specified further the nature of an existing modest relationship, rather than added substantially to its strength. But this seemingly unimpressive conclusion to a rather lengthy review should not be regarded as futile. The finding that the association between events and disturbance is due primarily to *major, time-clustered, undesirable events* has important theoretical implications, to be taken up in the following section.

LIFE-EVENT PROCESSES: THEORETICAL IMPLICATIONS

We have seen in this review that neither improved measurement nor specific qualities of events explain substantially more variance in psychological outcomes. These observations lead inexorably to another conclusion, that psychological disturbance is only partially determined by life events. Other factors clearly must be involved. What are these factors, and how might life events be related to them?

To answer these questions, it is important first to capitalize on pieces of our current knowledge. We know that symptom onset tends to occur soon after clusters of major undesirable events. This timing of onset suggests that recent disruptive experiences can be characterized as *precipitating or provoking factors* in the etiological process (Brown, 1979). That is, they may represent the most proximate causes of incipient psychological disorder. But, as our problematically low correlations imply, not all individuals who experience such events become ill.

What factors, then, may cause individuals to be more or less reactive to these precipitating events?

Two sets of *vulnerability—or resistance—factors* have been discussed in the stress literature. These might be distinguished as *predispositions* and *psychosocial resources*, respectively. Predispositions are remote, enduring physiological and psychological characteristics that should enhance or dampen the impacts of current life experiences. Included among predisposing factors are the biogenetic constitution of the individual (e.g., B. P. Dohrenwend and Egri, 1981; Kohn, 1968), personality traits (e.g., Kobasa *et al.*, 1981), and the psychological consequences of early life experiences, such as the loss of a parent during childhood (e.g., Lloyd, 1980a). Psychosocial resources refer to more recent and less stable psychological and social factors that might modify the disturbing impact of life events. These resources typically are subdivided into coping strategies thought to be more or less efficacious (e.g., Lazarus and Launier, 1978; Pearlin and Schooler, 1978) and social support availability (e.g., House, 1981). Briefly, researchers argue that individuals who face undesirable events or ongoing difficulties do not always become disturbed because they have stress-resistant biogenetic or personality characteristics, utilize efficacious coping responses, or draw on social support. These factors are believed to reduce, or buffer, the effects of current stressors. In short, disturbance may depend upon the joint occurrence, or interaction, of precipitating events and vulnerability (or resistance) factors. Vulnerable persons who face major undesirable events may become ill; resistant persons may not.

The ability of some of these resistance factors to reduce significantly the impacts of events and ongoing strains are reviewed extensively in the chapters by Turner and by Menaghan, and thus are not examined here. For our purposes, it is sufficient to note that such research efforts generally do not explain *why* events have disturbing impacts on individuals, but only *when* events will have such impacts. In Lazarsfeldian terms (Kendall and Lazarsfeld, 1950), the presence or absence of vulnerability factors specifies the relationship between events and disturbance; the relationship is weaker when resistance factors are relatively present and stronger when such factors are absent.

Thus, we have an initial causal model of event impacts. But, as Brown puts it, "What is going on? A causal model on its own, whatever its validity, is not enough" (1979:117). We must have a deeper theoretical understanding of the processes involved. Again in Lazarsfeldian terms, we must find variables that explain away these relationships (make them spurious) or intervene in these relationships (make them sensible) to have the beginnings of a theoretical understanding of them.

To accomplish this more difficult task, we must in some sense start over from the beginning. We must ask *how* events come to matter psychologically. Luckily, further clues to these processes lie in the dimensions of events found most closely associated with disturbance. Undesirability seems a particularly important dimension, especially when coupled with the findings of two studies that, surprisingly, have attracted little notice up to now.

Gersten and her colleagues (Gersten *et al.*, 1977) demonstrated that the association between undesirable family events and various measures of disturbance in children disappeared when ongoing stressful situational factors were controlled, where situational factors were composed primarily of measures of persistent difficulties (e.g., parents' unhappy marriage, economic dissatisfaction, low income status). Gersten *et al.* argued that these results showed the events–disturbance association to be spurious, due instead to the simultaneous event-producing and disturbance-producing effects of persistent difficult circumstances. However, because (1) their measures of difficulties consisted of scores obtained both before *and* after events had occurred, and (2) inspection of their tables showed events to be more highly correlated with later than earlier difficulties, another interpretation is possible. Events may have effects on disturbance *through* difficulties; that is, ongoing strains may intervene in the events–disturbance relationship. Thus, control for difficulties eliminated (explained) the association between events and disturbance.

Evidence from a study by Pearlin and Lieberman (1979) corroborates this latter interpretation. They found that two very disruptive undesirable events—the loss of employment and the loss of a marital partner through divorce, separation, or death—resulted in serious symptoms of psychological distress only when the intensity of difficulties following that event were high. Newly unemployed individuals and newly unmarried individuals who did not experience subsequent intense problems were not significantly different in symptomology from the stably employed or the stably married. Because controls for subsequent difficulties eliminated the relationships between events and distress, Pearlin and Lieberman concluded, "to an appreciable extent the impact of events is channeled through relatively durable problems impinging on the lives of people" (1979:240).

These studies suggest that major culturally undesirable events may not be disturbing in and of themselves. Rather, the *consequences* of such events may determine their disturbing quality. For example, the unexpected death of an apparently healthy spouse may leave the surviving spouse not only grief-stricken, but beset by a host of enduring financial, residential, and family problems. But the death of a spouse who has been painfully wasting away with cancer may eliminate the emotional torment, financial burdens, and disruptions in daily routine occasioned by a prolonged illness in the family. The event is nominally the same on a life-event scale, but its consequences are radically different. It is exactly this qualitative difference between two nominally identical events that Brown and Harris (1978) attempted to capture with their contextual measures of severe events—experiences that are threatening to an individual in the long term. And it is quite likely that measures of event magnitude (Holmes and Rahe, 1967) roughly tap the typical long-term consequences of events; note that undesirable events on such scales as the Holmes–Rahe SRRS have the greatest readjustment values associated with them. In short, experiences that generate or exacerbate ongoing strains may be what we actually mean by the phrase *major undesirable events* and what we may be measuring by our counts of the same.

So here we have, potentially, one explanatory piece of the puzzle: Multiple, clustered, major undesirable events may be associated with psychological disturbance because they generate or exacerbate enduring difficulties for the individual who experiences them. But why should such persistent problems have *psychological* effects? Why, for example, do individuals not break down physically, rather than psychologically?[12]

The usual pat answer is that the adjustments required by negative events and their attendant difficulties overwhelm the coping or supportive resources available to the person. Although this may be a valid answer, it is still incomplete. To repeat, why are these effects manifested in expressly psychological symptoms?

Several investigators have offered similar theoretical answers. Undesirable events and continuing difficulties may have psychological impacts because they cause individuals to view themselves negatively (Abramson et al., 1978; Brown and Harris, 1978; Kaplan, 1980; Kaplan et al., 1983; Lazarus and Launier, 1978; Mortimer et al., 1982; Pearlin et al., 1981; Sarbin, 1968; Thoits, 1982d, 1983). For these theorists, the maintenance and enhancement of self-regard is assumed either ex-

---

[12]Actually, this is a problematic rhetorical question. We do not know definitely that people are more likely to break down psychologically than physically following troubles due to life events. It is possible that both responses to strains may occur. Or, total amount of change may generate generalized anxiety and attendant health problems, whereas undesirable change may generate primarily psychological disorder through the processes described next in the chapter (see Gersten et al., 1974, and p. 59).

plicitly or implicitly to be a fundamental human need and to have important implications for one's psychological state.

Negative events (and the persistent undesirable consequences of those events) may decrease self-regard in two related ways. Failures to control the occurrence of events or their undesirable consequences may decrease a sense of mastery or control over life (Abramson et al., 1978). And the loss of valued social roles or inadequate performance in remaining roles may lower the value of individuals in their own and others' eyes (Kaplan, 1980). As Pearlin et al. state it,

> Persistent role strains can confront people with dogged evidence of their own failures—or lack of success—and with inescapable proof of their inability to alter the unwanted circumstances of their lives. Under these conditions, people become vulnerable to the loss of self-esteem and to the erosion of [a sense of] mastery. (1981:340)

In short, psychological symptoms may be the result of the meanings people attach to, or the cognitive interpretations people make of, events and their aftermaths with respect to the self. Lowered self-esteem and loss of a sense of control may generate the symptoms of anxiety and depression typically captured on psychological distress scales or diagnosed as neurotic disorders by practitioners. Efforts to regain self-regard by severely threatened individuals may result in unacceptable—pathological—behaviors or the deviant emotional and thought patterns of the more serious psychological disorders. Recent studies are beginning to supply evidence that self processes, in fact, are involved in the etiology of these disorders (Kaplan et al., 1983; Pearlin et al., 1981). Although it is clear that much more theoretical work is necessary to specify the forms or intensity of disturbance that might result from the self-implications people draw from their experiences (Abramson et al., 1978), at the very least, attention to self processes helps explain why psychological and not just physical symptoms follow from undesirable events and their consequences.

Self processes may also help explain the significant moderating, or buffering, effects of coping strategies and social support found in the empirical literature. As will become clear in the chapters by Turner and by Menaghan, not much is known about why or how certain coping responses and certain sources or types of social support work to alleviate the distress that people feel in response to events. It is possible that the self-denigrating impacts of events and continuing strains are mitigated to the extent that individuals' coping strategies or supportive contacts aid them in sustaining perceptions of mastery, self-worth, or both (Thoits, 1982d).

In brief, the *theoretical processes* through which events come to have serious psychological impacts require further explication and testing. Although more complex causal *models* of stress processes are currently developing—models in which events interact with vulnerability factors—unified theories of the interrelationships among these major sets of interacting factors have been noticeably lacking. Theoretical understanding is necessary not only for "pure" scientific purposes but for applied policy purposes as well. Causal models may have obvious policy implications, but their atheoretical nature may cause policy enactments to fail. For example, the finding that the possession of a confidant can reduce the distress felt by beleaguered individuals (Brown and Harris, 1978) suggests that, as a simple and inexpensive intervention strategy, mental health clinics might assign volunteers to befriend clients. But a volunteer friend program may obtain only limited success because how a confidant actually relieves distress is presently unknown and therefore unteachable to volunteers. Strategic successful intervention requires a thorough theoretical understanding of the processes linking the major factors in our models.

Moreover, attention to theoretical processes may suggest further links to be added to these models. For example, most researchers tacitly accept the postulate that life events overwhelm the coping resources of individuals. Unfortunately, because coping *capacities* cannot be directly measured, this hypothesis has never been tested. However, a closely related implication of this hypothesis is that events may alter *directly* the coping responses and/or social support resources of individuals. For example, repeated exposure to undesirable, uncontrollable events may discourage attempts at active coping in the future. The coping strategies of persons may change in response to events already experienced. Events also may alter the availability of social support. Loss of employment or a major residential move, for example, removes the person from frequent contact with potentially supportive co-workers, friends, or relatives. Many events on life-event scales are support losses almost by definition (e.g., death, divorce, decrease in the frequency of get-togethers with relatives or friends, Thoits, 1982a). Despite these implications, researchers have concentrated almost exclusively on the event-*moderating* effects of psychosocial resources, rather than on examining the direct influences of events and strains on these resources (for exceptions, see Lin et al., 1979; Menaghan, 1982; Pearlin et al., 1981; Thoits, 1982a; Turner and Noh, 1983). This lack of attention to the influences of events and strains on coping strategies and social support availability has not only impoverished our understanding of etiological processes in general, but, because of poorly specified models, may have produced biased estimates of the main and interactive effects of these factors as well (see Thoits, 1982a, for a detailed illustration of this problem).

Furthermore, if, as suggested earlier, life events and their aversive sequelae decrease a sense of mastery and self-esteem, these changes in self-regard may partially explain certain of the direct effects of events and strains on psychosocial resources. For example, exposure to uncontrollable events may erode a sense of mastery and therefore reduce the future likelihood that active coping attempts will be utilized. Rather, passive, potentially harmful forms of coping (e.g., denial, resignation, drug use) may be adopted, even when active efforts might be appropriate and rewarding. Similarly, an event-generated decrease in self-esteem may cause individuals, out of shame, to avoid potentially supportive others. Their bolstering regard and their coping advice thus are foregone, leaving the person less equipped to face further difficult circumstances. Obviously, direct and indirect (through self-esteem and mastery) influences of events and strains on psychosocial resources may not only perpetuate disturbance, but exacerbate or add to existing difficulties. A complex vicious cycle of effects may be engendered (Menaghan, 1982). Failure to consider the channels through which events and strains have an impact on disturbance have undoubtedly reduced the predictive power of current models of stress processes.

Theoretical understanding of the events–disturbance link has also been impoverished by a lack of attention to broader sociological, or epidemiological, patterns. It is well known that rates of mental illness are higher among disadvantaged sociodemographic groups, such as women, the unmarried, married women, and those of lower income, educational, and occupational status (Bachrach, 1975; B. P. Dohrenwend et al., 1980; Gove, 1972; Gove and Tudor, 1973). These distributions of disturbance suggest that members of lower-status groups must experience, at the very least, higher numbers of severe undesirable events. But remarkably little research has focused on the distribution of events among sociodemographic groups. And the results of such studies have not been consistent (see review by Thoits, 1982c). In fact, it appears that undesirable events are distributed more equally among groups than might be expected; certain advantaged groups (the married, those of higher income) actually report equal or even higher numbers of undesirable events than their disadvantaged counterparts (Thoits, 1982b, 1982c). Despite these departures from expectation, a growing body of research indicates that even though members of lower-status groups may not experience greater numbers of events, they are more psychologically reactive to the impacts of life events and chronic strains. That is, at each level of exposure, members of disadvantaged groups exhibit greater psychological distress or impairment than members of advantaged groups (Kessler, 1979a, 1979b; Langner and Michael, 1963; Pearlin and Johnson, 1977; Thoits, 1982b, 1982c). This differential reactivity to life difficulties cannot be explained entirely by a lack of social support in lower-status groups (Kessler and Essex, 1982; Thoits, 1982b, 1982c; Turner and Noh, 1983). Rather, it appears that lack of support in combination with deficiencies in self-esteem or mastery may account for differential vulnerability to life difficulties (Kessler and Essex, 1982; Turner and Noh, 1981).

As a set, these sociological findings are puzzling. Why, if they are not exposed to more undesirable events, do disadvantaged groups have higher rates of mental illness? Why are these groups more reactive to events and strains? And why should the combination of lack of support with deficiencies in self-regard be necessary to explain these differential vulnerabilities?

It is possible that lower-status groups are exposed to more undesirable, *uncontrollable* events (B. S. Dohrenwend, 1970, 1978). If uncontrollable negative events decrease a sense of mastery and self-esteem, and these effects in turn discourage active coping attempts or support utilization, then perhaps we have an explanation of differential reactivity to events. Lower-status groups may be more often exposed to a particular combination of event qualities that are more psychologically damaging not only in their direct impacts on the psyche but indirectly through their impacts on the self and on subsequent psychosocial resource utilization. Admittedly, these hypotheses at present are entirely speculative. But the point is that certain sociological phenomena suggest additional problems and issues that should help us refine our understanding of the link between life events and psychological disturbance. To date, few researchers have taken advantage of the theoretical implications that can be derived from these broader sociological patterns.[13]

In sum, we need to pay much more theoretical attention to why and how life events are related to psychological outcomes. Without explicit theory, we have tended to overlook important unexplored links in our models of stress processes. And, as a result, we have reduced our chances of explaining more variance in psychological outcomes as

---

[13]It might be added that it is important to control for the influences of individuals' sociodemographic characteristics simply to rule out the possibility that the events–disturbance association is a spurious product of these social characteristics (B. S. Dohrenwend, 1973).

well. It is now time to stop replicating and embroidering the basic life-events finding and to push on to generating and testing systematic theories of stress processes.

Despite its methodological limitations and atheoretical nature, life-events research still has taught us something at once simple and profound: The etiology of mental illness is partially environmental, or social, in origin. Like role theory, life-events research has led us to take seriously the link between the social environment and the person. Changes in the social environment produce changes in the psychological functioning of individuals. But unlike role theory, which has lacked dynamic processual propositions, developing stress theory offers the rich potential of not only explaining the etiology of mental illness at the individual level, but also simultaneously accounting for the unequal distributions of disorder in society. After all, what are these unequal distributions but a cross section of individual reactions to varying, yet patterned, life experiences? Our task is to understand better the social-psychological processes that translate patterned problematic social experiences into specific types of disorder. Ultimately, our theories should allow us to account for the higher incidence of disturbance among certain groups, particularly disadvantaged groups, in this society.

REFERENCES

Abramson, Lyn Y., Martin E. P. Seligman, and John D. Teasdale
  1978   "Learned helplessness in humans: Critique and reformulation." Journal of Abnormal Psychology 87:49–74.
American Psychiatric Association
  1952   Diagnostic and Statistical Manual of Mental Disorders. 1st edition. Washington, D.C.: American Psychiatric Association.
  1968   Diagnostic and Statistical Manual of Mental Disorders. 2nd edition. Washington, D.C.: American Psychiatric Association.
  1980   Diagnostic and Statistical Manual of Mental Disorders. 3rd edition. Washington, D.C.: American Psychiatric Association.
Antonovsky, Aaron, and R. Kats
  1967   "The life crisis history as a tool in epidemiological research." Journal of Health and Social Behavior 8:15–21.
Askenasy, Alexander R., Bruce P. Dohrenwend, and Barbara S. Dohrenwend
  1977   "Some effects of social class and ethnic group membership on judgments of the magnitude of stressful life events: A research note." Journal of Health and Social Behavior 18:432–439.
Bachrach, Leona L.
  1975   Marital Status and Mental Disorder: An Analytical Review. U.S. Depart-

ment of Health, Education, and Welfare (ADAMHA), Publication No. 75-217. Washington, D.C.: U.S. Government Printing Office.

Barrett, James E.
1979   "The relationship of life events to the onset of neurotic disorders." Pp. 87–109 in James E. Barrett (ed.), Stress and Mental Disorder. New York: Raven Press.

Barton, Allen
1969   Communities in Disaster: A Sociological Analysis of Collective Stress Situations. Garden City, N.Y.: Doubleday.

Beck, J., and K. Worthen
1972   "Precipitating stress, crisis theory, and hospitalization in schizophrenia and depression." Archives of General Psychiatry 26:123–129.

Birley, J. L. T., and George W. Brown
1970   "Crises and life changes preceding the onset or relapse of acute schizophrenia: Clinical aspects." British Journal of Psychiatry 116:327–333.

Bradley, Clare
1980   "Sex differences in reporting and rating of life events: A comparison of diabetic and healthy subjects." Journal of Psychosomatic Research 24:35–37.

Bremer, J.
1951   "A social psychiatric investigation of a small community in northern Norway." Acta Psychiatrica et Neurologica Scandinavica, Supplementum 62.

Brown, George W.
1974   "Meaning, measurement, and stress of life events." Pp. 217–243 in Barbara Snell Dohrenwend and Bruce P. Dohrenwend (eds.), Stressful Life Events: Their Nature and Effects. New York: Wiley.
1979   "A three-factor causal model of depression." Pp. 111–120 in James E. Barrett (ed.), Stress and Mental Disorders. New York: Raven Press.

Brown, George W., and J. L. T. Birley
1968   "Crises and life changes and the onset of schizophrenia." Journal of Health and Social Behavior 9:203–214.

Brown, George W., and Tirril Harris
1978   Social Origins of Depression: A Study of Psychiatric Disorder in Women. New York: Free Press.

Brown, George W., Tirril O. Harris, and J. Petro
1973   "Life events and psychiatric disorders, Part 2: Nature of causal link." Psychological Medicine 3:159–176.

Burgess, Ann Wolbert, and Lynda Lytle Holmstrom
1974   Rape: Victims of Crisis. Bowie, Md.: Brady.
1979   Rape: Crisis and Recovery. Bowie, Md.: Brady.

Cannon, W. B.
1929   Bodily Changes in Pain, Hunger, Fear, and Rage. New York: Appleton.

Carr, Leslie G., and Neal Krause
1978   "Social status, psychiatric symptomatology, and response bias." Journal of Health and Social Behavior 19:86–91.

Chiriboga, David A.
1977   "Life event weighting systems: A comparative analysis." Journal of Psychosomatic Research 21:415–422.

Clancy, Kevin, and Walter Gove
1974   "Sex differences in mental illness: An analysis of response bias in self-reports." American Journal of Sociology 80:205–216.

Clayton, Paula J., and Harriet S. Darvish
    1979   "Course of depressive symptoms following the stress of bereavement." Pp.
            121–136 in James E. Barrett (ed.), Stress and Mental Disorder. New York:
            Raven Press.
Clayton, Paula J., L. Desmarais, and G. Winokur
    1968   "A study of normal bereavement." American Journal of Psychiatry
            125:168–178.
Clayton, Paula J., James A. Halikas, and William L. Maurice
    1971   "The bereavement of the widowed." Diseases of the Nervous System
            32:597–604.
    1972   "The depression of widowhood." British Journal of Psychiatry 120:71–78.
Cleary, Patrick J.
    1980   "A checklist for life event research." Journal of Psychosomatic Research
            24:199–207.
    1981   "Problems of internal consistency and scaling in life event schedules."
            Journal of Psychosomatic Research 25:309–320.
Coates, D., S. Moyer, and B. Wellman
    1969   "Yorklea study: Symptoms, problems and life events." Canadian Journal of
            Public Health 69:471–481.
Coates, D. B., S. Moyer, L. Kendall, and M. G. Howat
    1976   "Life event changes and mental health." Pp. 225–250 in Irwin G. Sarason
            and Charles D. Spielberger (eds.), Stress and Anxiety. Volume 3. New York:
            Wiley.
Cobb, Sidney, and Stanislav V. Kasl
    1977   Termination: The Consequences of Job Loss. U.S. Department of Health,
            Education, and Welfare (NIOSH) Publication No. 77-224. Washington, D.C.:
            U.S. Government Printing Office.
Coddington, R. D.
    1972   "The significance of life events as etiologic factors in the diseases of chil-
            dren. II. A study of a normal population." Journal of Psychosomatic Re-
            search 16:205–213.
Cohen, Frances
    1975   "Psychological factors in the etiology of somatic illness." Unpublished
            manuscript, University of California, Berkeley.
Cohen, Frances, and Richard S. Lazarus
    1979   "Coping with the stresses of illness." Pp. 217–254 in George C. Stone,
            Frances Cohen, and Nancy E. Adler (eds.), Health Psychology: A Handbook.
            San Francisco: Jossey-Bass.
Conover, Donald, and Carlos E. Climent
    1976   "Explanations of bias in psychiatric case-finding instruments." Journal of
            Health and Social Behavior 17:62–69.
Cooke, D. J.
    1981   "Life events and syndromes of depression in the general population." So-
            cial Psychiatry 16: 181–186.
Cooke, D. J., and J. G. Green
    1981   "Types of life events in relation to symptoms at the climacterium." Journal
            of Psychosomatic Research 25:5–11.
Cooley, Eric J., Adam W. Miller, James C. Keesey, Mary J. Levenspiel, and Carol F. Sisson
    1979   "Self-report assessment of life change and disorders." Psychological Re-
            ports 44:1079–1086.

Crandell, Dewitt L., and Bruce P. Dohrenwend
  1967   "Some relations among psychiatric symptoms, organic illness, and social class." American Journal of Psychiatry 123:1527–1538.
Dekker, Daniel J., and James T. Webb
  1974   "Relationships of the Social Readjustment Rating Scale to psychiatric patient status, anxiety and social desirability." Journal of Psychosomatic Research 18:125–130.
Derogatis, Leonard R., R. S. Lipman, and L. Covi
  1973   "The SCL-90: An outpatient psychiatric rating scale." Psychopharmacology Bulletin 9:13–28.
Dohrenwend, Barbara Snell
  1970   "Social class and stressful events." Pp. 313–319 in E. H. Hare and J. K. Wing (eds.), Psychiatric Epidemiology. New York: Oxford University Press.
  1973   "Life events as stressors: A methodological inquiry." Journal of Health and Social Behavior 14:167–175.
  1977   "Anticipation and control of stressful life events: An exploratory analysis." Pp. 135–186 in John S. Strauss, Haroutun M. Babigian, and Merrill Roff (eds.), The Origins and Course of Psychopathology. New York: Plenum Press.
  1978   "Social status and responsibility for stressful life events." Pp. 25–42 in Charles D. Spielberger and Irwin G. Sarason (eds.), Stress and Anxiety. Volume 5. New York: Wiley.
Dohrenwend, Barbara Snell, and Bruce P. Dohrenwend
  1974   "A brief historical introduction to research on stressful life events." Pp. 1–5 in Barbara Snell Dohrenwend and Bruce P. Dohrenwend (eds.), Stressful Life Events: Their Nature and Effects. New York: Wiley.
  1981   "Life stress and illness: Formulation of the issues." Pp. 1–27 in Barbara Snell Dohrenwend and Bruce P. Dohrenwend (eds.), Stressful Life Events and Their Contexts. New York: Prodist.
Dohrenwend, Barbara Snell, Larry Krasnoff, Alexander R. Askenasy, and Bruce P. Dohrenwend
  1978   "Exemplification of a method for scaling life events: The PERI life events scale." Journal of Health and Social Behavior 19:205–229.
Dohrenwend, Barbara Snell, and John L. Martin
  1979   " Personal versus situational determination of anticipation and control of the occurrence of stressful life events." American Journal of Community Psychology 7:453–468.
Dohrenwend, Bruce P.
  1966   "Social status and psychological disorder: An issue of substance and an issue of method." American Sociological Review 31:14–34.
  1974   "Problems in defining and sampling the relevant population of stressful life events." Pp. 275–310 in Barbara Snell Dohrenwend and Bruce P. Dohrenwend (eds), Stressful Life Events: Their Nature and Effects. New York: Wiley.
  1979   "Stressful life events and psychopathology: Some issues of theory and method." Pp. 1–15 in James E. Barrett (ed.), Stress and Mental Disorder. New York: Raven Press.
Dohrenwend, Bruce P., and Barbara Snell Dohrenwend
  1969   Social Status and Psychological Disorder. New York: Wiley.
  1976   "Sex differences in psychiatric disorders." American Journal of Sociology 81:1447–1459.

Dohrenwend, Bruce P., Barbara Snell Dohrenwend, Madelyn Schwartz Gould, Bruce Link, Richard Neugebauer, and Robin Wunsch-Hitzig
    1980   Mental Illness in the United States: Epidemiological Estimates. New York: Praeger.
Dohrenwend, Bruce P., and Gladys Egri
    1981   "Recent stressful life events and episodes of schizophrenia." Schizophrenia Bulletin 7:12–23.
Douglas, Jack D.
    1967   The Social Meanings of Suicide. Princeton, N.J.: Princeton University Press.
Eitinger, Leo
    1964   Concentration Camp Survivors in Norway and Israel. London: Allen and Unwin.
Ensel, Walter M., and Mark Tausig
    1982   "The social context of undesirable life events." Paper presented at the National Conference on Stress Research, Durham, New Hampshire.
Fairbank, Dianne Timbers, and Richard L. Hough
    1981   "Cross-cultural differences in perceptions of life events." Pp. 63–84 in Barbara Snell Dohrenwend and Bruce P. Dohrenwend (eds.), Stressful Life Events and Their Contexts. New York: Prodist.
Fava, G. A., F. Munari, L. Pavan, and R. Kellner
    1981   "Life events and depression: A replication." Journal of Affective Disorders 3:159–165.
Finlay-Jones, Robert
    1981   "Showing that life events are a cause of depression—a review." Australian and New Zealand Journal of Psychiatry 15:229–238.
Fontana, Alan F., Linda A. Hughes, Jonathan L. Marcus, and Barbara Noel Dowds
    1979   "Subjective evaluation of life events." Journal of Consulting and Clinical Psychology 47:906–911.
Fontana, Alan F., Jonathan L. Marcus, Barbara Noel, and John M. Rakusin
    1972   "Prehospitalization coping styles of psychiatric patients: The goal-directedness of life events." Journal of Nervous and Mental Disease 155:311–321.
Fried, M.
    1963   "Grieving for a lost home." Pp. 151–171 in L. J. Duhl (ed.), The Urban Condition. New York: Basic Books.
Fröberg, Jan, Claes-Göran Karlsson, Lennart Levi, and Lars Lidberg
    1971   "Physiological and biochemical stress reactions induced by psychosocial stimuli." Pp. 280–295 in Lennart Levi (ed.), Society, Stress, and Disease. Volume 1. London: Oxford University Press.
Garber, Judy, and Martin E. P. Seligman (eds.)
    1980   Human Helplessness: Theory and Applications. New York: Academic Press.
Gersten, Joanne C., Thomas S. Langner, Jeanne G. Eisenberg, and Lida Orzek
    1974   "Child behavior and life events: Undesirable change or change per se?" Pp. 159–170 in Barbara Snell Dohrenwend and Bruce P. Dohrenwend, Stressful Life Events: Their Nature and Effects. New York: Wiley.
Gersten, Joanne C., Thomas S. Langner, Jeanne G. Eisenberg, and Ora Simcha Fagen
    1977   "An evaluation of the etiologic role of stressful life-change events in psychological disorders." Journal of Health and Social Behavior 18:228–244.

Gibbs, Jack, and Walter Martin
    1964   Status Integration and Suicide. Eugene: University of Oregon Press.
Glass, David C., and Jerome E. Singer
    1972   Urban Stress: Experiments on Noise and Social Stressors. New York: Academic Press.
Gleser, Goldine C., Bonnie L. Green, and Carolyn Winget
    1981   Prolonged Psychological Effects of Disaster: A Study of Buffalo Creek. New York: Academic Press.
Gong-Guy, Elizabeth, and Constance Hammen
    1980   "Causal perceptions of stressful events in depressed and nondepressed outpatients." Journal of Abnormal Psychology 89:662–669.
Gore, Susan
    1978   "The effect of social support in moderating the health consequences of unemployment." Journal of Health and Social Behavior 19:157–165.
Gove, Walter
    1972   "The relationship between sex roles, mental illness, and marital status." Social Forces 51:34–44.
Gove, Walter R., and Michael R. Geerken
    1977   "Response bias in surveys of mental health: An empirical investigation." American Journal of Sociology 82:1289–1317.
Gove, Walter, and Jeannette F. Tudor
    1973   "Adult sex roles and mental illness." American Journal of Sociology 78:50–73.
    1977   "Sex differences in mental illness: A comment on Dohrenwend and Dohrenwend." American Journal of Sociology 82:1327–1336.
Grant, Igor, Marvin Gerst, and Joel Yager
    1976   "Scaling of life events by psychiatric patients and normals." Journal of Psychosomatic Research 20:141–149.
Grant, Igor, Hervey Sweetwood, Marvin S. Gerst, and Joel Yager
    1978a   "Scaling procedures in life events research." Journal of Psychosomatic Research 22:525–530.
Grant, Igor, Hervey L. Sweetwood, Joel Yager, and Marvin S. Gerst
    1978b   "Patterns in the relationship of life events and psychiatric symptoms over time." Journal of Psychosomatic Research 22:183–191.
    1981   "Quality of life events in relation to psychiatric symptoms." Archives of General Psychiatry 38:335–339.
Grinker, R. R., and J. P. Spiegal
    1945   Men under Stress. New York: McGraw-Hill.
Gurin, Gerald, Joseph Veroff, and Sheila Feld
    1960   Americans View Their Mental Health. New York: Basic Books.
Hastings, D. W.
    1944   "Psychiatry in Eighth Air Force." Air Surgeon's Bulletin I(8):4–5.
Heller, Kenneth
    1979   "The effects of social support: Prevention and treatment implications." Pp. 353–382 in Arnold P. Goldstein and Frederick H. Kanfer (eds.), Maximizing Treatment Gains: Transfer Enhancement in Psychotherapy. New York: Academic Press.
Hinkle, Lawrence, Jr.
    1974   "The effect of exposure to culture change, social change, and changes in

interpersonal relationships on health." Pp. 9–44 in Barbara Snell Dohrenwend and Bruce P. Dohrenwend (eds.), Stressful Life Events: Their Nature
and Effects. New York: Wiley.

Holmes, Thomas H.
1979   "Development and application of a quantitative measure of life change
        magnitude." Pp. 37–53 in James E. Barrett (ed.), Stress and Mental Disor-
        der. New York: Raven Press.

Holmes, Thomes H., and Minoru Masuda
1974   "Life change and illness susceptibility." Pp. 45–72 in Barbara Snell
        Dohrenwend and Bruce P. Dohrenwend (eds.), Stressful Life Events: Their
        Nature and Effects. New York: Wiley.

Holmes, Thomas H., and Richard H. Rahe
1967   "The Social Readjustment Rating Scale." Journal of Psychosomatic Re-
        search 11: 213–218.

Horowitz, Mardi J., Catherine Schaefer, and Paul Cooney
1974   "Life event scaling for recency of experience." Pp. 125–133 in E. K. Eric
        Gunderson and Richard H. Rahe (eds.), Life Stress and Illness. Springfield,
        Ill.: Thomas.

Horowitz, Mardi, Catherine Schaefer, Donald Hiroto, Nancy Wilner, and Barbara Levin
1977   "Life event questionnaires for measuring presumptive stress." Psychoso-
        matic Medicine 39:413–431.

Hough, Richard L., Dianne T. Fairbank, and Alma M. Garcia
1976   "Problems in the ratio measurement of life stress." Journal of Health and
        Social Behavior 17:70–82.

House, James S.
1981   Work Stress and Social Support. Reading, Mass.: Addison-Wesley.

Hudgens, Richard W.
1974   "Personal catastrophe and depression: A consideration of the subject with
        respect to medically ill adolescents, and a requiem for retrospective life-
        event studies." Pp. 119–134 in Barbara Snell Dohrenwend and Bruce P.
        Dohrenwend (eds.), Stressful Life Events: Their Nature and Effects. New
        York: Wiley.

Hudgens, Richard W., J. R. Morrison, and R. G. Barchha
1967   "Life events and onset of primary affective disorders: A study of 40 hospi-
        talized patients and 40 controls." Archives of General Psychiatry
        16:134–145.

Hudgens, Richard W., Eli Robins, and W. Bradford Delong
1970   "The reporting of recent stress in the lives of psychiatric patients." British
        Journal of Psychiatry 117:635–643.

Hurst, Michael W.
1979   "Life changes and psychiatric symptom development: Issues of content,
        scoring, and clustering." Pp. 17–36 in James E. Barrett (ed.), Stress and
        Mental Disorder. New York: Raven Press.

Hurst, Michael W., C. David Jenkins, and Robert M. Rose
1978   "The assessment of life change stress: A comparative and methodological
        inquiry." Psychosomatic Medicine 40:2:126–141.

Husaini, Baqar A., and James Alan Neff
1980   "Characteristics of life events and psychiatric impairment in rural commu-
        nities." Journal of Nervous and Mental Disease 168:159–166.

1981   "Social class and depressive symptomatology: The role of life change events and locus of control." Journal of Nervous and Mental Disease 169:638–647.

Jacobs, Selby, and Jerome Myers

1976   "Recent life events and acute schizophrenic psychosis: A controlled study." Journal of Nervous and Mental Disease 162:75–87.

Janis, I. L.

1951   Air War and Emotional Stress. New York: McGraw-Hill.

Jemmott, John B., and Steven E. Locke

1982   "Psychosocial factors, immunologic mediation, and human susceptibility to disease: How much do we know?" Unpublished manuscript, Department of Psychology, Princeton University.

Jenkins, C. David, Michael W. Hurst, and Robert M. Rose

1979   "Life changes: Do people really remember?" Archives of General Psychiatry 36:379–384.

Johnson, David Richard, and Richard L. Meile

1981   "Does dimensionality bias in Langner's 22-Item Index affect the validity of social status comparisons?" Journal of Health and Social Behavior 22:415–433.

Johnson, James H., and Irwin G. Sarason

1978   "Life stress, depression, and anxiety: Internal-external control as a moderator variable." Journal of Psychosomatic Research 22:205–208.

Kaplan, Howard B.

1980   Deviant Behavior in Defense of Self. New York: Academic Press.

Kaplan, Howard B., Cynthia Robbins, and Steven S. Martin

1983   "Toward the testing of a general theory of deviant behavior in longitudinal perspective: Patterns of psychopathology." Pp. 27–66 in James R. Greenley (ed.), Research in Community and Mental Health. Volume III. Greenwich, Conn.: JAI Press.

Kendall, Patricia L., and Paul F. Lazarsfeld

1950   "Problems of survey analysis." Pp. 133–196 in Robert K. Merton and Paul F. Lazarsfeld (eds.), Continuities in Social Research: Studies in the Scope and Method of "The American Soldier." New York: Free Press.

Kessler, Ronald C.

1979a   "A strategy for studying differential vulnerability to the psychological consequences of stress." Journal of Health and Social Behavior 20:100–108.

1979b   "Stress, social status, and psychological distress." Journal of Health and Social Behavior 20:259–272.

Kessler, Ronald C., and Marilyn Essex

1982   "Marital status and depression: The importance of coping resources." Social Forces 61:484–507.

Kobasa, Suzanne C., Salvatore R. Maddi, and Sheila Courington

1981   "Personality and constitution as mediators in the stress-illness relationship." Journal of Health and Social Behavior 22:368–378.

Kohn, Melvin

1968   "Social class and schizophrenia: A critical review." Pp. 155–173 in David Rosenthal and Seymour Kety (eds.), The Transmission of Schizophrenia. Oxford: Pergamon Press.

Langner, Thomas S.
    1962   "A twenty-two item screening score of psychiatric symptoms indicating
            impairment." Journal of Health and Human Behavior 3:269–276.
Langner, Thomas S., and Stanley T. Michael
    1963   Life Stress and Mental Health. New York: The Free Press of Glencoe.
Lazarus, Richard S., and Raymond Launier
    1978   "Stress-related transactions between person and environment." Pp.
            287–327 in L. A. Pervin and M. Lewis (eds.), Perspectives in Interactional
            Psychology. New York: Plenum Press.
Lefcourt, Herbert M.
    1981   "Locus of control and stressful life events." Pp. 157–166 in Barbara Snell
            Dohrenwend and Bruce P. Dohrenwend (eds.), Stressful Life Events and
            Their Contexts. New York: Prodist.
Lehman, Robert E.
    1978   "Symptom contamination of the schedule of recent events." Journal of
            Consulting and Clinical Psychology 46:1564–1565.
Lei, Hau, and Harvey A. Skinner
    1980   A psychometric study of life events and social readjustment. Journal of
            Psychosomatic Research 24:57–65.
Leighton, Dorothea C., J. S. Harding, D. B. Macklin, A. M. MacMillan, and A. H. Leighton
    1963   The Character of Danger: Psychiatric Symptoms in Selected Communities.
            New York: Basic Books.
Levi, Lennart
    1974   "Psychosocial stress and disease: A conceptual model." Pp. 8–33 in E. K.
            Eric Gunderson and Richard H. Rahe (eds.), Life Stress and Illness. Spring-
            field, Ill.: Thomas.
Levine, Sol, and Norman A. Scotch
    1970   "Social stress." Pp. 1–16 in Sol Levine and Norman A. Scotch (eds.), Social
            Stress. New York: Aldine.
Lifton, Robert Jay
    1968   Death in Life: Survivors of Hiroshima. New York: Random House.
Lin, Nan, Walter M. Ensel, Ronald S. Simeone, and Wen Kuo
    1979   "Social support, stressful life events, and illness: A model and empirical
            test." Journal of Health and Social Behavior 20:108–119.
Lindemann, Erich
    1944   "Symptomatology and management of acute grief." American Journal of
            Psychiatry 101:141–148.
Lloyd, Camille
    1980a   "Life events and depressive disorder reviewed. I. Events as predisposing
            factors." Archives of General Psychiatry 37:529–535.
    1980b   "Life events and depressive disorder reviewed. II. Events as precipitating
            factors." Archives of General Psychiatry 37:541–548.
Lorimor, Ronald J., Blair Justice, George W. McBee, and Maxine Weinman
    1979   "Weighting events in life-events research (Comment on Dohrenwend et al.
            JHSB, June 1978)." Journal of Health and Social Behavior 20:306–308.
Lundberg, Ulf, and Töres Theorell
    1976   "Scaling of life changes: Differences between three diagnostic groups and
            between recently experienced and nonexperienced events." Journal of
            Human Stress 2:7–17.

Macmillan, Allister M.
    1957   "The Health Opinion Survey: Technique for estimating prevalence of psychoneurotic and related types of disorder in communities." Psychological Reports 3:325–339.
Makosky, Vivian Parker
    1980   "Stress and the mental health of women: A discussion of research and issues." Pp. 111–127 in Marcia Guttentag, Susan Salasin, and Deborah Belle (eds.), The Mental Health of Women. New York: Academic Press.
Manis, Jerome, M. L. Brawer, C. L. Hunt, and L. C. Kercher
    1963   "Validating a mental health scale." American Sociological Review 28:108–116.
Markush, Robert E., and Rachel V. Favero
    1974   "Epidemiologic assessment of stressful life events, depressed mood, and psychophysiological symptoms—a preliminary report." Pp. 171–190 in Barbara Snell Dohrenwend and Bruce P. Dohrenwend (eds.), Stressful Life Events: Their Nature and Effects. New York: Wiley.
Mason, John W.
    1975a   "A historical view of the stress field, Part I." Journal of Human Stress (March):6–12.
    1975b   "A historical view of the stress field, Part II." Journal of Human Stress (June):22–36.
Masuda, Minoru, and Thomas H. Holmes
    1967   "Magnitude estimations of social readjustments." Journal of Psychosomatic Research 11:219–225.
    1978   "Life events: Perceptions and frequencies." Psychosomatic Medicine 40:236–261.
McCombie, S. L.
    1975   "Characteristics of rape victims seen in crisis interviewing." Smith College Studies in Social Work 46:137–158.
McFarlane, Allan H., Geoffrey R. Norman, David L. Streiner, Renjan Roy, and Deborah J. Scott
    1980   "A longitudinal study of the influence of the psychosocial environment on health status: A preliminary report." Journal of Health and Social Behavior 21:124–133.
McGrath, Joseph E.
    1970   "A conceptual formulation for research on stress." Pp. 10–21 in Joseph E. McGrath (ed.), Social and Psychological Factors in Stress. New York: Holt, Rinehart & Winston.
Mechanic, David
    1962   Students under Stress. Glencoe, Ill.: Free Press.
    1974   "Discussion of research programs on relations between stressful life events and episodes of physical illness." Pp. 87–97 in Barbara Snell Dohrenwend and Bruce P. Dohrenwend (eds.), Stressful Life Events: Their Nature and Effects. New York: Wiley.
Meile, Richard L., and Wayne E. Gregg
    1973   "Dimensionality of the index of psychophysiological stress." Social Science and Medicine 7:643–648.
Menaghan, Elizabeth
    1982   "Measuring coping effectiveness: A panel analysis of marital problems and coping efforts." Journal of Health and Social Behavior 23:220–234.

Meyer, Adolf
    1951   "The life chart and the obligation of specifying positive data in psycho-
            pathological diagnosis." Pp. 52–56 in E. E. Winters (ed.), The Collected
            Papers of Adolf Meyer. Volume III. Baltimore: Johns Hopkins Press.
Miller, F. T., W. K. Bentz, J. F. Aponte, and D. R. Brogan
    1974   "Perception of life crisis events: A comparative study of rural and urban
            samples." Pp. 259–273 in Barbara Snell Dohrenwend and Bruce P. Dohren-
            wend (eds.), Stressful Life Events: Their Nature and Effects. New York:
            Wiley.
Miller, Patrick M., and J. G. Ingham
    1979   "Reflections on the life-event-to-illness link with some preliminary find-
            ings." Pp. 313–336 in I. G. Sarason and C. D. Spielberger (eds.), Stress and
            Anxiety. Volume 6. New York: Wiley.
Miller, Suzanne M.
    1981   "Predictability and human stress: Toward a clarification of evidence and
            theory." Pp. 203–256 in Leonard Berkowitz (ed.), Advances in Experimen-
            tal Social Psychology. Volume 14. New York: Academic Press.
Monroe, Scott M.
    1982   "Life events and disorder: Event-symptom associations and the course of
            disorder." Journal of Abnormal Psychology 91:14–24.
Mortimer, Jeylan T., Michael D. Finch, and Donald Kumka
    1982   "Persistence and change in development: The multidimensional self-con-
            cept." Pp. 263–313 in Paul B. Baltes and Orville G. Brim (eds.), Life-Span
            Development and Behavior. Volume 4. New York: Academic Press.
Mueller, Daniel, Daniel W. Edwards, and Richard M. Yarvis
    1977   "Stressful life events and psychiatric symptomatology: Change or un-
            desirability." Journal of Health and Social Behavior 18:307–316.
    1978   "Stressful life events and community mental health center patients." Jour-
            nal of Nervous and Mental Disease 166:16–24.
Murphy, Elaine, and George W. Brown
    1980   "Life events, psychiatric disturbance, and physical illness." British Journal
            of Psychiatry 136:326–338.
Myers, Jerome, Jacob J. Lindenthal, and Max P. Pepper
    1971   "Life events and psychiatric impairment." Journal of Nervous and Mental
            Disease 152:149–157.
    1974   "Social class, life events, and psychiatric symptoms: A longitudinal
            study." Pp. 191–205 in Barbara Snell Dohrenwend and Bruce P. Dohren-
            wend (eds.), Stressful Life Events: Their Nature and Effects. New York:
            Wiley.
Myers, Jerome K., Jacob J. Lindenthal, Max P. Pepper, and David R. Ostrander
    1972   "Life events and mental status: A longitudinal study." Journal of Health
            and Social Behavior 13:398–406.
Nelson, P., I. N. Mensh, E. Hecht, and A. Schwartz
    1972   "Variables in the reporting of recent life changes." Journal of Psychosomat-
            ic Research 16:465–471.
Nettler, Gwynn
    1978   Explaining Crime. 2nd edition. New York: McGraw-Hill.
Neugebauer, Richard
    1981   "The reliability of life-event reports." Pp. 85–107 in Barbara Snell Dohren-

wend and Bruce P. Dohrenwend (eds.), Stressful Life Events and Their Contexts. New York: Prodist.

Norland, Stephen, and Tom Weirath
  1978   "Validating the Langner scale: A critical review." Social Problems 26:223–231.

Parkes, C. M.
  1972   Bereavement—Studies of Grief in Adult Life. New York: International Universities Press.

Paykel, Eugene S.
  1974   "Life stress and psychiatric disorder: Applications of the clinical approach." Pp. 135–149 in Barbara Snell Dohrenwend and Bruce P. Dohrenwend (eds.), Stressful Life Events: Their Nature and Effects. New York: Wiley.
  1979   "Causal relationships between clinical depression and life events." Pp. 71–86 in James E. Barrett (ed.), Stress and Mental Disorder. New York: Raven Press.

Paykel, Eugene S., Jerome K. Myers, Marcia N. Dienelt, Gerald L. Klerman, Jacob J. Lindenthal, and Max Pepper
  1969   "Life events and depression: A controlled study." Archives of General Psychiatry 21:753–760.

Paykel, Eugene, Brigitte Prusoff, and Jerome K. Myers
  1975   "Suicide attempts and recent life events." Archives of General Psychiatry 32:327–333.

Paykel, Eugene S., Brigitte A. Prusoff, and E. H. Uhlenhuth
  1971   "Scaling of life events." Archives of General Psychiatry 25:340–347.

Paykel, Eugene S., and J. Tanner
  1976   "Life events, depressive relapse, and maintenance treatment." Psychological Medicine 6:481–485.

Pearlin, Leonard I., and Joyce S. Johnson
  1977   "Marital status, life-strains, and depression." American Sociological Review 42:704–715.

Pearlin, Leonard I., and Morton A. Lieberman
  1979   "Social sources of emotional distress." In Roberta Simmons (ed.), Research in Community and Mental Health. Greenwich, Conn.: JAI Press.

Pearlin, Leonard I., Morton A. Lieberman, Elizabeth G. Menaghan, and Joseph T. Mullan
  1981   "The stress process." Journal of Health and Social Behavior 22:337–356.

Pearlin, Leonard I., and Carmi Schooler
  1978   "The structure of coping." Journal of Health and Social Behavior 19:2–21.

Phillips, Derek L., and Kevin J. Clancy
  1970   "Response biases in field studies of mental illness." American Sociological Review 35:503–514.
  1972   "Some effects of social desirability in survey studies." American Journal of Sociology 77:921–940.

Phillips, Derek L., and Bernard E. Segal
  1969   "Sexual status and psychiatric symptoms." American Sociological Review 34:58–72.

Pugh, William M., Jeanne Erickson, Robert T. Rubin, E. K. Eric Gunderson, and Richard H. Rahe
  1971   "Cluster analyses of life changes. II. Method and replication in Navy subpopulations." Archives of General Psychiatry 25:333–339.

Rabkin, Judith Godwin
    1980   "Stressful life events and schizophrenia: A review of the research litera-
            ture." Psychological Bulletin 87:408–425.
Rabkin, Judith G., and Elmer L. Struening
    1976   "Life events, stress, and illness. Science 194:1013–1020.
Radloff, Lenore Sawyer
    1977   "The CES-D Scale: A self-report depression scale for research in the general
            population." Applied Psychological Measurement 1:385–401.
Rahe, Richard H.
    1974   "The pathway between subjects' recent life changes and their near-future
            illness reports: Representative results and methodological issues." Pp.
            73–86 in Barbara Snell Dohrenwend and Bruce P. Dohrenwend (eds.),
            Stressful Life Events: Their Nature and Effects. New York: Wiley.
Rahe, Richard H., and Ransom J. Arthur
    1978   "Life change and illness studies: Past history and future directions." Jour-
            nal of Human Stress:3–15.
Rahe, Richard H., William M. Pugh, Jeanne Erickson, E. K. Eric Gunderson, and Robert T.
Rubin
    1971   "Cluster analyses of life changes. I. Consistency of clusters across large
            Navy samples." Archives of General Psychiatry 25:330–332.
Rahe, Richard H., M. Romo, L. K. Bennett, and P. Siltanen
    1973   "Finnish subjects' recent life changes, myocardial infarction, and abrupt
            coronary death." Unit Report 72–40. San Diego, Calif.: U.S. Navy Medical
            Neuropsychiatric Research Unit.
Redfield, Joel, and Arthur Stone
    1979   "Individual viewpoints of stressful life events." Journal of Consulting and
            Clinical Psychology 47:147–154.
Rosenberg, Emily J., and Barbara Snell Dohrenwend
    1975   "Effects of experience and ethnicity on ratings of life events as stressors."
            Journal of Health and Social Behavior 16:127–129.
Ross, Catherine E., and John Mirowski II
    1979   "A comparison of life event weighting schemes: Change, undesirability and
            effect-proportional indices." Journal of Health and Social Behavior
            20:166–177.
Rubin, R. T., E. K. E. Gunderson, and R. J. Arthur
    1971   "Life stress and illness patterns in the U.S. Navy—V. Prior life change and
            illness onset in a battleship's crew." Journal of Psychosomatic Research
            15:89–94.
Ruch, Libby O.
    1977   "A multidimensional analysis of the concept of life change." Journal of
            Health and Social Behavior 18:71–83.
Ruch, Libby O., Susan Meyers Chandler, and Richard A. Harter
    1980   "Life change and rape impact." Journal of Health and Social Behavior
            21:248–260.
Ruch, Libby O., and Thomas H. Holmes
    1971   "Scaling of life change: Comparison of direct and indirect methods." Jour-
            nal of Psychosomatic Research 15:221–227.
Sarason, Irwin G., James H. Johnson, and Judith M. Siegel
    1978   "Assessing the impact of life changes: Development of the life experiences
            survey." Journal of Consulting and Clinical Psychology 46:932–946.

Sarbin, Theodore R.
  1968   "Notes on the transformation of social identity." Pp. 97–115 in L. M.
          Roberts, N. S. Greenfield, and M. H. Miller (eds.), Comprehensive Mental
          Health: The Challenge of Evaluation. Madison: University of Wisconsin
          Press.
Scheff, Thomas J.
  1966   Being Mentally Ill. Chicago: Aldine.
Schless, Arthur P., and Joseph Mendels
  1978   "The value of interviewing family and friends in assessing life stressors."
          Archives of General Psychiatry 35:565–567.
Schless, Arthur P., L. Schwartz, C. Goetz, and Joseph Mendels
  1974   "How depressives view the significance of life events." British Journal of
          Psychiatry 125:406–410.
Schmale, A. H.
  1972   "Giving up as a final common pathway to changes in health." Advances in
          Psychosomatic Medicine 8:20–40.
Schuessler, Karl, David Hittle, and John Cardascia
  1978   "Measuring responding desirably with attitude-opinion items." Social Psy-
          chology 41:224–235.
Schwartz, Carol C., and Jerome K. Myers
  1977a   "Life events and schizophrenia. I. Comparison of schizophrenics with a
          community sample." Archives of General Psychiatry 34:1238–1241.
  1977b   "Life events and schizophrenia. II. Impact of life events and symptom
          configuration." Archives of General Psychiatry 34:1240–1245.
Schwartz, Carol C., Jerome K. Myers, and Boris M. Astrachan
  1973   "Comparing three measures of mental status: A note on the validity of
          estimates of psychological disorder in the community." Journal of Health
          and Social Behavior 14:265–273.
Scott, William A.
  1970   "Research definitions of mental health and mental illness." Pp. 13–27 in H.
          Wechsler, L. Solomon, and B. Kramer (eds.), Social Psychology and Mental
          Health. New York: Holt, Rinehart, & Winston.
Seiler, Lauren
  1973   "The 22-item scale used in field studies of mental illness: A question of
          method, a question of substance, and a question of theory." Journal of
          Health and Social Behavior 14:252–264.
Seligman, Martin E. P.
  1975   Helplessness: On Depression, Development, and Death. San Francisco: W.
          H. Freeman.
Selye, Hans
  1956   The Stress of Life. New York: McGraw-Hill.
Sheatsley, P. B., and J. Feldman
  1964   "The assassination of President Kennedy: Public reaction." Public Opinion
          Quarterly 28:189–215.
Shrout, Patrick E.
  1981   "Scaling of stressful life events." Pp. 29–47 in Barbara Snell Dohrenwend
          and Bruce P. Dohrenwend (eds.), Stressful Life Events and Their Contexts.
          New York: Prodist.
Silver, Roxanne L., and Camille B. Wortman
  1980   "Coping with undesirable life events." Pp. 279–340 in Judy Garber and

Martin E. P. Seligman (eds.), Human Helplessness: Theory and Its Applications. New York: Academic Press.

Skinner, Harvey A., and Hau Lei
1980a "Differential weights in life change research: Useful or irrelevant?" Psychosomatic Medicine 42:367–370.
1980b "The multidimensional assessment of stressful life events." Journal of Nervous and Mental Disorders 168:535–541.

Spiro, Herzl, R., Iradj Siassi, and Guido M. Crocetti
1972 "What gets surveyed in a psychiatric survey? A case study of the MacMillan Index." Journal of Nervous and Mental Disease 154:105–114.

Spitzer, Robert L., and J. L. Fleiss
1974 "A reanalysis of the reliability of psychiatric diagnosis." British Journal of Psychiatry 125:341–347.

Star, S. A.
1949 "The screening of psychoneurotics in the army: Technical development of tests." Pp. 486–547 in S. A. Stouffer, A. A. Lumsdaine, M. H. Lumsdaine, R. M. Williams, M. B. Smith, I. L. Janis, S. A. Star, and L. S. Cottrell (eds.), Studies in Social Psychology in World War II. Volume 4. Princeton, N.J.: Princeton University Press.

Stein, Zena, and Mervyn W. Susser
1970 "Bereavement as a precipitating event in mental illness." Pp. 327–333 in E. H. Hare and J. K. Wing (eds.), Psychiatric Epidemiology. London: Oxford University Press.

Sterling, Joyce, Thomas E. Draybek, and William H. Key
1977 "The long-term impact of disaster on the health self-perceptions of victims." Paper presented at the American Sociological Association, Chicago.

Streiner, David L., Geoffrey R. Norman, Allan H. McFarlane, and Ranjan G. Roy
1981 "Quality of life events and their relationship to strain." Schizophrenia Bulletin 7:34–42.

Surtees, P. G., and J. G. Ingham
1980 "Life stress and depressive outcome: Applications of a dissipation model to life events." Social Psychiatry 15:21–31.

Szasz, Thomas
1960 "The myth of mental illness." American Psychologist 15:113–118.

Tausig, Mark
1982 "Measuring life events." Journal of Health and Social Behavior 23:52–64.

Tennant, Christopher, and Gavin Andrews
1976 "A scale to measure the stress of life events." Australian and New Zealand Journal of Psychiatry 10:27–32.
1978 "The pathogenic quality of life event stress in neurotic impairment." Archives of General Psychiatry 35:859–863.

Tennant, Christopher, Paul Bebbington, and Jane Hurry
1981 "The short-term outcome of neurotic disorders in the community: The relation of remission to clinical factors and to 'neutralizing' life events." British Journal of Psychiatry 139:213–220.

Theorell, Töres
1974 "Life events before and after the onset of a premature myocardial infarction." Pp. 101–117 in Barbara Snell Dohrenwend and Bruce P. Dohrenwend (eds.), Stressful Life Events: Their Nature and Effects. New York: Wiley.

Thoits, Peggy A.
  1978   "Life events, social integration, and psychological distress." Unpublished
          Ph.D. dissertation, Stanford University, California.
  1979   "Income maintenance, life changes, and psychological distress: Implica-
          tions for life events theory." Research Memorandum 66, Socioeconomic
          Research Center. Menlo Park, Calif.: SRI International.
  1981   "Undesirable life events and psychophysiological distress: A problem of
          operational confounding." American Sociological Review 46:97–109.
  1982a   "Conceptual, methodological, and theoretical problems in studying social
          support as a buffer against life stress." Journal of Health and Social Behav-
          ior 23:145–159.
  1982b   "Lack of social support in the face of life stress: Explaining epidemiological
          distributions of psychological vulnerability." Paper presented at the Na-
          tional Conference on Stress Research, Durham, New Hampshire.
  1982c   "Life stress, social support, and psychological vulnerability: Epidemiologi-
          cal considerations." Journal of Community Psychology 10:341–362.
  1982d   "Transforming emotions: An extension of Hochschild's theory of emotion
          work, with applications to stress, coping, and social support." Un-
          published manuscript, Sociology Department, Princeton University.
  1983   "Multiple identities and psychological well-being: A reformulation and
          test of the social isolation hypothesis." American Sociological Review
          48:174–187.
Thoits, Peggy, and Michael Hannan
  1979   "Income and psychological distress: The impact of an income-maintenance
          experiment." Journal of Health and Social Behavior 20:120–138.
Tousignant, Michael, Guy Denis, and Rejean Lachapelle
  1974   "Some considerations concerning the validity and use of the Health Opin-
          ion Survey." Journal of Health and Social Behavior 15:241–252.
Turner, R. Jay, and John W. Gartrell
  1978   "Social factors in psychiatric outcome: Toward the resolution of interpre-
          tive controversies." American Sociological Review 43:368–382.
Turner, R. Jay, and Samuel Noh
  1982   "Social support, life events, and psychological distress: A three wave panel
          analysis." Presented at the annual meeting of the American Sociological
          Association, San Francisco.
  1983   "Class and psychological vulnerability among women: The significance of
          social support and personal control." Journal of Health and Social Behavior
          24:2–15.
Tyhurst, J. S.
  1951   "Individual reactions to a community disaster: The natural history of a
          psychiatric projective phenomena." American Journal of Psychiatry
          107:764–769.
Uhlenhuth, E. H., Shelby J. Haberman, Michael D. Balter, and Ronald S. Lipman
  1977   "Remembering life events." Pp. 117–134 in John S. Strauss, Haroutun M.
          Babigian, and Merrill Roff (eds.), The Origins and Course of Psychopathol-
          ogy. New York: Plenum Press.
Vaillant, G. E.
  1979   "Natural history of male psychologic health: Effects of mental health on
          physical health." New England Journal of Medicine 301:1249–1254.

Vinokur, Amiram, and Melvin L. Selzer
    1975   "Desirable versus undesirable life events: Their relationship to stress and
            mental distress." Journal of Personality and Social Psychology 32:329–337.
Wershow, Harold J., and George Reinhart
    1974   "Life change and hospitalization—a heretical view." Journal of Psychoso-
            matic Research 18:393–401.
Wheaton, Blair
    1980   "The sociogenesis of psychological disorder: An attributional theory."
            Journal of Health and Social Behavior 21:100–124.
White, Gilbert F., and J. Eugene Haas
    1975   Assessment of Research on Natural Hazards. Cambridge, Mass.: MIT Press.
Wildman, Richard C., and David Richard Johnson
    1977   "Life change and Langner's 22 item mental health index: A study and
            partial replication." Journal of Health and Social Behavior 18:179–188.
Wolff, Harold G., S. G. Wolf, Jr., and C. C. Hare (eds.)
    1950   Life Stress and Bodily Disease. Baltimore: Williams & Wilkins.
Zeiss, Antonette M.
    1980   "Aversiveness versus change in the assessment of life stress." Journal of
            Psychosomatic Research 24:15–19.

3

Direct, Indirect, and Moderating Effects of Social Support on Psychological Distress and Associated Conditions*

R. JAY TURNER

INTRODUCTION

A substantial convergence is observable in research findings produced in psychiatric sociology and epidemiology and those from the broader fields of medical ecology and social epidemiology. Collectively, this evidence strongly supports the assumption that the nature of the social environment is significant for health and emotional well-being. Numerous studies on the occurrence and prevalence of psychiatric distress and disorders and on a wide range of somatic diseases have reported associations with such factors as low socioeconomic status, geographic

*I acknowledge with gratitude the assistance and criticisms of my colleagues Gail Frankel, Samuel Noh, and Mark Speechley.

mobility, social isolation, marital status, minority-group status or social marginality, and social disintegration.

The apparent generality of these associations across a substantial majority of illnesses has important implications for the plausibility of alternative explanations of the individual distributions observed. Cassel (1976:111) has described this generality in terms of a complete absence of etiologic specificity and concluded that psychosocial processes must function to enhance or lower susceptibility to all disease and to disorder in general. Similarly, Syme and Berkman (1976) have interpreted the pervasiveness of social class–illness relationships as indicating class differences in general vulnerability. They suggest that the underlying factors involved must also be quite general in character.

Following Cassel (1974, 1976), this chapter starts from the assumption that psychosocial processes influence the vulnerability of the organism in general. The nature of psychological distress or of physical disorder that may be experienced is not, therefore, a function of particular social stressors or mediators. It is, rather, a function of the disease agents present and/or predisposing factors including developmental and constitutional elements. The focus is on the hypothesis that variations in social support or social-support networks are one factor that importantly influences susceptibility to psychological distress and illness.

This hypothesis has been enunciated by Mueller (1980) in relation to psychiatric disorder. Taking note of several well-known epidemiological findings linking social factors to mental illness, he suggested that the common themes in these relationships "are the absence of adequate social ties or social support and the occurrence of disruption in the individual's social support network"; it was proposed that "social network factors may be the underlying mechanisms explaining these relationships" (Mueller, 1980:148).

To summarize, the role and significance of social support and social-support networks are here considered in the context of a perspective composed of three assumptions: (1) that social factors must function to enhance or lower susceptibility to all disease and disorder generally; (2) that the continuity and generality of observed connections between social factors and health suggest the likelihood that the influential mechanisms involved must also be quite general in nature; and (3) that it is reasonable to propose that social support may represent one such general and influential factor. As will be apparent from the review presented later in this chapter, evidence for the role and significance of social support for health and well-being is both abundant and compelling.

The Concept of Social Support

The Oxford dictionary defines *support*, in part, as to "keep from failing or giving way, give courage, confidence, or power of endurance to. . . . Supply with necessities. . . . Lend assistance or countenance to" (1975:850). What presumably distinguishes social support from the broader concept is that it necessarily involves the presence and products of stable human relationships. The concept of social support has been variously addressed in terms of social bonds (Henderson, 1977, 1980; Henderson *et al.*, 1978a), social networks (Mueller, 1980), meaningful social contact (Cassel, 1976), availability of confidants (Brown *et al.*, 1975; Lowenthal and Haven, 1968; Miller and Ingham, 1976) and human companionship (Lynch, 1977), as well as social support (Cobb, 1976; Dean and Lin, 1977; Murawski *et al.*, 1978). Although these concepts are hardly identical, they share a focus upon the relevance and significance of human relationships.

This focus has been the subject of considerable attention and research effort among social scientists, psychiatrists, and epidemiologists. This intensified interest, however, hardly signals the discovery of a new idea. In Genesis (2:18) the Lord judges that "It is not good that man be alone" and philosophers from Aristotle to Martin Buber have emphasized that the essence of human existence is expressed in our relations with others. Social bonds, social integration, and primary-group relations in general are central concepts in sociological theory and have long been prime considerations in sociological analysis. As Hammer *et al.* have observed, social linkages "may be thought of as the basic building blocks of social structure; and their formation, maintenance, and severance are universal and fundamental social processes" (1978:523).

A central hypothesis of primary-group theory "holds that our morale, our sense of well-being, is sustained by membership in primary groups, and that without any primary group affiliations we would become despairing. . . . Withdrawal from primary contacts would be seen as dangerous to an individual's cognitive and emotional states" (Weiss, 1974:18). This same point has more recently been argued by Lynch with respect to physical illness, especially heart disease. From a review of wide-ranging evidence, he concludes that "there is a biological basis for our need to form loving human relationships. If we fail to fulfill that need, our health is in peril" (1977:xv).

Perhaps nowhere has the significance of human associations been more clearly demonstrated than with respect to developmental contingencies. The profound consequences of maternal deprivation observed by Spitz (1946), the implications of nonresponsive mothering suggested by Harlow's (1959) work, and Bowlby's (1969, 1973) disquisition on the importance of attachment in healthy human development suffice to illustrate this point. It is only a minor leap of faith to the pervasive assumption that these compelling developmental contingencies must also be significant with respect to general functioning and well-being.

Thus, the view that social bonds and supportive interactions are important to a person's health and well-being seems to have been long and widely shared. What appears to be comparatively new is the growing availability of hard evidence on the matter, signaled most importantly in the seminal reviews by Cassel (1974, 1976) and Cobb (1976). These papers have also enunciated a hypothesis that substantially stimulated the current level of interest and research effort: that social support may be an effective buffer or mediator of life stress.

Kessler observed that "the concept of social support is used to help make sense of the fact that people in what seem to be 'supported' social environments are in better health than their counterparts without this advantage" (1982:261). He noted, with Carveth and Gottlieb (1979:181), that there is little agreement among researchers on the definition of social support. DiMatteo and Hays pointed out that the concept "has been interpreted in several ways and includes a range of phenomena" (1981:119). As Ewalt (1960) has observed in relation to the concept of mental health, social support appears to mean many things to many people.

Despite this diversity, most definitions have focused on the helping elements and processes of the social-relational systems in which the individual is located (Eckenrode and Gore, 1981; Gore, 1980). Thus Gottlieb referred to the substance of social support as "the help that helpers extend" (1981:209), and Lin et al. defined it as "support accessible to an individual through social ties to other individuals, groups and the larger community" (1979b:109). Similarly, Pearlin et al. described social support as "access to and use of individuals, groups, or organizations in dealing with life's vicissitudes" (1981:340), and Johnson and Sarason referred to "the degree to which individuals have access to social resources, in the form of relationships, on which they can rely" (1979:155).

Gerald Caplan has considered social support in the context of his long-term interest in crisis theory and mental health (G. Caplan, 1974; Caplan and Killilea, 1976). He defined support systems in terms of "attachments among individuals or between individuals and groups that serve to improve adaptive competence in dealing with short-term challenges, stresses, and privations" (Caplan and Killilea, 1976:41). As House (1981:22) has suggested, Caplan's analysis of social support emphasizes more formal sources of support, such as professionals, paraprofessionals, and self-help groups, in contrast to most conceptualizations that view support as a product of natural social circumstance.

A number of researchers have described differing types or categories of social support. Dean and Lin (1977) differentiated instrumental and expressive support, whereas both Pinneau (1975) and Schaefer et al. (1981) distinguished tangible, informational, and emotional forms. The five distinct categories of cognitive guidance, social reinforcement, tangible assistance, socializing, and emotional support are specified by Hirsch (1980); and Funch and Mettlin (1982) add perceived potential support to the very concrete categories of professional support and financial support. Common to all of these taxonomies is an acknowledgment of the relevance of emotional or perceived support on the one hand, and of actual aid or its availability on the other.

House (1981:23) has distilled four broad classes of social support from the array of conceptualizations in the literature. These are (1) *emotional support*, involving empathy, love and trust; (2) *instrumental support*, involving behaviors that directly aid the person in need; (3) *informational support*, composed of information useful in coping with personal and environmental problems; and (4) *appraisal support*, involving information relevant to self-evaluation or social comparisons, exclusive of any affect that might accompany such information.

House acknowledged that emotional support is the common element across most conceptualizations, that it is what most people mean when they speak of being supportive, and that it seems to be the most important dimension. However, he saw the other three classes as worthy of attention, arguing that "all should be considered as potential forms of support and their impact on stress and health (and the relation between these) treated as an empirical question" (1981:24).

The emphasis upon emotional support is mirrored in such concepts as *social bonds* (Henderson, 1977, 1980), *meaningful social contact* (Cassel, 1976), *availability of confidants* (Brown et al., 1975; Lowenthal and Haven, 1968; Miller and Ingham, 1976), and *human companionship* (Lynch, 1977). Implicit in all of these is the assumption that they address a core human requirement. A crucial aspect of this requirement is the experience of being supported by others, because "social support is likely to be effective only to the extent perceived" (House, 1981:27). From this perspective, interest focuses upon social support as a social-psychological variable with what Henderson (1980) has described as significant affectional content and psychological function.

This interest is consistent with W. I. Thomas's (Thomas and Thomas, 1982:572) familiar admonition that situations that are defined as real are real in their consequences. It is, after all, an axiom of social psychology that events or circumstances in the real world affect the individual only to the extent and in the form in which they are perceived. As Ausubel has pointed out, "this does not imply that the perceived world is the real world but that perceptual reality is psychological reality and the actual (mediating) variable that influences behavior and development" (1958:277).

Perhaps the best-known conceptualization of perceived or experienced social support has been provided by Cobb. He viewed social support as "information belonging to one or more of the following three classes: (1) information leading the subject to believe that he is cared for and loved; (2) information leading the subject to believe that he is esteemed and valued; and (3) information leading the subject to believe that he belongs to a network of communication and mutual obligation" (1976:300). As Barrera has observed, "from this perspective, it is the cognitive appraisal of support that is regarded as the central target of [measurement]" (1981:71). Social support thus refers to the clarity or certainty with which the individual experiences being loved, valued, and able to count on others should the need arise.

Cobb (1979:94) explicitly distinguished social support from support that is "instrumental" (counseling, assisting), "active" (mothering), or "material" (providing goods and/or services). There is no suggestion that these other forms of support are not important or that they lack relevance for health or well-being. His view appears simply to be that it is worth distinguishing social support, as self-relevant information, from various support resources. From this perspective, social support, like crises (Miller and Iscoe, 1963), can usefully be regarded as a personal experience rather than as a set of objective circumstances or even a set of interactional processes.

Guttman (1974) has urged that, prior to attempts at operationalization, concepts be formulated specifying the facets or dimensions of the phenomenon being defined. The assumption underlying this prescription is that most social phenomena are best understood as multidimensional in nature. The mapping sentence presented in Table 3.1 is an effort to represent the array of conceptualizations that have been offered and is consistent with the view of many researchers that support

TABLE 3.1

Mapping-Sentence Definition of Social Support[a]

The domain of social support is defined as:

	A		B
The assessment by the	1. respondent	of the	1. objective
	2. investigator		2. subjective

C		D
1. intensity	of the	1. love and/or affection
2. frequency		2. status and/or esteem
3. durability		3. information and/or interpretation
		4. aid and/or guidance

E		F	G
1. accessible	from	1. wife or husband	1. in general
2. utilized		2. intimates	2. with respect
		3. confidants	to a focused
		4. parents	problem
		5. children	
		6. friends	
		7. acquaintances	
		8. neighbors	
		9. co-workers	
		10. associates	
		11. professionals	
		12. unspecified significant others	

[a]Most of the mapping sentence was suggested by Peter Stemp (personal communication 1983).

is a multidimensional concept (R. Caplan, 1979; Dean and Lin, 1977; Henderson, 1977; House, 1981; Kaplan *et al.*, 1977; Thoits, 1982).

This mapping sentence summarizes most of the elements found in the literature and identifies the major facets represented and the alternatives within each facet that have to varying degrees been debated. Is information from the respondent the only real basis for assessing social support or is information from other sources also relevant, or even to be preferred? Is social support by nature subjective, objective, or both? Is amount of support important, and, if so, what quantitative dimensions make a difference? Are there different types of support and is the relevant content psychological or tangible in character? Finally, the sentence calls attention to the possible importance of source of support and whether the issue is general support or support with respect to a focused problem.

The mapping sentence is not presented as an ideal definition, and I am aware of no conceptualizations or measurement efforts that have incorporated all elements of all facets depicted. However, to the extent that the ingredients of most conceptualizations are represented, it provides a basis for examining measurement approaches in terms of the extent to which various aspects of the concept are indexed or assumed.

Measuring Social Support

A variety of approaches to the estimation of social support have proven useful in predicting mortality and both psychiatric and psychological morbidity. These approaches appear to fall into three distinguishable categories: the social-integration approach, social-network analysis, and the social-psychological or perceptual approach.

The Social-integration Approach. This approach assesses support in terms of the individual's connections with others, including primary and secondary relationships and both formal and informal group associations. Some researchers have simply used marital status as a complete or partial index (Eaton, 1978; Gore, 1978; Lynch, 1977). Berkman and Syme (1979) are among those who have attempted a more comprehensive estimate of availability and use of social resources. Data were obtained on four kinds of social ties: marriage, contacts with close friends and relatives, church membership, and formal and informal voluntary associations (see also Brown *et al.*, 1979; Myers *et al.*, 1975).

It can be seen by referring to Table 3.1 that social-integration approaches assume that some quantity of some type of support is accessible from the connections specified. Although it seems a reasonable assumption that individuals who are married and/or have other social relationships will, on the average, have higher social support, such an assumption in the individual case must be recognized as hazardous. Surely some marriages, for example, are by their nature less supportive than no relationship. Nevertheless, such social connections are crucial because the "minimum condition for experiencing social support . . . is to have one or more stable relationships with others. Hence, the crudest approach to the measurement of support is to measure the quantity and structure of social relationships" (House, 1981:29). In this connection, it should be noted that crudeness is another term for measurement error and that evidence based on such measures therefore yields conservative estimates of the significance of social support for physical and emotional health.

Social-network Analysis. This appears to represent a distinct and promising approach to estimating the capacity or potential of social environments for providing support. Rather than defining social support simply in terms of the quantity and/or quality of social contact, this approach attempts a more complex and comprehensive analysis of social environments. Mitchell and Trickett expressed this distinction as follows:

> Although social support systems are often thought of in terms of some formally recognized entity (i.e., family, neighbourhood, church, or social organizations . . .) it is often some unique configuration of these that comprises the salient reference group of the individual. The concept of social network presents one way of getting across these formal boundaries and examining the total social field within which the individual is embedded. (1980:28)

Walker *et al.* defined an individual's social network as "that set of personal contacts through which the individual maintains his social identity and receives emotional support, material aid and services, information and new social contacts" (1977:35). They suggested that the network characteristics most relevant to personal support are (*a*) size: the number of persons with whom the individual maintains social contact; (*b*) strength of ties: which can include intimacy as well as time and intensity involved in the tie; (*c*) density: connectedness in terms of the extent to which network members know and contact one another independently of the individual; (*d*) homogeneity of membership: the social and demographic similarity of network members; and (*e*) dispersion of membership: the ease with which network members can get together. Although other characteristics have been considered, these five represent the major dimensions along which social support networks have been described. In a useful review of the social-network literature, Mitchell and Trickett (1980) detailed the diversity of specific approaches used by researchers in assessing these dimensions.

Enthusiastic endorsements of social-network analysis coupled with serious criticism of both the social-intimacy and social-integration approaches have been presented by both Gottlieb (1981) and Wellman (1981). In Gottlieb's view, these latter approaches "yield little useful information about social support; at most, they have generated hypotheses that can best be examined through the use of network analysis" (1981:204). Starting from the intuitive knowledge that social ties are not always supportive, Wellman argued that the focus on availability of supportive ties weakens and distorts by oversimplifying. He suggested that "to study the conditions under which individuals do get support, we must allow for the possibility that many of their ties are not necessarily supportive" (1981:172).

Hammer has noted that:

> The difference between social networks and social supports is not a mere terminological distinction, since it leads to different formulations of the research problems, different choices of the kinds of measures to be used, different perspectives on the role of basic social research, and a different potential for theoretical analysis. (1981:46)

She argues that we might more profitably study social connections because, unlike social support, such connections "are distinctively social and definitively neutral" (1981:47).

It seems that there is much to recommend the social-network approach. Setting aside the practical difficulties associated with its use in large-scale research, it seems clear that the assessment of social connections or networks can provide the most complete and unconfounded data on the capacity or potential of the social environment for "radiating supportive functions to its members" (Gottlieb, 1981:210).

There is, then, basis for arguing that analysis of the parameters of social networks is important and even indispensible for both theoretical and practical development. Whether social support is conceived as emotional support or as including a wider range of phenomena, practical intervention requires that we understand the contexts in which support is more and less likely to arise. However, it is far from clear that social-network analysis provides a wholly adequate basis for assessing social support as Gottlieb (1981), among others, has implied. As Pearlin et al. have noted, "being embedded in a network is only the first step toward having . . . support; the final step depends on the quality of the relations one is able to find within the network" (1981:340).

Although the social-network approach appears comprehensive and avoids the pitfall of assuming that ties are necessarily supportive, like the social integration approach it remains a proxy measure for social support. As Kessler (1982:263) implied, network analysis is properly concerned with the prediction of support and predictive factors should not be confused with the phenomenon being predicted. To estimate the potential of social environments for, in Gottlieb's terms, "radiating supportive functions to its members" (1981:210) is to predict level of social support, which surely must be measured on other grounds.

From these considerations it follows that social-network analysis, although promising and important, is also insufficient. Such analyses do not address a central and crucial aspect of social connectedness—the extent to which the individual experiences the support of others.

The Social-psychological or Perceptual Approach. This approach focuses, in one way or another, on the experience of being supported by others. This focus is expressed in such terms as emotional support, experienced support, attachment, need satisfaction, and satisfaction with one's marriage or other significant relationships. The vast majority of investigators in this field have attempted to index such experiences as at least part of their assessment of social support. One prominent procedure has been to assess the presence or availability of a confiding relationship (Andrews *et al.*, 1978; Dean *et al.*, 1980; B. H. Kaplan, 1975; Lin *et al.*, 1981; Miller and Ingham, 1976).

Lowenthal and Haven asked respondents if there was "anyone in particular you confide in or talk to about yourself or your problems" (1968:22). Although typical kinds of social-interaction questions were also employed, the major findings were in relation to the confidant question. Brown *et al.* (1979) obtained information on frequency of contact and on satisfaction with various relationships while ascertaining whether a husband or boyfriend was mentioned as a confidant. Although these reports were to some extent edited on the basis of evidence from the total interview, the presence or absence of a confidant again proved to be the most powerful element in their analyses.

Many researchers who have addressed social support as a multidimensional concept have, in some fashion, included perceived support as a significant element. In a major longitudinal study Dean and Lin and their colleagues (Dean *et al.*, 1981; Lin *et al.*, 1981) included, in addition to items assessing the availability and utilization of confidants, "a set of 26 items focussing on the activities and aspects which might provide (or jeopardize) either instrumental or expressive support to the respondent" (Lin *et al.*, 1981:78). One of five factors derived from these items is labeled "lack of companionship" and includes items assessing the frequency with which respondents had been bothered by such things as "no close companion," "not enough close friends," and "no one to show love and affection." These items appear to tap the experiences of being supported by others. Interestingly, in a more recent publication (Dean and Ensel, 1982) social support is indexed solely in terms of "strong tie support" measured by the two items "not having a close companion" and "not having enough close friends." Presumably, the decision to employ only these 2 out of the 26 items in the scale was based upon their performance in analyses of the previous data wave.

As part of a multidimensional index that includes elements of the subject's network and items assessing both social integration and access to instrumental assistance, Husaini *et al.* (1982) have also included subjective or perceptual aspects. Specifically, questions are employed assessing the extent to which the subject's spouse is experienced as being very good at understanding problems and satisfaction and happiness with spouse and marriage. Similarly, Aneshensel and Frerichs (1982) have adopted a Sense of Support Scale from the work of Panagis and Adler (1977) that assesses socioemotional as well as instrumental assistance in addition to information on available connections with friends and relatives.

One additional example of a measurement effort that incorporates perceptual aspects will suffice for present purposes. A comprehensive attempt at assessing the role and significance of the individual's immediate social environment is the work of Henderson and his colleagues at the Social Psychiatry Research Unit of Australian National University (Henderson, 1977, 1980; Henderson et al., 1978a, 1978b, 1980a, 1980b, 1981). They developed the Interview Schedule for Social Interaction (ISSI) with the goal of considering the whole array of social bonds based on a fusion of aspects of attachment theory and social-network theory.

The development of their schedule was substantially guided by Weiss's (1974) views on the "provisions of social relationships." Weiss proposed six categories of such provisions, each generally associated with a particular type of relationship. These are (a) sense of attachment or belonging most often provided by marriage or other cross-sex relationships; (b) social integration, provided by a network of friends and colleagues who offer companionship and opportunity to share interests and values; (c) opportunity for nurturing others, most often children, which provides a sense of being needed; (d) reassurance of worth, provided by family, friends and colleagues who attest to an individual's competence in a given role; (e) a sense of reliable alliance, provided primarily by kin relationships; and (f) the opportunity for obtaining guidance from trustworthy and supportive friends and relatives. Weiss suggested that all of these provisions may be required, at least under some circumstances, and that their absence gives rise to various forms of distress.

Weiss's "provisions" thus incorporate both social support resources in the form of availability of friends and opportunities for guidance and for nurturing others, and experienced support in the form of a sense of attachment and reliable alliance and the reassurance of worth. Clearly these latter provisions of social relationships closely correspond with Cobb's view of social support as emotional and perceptual in character. The two major foci of the ISSI are the availability of social relationships determined largely by the actual conditions of the social environment as reported by the respondent and their adequacy as judged or perceived by the individual.

In the view of these researchers the ideal is to obtain two categories of information about the individual's social environment: "objective knowledge about it and, by contrast, how the individual construes it" (Henderson et al., 1981:33). They thus appear to be in agreement with the view presented earlier that future progress in determining the role, significance, and modifiability of social support requires that we measure and understand both the social context in which the individual operates and the extent to which this environment is experienced as supportive.

The Interview Schedule for Social Interaction (ISSI) is a 52-item instrument with an "attachment table" for use in obtaining information on the whole array of persons with whom social bonds exist. The schedule and information on reliability, stability and validity are presented in Henderson et al. (1981).

EVIDENCE FOR THE RELEVANCE OF SOCIAL SUPPORT

Following John Cassell (1974, 1976) it was suggested earlier that social factors must function to enhance or lower susceptibility to all disease and disorder in general and that the influential mechanisms involved must also be general in nature. The hypothesis addressed in this chapter is that social support may represent one such general and influential factor. A minimum requirement for this proposition to remain tenable is that social support be associated with the occurrence of diverse forms of distress, disorder and illness. I now turn to evidence on this matter.

Mortality and Physical Disorder

A number of authors have argued that animal studies provide strong evidence for the significance of social support in buffering or ameliorating the effects of stress. These studies form an important part of the basis for Cassel's admonition that "we should no longer treat psychosocial processes as unidimensional stressors or non-stressors, but rather as two-dimensional, one category being stressors, and another being protective or beneficial" (1976:112). Bell et al. stated that "the groundwork, and indeed some of the most persuasive evidence for the power of social support factors in influencing the individual's susceptibility to illness, comes from animal studies" (1982:326).

The availability of these and other reviews (Dean and Lin, 1977; House, 1981) make it unnecessary to detail these studies here. It will simply be noted that, under conditions of laboratory-induced stress, the presence of littermates or of other animals who were not strangers, or of the mother, or of affection provided by humans, reduced or eliminated gastric ulcer formation in rats (Conger et al., 1958), hypertension in mice (Henry and Cassel, 1969), experimental neurosis in a goat (Liddell, 1950), and arteriosclerotic heart disease in rabbits (Nerem et al., 1980).

Less direct evidence is provided by studies that have considered the consequences of social disorganization, one expression of which is the disturbance of relationships within animal communities. Such disorganization has been shown to raise the vulnerability of animals to radiation (Ader and Hahn, 1963), diabetes (Ader et al., 1963), cancer (Andervont, 1944), trichinosis (Davis and Read, 1958), and arteriosclerosis (Ratcliffe and Cronin, 1958). Although, as Pinneau has noted, "it remains unclear by what processes the other animals influence the reactions of subjects under stress" (1975:7), these studies make clear that bonds or relationships, or social support, matter significantly for health, at least for lower animals.

As noted earlier, marital status has been widely viewed as a proxy measure indexing gross differences in social support. The evidence for an important association between marital status and mortality is widespread and incontrovertible. In the 1950s Kraus and Lillienfeld concluded from existing medical evidence that "married people experienced a lower mortality rate from all causes than did single persons, the widowed, and the divorced for every specific age group in each sex and color" (1959:207). They also examined the consequences for men of loss of marital partner. Widowers were found to have a death rate three to five times that for married men of the same age for all causes of death including such diverse conditions as peptic ulcer, cancer, infectious diseases, and heart disease.

Based on United States mortality data for the period 1959–1961, Carter and Glick (1970) reported findings wholly consistent with those of Kraus and Lillienfeld. Although the relationships were substantially stronger for men than for women, death rates were significantly lower for married people for all causes of death across both sex and race.

The relationship between social support and subsequent all-cause mortality has more recently been examined by Berkman and Syme (1979). Their study covered the 9-year period between 1965 and 1974 and involved large representative samples of both men and women from Alameda County, California, who were between 39 and 65 years of age in 1965. Berkman and Syme addressed social support in terms of social integration as reflected in marital status, contacts with close friends and relatives, church membership, and informal and formal group associations. Each of these measures was found to be independently associated with risk of mortality over the 9-year follow-up period.

The presumably more intimate aspects of integration embodied in marriage and friendship ties were more powerful predictors than the other two dimensions. Marital status yielded the strongest relationships, with lower mortality rates observed for the married in all age and sex categories. As in previous research, marriage was found to be more protective for men than for women, for whom contact with friends was the most significant factor.

Blazer (1982) examined the social support–mortality relationship within a sample of persons 65 and older. Three distinct types of social support were assessed: frequency of social interaction, roles and availability of attachment, and perceived social support. Data on these 3 dimensions and on 10 potentially confounding variables were obtained 30 months before a telephone follow-up that assessed mortality status. The 10 potentially confounding variables considered were age, sex, race, economic status, physical health status, self-care capacity, depressive symptoms, cognitive functioning, stressful life events, and cigarette smoking.

All three dimensions of support were found to be significantly related to 30-month mortality, with perceived social support being the most powerful predictor. With all 10 potentially confounding variables controlled, the relative mortality risks were 1.88, 2.04, and 3.40 for those deficient in frequency of interaction, roles and availability of attachment, and perceived social support, respectively.

This longitudinal study and that by Berkman and Syme (1979) combine to make a powerful case for an association between social support, variously indexed, and mortality. Here, as in other mortality studies, the temporal ordering of variables can hardly be questionned. More importantly, the controls implemented, especially in the Blazer study, bear on the possibility that a third variable or set of variables influence both support and risk of mortality. Although the factors considered certainly do not exhaust such possibilities, they do contribute to reducing the range of plausible alternative explanations.

Before leaving this overview of mortality studies focusing on marital status as a predictor, one additional point requires consideration. Although marital status is related to mortality within all age and racial groupings and for both sexes, these and other studies (e.g., Ernster *et al.*, 1979; Ortemeyer, 1974) suggest that the apparent protection conferred by marriage is substantially greater for men than for women. This, of course, is precisely the observation made by Durkheim with respect to suicide nearly a century ago (Durkheim, 1951).

Since Durkheim's classic statement the occurrence of suicide has been repeatedly linked with social integration and isolation (Gibbs and Martin, 1964; Sainsbury, 1956). Within this tradition, Cumming and Lazer have addressed the issue of sex differences in the apparent protectiveness of marriage. Using Canadian suicide data for the years 1951, 1956, 1961, 1966, and 1971, they began by showing that the apparently greater protectiveness of marriage for men with respect to suicide is consistent through time. A social network interpretation for this finding was offered and examined to the extent allowed by availability of data from differently organized societies. This evidence was found to be consistent with the conclusion that "the particular role of women in modern western society in maintaining kinship affiliations is one reason for their lower suicide rates and the major reason for their lesser protection through marriage" (1981:281). In other words, because women in our society tend to maintain both normative and interactive integration of kinship systems (and perhaps of wider social networks as well) on behalf of men and themselves, the implications of loss of spouse for men tends to be multiplied. Widows lose only their husbands, but widowers also tend to suffer the loss of some portion of tbeir wider support network.

Clearly Durkheim's theory and the work of Cumming and Lazer (1981) are consistent with the hypothesis that marital status roughly indexes variations in social support and that social support matters for suicide. Moreover, it seems reasonable to propose that the explanation offered by Cumming and Lazer with regard to suicide can be applied with equal cogency to observed sex differences in the protectiveness of marriage with respect to diverse forms of mortality.

A detailed consideration of the significance of personal relationships for heart disease was presented by Lynch (1977). He employed diverse forms of evidence to argue that social isolation impacts dramatically on the occurrence of the disease. The evidence reviewed included differences in rates of heart disease by marital status and by the degree of social integration and stability of one's community of residence, animal laboratory studies, studies of the effects of the presence of others in life-threatening situations, and studies on the sudden-death syndrome. Although much of this evidence is indirect and no single study can be said to constitute compelling evidence, collectively it suggests the appropriateness of Lynch's conclusions that human companionship is associated with lower rates of all types of coronary disease.

The influence of social support on risk for angina pectoris was investigated by Medalie and Goldbourt (1976) in a 5-year prospective study of 10,000 men. Social support was assessed using measures of family interaction and spousal demonstrations of love. Those who reported favorable love relationships with their wives were significantly less likely to present symptoms of angina pectoris even in the presence of physiological risk factors.

Social support has also been found to interact with life stress to reduce the negative impact of stress on physical health. In the interesting study of Nuckolls et al. (1972) the relationships among social stresses, social support (as indexed by a psychosocial-assets score), and complications of pregnancy was assessed. Neither life-change scores nor social-support scores were significantly related, by themselves, to pregnancy complications. However, when these two variables were considered conjointly, it was found that among women with high life-change scores, those who had high social-support scores had only one-third the complication rate of women with low social-support scores. In the absence of high life change, there was no significant relationship between social support and complications.

Termination of employment constitutes a major source of stress among men with stable work histories. Using an index primarily assessing emotional support, Cobb and Kasl (1977) and Gore (1978) reported on the stress-moderating effects of support among a sample of men whose jobs were abolished. Subjects were studied over time including an assessment during the anticipatory period and at several points up to 24 months after the plant closing. They found high levels of social support to be protective against certain physical difficulties. One interesting finding was that low levels of social support were associated with significantly higher rates of physical indicators of arthritis (Gore, 1978).

A number of studies have demonstrated an association between social support and the course or outcome of illness. De Araujo et al. (1973) have shown that asthmatic individuals with high levels of stress and low levels of social support required nearly four times the dosage of steroids compared with similar individuals who had high stress and high levels of support. Finlayson (1976) assessed the impact of wife's level of social support from friends and family on her husband's recovery from myocardial infarction. Husbands whose wives felt most supported had higher rates of recovery.

Based on a careful review of the available literature, DiMatteo and Hays concluded that, "taken as a whole, the research suggests that social support, may, in fact, be associated with recovery, and coping with serious physical illness and injury" (1981:121). Although most studies considered show a social-support impact on psychological adaptation, evidence is also summarized suggesting an effect on symptom change in essential hypertension (Berle et al., 1952), survival in myocardial infarction (Jarvinen, 1955), length of survival beyond expected in cancer (Weisman and Worden, 1975), and blood pressure in hypertension (Earp, 1979; Wellons et al., 1979).

Psychological Distress and Disorder

There is now a considerable and growing body of evidence linking social support with psychological distress generally and suggesting that level of support may be particularly relevant for depression (Brown et al., 1975; Dean et al., 1981; Miller and Ingham, 1976). This research, only a portion of which can be reviewed here, seems to have been substantially stimulated by the hypothesis that social support may serve as a buffer against the effects of life stress.

Brown and his colleagues have considered factors that might influence vulnerability to depression in the face of adversity (Brown et al., 1975; Brown and Harris, 1978). Specifically, they examined the influence of a close, confiding relationship in reducing the risk of depression following a major life event or long-term difficulty. Among those women who lacked a confiding relationship with a husband or boyfriend, 38% developed depression following life stress or major difficulties, compared with only 4% of women with such a confiding relationship.

In a related study conducted on the Hebridean island of North Uist, women who were socially integrated into the island society were found to have significantly lower rates of depression but higher rates of anxiety (Brown et al., 1979). Social integration was defined in terms of having grown up on the island, living in a household engaged in one of the two dominant economic–occupational activities, and attending church regularly.

The beneficial mental-health effects of having a confidant were also demonstrated by Lowenthal and Haven (1968) and Miller and Ingham (1976). Studying an aged population, Lowenthal and Haven found the availability of a confidant to reduce the occurrence of depression significantly. Miller and Ingham considered the significance of friends as well as confidants in a study of health-center clientele in Edinburgh. They found more severe psychological symptoms among both men and women who had no intimate contact. This relationship, however, was more pronounced for women.

Pearlin *et al.* (1981) examined social support and coping in an attempt to understand how life events, chronic life strains, and self-concept influence depression. Their results indicated that both social support and coping are mediators in the stress–distress process. They suggested that these factors can reduce chronic strains that may occur following a life event and prevent the loss of self-esteem and sense of mastery that chronic strains and life events may produce. In the view of Pearlin and his colleagues, social support and coping influence the risk of depression through this effect on self-concept. They were unable to demonstrate direct effects of social support on depression.

Several additional studies have considered the interplay between social support and life stress with respect to depression. Based upon a major community epidemiologic study involving 2029 residents of the southeastern portion of the United States, Bell *et al.* (1982) considered the impact on depressive symptoms of social support, stressful life events, and socioeconomic status. All three variables were found to exert significant independent effects. Despite some inconsistencies in results, these authors concluded that support has main effects and also tends to mediate the effects of life stress.

Aneshensel and Frerichs (1982) have attempted to determine the causal interrelationships among stress, social support, and depression. Using data obtained at 4-month intervals over 1 year from 740 adults, a "longitudinal latent causal variable model" was assessed. Social support was found to have direct negative effects on current depression and indirect effects in subsequent depression.

In a cross-sectional study, Husaini and his colleagues (Husaini *et al.*, 1982) found social support to have both direct independent effects and buffering effects on depression. These findings held for the total group, but results were more pronounced among females. The sample for this study included nearly 1000 white, married adults from rural Ohio, Oklahoma, and Tennessee.

The relationship between social support and psychological distress has been examined from a number of perspectives by Dean and Lin and their associates (Dean and Lin, 1977; Dean *et al.*, 1980; 1981; Lin *et al.*, 1979b). They developed a scale to assess what they term the instrumental and expressive dimensions of support (Lin *et al.*, 1979a). The instrumental system is directed toward the completion of tasks, and the expressive system is concerned with the satisfaction of individual needs.

A significant relationship was observed between social support thus measured and psychological distress (Dean et al., 1981).

In one analysis Dean et al. (1980) found that lack of companionship support showed the strongest association with depression for all age groups. Other types of support varied in their strength as predictors of depression across age groups. Social support was indexed wholly in terms of companionship support in a more recent publication (Dean and Ensel, 1982). From analyses in which personal competence and life-events scores were simultaneously considered, they found social support to have the strongest effects on depression for both sexes and within all three of the age groupings considered. They concluded that their findings point toward the significance of social support for understanding the epidemiology of depression.

A series of studies by Henderson and his colleagues provide additional evidence for a positive relationship between social support and psychological health status (Henderson et al., 1978a, 1978b, 1980a, 1980b). An instrument designed to assess availability and adequacy of attachment and social integration was employed in a large community survey of the prevalence of nonpsychotic psychiatric morbidity. Availability and adequacy of both attachment and social integration were significantly related to neurosis and depression for both men and women, although there was some variation in the relationships between support and the dimensions of psychological health across the sexes (Henderson et al., 1980a).

Further work by this team of investigators focused on neurosis, conceptualized as "those non-psychotic disorders which are characterized mainly by mild to moderate depression and the psychological and somatic manifestations of morbid anxiety" (Henderson et al., 1981:91). The 30-item version of Goldberg's (1972) General Health Questionnaire (GHQ) was employed to assess neurotic symptomatology. A three-wave panel design was employed to study a subset of the original community sample over time. This strategy allowed examination of the relationship between changes in GHQ scores and change in various dimensions of social support. Social-network characteristics assessing the availability of social relationships were not found to be associated with risk for later neurotic symptoms. However, a clear link was found between perceived adequacy of relationships and subsequent morbidity, at least in the presence of adversity (Henderson et al., 1981).

LaRocco et al. (1980) examined the influence of several sources of support and job stress on general mental health and job strain. They found that social support buffered the effects of job stress on overall mental health, but that social support did not protect against the effect of job stress on job-related strain. They also found that job stress and strain were primarily influenced by job-related sources of support and that the effects on job strain were largely direct rather than buffering effects. However, mental-health outcomes were found to be influenced by a wider range of sources of support that appeared to exert their influence primarily by buffering the effects of stress.

There is some evidence that variable types of social networks, generally defined in terms of the interpersonal linkages among a set of individuals, are associated with differential psychological well-being. Hammer et al. (1978) reported that among a general population sample the primary network usually consists of 25–40 people, and of these 6–10 are known intimately. Within the social network there are typically several clusters with 6 or 7 highly interconnected individuals in each cluster.

A similar network pattern among normals was reported by Pattison et al. (1975). The primary networks of neurotics, in contrast, were smaller (10–12 people) and often included significant persons who were no longer living or who lived far away. There was also a low level of interconnectedness among members, and personal relations with network members were more often rated negatively by neurotics than by normals.

In their study of the social networks of neurotics and normals, Henderson et al. (1978b) also found neurotics to have smaller networks and to experience more negative interaction than normals. Similarly, in a comparison of 50 psychiatric outpatients in Toronto with 50 family-practice clients, Silberfeld (1978) found the psychiatric patients to have fewer persons in their personal networks and to spend less time in social interaction.

The social networks of psychotics appear to be clearly differentiated from those of both neurotics and normals (Pattison et al., 1975; Sokolovsky et al., 1978; Tolsdorf, 1976). The networks of psychotics are characterized by their small size, domination by kin, and large proportion of dependent relationships. Additional evidence for a relationship between mental-health status and the character of one's social network has been presented by Mueller (1980) in a review of a broad array of studies.

Although there seems little doubt that the nature and size of the social networks of psychologically distressed individuals differ from the norm, the meaning of this association is difficult to determine. It may be that network resources influence mental health, but it can be argued with equal cogency that the restricted networks found among neurotics and schizophrenics, for example, are a consequence or expression of the disorder. Clearly longitudinal designs are required to establish the time ordering of network and mental-health variables. However, even with definite information that the network characteristics reported preceded the onset of symptoms, the causal issue would remain unresolved. It is well known that the social-relational characteristics of individuals who later become schizophrenic and, to a lesser extent, those who later become neurotic are likely to result in a diminished number and variety of social relationships. Thus premorbid social characteristics may account largely or wholly for the observed association between network characteristics and mental-health status.

As both Mueller (1980) and Henderson et al. (1981) have observed, studies are required that measure both networks and disorder at several points in time so that changes in network characteristics can be related to changes in psychiatric status. To my knowledge only Henderson et al. (1981) have examined network characteristics within such a design, and they were unable to demonstrate any network effects on neurotic symptoms. To this point, therefore, the argument that formal network characteristics matter with respect to the occurrence of psychological disorder must be accepted largely on faith.

Overall, the evidence for the role and significance of human companionship, associations, and connectedness is truly diverse and pervasive. In addition to the evidence already sampled that suggests the importance of social support for physical health, psychological well-being, and the prevention of psychiatric disorder, a substantial body of literature suggests its relevance for the prevention of hospitalization and for posthospital community adjustment (Gruenberg et al., 1969; Holman and Shore, 1978; Jessner et al., 1952; Turner et al., 1970; Wagenfeld et al., 1967).

DiMatteo and Hays (1981) have reviewed an array of studies suggesting the relevance of social support for psychological adaptation to serious illness and injury. Moreover, social support has been related to lessening the anxiety caused by natural disasters (Bowlby, 1973), to adjusting emotionally to abortion (Belsey et al., 1977) to aiding the process of bereavement (Burch, 1972), and to the adjustment involved in aging and retirement (Lowenthal and Haven, 1968). Social support has also been recognized as the basis for such mutual-help organizations as Alcoholics Anonymous (Caplan and Killilea, 1976) and self-help groups organized for ex-drug addicts (Dumont, 1974). The concept has also been incorporated into innovative models for community mental health (G. Caplan, 1974) and health-care delivery (Croog et al., 1968).

A PROGRAM OF RESEARCH ON SOCIAL SUPPORT

From the foregoing overview of currently available evidence, it can hardly be doubted that social support, variously indexed, is associated with significant variations in physical health, psychological health, and general well-being. Further, it appears, as House has suggested, "that it is the presence of significant, *emotionally supportive* relationships that is responsible for most of the documented relationships" (1981:84; emphasis added).

If these two broad conclusions are accepted, two research directions follow. First, whether instrumental or material forms of support are seen as a part of social support, as many prefer, or as distinct from social support, as Cobb (1979) has argued, more evidence is required of their role and significance for health, net of the affective or emotional by-products of such support. Second, the apparent potency of emotional support—despite the fact that it has typically been assessed indirectly, or directly by a single or a few items—suggests the need for research in which emotional or experienced social support is more deliberately and adequately indexed.

This latter need forms the basis for a program of research on social support with which the Health Care Research Unit of the University of Western Ontario has been preoccupied since 1978. The efforts of my colleagues & myself have been guided, in part, by the wide agreement that future progress in determining the role and significance of social support requires the development of effective measuring instruments (Cassel, 1974; Dean and Lin, 1977; Kaplan et al., 1977; Thoits, 1982).

Although we acknowledged the relevance of social-integration measures and the promise of network analysis for estimating support resources, we viewed the measurement of experienced social support as the central and most significant objective. Given this interest we were attracted by Cobb's (1976) conceptualization and some of our measurement efforts have followed directly from that conceptualization. An instrument developed by A. Kaplan (1977) as part of a thesis done under the supervision of Cobb was one starting point. Kaplan proposed and partially tested a story-identification technique composed of 16 sets of vignettes. We initially adopted 7 of these sets that, in our judgment, most effectively addressed the experience of being supported by others. For some studies a 9-item version of this instrument was developed involving 2 new sets of vignettes and slight modifications to 5 of Kaplan's originals.

Three other instruments developed at the Health Care Research Unit have also been employed: the Reflected Love Scale, the Reflected Esteem Scale, and the Provisions of Social Relations Scale (PSR). This latter instrument is a 15-item scale that addresses several of the provisions described by Weiss (1974). These four measures have been described and evaluated elsewhere using data from four major studies involving diverse populations (Turner et al., forthcoming). All were shown to be highly reliable internally. Addressing the issue of construct validity, we found the four indices to be appropriately associated with one another, to show the expected relationships with various measures of social support resources consistently, and to be associated with theoretically relevant external variables.

Based on both our field experience with these instruments and analyses of their formal properties, our conclusion is that the Revised Kaplan Scale (both versions) and the Provisions of Social Relations Scale are highly promising as global indices of social support. These two instruments may also provide a means for measuring some important subcomponents of the construct.

Several studies are being conducted at the Health Care Research Unit in which one or more of these measures has been employed. Results available from three of these studies provide additional evidence for the prominent role of social support in relation to psychological distress.

Adaptation and the Mothering Role

Factors influencing adaptation in the mothering role were examined in a 3-year study involving 312 women who had recently given birth at a major hospital in London, Ontario. A longitudinal (prospective) design involving three data-gathering points was utilized. Base-line information was gathered 2–4 weeks after the birth and follow-up questionnaires were administered at 6 and 12 months after base line.

Level of psychological distress was one major dimension of adaptation examined. Distress was indexed using 19 symptom items designed to assess the constructs of anxiety, depression, and anger/aggression (Petersen and Kellam, 1977). This scale shows very good internal reliability (Turner, 1981; Turner et al., forthcoming), good 6-month stability (Turner and Noh, 1982), and some evidence for validity has been reported (Petersen and Kellam, 1977).

In a series of analyses the seven-item Kaplan scale was found to be the most powerful predictor of psychological distress of a wide range of variables considered. The salience of social support was demonstrated at all three data-gathering points and held independent of the effects of levels of life stress and role strain. Both life stress and role strain were associated with higher levels of distress whereas social support was importantly associated with lower levels (Turner and Noh, 1982). Strong social-support effects were also observed when social class, stressful life events, and personal control were simultaneously controlled (Turner and Noh, 1983).

These data were also employed to assess directly the hypothesis that social support may be one factor underlying the well-known relationship between social class and psychological distress (Turner and Noh, 1983). Analyses confirmed the presence of class differences in responsiveness or vulnerability to life stress and provided evidence that variations in social support contribute to this differential responsiveness.

One additional set of findings from this study bears compellingly on the relevance of social support, as indexed, for general adaptation. These findings derive from analyses addressed to the additional objective of contributing to development of more effective procedures for distinguishing mothers who are at elevated risk for problem parenting (Turner and Associates, 1982). To this end, data were obatined from an additional sample composed of women identified as manifesting some form of maladaptation in their parenting role (some degree of child abuse or neglect). A total of 78 women from the child-protection case load of London Family and Children's Services were interviewed by their caseworkers and responded to the full set of measures employed in the larger study. The availability of this sample allowed case-comparison analyses to assess the capacity of various measures to distinguish those having parenting difficulties from those who are not.

Consistent with the goal of improving on previous capacity, our starting point was the Michigan Screening Profile of Parenting (MSPP) (Helfer et al., 1978a, 1978b), recognized by many as the most advanced and promising screening instrument available. The potential significance of attitudes led us to also consider the well-known Parental Attitude Research Instrument (PARI) (Schaefer and Bell, 1958), even though it has only occasionally been employed in this kind of screening context.

For all assessments, two parallel sets of analyses were conducted—one set involving all subjects in both samples and one involving a subset of 78 mothers from the larger study, matched as closely as possible with the substudy sample of maladapting mothers on age, education, and socioeconomic circumstance. Inspection of the results of the parallel analyses revealed few variations and no substantial differences.

Discriminant function analysis showed that the MSPP accurately discriminated 69% of the cases and that this accuracy rate was not improved when the PARI was also considered. In sharp contrast, the three social-support measures involved in this study (Kaplan scale, Reflected Love, Reflected Esteem) combined to produce a total accuracy rate that approached 90%. Moreover, when these indices were considered, neither the MSPP nor the PARI scales made any contribution to the discriminating power of the resulting function (Turner and Associates, 1982).

Perhaps the most noteworthy observation to emerge from this case-comparison analysis was the apparent importance and potential of the Kaplan scale. In every analysis in which this measure was considered, it was by far the most powerful in the discriminant function.

The array of analyses conducted suggest that a linear combination of the three indices of social support constitutes a reasonably efficient and highly promising screening dimension. Moreover, these measures of this dimension appear to represent a clear advance over previous instruments in capacity to distinguish mothers who may be exhibiting problems in their parenting role. Thus the collective evidence from this study suggests that experienced social support has substantial theoretical significance and potential for important practical utility.

Adult-Onset Hearing Loss

A study designed to assess factors associated with the adjustment of individuals with adult-onset hearing loss provides additional evidence for the relevance of social support to psychological distress. This investigation was partly guided by the assumption that the availability and experience of social support may be an issue of special salience for the hearing-impaired who are reported to have somewhat limited social interaction, to feel socially isolated, and to be socially withdrawn. The study involved some 420 adults aged 18–50 with clinically significant hearing loss diagnosed after the age of 15.

Social support was measured using the 7-item Kaplan scale and Reflected Esteem, and marital status was examined as an additional index. Psychological distress was assessed by a 21-item scale developed at the Social Psychiatry Study Center of the University of Chicago (Petersen and Kellam, 1977). The scale was composed of three separate dimensions indexing anxiety, depression, and paranoia. All measures demonstrated satisfactory internal reliability, with Cronbach's alphas ranging from .72 to .83.

Initial analyses examined a range of hearing-related variables, social and structural variables, and social support in an effort to explain variation in psychological distress (Frankel and Turner, 1983). Out of the whole range of variables considered, social support emerged as a consistently powerful predictor of psychological distress. For the summary measure of distress, the Kaplan scale, Reflected Esteem, and marital status each made significant independent contributions and together explained approximately 25% of the variability in distress. The Kaplan scale was by far the most important and powerful predictor, alone accounting for 20% of the total variance.

These data were also utilized to reassess the model proposed by Pearlin et al. (1981) specifying the process by which stress is translated into distress (Frankel and Nuttall, 1982). Pearlin and his colleagues considered a number of factors thought to influence the process, finding an intervening effect for social support but no direct effect on distress. The major finding from this replication was that social support has a more pronounced effect than the work of Pearlin et al. (1981) suggested. Both indirect and strong direct effects on distress were observed. In subsequent analyses these findings were observed to hold when the variables of age, sex, marital status, and social class were controlled.

Adaption among the Physically Disabled

This investigation examines social and psychological adjustment, variously defined, among physically disabled community residents. Subjects were obtained using a screening interview conducted at households identified by a multistage cluster sampling technique applied to the 10 counties of Southwestern Ontario.

Initial analyses of these data focused on depressive symptomatology as assessed by the Centre for Epidemiology Studies Depression Scale (CES-D) (Radloff, 1977). Social support was included among the variables hypothesized to be relevant on the basis of evidence suggesting that interpersonal relationships (and presumably the experienced products of such relationships) are likely to be especially problematic for the physically disabled (Kleck et al., 1966; Zahn, 1973). Both the nine-item Revised Kaplan Scale and the Provisions of Social Relations Scale were utilized. Scores were first standardized and then summed to form a single global estimate of experienced social support.

Consistent with findings from the other studies reviewed, we observed a compelling relationship between social support and depressive symptomatology (Levin and Turner, 1982; Turner et al., forthcoming). This relationship remained both statistically significant and substantial when life stress, age, sex, and disability-related variables (duration, perceived severity, and functional status) were controlled. Moreover, using a score of 16 or more on the CES-D as a criterion for identifying persons with clinically relevant depression (Radloff, 1977), analysis indicated that an important factor distinguishing depressed patients from others may be level of experienced social support.

On the issue of whether social support is of significance for depression independent of stress level or is important only in stressful circumstances, our findings are mixed. A stronger relationship was found where stress was high, supporting the buffering hypothesis, but a clear relationship was also observed in the lower-stress group. Thus there is evidence for both main and interactive effects.

As noted earlier, the quantity and range of available evidence leaves little doubt that social support, at least when conceived as an emotional or perceptual dimension, is importantly connected with mortality and with diverse forms of physical morbidity and psychological distress and disorder. Evidence from our own research strongly reinforces this conclusion with respect to depressive symptomatology, general psychological distress, and adaptation in the core mothering role. Despite this degree of clarity, a number of theoretically contentious issues lie in the path of a full understanding of the nature and meaning of these associations.

THEORETICAL CONSIDERATIONS

Operational Confounding

Several investigators have addressed the issue of operational confounding between social-support measures and stressful life events, raising the possibility that the health impact of loss events included in event lists may derive more, or as much, from support loss as from associated stress (Mueller, 1980; Schaefer et al., 1981; Thoits, 1982). The possibility that this circumstance impedes effective assessment of the buffering hypothesis as Schaefer et al. (1981) and Thoits (1982) have suggested will be considered subsequently. Here it will simply be noted that operational (as opposed to theoretical) confounding is a problem limited largely to research in which social support is indexed in terms of support resources using social-integration or social-network approaches. Assessments of social support in terms of the perception or experience of being supported by others clearly is operationally distinct from stress measured by a count of life events.

This methodological advantage of perceptual measures, however, must be weighted against the possibility of redundancy or operational confounding between such measures and psychiatric outcomes such as depression or general psychological distress. It is arguable, after all, that experiences of being loved and esteemed and able to count on others may be an integral aspect of mental health or emotional well-being, at least when broadly conceived. It might even be suggested that the absence of such perceptions may be an expression of, or accompaniment to, depressive affect.

In an attempt to obtain evidence bearing on this issue, a series of confirmatory factor analyses were applied to each of four data sets to assess whether the apparently similar constructs of social support and psychological well-being could be empirically differentiated (Turner, 1981; Turner et al., forthcoming). These data sets were taken from the three Health Care Research Unit studies described earlier and from an ongoing study of 523 discharged psychiatric patients who had been diagnosed as functionally psychotic. In this latter study social support was measured by both the nine-item Revised Kaplan Scale and the Provisions of Social Relations Scale, and psychiatric status was assessed using the Brief Symptom Inventory Scale, which is a short form of the Symptom Check List-90 (SCL-90) (Derogatis, 1977).

Our factor-analytic studies thus involved all pairings allowed by the data of four perceptual measures of social support with differing indices of psychological distress across four diverse populations. The results were remarkable in their clarity and very persuasive in their consistency. The most important underlying determinants of the social-support and psychological-distress items differed in every instance. Even though, in some computations, the support scales and distress measures divided into subscales, the distinction between support and distress remained constant throughout these confirmatory factor analyses (Turner et al., forthcoming).

Thus, on the question of some possible redundancy between perceptual measures of social support and measures of psychological distress, we view these results as demonstrating that social support is a separate and distinguishable dimension. Although it is accepted that experienced social support cannot be wholly divorced from the general domain of psychological well-being, this evidence supports the argument that the construct of social support warrants separate consideration within both theory, and efforts at measurement and research.

Causal Interpretation

A fundamental assumption among those who investigate the social correlates of psychological distress and disorder is that there is an etiological message to be found within the linkages discovered. There is, however, often difficulty in determining the nature of this message. This is clearly the case with the relationship between social support and psychological distress and disorder that has been demonstrated.

Many of the studies reporting this relationship have been epidemiological in character and, accordingly, confront the classic dilemma of whether findings are to be interpreted from a social-causation or a social-selection perspective (Dohrenwend and Dohrenwend, 1969; Turner, 1972; Turner and Wagenfeld, 1967). Does the support implicit in being married, being socially integrated, or having a confidant makes psychological distress or disorder less likely, or does distress and disorder limit the likelihood that the individual will secure and maintain social relationships? The former set of possibilities are social-causation hypotheses whereas the latter set point to social-selection processes.

A second form of selection interpretation proposes that such relationships are artifacts deriving from personal inadequacies of persons who later become disordered. For example, such inadequacies are seen as reducing the likelihood of marriage or, given marriage, as increasing the likelihood of separation or divorce. Indeed, there is some evidence to suggest that such selection processes substantially account for the well-known relationship among men between marital status and both the incidence and prognosis of schizophrenia (Turner and Gartrell, 1978; Turner et al., 1970). There is reason for giving this latter form of the social-selection hypothesis special attention when addressing the issue of causal interpretation. This is so because, although studies establishing that social support is related to the later onset of disorder effectively rule out the possibility that level of support is a consequence of disorder, they cannot rule out the hypothesis that personal characteristics influence both support level and the occurrence of distress or disorder.

It seems clear that the interpretative dilemma surrounding the connection between social support and health cannot be currently resolved with confidence and that it is unlikely to be fully resolved by future research. As House has correctly pointed out, a definitive answer to this question would require "carefully controlled experiments which manipulate the levels of social support experienced by people over a long period of time—experiments that are impractical and/or unethical" (1981:55).

Despite this circumstance and the related fact that no single study is persuasive on the matter, the total body of available evidence suggests that "much . . . of the causal flow is from social relationships to health rather than vice versa" (House, 1981:51).

This evidence varies widely in both strength and directness. On the most general level, the pattern of well-known epidemiological findings alluded to at the outset of this chapter bears upon the issue. It was suggested that the generality of associations with such factors as social class, marital status, geographic mobility, and minority-group status across a substantial majority of illnesses that have been studied has implications with respect to the plausibility of alternative interpretations of such relationships. Specifically, social-selection interpretations are quite plausible in relation to relationships between these social factors and schizophrenia. However, such explanations are not nearly so appealing with respect to mortality or various forms of morbidity such as heart disease, or even with respect to subclinical depression or general psychological distress. Surely mortality cannot be a cause of previous marital status, class position, and so forth, and it is not easy to imagine that all of the various forms of morbidity that have been studied would tend to influence such social statuses and circumstances. Moreover, it is difficult to identify personal characteristics or inadequacies that are likely to reduce for example, socioeconomic achievement, the likelihood of being married, or level of social integration, on the one hand, and increased risk for a wide range of illnesses and for the early death on the other.

The foregoing indirect and intuitive evidence, of course, is insufficient to argue the causal relevance of variations in social support. Fortunately, there are several additional forms of evidence that bear upon the matter.

1. *Animal studies.* Cassel's (1974, 1976) perspective on the relevance of social support derived substantially from evidence on the physical effects of laboratory-induced stress. He was impressed by Liddell's (1950) finding suggesting that the presence of the mother protects young goats from experimental neurosis, by the Conger et al. (1958) observation of the relevance of isolation for the occurrence of ulcera-

tion in rats, and the Henry and Cassel (1969) report on the significance
of littermate presence for the prevention of persistent hypertension in
mice. To these can be added the recent work of Nerem et al. (1980)
demonstrating that cuddling, fondling, and talking to rabbits on a high-
fat diet prevented arteriosclerotic heart disease that was produced in
rabbits on the same diet but not given such attention. Although the
internal reliability of these animal studies leaves no doubt about the
causality involved, the applicability of the findings to the human circumstance can hardly be assured.

2. *Laboratory analogue studies with humans.* As House has noted,
"social psychological experiments on humans have also documented
beneficial effects of other people in buffering the impact of stress"
(1981:46). One study especially pertinent here is that by Back and
Bogdonoff (1967), which showed that stress-induced physiological
arousal was significantly lower when friends were present than when
subjects were alone. As with the animal studies the experimental nature of this investigation allows unambiguous interpretation. This
study is clearly consistent with the hypothesis of social-support effects
on health, but such studies have not tended to travel well from the
laboratory to complex social life and, accordingly, should be interpreted with caution.

3. *Intervention studies.* A small amount of relevant experimental
evidence is available from intervention studies. Egbert et al. (1964)
found that supportive care given by the anesthetist to one of two randomly formed groups of surgical patients significantly reduced both
the amount of medication required for pain and the length of hospitalization. A supportive intervention with recently widowed women involving nondirective counseling has been shown by Raphael (1977) to
reduce the rate of experienced physical and mental illnesses over the
subsequent 13 months. The number of instances in which experimental
social-support interventions have not produced measurable effects is
difficult to estimate given the current bias against publishing negative
results. However, these studies are too well designed not to be taken
seriously.

4. *Longitudinal studies.* There are now a number of studies that provide evidence for the temporal priority of social support, variously
indexed, in social-support–health-outcome relationships. Examples
include the all-cause mortality studies by Berkman and Syme (1979),
who demonstrated the relationship of social integration with outcomes
over a 9-year period, and Blazer's (1982) report that experienced social
support predicts mortality 3 years later. The relevance of prior levels of
social support for psychological distress has been demonstrated by,

among others, Pearlin *et al.* (1981) and Schaefer *et al.* (1981). These and similar studies clearly contribute to clarifying the causation issue because they limit the range of plausible interpretations. What cannot be wholly ruled out from such evidence is the possibility that some third variable, presumably developmentally or constitutionally determined personal characteristics, influences both level of support and health risk.

5. *Panel studies.* One more form of relevant evidence is provided by studies in which both social support and psychological distress are measured over time and quantitative changes in one variable can be related to changes in the other. Although Dean and Lin and their colleagues (Dean and Ensel, 1982; Dean et al., 1980; Lin et al., 1979b) have conducted a three-wave community panel study, findings on the relationship between changes in support and distress have not yet been presented. However, Henderson et al. (1981) have fully applied this strategy in assessing the impact of social support on neuroses. Although there was no evidence that lack of social relationships influenced the subsequent development of neurotic symptoms, perceived adequacy of social relationships was found to be linked to subsequent morbidity.

We applied a similar form of analysis to the three-wave panel data obtained in the study of mothers described earlier (Turner and Noh, 1982). Figure 3.1 presents a linear model displaying only lagged effects between social support, indexed by the Kaplan scale, and psychological distress. In a more general model that included measures of stressful life events and chronic role strain, these are the only such effects that were consistently observed. This pattern of consistent lagged effects in both directions and the fact that the coefficients in each case are virtually identical are, at a minimum, suggestive with respect to the question of the causal direction involved.

In considering the issue of causation, it seems well to begin by acknowledging that neither human development nor functioning is very likely to proceed in terms of linear or clear-cut causes and effects. To a substantial extent and in a substantial number of social-psychological arenas, it seems probable that causes and effects are reciprocal. M. B. Smith has conceptualized development as a matter of benign circles or of vicious ones, viewing causation in personal and social development as "inherently circular or spiral, rather than linear, in terms of neatly isolable causes and effects" (1968:277). In the present case, it seems probable that the availability, use, and experience of social support has consequences for psychological well-being. It also seems probable that

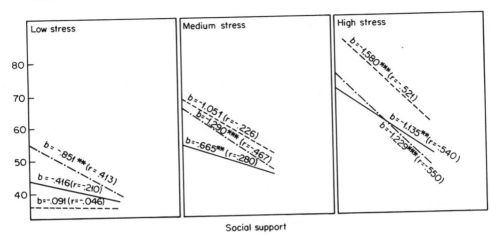

Figure 3.1. A three-wave panel analysis of cross-lagged effects: social support and psychological distress. ————, upper class; – – –, middle class; —·—, lower class. **p ≤ .05; ***p ≤ .01.

psychological status or condition will affect the availability of social support and the tendency to experience that support.

The findings presented in Figure 3.1 and those reported by Henderson and his colleagues are consistent with the assumption that at least some important part of the causation involved goes from support to psychological distress. However, the possibility that premorbid social and personal characteristics might influence both the occurrence of distress and disorder and perceptions of the extent or adequacy of social support still cannot be ruled out.

It seems clear that no single study or type of study is sufficient to resolve the interpretative dilemma surrounding the well-established relationship between social support and psychological distress and disorder. Moreover, practical and ethical barriers make it unlikely that wholly convincing evidence on the matter will be forthcoming. Nevertheless, as House (1981:55) has observed, the collective evidence from diverse research approaches constitutes a compelling case for the causal impact of social support.

Main versus Buffering Effects

As noted earlier, much of the recent interest and research attention devoted to the concept has been associated with the hypothesis that social support may constitute a buffer or mediator of the effects of life stress. This is the central thesis of the provocative reviews by both Cassel (1976) and Cobb (1976) and, given his focus upon normative and imposed crises, is clearly the view favoured by Caplan (G. Caplan, 1974; Caplan and Killilea, 1976). Cobb has argued that

> social support facilitates coping with crises and adaptation to change. Therefore, one should not expect dramatic main effects from social support. There are, of course, some main effects simply because life is full of changes and crises. The theory says that it is in moderating the effects of the major transitions in life and of the unexpected crises that the effects should be found. (1976:502)

The view that stressors are an omnipresent accompaniment to life has been strenuously argued by Antonovsky. In his view, "all of us . . . even in the most benign and sheltered environments, are fairly continuously exposed to what we define as stressors. The range of human experience in exposure to stressors is not from very low to very high" (1979:77). Rather it runs from fairly serious and life-long to "unbelievable hell on earth. . . . We are able to get low scorers on stress experience because we do not ask the right questions or do not ask patiently enough and not because there really are any low scorers" (1979:77). Antonovsky's insistence that "even the most fortunate of people . . . know life as stressful to a considerable extent" (1979:84) is consistent with Cobb's suggestion that it is "not worth worrying about the distinction between main effects and interaction effects" (1979:99). If the constancy-of-stress argument is accepted, both direct and interactive effects would be theoretically interpretable in terms of the buffering hypothesis.

However persuasive or unpersuasive one views this argument theoretically, it hardly resolves all of the issues that underlie the buffering-versus main-effects debate. Even if what look like main effects are really buffering effects, it would remain crucial that we determine whether support is of greater significance where stress is relatively high than when relatively low. Given the inevitability of limited resources, it seems important and useful to be able to distinguish those who most need and who might most benefit from an effective social-support intervention. Thus, although all might benefit from enhanced social support, the issues of relative need and relative benefit with respect to psychological distress or disorder remain salient.

Available empirical evidence on this question is highly conflicting and, for me, impossible to resolve at this juncture of research progress. Substantial evidence consistent with the buffering hypothesis can be assembled (Brown *et al.*, 1975; Cassel, 1976; Cobb, 1976; De Araujo et al., 1973; Dean and Lin, 1977; Nuckolls et al., 1972), whereas a number of studies report finding primarily main effects (Andrews et al., 1978; Aneshensel and Frerichs, 1982; Bell et al., 1982; Dean and Ensel, 1982; Husaini et al., 1982; Schaefer et al., 1981; Williams et al., 1981). Interestingly, although Dean and Lin (1977) favored the buffering hypothesis, their subsequent work revealed only main effects (Dean and Ensel, 1982; Dean et al., 1980, and Henderson (1980) eloquently argued the significance of social bonds independent of level of adversity but found support to influence neurotic symptoms only in the presence of adversity (Henderson et al., 1980a).

A further indication of the complexity of the matter is revealed in the contrary conclusions drawn by Thoits (1982) and by Schaefer et al. (1981). Both considered the implications for the hypothesis of confounding between measures of life stress and of social support. However, Thoits (1982:148) saw this confounding as biasing results in favor of the buffering hypothesis while Schaefer et al. (1981:387) concluded that such confounding could disguise or wash out interaction effects.

In a closely reasoned assessment of this issue House (1981:56) implied that there is a tendency for buffering effects to be observed in the technically stronger studies and proposed an explanation for the failure of many cross-sectional studies to observe such effects. Although a detailed technical discussion was also presented, the general argument was that although the stress-buffering effects of support tend to occur over time, they will at some point be completed.

> At the time the coping or reinterpretation involved in the buffering process are occurring, researchers would observe differences in the impact of the objective stressor or perceived stress on health between persons with high and low social support. But once the buffering process is complete observers would merely note lower stress levels or better health among persons with greater versus lesser social support (1981:57)

Thoits (1982) has criticized the usual practice of forming support-interaction terms using scores for previously occurring events. In her view, the appropriate test requires the use of event scores with previously measured social support. This point seems well taken and to be consistent with the conceptualization of buffering that sees the impact of stressors as determined by the soil on which stressors fall (Paykel, 1978).

Evidence from our study of mothers may shed additional light on the inconsistency of findings relating to the buffering hypothesis. In initial analyses social support was found to relate to psychological distress independent of stress level, and the life-stress by social-support interaction term was not significant when the main effects were controlled (Turner, 1981; Turner and Noh, 1982). This finding, of course, is consistent with the hypothesis of direct social-support effects and is highly similar to findings of other investigators who have concluded that there is no evidence for a stress-buffering role.

Further analyses of these same data, however, indicated that the question of whether social support is of influence in its own right or is important wholly, or largely, as a buffer against unusual stress may not be so simply answered. With the sample divided into three broad so-cial-class groupings, social support was regressed on psychological dis-tress within each of three stress-level categories (Turner and Noh, 1983). Figure 3.2 displays the results.

Although the small *n* sizes involved advise caution in interpreting these results, they are quite compelling in their clarity. Looking first at the slopes for social support among the lower-class group, it is obvious that the significance of support varies by level of stress. No significant relationship is observed for the lower class in either the low- or medi-um-stress circumstance. However, social support is clearly of dramatic significance in the high-stress circumstance (r = .52). The regression coefficients are significantly different across stress levels for the lower class but not for the other class groupings.

The middle-class group provides the sharpest contrast with the lower class in these results. Clear social-support effects are observed regard-less of stress level. It can be seen that the answer to the question of

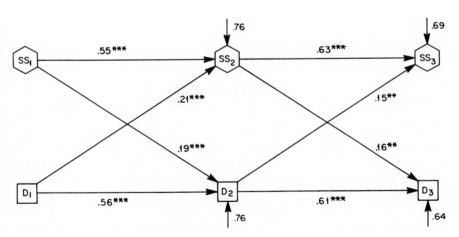

Figure 3.2. Regressions of psychological distress on social support for three catego-ries of stress by social class level (*N* = 293). **p < .01; ***p < .001. (From Turner & Noh, 1983.)

whether social support has main or buffering effects is both conditional and complex. The significant support coefficients observed for the middle class at all three stress levels demonstrate a main effect. In sharp contrast, no main effects are observed for the lower class, as evidenced by the small (and nonsignificant) support coefficients within the low- and medium-stress conditions. Social support matters, and matters importantly, only among those experiencing a high level of stress. This finding provides clear support for the buffering hypothesis. Thus, the significance of social support appears to vary with both social class and stress level.

As noted earlier, it does not currently seem possible to resolve the direct- versus buffering-effects question with confidence. However, the collective available evidence points to the appropriateness of three assumptions or working hypotheses: (1) social support tends to matter for psychological well-being independent of stressor level, (2) support tends to matter more where stressor level is relatively high, and (3) the extent to which (1) and (2) are true varies across subgroups of the population defined by class level and, probably, by other variables. Further progress in resolving this issue will require that future research consider the possibility of subgroup variation, consider the circumstances described by House (1981) that might obscure buffering effects, and address the need emphasized by Thoits (1982) for establishing the temporal priority of social support when forming support by life-stress interaction terms.

SUMMARY AND CONCLUSIONS

The material considered in this chapter makes it clear that social support means many things to many people, with both conceptualizations and measurements varying substantially. A number of authors have distinguished differing dimensions of support, arguing that each should be regarded as of potential significance and included in future studies. This point is fully accepted here and consideration in research of material and instrumental support, as well as formal network characteristics, is certainly to be recommended. However, consistent with Cobb's (1976, 1979) view, there seems little to be gained and much to be lost in the current tendency to group these several dimensions under the common label of social support. Surely both communication and scientific progress would be advanced if support that is instrumental or material or that flows from particular network characteristics were so labeled. Such clarification could only assist the necessary process of determining the impact on health and well-being of these sources of support.

House (1981:84) has suggested, and the review presented here confirms, that most of the documented association between social support and health derives from reported relationships with emotional or perceived support. It is recommended therefore that the term *social support* be reserved to refer to the experience or cognition of being supported by others, comprised of self-relevant information as processed and held by the individual. Thus conceived, social support cannot be reduced to, or adequately captured by, level of instrumental or material assistance, availability of resources, or system capacity or potential, no matter how elegantly assessed.

There are at least two additional important reasons why reductionistic tendencies and tendencies to conglomerate support dimensions should be resisted. First, effective and reliable measures of experienced social support constitute useful and direct criteria for assessing the relative personal utility of various resource or network characteristics. Such measures also provide a lever for identifying and evaluating relevant aspects of "process" where this "black box of support research" (Gore, 1980:11) is studied. Second, and more importantly, the reduction or confounding of this cognitive–perceptual variable would obviate the possibility of understanding the impact on health of interactions between experienced social support and significant similar-level variables such as locus of control (Rotter, 1966) or mastery (Pearlin and Schooler, 1978), orientational system (Kohn, 1969) or the attitudes toward self and world that Smith (1968) sees as defining the competent self.

Although their interests appear quite different, Liem and Liem have expressed a similar view. They noted the interesting finding "that the amount of help received is not always related to perceptions of being supported." In their view the chief significance of this finding "lies in the need it suggests for the development of social support measures that include . . . behaviorally oriented indices as well as subjective estimates of social support" (1978:19, cited in Barrera, 1981).

The starting point of this chapter was a perspective suggested by the work of Cassel (1974, 1976) and others involving three propositions: (1) social factors must function to enhance or lower susceptibility to all disease and disorder generally, (2) the continuity and generality of observed connections between social factors and health suggests the likelihood that the influential mechanisms involved must also be general in nature, and (3) that it is reasonable to propose that social support may represent one such general and influential factor. A review of part of the considerable body of available evidence confirms and substantially extends Cassel's observation that "a remarkably similar set of circumstances characterizes people who develop tuberculosis, schizophrenia, multiple accidents, suicide and alcoholism" (1976:110).

My most general conclusion is that the quantity and range of available evidence leaves little doubt that social support, at least when conceived as an emotional or perceptual dimension, is importantly connected with mortality and with diverse forms of physical morbidity and psychological distress and disorder. Evidence from our research involving sharply contrasting populations strongly reinforced this conclusion with respect to depressive symptomatology, general psychological distress, and adaptation in the mothering role.

Despite the clarity of this evidence, there are certain theoretically contentious issues that must be resolved before the meaning of the connections between social support and distress and disease can be interpreted with confidence. Although the data on these matters are hardly definitive, tentative conclusions were drawn on the questions of operational and theoretical confounding, causal direction, and main versus buffering effects. The evidence suggests (1) that social support is a dimension distinct from psychological distress and that warrants separate and careful consideration within both theory and research; (2) that at least some significant portion of the causation involved in the association goes from social support to psychological distress and disorder; and (3) that level of social support is of influence independent of degree of adversity, that it matters more when adversity is high, and that the extent to which one or both of these are so varies across subgroups of the population defined by socioeconomic status and perhaps other factors.

The central hypothesis addressed in this chapter is that social support may represent a significant element in the differential vulnerability to illness implied in the wide array of epidemiological findings on the social distribution of diverse forms of distress, disorder, and disease. Collectively, the evidence reviewed appears consistent with and to support this hypothesis. If this conclusion is accepted, then Dean and Lin's assertion that "social support is . . . the most important concept for future study" (1977:408) would certainly follow.

A complete agenda for future research would necessarily be complex, speculative, and changeable in the light of new information. In closing, I will mention a few general issues that appear to be particularly salient and in need of research attention.

What information is available indicates that the fit between level of environmental-support resources and perceived social support is modest at best. Clearly research is required that more closely examines what type of environmental supports or social networks best predict the experience of social support, and under what social circumstances. A related but distinct question is what developmentally and/or constitutionally determined characteristics filter the experience or perception of environmental supports?

It seems clear that the nature of the operant milieu significantly influences the experience of social support. We have found substantial stability over time in social-support scores, but only about 50% of the variance in such scores is accounted for by the same measure taken 6 months earlier. Assuming that some aspects of social environment are stable over a 6-month interval, this suggests that something well in excess of half the variability in experienced social support derives directly or indirectly from contemporaneous or recent life circumstances and occurrences.

It seems equally apparent that other factors must combine with environmental features in producing differing perceptions of social support. A consideration of Cobb's (1976) compelling conceptualization of the construct reinforces this point. Cobb defines social support as the information or experience of being loved and wanted, valued and esteemed, and able to count on others should the need arise. Clearly the likelihood of such perceptions cannot be independent of self-esteem and self-love or of historically based expectancies with respect to the responsiveness of the social network.

Although the full range of relevant personal attributes remains to be established, it seems probable that the more crucial among these are expressed in attitudes toward self and world forged in social encounters and determined by the general responsiveness of the social environment. Ryan (1967) has argued that self-esteem is largely dependent on the experience of self as at least minimally powerful personally. This perception is based upon the real-life exercise of influencing outcomes and is thus determined by the individual's history of efficacies and inefficacies.

In setting forth his view of the competent self, Smith points to the perception of the self as "causally important, as effective in the world . . . as likely to be able to bring about desired effects and as accepting responsibility when effects do not correspond to desire" (1968:281). To this he adds the crucial insight that such attitudes are closely and reciprocally linked to a perception of the world as trustable and reasonably fair. "Coordinate with the feeling of efficacy is an attitude of hope—the world is the sort of place in which, given appropriate efforts, I can expect good outcomes" (Smith, 1968:282).

Emphasized here, in complementary conceptualizations (Kohn, 1969, 1972), is the significance of the responsiveness of the environment developmentally and throughout the life course. It seems reasonable to propose that both the availability of social support and the extent to which support is perceived must be conditioned by prior experiences and the attitudes toward self and world that are the necessary products of such experience. That such attitudes are clearly related to location in the social structure, and perhaps to other statuses that are known to be associated with the occurrence of distress and disorder, is consistent with this hypothesis. Clearly, research assessing the role and significance of various personal attitudes in relation to the tendency to experience social support is greatly needed.

Finally, for both theoretical and practical purposes, substantial additional research is required to determine the extent to which perceived social support is programmatically malleable. We need to know what kinds of interventions with what kinds of subjects are most likely to positively influence this apparently crucial variable.

REFERENCES

Ader, R., and E. W. Hahn
    1963   "Effects of social environment on mortality to whole body—x—irradiation in the rat." Psychological Reports 13:211–215.
Ader, R., A. Kreutner, and H. L. Jacobs
    1963   "Social environment, emotionality and alloxan diabetes in the rat." Psychosomatic Medicine 25:60–68.
Andervont, H. B.
    1944   "Influence of environment on mammary cancer in mice." Journal of the National Cancer Institute 4:579–581.
Andrews, G., C. Tennant, D. M. Hewson, and G. E. Vaillant
    1978   "Life event stress, social support, coping style, and risk of psychological impairment." Journal of Nervous and Mental Disease 166:307–316.
Aneshensel, C. S., and R. R. Frerichs
    1982   "Stress, support, and depression: A longitudinal causal model." Journal of Community Psychology 10:363–376.
Antonovsky, A.
    1979   Health, Stress, and Coping. San Francisco: Jossey-Bass.
Ausubel, D. P.
    1958   Theory and Problems of Child Development. New York: Grune & Stratton.
Back, K. W., and M. D. Bogdonoff
    1967   "Buffer conditions in experimental stress." Behavioral Science 12:384–390.

Barrera, M., Jr.
   1981   "Social support in the adjustment of pregnant adolescents: Assessment issues." Pp. 69–96 in B. H. Gottlieb (ed.), Social Networks and Social Support. Beverly Hills, Calif.: Sage.
Bell, R. A., J. B. LeRoy, and J. J. Stephenson
   1982   "Evaluating the mediating effects of social support upon life events and depressive symptoms." Journal of Community Psychology 10:325–340.
Belsey, E. M., H. S. Greer, S. Lal, S. C. Lewis, and R. W. Beard
   1977   "Predictive factors in emotional response to abortion: King's termination study IV." Social Science and Medicine 11:71–82.
Berkman, L., and S. L. Syme
   1979   "Social networks, host resistance and mortality: A nine-year follow-up study of Alameda County residents." American Journal of Epidemiology 109:186–204.
Berle, B. B., R. H. Pinsky, S. Wolf, and H. G. Wolff
   1952   "A clinical guide to prognosis in stress diseases." Journal of the American Medical Assocation 149:1624–1628.
Blazer,D. G.
   1982   "Social support and mortality in an elderly population." American Journal of Epidemiology 115:684–694.
Bowlby, J.
   1969   Attachment and Loss: Attachment. Volume 1. London: Hogarth Press.
Bowlby, J.
   1973   Attachment and Loss: Separation, Anxiety and Anger. Volume 2. London: Hogarth Press.
Brown, G. W., M. Bhrolchain, and T. Harris
   1975   "Social class and psychiatric disturbance among women in an urban population." Sociology 9:225–254.
Brown, G. W., S. Davidson, T. Harris, U. Maclean, S. Pollock, and R. Prudo
   1979   "Psychiatric disorder in London and North Uist." Social Science and Medicine 11:367–377.
Brown, G. W., and T. Harris
   1978   Social Origins of Depression. New York: The Free Press.
Burch, J.
   1972   "Recent bereavement in relation to suicide." Journal of Psychosomatic Research 16:361–366.
Caplan, G.
   1974   Support Systems and Community Mental Health. New York: Behavioral Publications.
Caplan, G., and M. Killilea
   1976   Support Systems and Mutual Help: Multidisciplinary Explorations. New York: Grune & Stratton.
Caplan, R.
   1979   "Patient, provider, and organization: hypothesized determinants of adherence." In S. J. Cohen (ed.), New Directions in Patient Compliance. Lexington, Mass.: Health.
Carter, H., and P. C. Glick
   1970   Marriage and Divorce: A Social and Economic Study. American Public Health Association, Vital and Health Statistics Monograph. Cambridge, Mass.: Harvard University Press.

Carveth, W. B., and B. H. Gottlieb
    1979   "The measurement of social support and its relation to stress." Canadian
            Journal of Behavioral Science 11:179–187.
Cassel, J.
    1974   "Psychosocial processes and 'stress': Theoretical formulations." Interna-
            tional Journal of Health Services 4:471–482.
Cassel, J.
    1976   "The contribution of the social environment to host resistance." American
            Journal of Epidemiology 104:107–123.
Cobb, S.
    1976   "Social support as a moderator of life stress." Psychosomatic Medicine
            38:300–314.
Cobb, S.
    1979   "Social support and health through the life course." Pp. 93–106 in M. W.
            Riley (ed.), Aging from Birth to Death. Boulder, Colo.: Westview Press.
Cobb, S., and S. V. Kasl
    1977   Termination: The Consequence of Job Loss. Publication N10SH 77-224.
            Washington, D.C.: U.S. Department of Health, Education and Welfare.
Conger, J. J., W. Sawrey, and E. S. Turrell
    1958   "The role of social experience in the production of gastric ulcers in hooded
            rats placed in a conflict situation." Journal of Abnormal Psychology
            57:214–220.
Coulson, J. et al. (eds.)
    1975   The Oxford Illustrated Dictionary. London: Oxford University Press.
Croog, S. H., S. Levine, and Y. Lurie
    1968   "The heart patient and the recovery process." Social Science and Medicine
            2:111–164.
Cumming, E., and C. Lazer
    1981   "Kinship structure and suicide: A theoretical link." Canadian Review of
            Sociology and Anthropology 18:271–282.
Davis, D. E., and C. P. Read
    1958   "Effect of behavior on development of resistance in trichinosis." Proceed-
            ings of the Society for Experimental Biology and Medicine 99:269–272.
De Araujo, G., P. Van Arsdel, Jr., T. H. Holmes, and D. Dudley
    1973   "Life change, coping ability and chronic intrinsic asthma." Journal of Psy-
            chosomatic Research 17:359–373.
Dean, A., and W. M. Ensel
    1982   "Modelling social support, life events, competence and depression in the
            context of age and sex." Journal of Community Psychology 10:392–408.
Dean, A., N. Lin, and W. M. Ensel
    1981   "The epidemiological significance of social support systems in depres-
            sion." Pp. 77–109 in R. G. Simmons (ed.), Research in Community and
            Mental Health. Greenwich, Conn.: JAI Press.
Dean, A., and N. Lin
    1977   "The stress-buffering role of social support: Problems and prospects for
            systematic investigation." Journal of Nervous and Mental Disease 165:403–
            417.
Dean, A., N. Lin, M. Tausig, and W. M. Ensel
    1980   "Relating types of social support to depression in the life course." Paper
            presented at the annual meeting of the American Sociological Association,
            New York.

Derogatis, L. R.
  1977   SCL-90 Scoring Manual. Baltimore: Johns Hopkins University School of Medicine.
DiMatteo, M. R., and R. Hays
  1981   "Social support and serious illness." Pp. 117–148 in B. H. Gottlieb (ed.), Social Networks and Social Support. Beverly Hills, Calif.: Sage.
Dohrenwend, B. P., and B. S. Dohrenwend-
  1969   Social Status and Psychological Disorder: A Causal Inquiry. New York: Wiley–Interscience.
Dumont, M. P.
  1974   "Drug problems and their treatment." Pp. 287–293 in G. Caplan (ed.), American Handbook of Psychiatry. Volume 11. New York: Basic Books.
Durkheim, E.
  1951   Suicide: A Study in Sociology. Glencoe, Ill.: The Free Press.
Earp, J. A. L.
  1979   "The effects of social support and health professional home visits on patient adherence to hypertension regiments." Preventive Medicine 8:155. Abstract.
Eaton, W. W.
  1978   "Life events, social supports, and psychiatric symptoms: A re-analysis of the New Haven data." Journal of Health and Social Behavior 19:230–234.
Eckenrode, J., and S. Gore
  1981   "Stressful events and social supports: The significance of context." Pp. 43–68 in B. H. Gottlieb (ed.), Social Networks and Social Support. Beverly Hills, Calif.: Sage.
Egbert, L. D., G. E. Battit, C. E. Welch, and M. K. Bartlett
  1964   "Reduction of post-operative pain by encouragement and instruction of patients." New England Journal of Medicine 270:825–827.
Ernster, V. L., S. T. Sacks, S. Selvin, and N. L. Petrakis
  1979   "Cancer incidence by marital status: U. S. Third National Cancer Survey." Journal of the National Cancer Institute 63:567–585.
Ewalt, J. R.
  1960   "Introduction." Pp. 3–16 in G. Gurin, J. Veroff, and S. Feld (eds.), Americans View their Mental Health. New York: Basic Books.
Finlayson, A.
  1976   "Social networks as coping resources: Lay help and consultation patterns used by women in husbands' post-infarction career." Social Science and Medicine 10:97–103.
Frankel, B. G., and S. Nuttall
  1982   "The role of social support in the stress process: Further explication of a model." Paper presented at the annual meeting of the American Sociological Association, San Francisco.
Frankel, B. G., and R. J. Turner
  1983   "Psychological adjustment in chronic disability: The role of social support in the case of the hearing impaired." Canadian Journal of Sociology 8:273–291.
Funch, D. P., and C. Mettlin
  1982   "The role of support in relation to recovery from breast surgery." Social Science and Medicine 16:91–98.
Gibbs, J., and W. T. Martin
  1964   Status Integration and Suicide. Eugene: University of Oregon Press.

Goldberg, D. P.
    1972   The Detection of Psychiatric Illness by Questionnaire. Institute of Psychia-
            try, Maudsley Monographs No. 21. London: Oxford University Press.
Gore, S.
    1978   "The effect of social support in moderating the health consequences of
            unemployment." Journal of Health and Social Behavior 19:157–165.
Gore, S.
    1980   "Stress buffering functions of social supports: An appraisal and clarifica-
            tion of research models." Pp. 202–222 in B. S. Dohrenwend and B. P.
            Dohrenwend (eds.), Stressful Life Events and Their Contexts. New York:
            Prodist.
Gottlieb, B. H.
    1981   "Social networks and social support in community mental health." Pp.
            11–42 in B. H. Gottlieb (ed.), Social Networks and Social Support. Beverly
            Hills, Calif.: Sage.
Gruenberg, E., H. B. Snow, and C. L. Bennett
    1969   "Preventing the social breakdown syndrome." In F. C. Redlich (ed.), Social
            Psychiatry. Baltimore: ARNMD.
Guttman, L.
    1974   "Measurement as structural theory." Psychometrika 36:329–347.
Hammer, M.
    1981   "Social supports, social networks, and schizophrenia." Schizophrenia Bul-
            letin 7:45–57.
Hammer, M., S. Makiesky-Barrow, and L. Gutwirth
    1978   "Social networks and schizophrenia." Schizophrenia Bulletin 4:522–545.
Harlow, H. E.
    1959   Love in infant monkeys. Scientific American 200:68–74.
Helfer, R., J. K. Hoffmeister, and C. Schneider
    1978a   MSPP (Michigan Screening Profile of Parenting). Boulder, Col.: Test Analy-
            sis and Development Corporation.
Helfer, R., C. Schneider, and J. K. Hoffmeister
    1978b   Report on the Research Using the Michigan Screening Profile of Parenting
            (MSPP). Boulder, Col.: Test Analysis and Development Corporation.
Henderson, S.
    1977   "The social network, support and neurosis: The function of attachment in
            adult life." British Journal of Psychiatry 131:185–191.
Henderson, S.
    1980   "A development in social psychiatry: The systematic study of social
            bonds." Journal of Nervous and Mental Disease 168:63–69.
Henderson, S., D. G. Byrne, and P. Duncan-Jones
    1981   Neurosis and the Social Environment. New York: Academic Press.
Henderson, S., D. Byrne, P. Duncan-Jones, R. Scott, and S. Adcock
    1980a   "Social relationships, adversity and neurosis: A study of associations in a
            general population sample." British Journal of Psychiatry 136:574–583.
Henderson, S., P. Duncan-Jones, S. Adcock, R. Scott, and G. Steele
    1978a   "Social bonds in the epidemiology of neurosis: A preliminary communica-
            tion." British Journal of Psychiatry 132:463–466.
Henderson, S., P. Duncan-Jones, D. Byrne, and R. Scott
    1980b   "Measuring social relationships: The interview schedule for social interac-
            tion." Psychological Medicine 10:723–734.

Henderson, S., P. Duncan-Jones, H. McAuley, and K. Ritchie
    1978b   "The patient's primary group." British Journal of Psychiatry 132:74–86.
Henry, J. P., and J. C. Cassel
    1969   "Psychosocial factors in essential hypertension." Journal of Epidemiology
            90:171–200.
Hirsch, B.
    1980   "Natural support systems and coping with major life changes." American
            Journal of Community Psychology 8:159–172.
Holman, T., and M. F. Shore
    1978   "Halfway house and family involvement as related to community adjust-
            ment for ex-residents of a psychiatric halfway house." Journal of Communi-
            ty Psychology 6:123–129.
House, J. S.
    1981   Work Stress and Social Support. Reading, Mass.: Addison-Wesley.
Husaini, B. A., J. A. Neff, J. R. Newbrough, and M. C. Moore
    1982   "The stress-buffering role of social support and personal competence
            among the rural married." Journal of Community Psychology 10:409–426.
Jarvinen, K. A. J.
    1955   "Can ward rounds be a danger to patients with myocardial infarction."
            British Medical Journal 1:318–320.
Jessner, L., G. E. Blom, and S. Waldfogel
    1952   "Emotional implications of tonsillectomy and adenoidectomy on chil-
            dren." Psychoanalytic Study of the Child 7:126–169.
Johnson, J. H., and I. G. Sarason
    1979   "Moderator variables in stress research." Pp. 151–167 in I. G. Sarason and
            C. D. Spielberger (eds.), Stress and Anxiety. Volume 6. Washington, D.C.:
            Hemisphere.
Kaplan, A.
    1977   "Social support: Construct and its measurement." Unpublished B.A. thesis,
            Brown University, R.I.
Kaplan, B. H.
    1975   "Toward further research on family and health." Pp. 89–106 in B. H.
            Kaplan and J. C. Cassel (eds.), Family and Health: An Epidemiological
            Approach. Chapel Hill: Institute for Research in Social Science, University
            of North Carolina.
Kaplan, B. H., J. C. Cassel, and S. Gore
    1977   "Social support and health." Medical Care 15:47–58. Supplement.
Kessler, R. C.
    1982   "Life events, social supports, and mental health." Pp. 247–271 in W. R.
            Gove (ed.), Deviance and Mental Illness. Beverly Hills, Calif.: Sage.
Kleck, R., H. Ono, and A. H. Hastorf
    1966   "The effects of physical deviance on face-to-face interaction." Human Rela-
            tions, 19:425–436.
Kohn, M. L.
    1969   Class and Conformity: A Study in Values. Homewood, Ill.: Dorsey.
Kohn, M. L.
    1972   "Class, family and schizophrenia: A reformulation." Social Forces
            50:295–313.
Kraus, A. S., and A. M. Lillienfeld
    1959   "Some epidemiologic aspects of the high mortality rate in the young wid-
            owed group." Journal of Chronic Diseases 10:207–217.

LaRocco, J., J. House, and J. French, Jr.
    1980   "Social support, occupational stress and health." Journal of Health and
            Social Behavior 21:202–219.
Levin, D., and R. J. Turner
    1982   "The influence of social support on depression among the physically dis-
            abled." Paper presented at the 17th annual meeting of the Canadian Sociol-
            ogy and Anthropology Association, Ottawa, Ontario.
Liddell, H. S.
    1950   "Some specific factors that modify tolerance for environmental stress." Pp.
            155–171 in H. G. Wolff, S. Wolf, and C. Hare (eds.), Life Stress and Bodily
            Disease. Baltimore: Williams & Wilkins.
Liem, R., and J. Liem
    1978   "Social support and stress: Some general issues and their applications to
            problems of unemployment." Unpublished manuscript, Boston College.
Lin, N., A. Dean, and W. M. Ensel
    1979a   "Development of social support scales." Paper presented at the Third Bien-
            nial Conference on Health Survey Research Methods, Reston, Va.
Lin, N., A. Dean, and W. M. Ensel
    1981   "Social support scales: A methodological note." Schizophrenia Bulletin
            7:73–89.
Lin, N., R. Simeone, W. M. Ensel, and W. Kuo
    1979b   "Social support, stressful life events and illness: A model and an empirical
            test." Journal of Health and Social Behavior 20:108–119.
Lowenthal, M. F., and C. Haven
    1968   "Interaction and adaptation: Intimacy as a critical variable." American So-
            ciological Review 33:20–30.
Lynch, J.
    1977   The Broken Heart. New York: Basic Books.
Medalie, J. H., and U. Goldbourt
    1976   "Angina pectoris among 10,000 men: Psychosocial and other risk factors as
            evidenced by a multivariate analysis of a five-year incidence study." Amer-
            ican Journal of Medicine 60:910–921.
Miller, P., and J. Ingham
    1976   "Friends, confidants and symptoms." Social Psychiatry 11:51–57.
Miller, K., and I. Iscoe
    1963   "The concept of crisis: Current status and mental health implications."
            Human Organization 22:195–201.
Mitchell, R., and E. Trickett
    1980   "Task force report: Social networks as mediators of social support." Journal
            of Community Mental Health 16:27–44.
Mueller, D. P.
    1980   "Social networks: A promising direction for research on the relationship of
            the social environment to psychiatric disorder." Social Science and Medi-
            cine 14A:147–161.
Murawski, B., D. Penman, and M. Schmitt
    1978   "Social support in health and illness: The concept and its measurement."
            Cancer Nursing 1:365–371.
Myers, J., J. Lindenthal, and M. Pepper
    1975   "Life events, social integration and psychiatric symptomatology." Journal
            of Health and Social Behavior 14:421–427.

Nerem, R., M. J. Levesque, and J. F. Cornhill
    1980   "Social environment as a factor in diet-induced atherosclerosis. Science 208:1475–1476.
Nuckolls, K. B., J. C. Cassel, and B. H. Kaplan
    1972   "Psychosocial assets, life crisis and the prognosis of pregnancy." American Journal of Epidemiology 95:431–441.
Ortmeyer, C. F.
    1974   "Variations in mortality, morbidity, and health care by marital status." Pp. 159–188 in C. L. Erhardt and J. E. Berlin (eds.), Mortality and Morbidity in the United States. Cambridge, Mass.: Harvard University Press.
Panagis, D. M., and L. M. Adler
    1977   "Sense of support scale (SOS)." Unpublished.
Pattison, E. M., D. DeFrancisco, and P. Wood
    1975   "A psychosocial kinship model for family therapy." American Journal of Psychiatry 132:1246–1251.
Paykel, E. S.
    1978   "Contribution of life events to causation of psychiatric illness." Psychological Medicine 8:245–253.
Pearlin, L., M. Lieberman, E. Menaghan, and J. Mullan
    1981   "The stress process." Journal of Health and Social Behavior 22:337–356.
Pearlin, L., and C. Schooler
    1978   The structure of coping. Journal of Health and Social Behavior 19:2–21.
Petersen, A., and S. Kellam
    1977   "Measurement of the psychological well-being of adolescents: The psychometric properties and assessment procedures of the How I Feel." Journal of Youth and Adolescence 6:229–247.
Pinneau, S. R., Jr.
    1975   "Effects of social support on psychological and physiological stress. Unpublished Ph.D. dissertation, University of Michigan.
Radloff, L. S.
    1977   "The CES-D Scale: A self-report depression scale for research in the general population." Applied Psychological Measurement 1:385–401.
Raphael, B.
    1977   "Preventive intervention with the recently bereaved." Archives of General Psychiatry 34:1450–1454.
Ratcliffe, H. L., and M. T. I. Cronin
    1958   "Changing frequency of arteriosclerosis in mammals and birds at the Philadelphia Zoological Garden." Circulation 18:41–52.
Rotter, J. B.
    1966   "Generalized expectancies for interal vs. external control of reinforcement." Psychological Monographs 80:1–28.
Ryan, W.
    1967   "Preventive services in the social context: Power, pathology, and prevention." Pp. 9–30 in Proceedings of a Mental Health Institute (Salt Lake City). Boulder, Colo.: Western Interstate Commission for Higher Education.
Sainsbury, P.
    1956   Suicide in London. New York: Basic Books.
Schaefer, E. S., and R. Q. Bell
    1958   "Development of Parental Attitude Research Instrument." Child Development 29:339–361.

Schaefer, C., J. C. Coyne, and R. S. Lazarus
    1981   "The health-related functions of social support." Journal of Behavioral
            Medicine 4:381–406.
Silberfeld, M.
    1978   "Psychological symptoms and social supports." Social Psychiatry
            13:11–17.
Smith, M. B.
    1968   "Competence and socialization." Pp. 270–320 in J. A. Clausen (ed.), Social-
            ization and Society. Boston: Little, Brown.
Sokolovsky, J., J. Cohen, D. Berger, and J. Geiger
    1978   "Personal networks of ex-mental patients in a Manhattan SRO hotel."
            Human Organization 37:5–15.
Spitz, R. A.
    1946   "Anaclitic depression: An inquiry into the genesis of psychiatric condi-
            tions in early childhood II." Psychoanalytic Study of the Child 2:313–342.
Syme, S. L., and L. F. Berkman
    1976   "Social class, susceptibility and sickness." American Journal of Epidemiol-
            ogy 104:1–8.
Thoits, P. A.
    1982   "Conceptual, methodological, and theoretical problems in studying social
            support as a buffer against life stress." Journal of Health and Social Behav-
            ior 23:145–158.
Thomas, W. I., and D. S. Thomas
    1928   The Child in America: Behavior Problems and Programs. New York: Knopf.
Tolsdorf, C. C.
    1976   "Social networks, support and coping: An exploratory study." Family Pro-
            cess 15:407–418.
Turner, R. J.
    1972   "The epidemiological study of schizophrenia: A current appraisal." Journal
            of Health and Social Behavior 13:360–369.
Turner, R. J.
    1981   "Experienced social support as a contingency in emotional well-being."
            Journal of Health and Social Behavior 22:357–367.
Turner, R. J., and Associates.
    1982   The Family Volunteer Study. Final Report for the Ministry of Community
            and Social Services. Unpublished.
Turner, R. J., L. Dopkeen, and G. Labreche
    1970   "Marital status and schizophrenia: A study of incidence and outcome."
            Journal of Abnormal Psychology 76:110–116.
Turner, R. J., B. G. Frankel, and D. Levin
    Forth- "Social support: Conceptualization, measurement and implications for
    coming mental health." In J. R. Greenley (ed.), Research in Community and Mental
            Health. Volume III. Greenwich, Conn.: JAI Press.
Turner, R. J., and J. W. Gartrell
    1978   "Social factors in psychiatric outcome: Toward the resolution of interpre-
            tive controversies." American Sociological Review 43:368–382.
Turner, R. J., and S. Noh
    1982   "Social support, life events and psychological distress: A three wave panel
            analysis." Paper presented at the annual meeting of the American So-
            ciological Association, San Francisco.

Turner, R. J., and S. Noh
   1983   "Class and psychological vulnerability among women: The significance of
            social support and personal control." Journal of Health and Social Behavior
            24:2–15.
Turner, R. J., and M. O. Wagenfeld
   1967   "Occupational mobility and schizophrenia: An assessment of the social
            causation and social selection hypothesis." American Sociological Review
            32:104–113.
Wagenfeld, M. O., R. J. Turner, and G. P. Labreche
   1967   "Social relations and community tenure in schizophrenia." Archives of
            General Psychiatry 17:428–434.
Walker, K. N., A. MacBride, and M. L. S. Vachon
   1977   "Social support networks and the crisis of bereavement." Social Science
            and Medicine 11:35–41.
Weisman, A. D., and J. W. Worden
   1975   "Psychosocial analysis of cancer deaths." Omega 6:61–75.
Weiss, R.
   1974   "The provisions of social relationships." Pp. 17–26 in Z. Rubin (ed.), Doing
            unto Others. Englewood Cliffs, N.J.: Prentice-Hall.
Wellman, B.
   1981   "Applying network analysis to the study of support." Pp. 171–200 in B. H.
            Gottlieb (ed.), Social Networks and Social Support. Beverly Hills, Calif.:
            Sage.
Wellons, R. V., R. D. Caplan, R. Van Harrison, and J. R. P. French, Jr.
   1979   "Effects of social support on adherence to therapeutic regimens." Preven-
            tive Medicine 8:248. Abstract.
Williams, A. W., J. E. Ware, and C. A. Donald
   1981   "A model of mental health life events, and social supports applicable to
            general populations." Journal of Health and Social Behavior 22:324–336.
Zahn, M. A.
   1973   "Incapacity, impotence and invisible impairment: Their effects upon inter-
            personal relations." Journal of Health and Social Behavior 14:115–123.

Individual Coping Efforts: Moderators of the Relationship between Life Stress and Mental Health Outcomes*

ELIZABETH G. MENAGHAN

INTRODUCTION

Whether stressors are conceptualized in terms of life events or chronic role problems, coping efforts have been posited as key intervening variables in the relationship between life stress and life outcomes. Yet empirical investigation of coping variables has lagged behind these theoretical claims. The general question considered here is how and under what conditions various types of coping variables are effective in modifying the linkage between stress and outcomes. The chapter focuses on three aspects of this question: conceptual issues, determinants of coping usage, and evidence for coping effectiveness.

*Preparation of this manuscript was assisted by a research grant from the Graduate School of The Ohio State University. Portions of this paper have been adapted from an article that considered the implications of coping research for the field of family studies (Menaghan, 1983c).

CONCEPTUAL ISSUES

If we hope to discover how coping mediates between life stress and outcomes, we must initially specify what we mean by these terms.

Stress

Although some research clings to the early homeostatic models of Selye (1956) and considers all demand for change as stressing, accumulating research using both physiological and psychological outcome measures (e.g., Pearlin and Lieberman, 1979) suggests that change per se may be neither necessary nor sufficient for the experience of stress. Rather, stress occurs to the extent that there is some mismatch—actual or perceived—between the person and his or her environment: Environmental demands tax or exceed the adaptive capacities or resources of the person, and/or environmental opportunities constrain the satisfaction of individual needs (Fletcher and Payne, 1980; Lazarus, 1981; Stagner, 1981).

Consensus at this abstract level, of course, does not imply agreement about the optimal categorization of either environmental presses or individual capacities. Other pivotal questions are whether to focus on "objective" versus "perceived" mismatch, and thus whether to seek some objective measures of situational demands or to utilize individuals' self-reports of life event or situation characteristics. As Rutter (1981:328) and others have remarked, physiological and psychological responses to "presumed stressors" show marked individual differences that seem to be linked to how people perceive events and how they respond emotionally to situations. Similarly, Lazarus (1981) has restricted his definition of psychological stress to demands that exceed resources *as cognitively appraised by the person.* Of course, such measures necessarily combine, in unknown proportions, both initial perceptions of stressfulness and filtering appraisals that have already begun to try to reduce stress. Finally, conceptions of stress may emphasize discrete life events that introduce change to individual lives, or they may focus instead on less bounded, more chronic and socially structured sources of possible stress, especially those that cling to the normative adult social positions of spouse, parent, and worker. Although much of the last-mentioned research has focused on problems within a given social role (e.g., Menaghan 1982b; Needle *et al.*, 1981; Pearlin *et al.*, 1981), a few studies have explored the intersection of role demands and opportunities from several social roles, such as the possible conflicts between occupational and family roles (e.g., Hall, 1972; Harrison and Minor, 1978). In this chapter, the emphasis is on perceived mismatch between environment and self because this is what most studies have measured and what most notions of coping have assumed.

Coping

Like the concept of stress, *coping* has been used as an umbrella term encompassing a wide range of variables. It seems useful at the outset at least to distinguish three broad categories of coping variables: coping resources, coping styles, and coping efforts.

Resources are generalized attitudes and skills that are considered advantageous across many situations; they include attitudes about self (esteem, ego strength), attitudes about the world (sense of coherence, belief in mastery), intellectual skills (cognitive flexibility and complexity, analytic abilities, knowledge), and interpersonal skills (communication skills, competence and ease in interpersonal interaction). *Coping styles* are generalized coping strategies, defined as typical, habitual preferences for ways of approaching problems: for example a tendency to withdraw from rather than move toward people, to deny rather than ruminate over difficulty, to be active rather than reactive, or to blame others rather than oneself. Such coping-style typologies, by definition, assume some cross-situational, relatively stable problem-solving tendencies in individuals. *Coping efforts* are specific actions (covert or overt) taken in specific situations that are intended to reduce a given problem or stress (e.g., appraise the problem, express or inhibit emotions, begin a new activity, ask for help, or refuse to think about it). Situational specificity, of course, can vary in degree; studies may examine strategies specific to a single role or relationship (Pearlin and Schooler, 1978), a single event such as reaction to an exam (Morris and Engle, 1981) or a reprimand at work (Andrews et al., 1978), or recurrent experiences, such as a spouse's business trips (Boss et al., 1979).

Outcomes

Within each of these very broad divisions there are multiple candidates for inclusion and multiple ways of categorizing such candidates. In part what is considered coping depends on the criteria used for judging its effectiveness: to cope is to manage a stress successfully, and coping responses ought to show some evidence of effectiveness. Assessments of coping effectiveness have used a wide array of possible outcome criteria; the three most common indicators in the studies reviewed here are perceived helpfulness, reduction in emotional distress, and reduction in problem level.

Studies (e.g., Berman and Turk, 1981; McCubbin et al., 1976) focusing on perceived helpfulness—respondents' claims that this or that strategy was helpful to them in some way—are difficult to interpret because such testimonies stand in an uncertain relationship to actual effects. For example, Videka (1979) found that participants in Mended Hearts self-help groups considered their participation very helpful, but they could generally not be distinguished from similar nonparticipating heart surgery patients on a wide variety of social and psychological measures. Averill (1973) similarly reported essential independence in laboratory stress studies between what respondents asserted was helpful and what improved their actual physiological or self-reported response. For example, most respondents preferred self-administration of shocks to other-administration and preferred having information about shock timing to not having such information; but these conditions did not reduce negative response, at least in the studies Averill has reviewed.

Studies that attempt some measure of effectiveness less subjective than perceived helpfulness, such as the reduction of feelings of distress or depressive affect (e.g., Pearlin and Schooler, 1978), still do not capture the implied expectation that coping might actually reduce problems or lead to some optimal solution.

The few studies that have looked at problem reduction over time (e.g., Menaghan, 1982b, 1983b) as well as at reduction in ongoing feelings of distress, or that have contrasted effects on a target individual with effects on involved others (such as spouses and children), suggest that the effectiveness of the same coping resource, style, or effort may vary dramatically depending on one's choice of indicator. For example, Stern and Pascale (1979) found that heart attack patients who denied the seriousness of their illness were overtly less anxious and depressed and more likely to resume their role responsibilities, but their wives were more prone to depression. Similarly, the same response positively associated with short-term well-being (e.g., maintaining hope that a missing-in-action husband will be found) may be negatively associated with well-being if it persists years afterward (Boss, 1980). Thus conclusions about the effectiveness of coping may vary depending on the choice of outcome criteria and the time frame in which effects are examined.

Such specificity of findings has led some researchers to question the entire effort to identify generally effective coping variables. For example, Barofsky argued that what is adaptive varies by domain, situation, time period, and measurement choices, and concluded that "the core question raised by the study of coping ('Is some behavior or thought adaptive?') may not be completely answerable" (1981:6). Turk (1979), discussing adaptation to chronic illness, spoke of adaptation processes specific to each illness, and argued that we must specify the adaptive tasks posed by each illness and the range of response options available for task accomplishment. Similarly, Hackman (1970) argued that until we have some classificatory system for describing task demands, we will be unable to assess how well a person's coping strategy is working. And Hirsch (1981) sees the task of coping researchers as identifying specific criteria of social adaptation for particular subgroups and using these criteria to specify particular coping objectives, adaptive tasks, and useful strategies and resources. For example, he argues that the coping objective for mature women attending college is to develop a repertoire of satisfying social roles appropriate to their life circumstances; that is, to cultivate activities and relationships outside the family sphere (which has presumably been the base of their role identity up to this point). For people with these objectives, Hirsch identifies such diverse resources as values (do they value independence from their families?), behavior setting (does it foster friendship development?), and cultural movements (is there support for women's participation in nonfamily activities?). Clearly, these are not generally adaptive resources, but ones that may aid adaptation for certain people in certain situations.

In contrast, others maintain that for all those in stress there is a finite number of general adaptive tasks that constitute general criteria for assessing effectiveness as well as for categorizing coping efforts. These tasks essentially flow from the notion of stress itself. We have defined stress as a mismatch or discrepancy between environmental demands and individual capacities, or between environmental opportunities and individual needs or goals. Efforts at stress reduction, then, must try to alter one of the two major elements involved—environmental demands or opportunities, and individual needs or goals—either by actually reducing demands or increasing capacities or by altering one's interpretation of either demands or capacities. These two approaches to problem resolution—direct action and interpretive appraisal—may occur simultaneously or sequentially.

At the same time, such mismatch can be an unpleasant, anxiety-arousing, and tension-producing experience, and efforts at problem resolution are probably ordinarily preceded by or accompanied by efforts to avoid being overwhelmed by negative affect. Haan (1977) has pointed out that there is a rather small and fairly exhaustive set of possible approaches here; she distinguishes three general approaches: expression or release, suppression or restraint, and diversion, substitution, or displacement. Again, it seems important to avoid the assumption that one either manages emotions or resolves problems; the temporal ordering and interrelationships among these approaches remain empirical questions.

Most of the coping variables studied thus far essentially fall into one of these three major groupings: direct action on environment or self; interpretive reappraisal regarding environment or self; or emotion management. For example, Haan (1977), discussing what individuals must do to cope with stress, argued one needs at minimum to (1) regulate affect (manage tension), (2) focus attention and interpretively simplify the problem, and (3) engage in cognitive-processing or problem-solving efforts. In their studies of wives, McCubbin and his colleagues (Boss et al., 1979; McCubbin et al., 1976) emphasized efforts to increase independence and resources, efforts to use the norms of some group to guide the subjects' own interpretations, and efforts at tension release.

Several authors have also stressed more long-range goals, essentially aimed less at the specific problem than at preserving or enhancing individuals' overall capacities and resources for future use. These resources involve a sense of self as competent and valuable, a sense of life as meaningful and coherent, and a sense of social integration. For example, Moos (1977) mentioned as general adaptive tasks the preservation of a satisfactory self-image, with a sense of competence and mastery, and the preservation of relationships with family and friends; McCubbin and his associates stressed efforts to develop or maintain interpersonal supports; Dimsdale (1979) emphasized maintaining self-worth and a sense of unity with the past and future; Benner, Roskies, and Lazarus (Benner et al., 1980) mentioned maintaining active, mutually responsive relationships; Folkman, Schaefer, and Lazarus (Folkman et al., 1979) stressed maintaining integrity and morale; and Kaplan (1975, 1980) argued that defensive interpretations, devaluation of particular groups and values, and participation in deviant behaviors may all be seen as efforts to maintain self-esteem.

In summary, stress may be defined as perceived mismatch between environment and self; coping embraces actions to reduce that mismatch (directly or by altering the interpretation of environment or self), to avoid or manage associated emotional distress, and to maintain or enhance the overall sense of self. Key outcomes, then, are reduction in presenting problems, avoidance of distress, and maintenance of sense of self.

DETERMINANTS OF COPING USAGE

At a very general level, individual characteristics and material resources have been linked theoretically to the psychosocial resources individuals are likely to possess. These in turn may influence generalized coping styles or dispositions. Both the situation one faces and one's general style may in turn shape one's appraisal of the situation and choice of specific coping efforts. Key questions here involve the extent to which research has thus far identified linkages between individual characteristics, situational properties, coping resources, and coping styles on the one hand, and specific coping efforts on the other. Also involved is the extent of support for the assumed linkages among coping resources, styles, and efforts.

Demographic Correlates

Coping Resources

The predictors of such coping resources as self-esteem, mastery, coherence, and analytic and interpersonal skills have generally stressed socioeconomic and demographic variables. For example, George noted that more education "appears to foster a cognitive complexity that facilitates realistic stress perception and problem-solving skills" (1980:27). Shanan (Shanan *et al.*, 1976) also found more education related to more positive self-perceptions and a greater readiness to deal with complexity and novelty. And Kohn and his associates (Kohn and Schooler, 1978; Miller *et al.*, 1979) found that more education and more autonomous occupations seem to increase intellectual flexibility for both men and women.

Worden and Sobel (1978) reported that socioeconomic status was positively related to greater ego strength among their sample of cancer patients, and in the Pearlin data (Pearlin *et al.*, 1981; Pearlin and Schooler, 1978), being male, currently married, better educated, and having a higher income were associated with higher self-esteem and a greater sense of personal mastery. Kessler and Cleary, in an effort to explain the frequently observed association between socioeconomic status and symptom-screening scales, reported that the upwardly mobile are less affected by undesirable life events, and suggested that they have "the sort of personal characteristics—feelings of self-esteem, confidence, perseverance—that are the stuff of competent problem management" (1980:472). As Vanfossen, Spitzer, and Jones (Vanfossen et al., 1981) pointed out, however, Kessler and Cleary did not directly measure these coping resources and so could not establish that these resources do vary by social class or mobility experience. Eron and Peterson (1982) reviewed literature suggesting that low socioeconomic origins in childhood are associated with a poorer learning environment for acquiring coping resources, resulting in deficits in cognitive development and language skills.

Coping Styles and Efforts

In research on more specific coping variables, Kandel (1980) has reported sex differences in the substances used for emotion management, with men more likely to report using alcohol to cope with life crises and women more likely to use prescribed psychoactive drugs. There also seem to be life-course differences in the tendency to turn toward such substances: use of both legal and illegal substances appears to peak at ages 18–21 and decline thereafter.

Studies of parallel coping efforts in the specific roles of marriage, parenting, and work yield some insight into the role specificity of linkages between demographic variables and coping efforts (Menaghan, 1982a, 1983a, 1983b). In all three roles, questions were asked about four similar approaches: optimistic comparisons, selective inattention, restricted expectations, and direct action. Optimistic comparisons is essentially an interpretive appraisal strategy, in which the individual uses comparative frames of reference—with others and with one's own past and future—in such a way that one's own situation is judged in a positive light. Selective inattention involves attempting to focus on positive attributes of a situation and trying to minimize the importance of more negative aspects. Individual items include such statements as "tell yourself the difficulties are not important," "remind yourself that for everything bad there is also something good," and "tell yourself that something in your children's behavior is not really important." Restricted expectations involves a passive resignation to the inevitability of problems and a lowering of expectations for problem resolution in that role. In occupational life, it includes such statements as "I really don't expect to get much pleasure out of work" and "I can put up with a lot on my job as long as the pay is good." In parenting one agrees that "the way my children are turning out depends on their inner nature and there is very little I can do about it," and in marriage one decides to "just keep hurt feelings to yourself" and "keep out of your husband's/wife's way for a while." Direct action approaches all involve efforts to alter the situation, generally by influencing the behavior of the relevant role complements. In occupation, one "takes some action to get rid of the difficulties in your work situation" and "talks to others to find a solution." In marriage, one "sits down and talks things out" and "tries to find a fair compromise." In parenting, one "scolds," "threatens some kind of punishment," or "takes away a privilege."

In each role area, the use of specific coping efforts was predicted in a multiple regression equation including the initial level of role problems reported and key demographic and contextual variables. There were few role-invariant predictors for parallel efforts. For example, gender differences were found for 5 of the 12 efforts: women were more apt than men to use optimistic comparisons in parenting but not in work or marriage, more apt to use selective inattention in work and marriage but not in parenting, less apt to restrict their expectations at work but not in marriage or parenting, and more apt to attempt direct negotiations in marriage but not in work or parenting. Socio economic status (SES) affected all four occupational efforts: Those of higher status made more optimistic comparisons, were more apt to try direct action, and less often used selective inattention and restricted expectations. However, except for higher-SES parents being somewhat less likely to make positive comparisons, SES was unrelated to coping choices in other role areas.

At least from these studies, then, location in the social structure, as indicated by gender, education, and SES, seems to be more reliably linked to such broadly defined psychosocial coping resources as self-esteem and mastery than to specific coping efforts.

Situational Correlates

A major predictor of more specific coping efforts is the problem being faced. For example, Coyne, Aldwin, and Lazarus (Coyne et al., 1981) asked respondents to appraise their situations as one that could be changed, one that must be accepted or gotten used to, one that they needed to know more about, or one in which they had to refrain from doing what they wanted. Respondents engaged in more problem-focused coping in situations they thought could be changed, and were more apt to try interpretive reappraisals to minimize threat for situations that seemed to require acceptance.

Using the same data from repeated measurements of a sample of 100 white, middle-aged, nonpoor respondents, Folkman and Lazarus (1980) divided usage or nonusage of the 68 coping efforts queried about into those indicating a predominant focus on problem-resolving efforts and emotion-management efforts. They reported that situations in which more information was needed also generated higher levels of problem-focused coping. There were some differences in coping usage by the kind of problem (occupational, family, or health-related) respondents faced, with health problems marked by less frequent problem-solving efforts and more frequent emotion-focused efforts, family problems eliciting a moderate amount of both sorts of coping, and work-related problems characterized by more frequent problem-solving efforts and less frequent emotion-focused efforts. Across all the episodes reported by their 100 respondents, problem-focused coping and emotion-focused coping were not alternative or mutually exclusive; they report an approximate correlation coefficient of .44.

Within a given role area, the *severity* of problems exerts a strong influence on coping usage (Menaghan, 1982a, 1983a, 1983b). For the four types of coping efforts described earlier (optimistic comparisons, selective inattention, restricted expectations, and direct action), 9 of the 12 regression coefficients for problem level were significant. Greater marital problems were associated with lower use of optimistic comparisons, more selective inattention, more restriction of expectations, and less direct action through negotiations. Greater parental problems were also associated with lower use of optimistic comparisons and more selective inattention, but they were accompanied by more direct action efforts. The difference here may reflect the particular direct action effort assessed in parenting, which is essentially a coercive, punitive disciplinary approach rather than the compromise–negotiation efforts assessed in marriage. Greater occupational problems were also associated with more selective inattention and more restriction of expectations, but they did not influence the usage of optimistic comparisons or of direct actions. Thus, the general pattern of findings suggests that more severe problems make optimistic comparison and direct action through compromise or discussion less likely, and increase the usage of selective inattention and restriction of expectations.

Other aspects of a situation beyond the sheer level of difficulty also influenced coping choices in these studies. Holding level of difficulty constant, those married longer engaged in more selective inattention, for example (Menaghan, 1982a). Family composition (ages and number of children) influenced parental coping efforts; disciplinary action increased and optimistic comparisons decreased as the number of children increased and their average age decreased. The older the average age of children, the more likely parents also were to restrict their expectations in that role (Menaghan, 1982b). In contrast, family composition variables had little impact on coping responses to marital and occupational problems; marital variables similarly had little impact on coping choices in nonmarital roles (Menaghan, 1983a, 1983b). And as reported earlier, SES, largely reflecting rank of occupation, influenced all four occupational variables but made little difference for coping with marital or parental problems. Thus, the impact of such contextual variables seems to reflect variations in the kinds of problems faced in particular roles, and presumably in the kinds of coping approaches intuitively judged as appropriate to that kind of problem. Their predictive power does not generalize across roles, at least not in these data.

Linkages among Resources, Styles, and Efforts

In labeling attitudes about self, analytic and interpersonal skills, and views of the world as coping resources, we make the assumption that they in fact shape more problem-focused coping styles and efforts. How well does empirical research support this claim? Worden and Sobel's (1978) study did indicate that a general measure of ego strength is associated with coping styles: Those with higher ego strength tended more toward problem redefinition and less toward emotion suppression, externalization of blame, and fatalistic acceptance of problems. Tyler (1978), in presenting a model of "the competent self," argued that favorable self-attitudes, a sense of self-efficacy, and optimistic trust in the world are accompanied by an "implementing and fulfilling set of behavioral attributes"; these include an active, planful orientation, high initiative, realistic goalsetting, and substantial forbearance and effort in goal attainment. His measure of such behavioral attributes was moderately correlated with Rotter's locus-of-control scale, with the more internally oriented college and high-school students studied also having a more active, planful coping style.

Resources have also been linked to more specific coping efforts. Pearlin, Lieberman, Menaghan, and Mullan (Pearlin et al., 1981) reported that individuals with higher self-esteem and a more internal sense of mastery used more optimistic comparisons and more devaluation of monetary success in dealing with economic problems. In the role areas of marriage, parenting, and occupational life, zero-order correlations consistently suggested that higher self-esteem and a more internal sense of mastery were associated with more optimistic comparisons, less use of selective inattention, and less use of restricted expectations. They were associated with more direct action efforts except in the parental area; here, those with higher self-esteem and mastery were less likely to use the punitive disciplinary approaches that constituted action in this area (see Table 4.1). Thus, broad attitudes did have consistent linkages with specific coping efforts.

Attempts to ascertain linkages between such psychosocial resources and coping styles, and between styles and efforts, have been hampered by methodological and theoretical problems in the measurement of coping styles. Although many writers agree with Kaplan (1975) that we should distinguish between the use of more or less effective response patterns in a given situation and the predisposition to employ such defenses in general circumstances, others (e.g., Folkman and Lazarus,

TABLE 4.1

Linkages among Coping Resources and Coping Efforts: Chicago Panel Data[a]

Coping effort	(1) Zero-order correlations with coping resources		(2) Zero-order inter- correlations[b]			(3) Residual inter- correlations[b]		
	Self-esteem	Mastery	M	P	O	M	P	O
Optimistic comparisons								
Marital	.20	.24	1.00			1.00		
Parental	.09	.09	.19	1.00		.08	1.00	
Occupational	.07	.14	.21	.08	1.00	.18	.01	1.00
Selective inattention								
Marital	−.15	−.28	1.00			1.00		
Parental	−.08	−.21	.29	1.00		.15	1.00	
Occupational	−.12	−.14	.27	.04	1.00	.07	.09	1.00
Restricted expectations								
Marital	−.18	−.23	1.00			1.00		
Parental	−.16	−.28	.11	1.00		.05	1.00	
Occupational	−.23	−.28	.04	.18	1.00	−.05	.13	1.00
Direct action								
Marital	.16	.23	1.00			1.00		
Parental	−.10	.01	.02	1.00		.01	1.00	
Occupational	.22	.28	.20	.04	1.00	.12	.13	1.00

[a]All correlations shown are based on the role-specific samples used in regression equations predicting coping usage and effectiveness; n for marriage is approximately 755, for parenting 410, and for occupation 495. For specific sample restrictions for the three roles see Menaghan, 1982a, 1983a, 1983b.

[b]M, marital, P, parental, O, occupational.

1980) either doubt the existence of such stable role-invariant dispositions or doubt their linkage with specific coping efforts. Regarding the latter, Epstein argued convincingly that much of the failure to link behavioral disposition measures with behavior in specific situations is an artifact of the unreliability and instability of the single-item behavior measures used. He argued that specific behaviors must be "sampled over an appropriate level of generality and averaged over a sufficient number of occurrences" (1979:1121), and presented evidence that averaging over a number of reports (for example, behavior checklists repeated daily for 14 days) produces behavior measures that are highly related to similarly averaged self-report measures of behavioral dispositions. However, Epstein was not assessing coping variables per se in his argument or data.

Vickers and Hervig (1981), reviewing extant measures of coping styles (Gleser and Ihilevich's (1969) Defense Mechanisms Inventory, Joffe and Naditch's (1977) coping–defense scales derived from the California Personality Inventory, and Schultz's (1967) Coping Operations Preference Enquiry), identified problems with all of them. Measures of the "same" defense across scales showed little convergence, and measures of "different" styles showed high (up to .88) correlations, even within the same research instrument. As noted earlier, some researchers (e.g., Vaillant, 1976) measure styles by summing up respondents' coping responses to specific problems, thus making assessments of how well style predicts specific efforts impossible.

An indirect but suggestive approach exploring the existence of relatively problem-invariant coping styles is to explore the associations among role-specific coping efforts that are parallel in content. Table 4.1 shows the pattern of association across marital, parental, and occupational roles of the four coping efforts—optimistic comparisons, selective inattention, restricted expectations, and direct action—in the Chicago panel data. Zero-order correlations among similar measures are shown in the second panel of information. Although all of the associations are in the expected direction, their magnitude is low. Marital and occupational coping seems most similar, with the use of optimistic comparisons, selective inattention, and direct action being positively associated at an r of about .20. Marital and parental coping choices also show some overlap, especially in the use of optimistic comparisons (r = .19) and selective inattention (r = .29). Occupational and parental coping efforts show little patterning, except for a weak (r = .18) association in use of restricted expectations. The pattern of interrole correlations for direct action—little association between parental direct action and direct action in either of the other two roles—suggests that

the punitive efforts involved in parental action differ from the negotiation efforts assessed in marriage and occupation, a conclusion also
suggested by the different association of parental direct action with the
coping resources.

It could be argued that such zero-order correlations probably under-
estimate the extent of similarity in coping choices. Coping efforts are
also responsive to the severity of the problem being faced and to such
contextual variables as family composition in parenting and occupational type in work; thus it could also be argued that if such zero-order
effects were controlled greater similarity in coping choices might be
uncovered, and one would be more justified in positing the influence of
some relatively stable and relatively role-invariant coping predispositions or styles.

One way to assess this possibility is to calculate the residual values
for each coping variable from their predictive equations. Thus, for each
person the deviation of his or her response from the value predictable
from the severity of problems, the situational context, and that person's
demographic characteristics are obtained. For example, our set of residual scores in marriage reflect the variation in use of optimistic comparisons that is not explained by variation in problem level, marital
duration and family composition, gender, or SES. In parenting, we
assess residual variation net of that attributable to parental problem
level, marital situation and family composition, gender, and SES, and
in occupation we assess residual variation net of that explained by
occupational problem level, full- or part-time work status, marital status, family composition, age, gender, and SES. The intercorrelation of
such residuals, then, reflects a provisional estimation of the extent to
which the variation in coping efforts not explained by demographic
and situational factors shows some intrapersonal consistency across
roles.

Table 4.1 displays these residual intercorrelations in the third panel.
As comparison with the second panel makes clear, this procedure generally results in slightly weaker interrole correlations; the average correlation is about .08, compared with an average zero-order correlation
of about .13. Further, the pattern of intercorrelations does not suggest
any single pair of roles for which there is greater average overlap, or any
single kind of coping effort for which interrole associations are even
moderate. At least from these data, then, there is greater support for the
role specificity of coping efforts than for the operation of some generalized coping styles across role areas.

Although there are associations between coping resources and
efforts, then, there are so far few empirically based linkages between

resources and styles or between styles and efforts. The evidence that does exist for all of these linkages is cross-sectional, and certainly does not establish the direction of association. Yet they are at least consistent with expected relationships.

Some researchers (e.g., Shalit, 1977) have suggested that the linkages among generalized resources, styles, and specific efforts may be particularly strong in ambiguous situations, where the problem itself does not powerfully press for particular responses. Similarly, Klein and Hill (1979) argued that in the face of uncertainty the best predictor of a family's initial attempts to solve a problem may be its established interaction preferences. Reiss (1981) also argued that the task he presented to families was intentionally ambiguous in order to elicit problem-solving efforts flowing from a family's conception of itself and its social world rather than from the demand properties of the task itself. In contrast, Folkman *et al.* (1979) argued that ambiguity itself has certain demand properties: it inordinately encourages avoidance, denial, and defensive distortion of threatening information. Thus far, the direction and extent of influence of such other characteristics of problems as ambiguity, expectedness, or felt responsibility are matters of assertion rather than evidence.

THE EFFECTIVENESS OF COPING

Whether coping is assessed at the level of resources, styles, or efforts, a critical question is how effective such variables really are in enhancing outcomes when stress occurs. As argued in the section "Conceptual Issues," three key criteria for effectiveness are reductions in emotional distress or upheaval, resolution of or reduction in problems, and maintenance of a sense of self as worthwhile and potent.

Maturity versus Effectiveness

Especially at the level of coping styles, however, some researchers prefer to use more intrinsic criteria to evaluate coping. For example, Andrews *et al.* (1978) and Frydman (1981) followed Vaillant (1976) in ranking coping styles as more or less mature and deriving an overall maturity of coping style score from specific responses to specific situations, or from endorsements of various responses to hypothetical vignettes. These theorists implicitly or explicitly questioned the use of empirical assessments of effectiveness to judge the adequacy of coping. Even if efforts or styles fail to overcome particular problems, they argued, some styles are preferable to others because they are intrinsically better or more mature approaches.

Several criteria underlie such judgments about the relative maturity of particular coping styles or efforts. Vaillant (1976) derived his hierarchizing in part from age trends in relative usage. The use of immature styles (acting out, denial through fantasy) decreased from late adolescence to middle age, and the use of mature styles (sublimation, altruism, anticipation, and suppression) increased. (Several of the intermediate approaches, notably intellectualization, accounted for a fairly constant proportion of responses over time.) Antonovsky (1979) stressed three intrinsic critieria: (1) rationality, including the accuracy and objectivity with which one appraises one's situation; (2) flexibility, defined as the extent to which one creates contingent plans and tactics and is willing to consider implementing them; and (3) farsightedness, the extent to which one anticipates the long-range as well as immediate responses to actions one is envisaging. Buehler and Hogan (1980) similarly prefer long-range over short-range orientations and comprehensive over piecemeal approaches to problems.

Haan (1977) offered the most detailed and multifaceted set of criteria for maturity in her categorization of ego processes as reflecting either an adaptive or maladaptive mode. Adaptive coping must be characterized by relative freedom from reality distortion, flexibility, and future orientation; it is also more complex, allows for some gratification of impulses, and permits some expression of affect. In her later writing she stressed in particular the first criterion, arguing that "unrestricted, undistorted communication with the self, others, and the world is the unacknowledged core value of psychoanalysis" (Haan, 1981:161). It is also seen as the critical criterion for coping: "The core value of coping, as we commonly use the word, is being accurate about one's self to one's self (self-insight in psychoanalytic theory), [and] about others to one's self, (Habermas', Piaget's, and Swanson's intersubjective integrity). . . . The scientific ethic also rests on this notion of intersubjective accuracy" (1981:161–162)

Others have vigorously disagreed, pointing to theoretical and empirical support for the usefulness of, for example, less rational and more distorted assessments that minimize the seriousness of one's situation. Hansen and Johnson (1979:588) argued that misperceptions may make it easier to cope with problems, in part through fostering illusions of competence or control, and Rosenstiel and Roth (1981) found denial associated with better outcomes.

Haan cited Frenkel-Brunswick in her own arguments: "There are richer and poorer, more efficient and less efficient orientations or ways of dealing with reality, and as scientists we are not entitled to obscure or circumvent this fact" (1954:468). If these are not just intrinsically preferable but also more efficient orientations, however, then it does not seem inappropriate to assess empirically the relative effectiveness of more and less mature coping approaches. Among the studies that have done so, Frydman (1981) examined the psychological distress of parents with a child suffering from either leukemia or cystic fibrosis and reported that greater overall maturity of coping styles was associated with lower distress in one group but not the other. Andrews et al. (1978) reported that a similar score was related to lower psychiatric impairment in a community sample. And Vaillant (1976) reported the most sweeping claims for effectiveness: His overall score correlated with better career progress, greater marital enjoyment, better interpersonal and psychological functioning, and greater subjective happiness.

Unfortunately, such correlations between coping patterns and various outcomes do not directly address the question of how such coping may intervene in the relationship between stress and outcomes. These studies do not measure the stress individuals are facing, so we do not know whether, given equivalent stress, persons with more mature coping styles will show better outcomes. The same problem recurs in studies of coping resources and efforts, which limits our knowledge of effectiveness.

Perceived Helpfulness versus Effectiveness

Other studies confound the usage of particular coping variables with their effectiveness and/or equate perceived helpfulness with effectiveness.

For example, helpfulness ratings characterize a series of small-sample studies carried out by McCubbin and a variety of collaborators (Boss et al., 1979; Maynard et al., 1980; McCubbin, 1979; McCubbin et al., 1976). All used wives as respondents, and explored the impact on them of various aspects of their husbands' work lives; all assessed coping with measures that asked the wives to rate how helpful (not at all, minimally, or very) they found each of several possible coping behaviors to be to them, rather than how often they performed such actions.

Unfortunately, when what people do and what they consider helpful are assessed separately, the two are not necessarily identical. Horowitz

(1978) illustrated this quite nicely. Presenting respondents with 33 possible responses to life events he asked them first to identify which they utilized, and of those to identify those that were very helpful. There were large variations: for example, in a sample of people facing bereavement, 46% tried to find new interests and 69% tried to look at their situation as realistically as possible, but not a single respondent thought either of these very helpful. The exact figures, of course, are less important than the general lack of association between perceived helpfulness and reported usage.

Part of the problem is the ambiguity involved in a rating of "not helpful." Were strategies judged less helpful tried and found wanting, avoided because they were judged unlikely to be helpful, or used extensively despite their perceived ineffectiveness? Thus, with no separate measure of usage the relationship between patterns used and either perceived helpfulness or observed effectiveness cannot be ascertained.

Such data may, however, suggest how perceived helpfulness ratings compare with other outcome measures. For example, Berman and Turk (1981) reported that respondents with lower life satisfaction and worse mood state considered engaging in social activities and trying to increase autonomy less helpful, and expressing their negative feelings more helpful, than did more positive respondents; considering home and family activities less helpful was an additional predictor of negative life satisfaction. In this case, however, as with the correlations between maturity of coping styles and measures of outcomes, the respondents studied (divorced parents) also varied in the problems they were facing, and such differences may have influenced both ratings of helpfulness and measures of mood state and life satisfaction. Without some control for problem level, the meaning of these associations between perceived helpfulness and mental health outcomes remains ambiguous.

McCubbin and his colleagues also reported some associations between measures of perceived helpfulness and other outcome variables selected to reflect the psychological functioning and role performance of the respondent wives and their children: Wives who perceived tension-management behaviors as more helpful reported more symptoms, wives who rated relying on religion and the past as helpful reported more role adjustment problems, and there was no relationship between children's difficulties and any of the perceived helpfulness measures. Once more, the confounding of usage and helpfulness and the absence of controls for level of problems make it difficult to evaluate such findings.

Evidence for Effectiveness

Coping Resources: Beliefs, Attitudes, and Skills

Evidence for the effectiveness of coping resources is rather limited and often indirect. For example, Linden and Feuerstein (1981) discussed the significance of social incompetence, which seems to be a mixture of inappropriate *behaviors* when in distressing social situations, increased *anxiety* when in those situations, and a pessimistic cognitive set or *belief* that one doesn't handle interpersonal encounters very well. They asserted that whether one measures behavioral skills, cognitive self-perceptions, or situational evaluations, essential hypertensives emerge as less socially competent than their normotensive peers. The implicit argument is that hypertension is a negative physiological outcome of inadequate coping resources.

There is also scattered support for the importance of interpersonal skills in accounting for variations in the amount of distress versus satisfaction experienced in major life roles. For example, Wampler and Sprenkle (1980), discussing marital improvement techniques, claimed that learning how to communicate in an "open" style—with high self-disclosure, high receptivity to partner's disclosure, and "speaking for self"—provides resources that will aid in the resolution of any interpersonal conflict. They also reviewed evidence that couples learning such skills do report greater marital satisfaction than couples not so trained. Once more, there is no direct measurement of the kind or severity of problems facing these couples, so that we cannot be certain that the groups are similar in perceived stress.

The most studied personal resource variables are measures of locus of control and sense of mastery. These are conceptualized as general orientations to the world. For example, Turk (1979) reported that a greater sense of personal mastery is related to better adjustment to illness; Johnson and Sarason (1979) argued that perceiving events as controllable is associated with less adverse outcomes; and Pearlin et al. (1981), in an analysis controlling for exposure to key life events and for level of problems, found that a greater sense of personal mastery predicts less depressive affect. (In the same analysis, greater self-esteem was also linked to less depressive affect.) In an earlier study using wave one of the same data, Pearlin and Schooler (1978) examined the effectiveness of self-esteem and personal mastery in reducing role-related distress in each of four—marital, parental, economic, and occupational—role areas. Controlling for the level of problems in that role, both self-esteem and mastery had significant independent effects on role distress in each area. Even after also controlling for a summary measure of role-specific coping efforts, these psychological resources exerted a significant direct impact on emotional distress.

It seems difficult to argue against notions that more positive and potent views of the self, more orderly conceptions of the world, better skills in information gathering and analysis, and greater interpersonal ease and skills are better than their opposites. Nevertheless, it is notable that demonstrations of their effectiveness, especially demonstrations also assessing level of stress rather than simply correlating resources with outcome measures, are relatively meager.

Coping Styles

Coping styles, like personal resources, are considered to be general and relatively stable qualities of individuals that they bring to situations, in contrast to more situationally variable coping efforts. In practice this distinction is hard to maintain, because some researchers reach their conclusions about general style by empirically generalizing across specific situations (Vaillant, 1976; Worden and Sobel, 1978). Others ask respondents to report their "usual" tendencies directly. Typically, the categories used reflect a psychoanalytic scheme of defense mechanisms such as denial, displacement, and suppression.

Once more, evidence for the effectiveness of such styles is not abundant. Worden and Sobel (1978) did link coping styles and emotional distress among cancer patients; emotional distress was inversely related to a tendency to redefine problems and positively related to tendencies to blame others, suppress emotions, and accept problems fatalistically. Stagner (1981) discussed near-zero correlations between life satisfaction and such coping styles as confrontation and displacement, and moderate inverse correlations for avoiding, enduring, and escaping. Again, of course, such correlations do not directly address the stress–coping–outcome question. Rosenstiel and Roth (1981), studying respondents who had in common the rather massive stressor of spinal-cord injury and subsequent paralysis, report that rationalization and denial were related to better subsequent life satisfaction, higher productivity, and greater maintenance of optimum physical health and functioning; extensive preoccupation and catastrophizing were negative predictors. And, as reviewed earlier in the section "Maturity versus Effectiveness," overall maturity measures of coping style have been shown by several researchers to be correlated with an assortment of positive outcomes.

Coping Efforts

Distress and Satisfaction Outcomes. There is a greater accumulation of knowledge about the effectiveness of specific coping efforts. For example, Rosenstiel and Roth also measures specific behaviors engaged in as their spinal-cord-injured respondents prepared to leave their rehabilitation unit and resume living in their communities. These were anticipatory problem solving (assessed by the number of concrete goals the person had set for the new situation and by the extent of means–end thinking about how to obtain those goals) and mental rehearsal (imagining how one would behave in the new situation). They report that having a greater number of concrete goals predicted better outcomes. (Turk, 1979, also linked greater short-to-moderate-range goal setting to better adjustment to illness.) Neither the extent of mental rehearsal nor the extent of means–end thinking, however, were related to their outcome measures.

Colletta and Gregg (1981) assessed efforts in the three categories of those modifying the situation (direct action), those modifying the meaning of the situation (interpretive appraisal), and those that manage stress-related tension and distress (emotion management). However, rather than assessing empirically the extent of covariation among these categories or their effects, they conceptualized a continuum of active coping on which both interpretive appraisal and stress management are low and only direct action is high. With self-esteem and available social supports held constant, this omnibus measure of active coping was related to lower emotional distress in their sample. They did not directly assess the level of stress or problems faced, but variation was probably reduced by restricting their sample to adolescent black women who had recently given birth.

Both Hall (1972) and Harrison and Minor (1978) examined the coping efforts of women in multiple roles. Both studies posited three possible coping approaches to dealing witb conflict among wife, mother, and work roles: (1) structural role redefinition through altering the role demands of others (essentially direct action on environmental demands), (2) personal role redefinitions through altering one's personal role conceptions even if no new understandings are reached with role senders (interpretive appraisal of environmental demands), and (3) reactive role behavior through accepting all role demands as unalterable and focusing attention on finding more efficient or more successful ways to meet the entire set of role demands (direct action on self). Neither study reported the extent to which such approaches were alternative or simultaneous strategies, although it was apparently assumed that they are alternatives. Harrison and Minor did note that the use of structural role redefinition varies by the particular role pair in conflict: It is highest for wife–worker conflict, less common for wife–mother conflict, and least common for conflicts between work and mothering. Hall reported that such structural redefinition tended to be associated with higher reported satisfaction with "the way you deal with the roles in your life," and the greater use of reactive role behavior was related to lower satisfaction. Harrison and Minor, on the other hand, reported no association between the use of particular strategies and women's satisfaction. In neither case was there any measure of the extent of role conflict being managed, however, so the meaning of the findings remains ambiguous.

In the first of the series of coping analyses using the Chicago-area sample, Pearlin and Schooler (1978) reported the impact of role-specific coping efforts on emotional distress. They assessed coping efforts separately in the four major role areas of occupation, economic life, marriage, and parenting, and classified the 19 coping factors as (1) action to alter the situation, (2) reinterpretation of the problem (e.g., selective ignoring, making optimistic comparisons), and (3) efforts to manage negative emotions (e.g., helpless resignation). They assessed the effectiveness of each factor in reducing role-related distress net of initial role problems and net of each of the others. Their findings are interesting in themselves and also relevant to the usage–helpfulness–effectiveness relationships: All of their items were initially culled from open-ended interviews concerning how people dealt with their role problems, but of the 19 strategies delineated, 8 (advice seeking in marriage and in parenting, selective ignoring in marriage and in parenting, passive forbearance in marriage, helpless resignation in parenthood, emotional discharge in marriage, and reliance on discipline in parenting) were related to *greater* role distress at any given level of strain. The *lesser* use of such efforts, along with the greater use of others (negotiation in marriage and optimistic comparisons in both marriage and parenting), predicted lower distress.

In a partial replication of this study, Needle, Griffin, and Svendsen (1981) assessed parallel occupational coping efforts (optimistic comparisons, selective ignoring, restriction of occupational expectation, and direct action) in a randomly selected sample of 937 Minnesota public-school teachers. They measured the level of occupational stress experienced in terms of the availability or unavailability of the work conditions each teacher judged most important to doing his or her job well, and statistically controlled for variations in occupational stress when assessing the effectiveness of coping efforts. Pearlin and Schooler had found both optimistic comparisons and restricted expectations related to lower role-related distress. Needle *et al.* reported that only optimistic comparisons were associated with better outcomes. In their case, positive outcome was indexed by greater general well-being and fewer somatic symptoms, rather than by role-related emotional distress.

Mastery and Self-esteem Outcomes. Whether particular coping efforts serve to maintain one's self-esteem, sense of coherence, or personal mastery has not yet been extensively studied. Kaplan (1975, 1980) has given the greatest systematic attention to self-esteem. He essentially posited a universal desire to maximize self-esteem, and he argued that this motive leads those who perceive themselves to be underesteemed by normal societal standards to turn to deviant forms of behavior and to adopt the normative standards of deviant reference groups in order to enhance their self-esteem. In his longitudinal study of adolescents, he reported a complex set of findings suggesting that the decision to adopt deviant behavior patterns, and the impact of such a decision on self-esteem, varies depending on the initial characteristics of the person and other variables. For example, deviance increased self-esteem among males when psychological defenses were weak but was associated with decreased self-esteem when defenses were strong. Kaplan also found that adolescents with lower self-esteem were more likely to experiment with deviant behavior patterns than were those with higher self-esteem.

Pearlin, Lieberman, Menaghan, and Mullan (Pearlin *et al.*, 1981) examined the impact of undesirable disruptions of occupational life (being fired, demoted, laid off, or forced to leave work because of illness) on one's self-esteem and mastery. Reasoning that such events exert their impact partly through impact on economic strain, they assessed the effectiveness of two economic coping efforts—optimistic comparisons and devaluation of economic success—in bolstering self-esteem and mastery. They found that such coping efforts are associated with a greater sense of self-esteem and mastery, even when one's levels of initial mastery and self-esteem, experience with job disruption, and initial and later economic strain are statistically controlled. Although economic coping efforts had no direct impact on depressive symptoms, they indirectly protect against depression through bolstering the resources of mastery and self-esteem: when respondents were statistically equated on initial and later problems, job disruption experience, and a variety of demographic variables, those with less negative change in self-esteem and mastery also reported fewer depressive symptoms.

Problem Reduction versus Distress Outcomes. A series of panel analyses of role-specific coping efforts (Menaghan, 1982b, 1983a, 1983b),
make it possible to compare the effectiveness of coping efforts by using
the two criteria of reduction in role-related distress and reduction in
reported role problems over time. The three analyses of marital, parental, and occupational coping efforts each conceptualized initial problem levels as partially determined by situational context variables such
as gender, SES, marital and parental statuses; the level of problems, as
well as the situational context, in turn influences the choice of coping
efforts. (The pattern of findings concerning coping choice has been
reported here in the section "Determinants of Coping Usage"). Such
coping efforts, as well as situational context and problem level, in turn
shape the extent of role-related distress. Over time, initial problem
levels, situational context, and experienced distress, along with coping
efforts, are expected to shape later problems.

Table 4.2 summarizes the pattern of results across the three role
areas, as indicated by the estimated regression coefficients of the coping efforts when entered into predictive equations with initial problem
level and relevant contextual variables. It is clear that the direct impact
of these coping efforts on later problem level is much less impressive
than their effectiveness in reducing role-related distress. Of course,
because lower distress at any given initial problem level is generally
associated with a decline in problem levels over time, there is some
indirect linkage between coping and problem reduction through its
effect on distress.

In every role area examined, optimistic comparisons—the use of
comparative temporal and interpersonal points of reference to achieve
a relatively positive view of one's own situation—is associated with
lower emotional distress. Only in marriage, however, does it directly
reduce later problems. Selective ignoring—the effort to minimize the
importance of problems and focus one's attention on the positive aspects of one's situation—seems neither an assert nor a liability in most
role areas; only in marriage does it have any significant impact. Notably, despite its apparent focus on achieving a more positive assessment
of one's situation, selective ignoring is actually associated with greater
marital distress rather than with less. Restriction of expectations is also
generally inversely related to distress, with such efforts linked to greater negative feelings in three of the four analyses. In no case, however,
does it have any direct impact on later problem level. Finally, direct
action in parenting is associated with increased distress; in other areas,
there is no strong impact on distress. The direct action of negotiation in

TABLE 4.2

The Effect of Role-Specific Coping Efforts on Role-Related Emotional Distress and Later Problem Level: Chicago Panel Data[a]

	Outcome measure	
Coping effort	Role distress	Subsequent problem level
Optimistic comparisons		
Marital	Reduction	Reduction
Parental: younger children	Reduction	n.s.
Parental: older children	Reduction	n.s.
Occupational	Reduction	n.s.
Selective inattention		
Marital	Increase	n.s.
Parental: younger children	n.s.	n.s.
Parental: older children	n.s.	n.s.
Occupational	n.s.	n.s.
Restricted expectations		
Marital	Increase	n.s.
Parental: younger children	n.s.	n.s.
Parental: older children	Increase	n.s.
Occupational	Increase	n.s.
Direct action		
Marital	n.s.	Reduction
Parental: younger children	Increase	n.s.
Parental: older children	Increase	n.s.
Occupational	n.s.	n.s.

[a]Summarized from Menaghan (1982b, 1983a, 1983b).

marriage does reduce later marital problems. Contrary to the assumptions of those who stress active efforts to resolve presenting problems directly, however, such efforts have no significant impact in either direction on later problem level.

Except for marital problems, then, the coping variables assessed in these studies had no direct impact on later problems. In parenting, the key influences on altered problem levels were family composition variables such as the number of children, their average age, and their residence at home or away. In work life, net of greater initial problems, only younger age predicted greater later problems. In marriage, shorter marital duration and being female were associated with more problems. Thus, problem level seems more responsive to contextual variables and initial problem levels than to individual coping efforts. Emotional distress is more readily affected by coping variables, but here a substantial proportion of the significant relationships are negative: they actually worsen distress feelings for any given level of problems.

Interactive Effects: Problem Level and Context. For all levels of coping it is important to ask whether the impact of coping may vary systematically, either at different levels of situational stressfulness or for people in different situational contexts. This is both theoretically interesting and practically important. As House puts it in developing a parallel argument about the relationships among social supports, situations, and outcomes, to the extent that support (or coping) has largely main effects, everyone would benefit from enhancing those levels; but if it has primarily buffering effects, enhancement "will be of significant value to people experiencing moderate to high levels of stress, but of lesser, or even no, value to people experiencing little or no stress" (1981:37).

Such interactions might take a variety of forms. For example, a given coping variable could have a great impact in low-stress situations but be increasingly impotent as troubles mount; coping efforts could be maximally effective at some moderate level of stress, and less so at both extremely high and extremely low levels of stress—at high levels because they are not enough, and at low levels because they are not necessary. If interaction is present, of course, conclusions about its form may vary depending on the particular range of stressfulness sampled. Thus, any interpretation of findings of interaction must consider where the sample fits on the broad continuum of stressfulness.

There has been little analysis aimed at identifying the optimum range of situations for specific coping variables or at assessing the presence or form of interactions. Menaghan (1982b, 1983a, 1983b) found no evidence for interactions of coping and problem level in marital, parental, or work roles. And Pearlin et al. (1981) found that the effectiveness of coping on self-esteem, mastery, and depression does not vary with level of economic problems. There are some variations by situational context. Pearlin et al. reported that coping was particularly effective— in reducing economic problems, in maintaining self-esteem, and in reducing depression—for those who had suffered job disruption. Menaghan (1982b) found that the effects of direct action and optimistic comparisons in reducing later marital problems were more powerful for those of higher SES. In parenting, the exacerbating role of restricted expectations was largely confined to fathers rather than to mothers (Menaghan, 1983b); in occupation, there was some suggestion that direct action might actually worsen problems for those who had also had negative job changes (Menaghan, 1983a).

Given the high number of possible interactions tested, these scattered findings may be attributable to chance fluctuations; certainly, replication of such variations is essential before they can be taken too seriously. Nevertheless, they offer some empirical encouragement that effects may not be simply additive in nature. Researchers need at least to entertain the possibility of interactions of problem levels and coping, and of situations and coping, for the various dependent variables they examine if evidence about the form of the stress–coping–outcome relationship is to be found.

In summary, findings about effectiveness are marred by some confusion among usage, helpfulness, and effectiveness measures; by the a priori belief that some coping approaches are preferable to others; and by the failure to assess all three components—stress as well as coping and outcomes—involved in the stress–coping–outcome relationship. The most extensive body of findings is at the level of coping efforts. There is little support for 'the belief that such efforts powerfully enhance problem resolution, although they may help to maintain sense of self and to control levels of emotional distress. Clearly, more, and more adequate, studies of effectiveness will be needed before firm conclusions can be drawn about these relationships.

FUTURE DIRECTIONS

Although research on stress and life outcomes is abundant, and coping is a frequently posited intervening variable in this relationship, empirical multivariate assessments of the life-stress–coping–outcome relationship are still in their infancy. It may be useful to outline some of the outstanding unanswered questions as a sort of agenda for the future.

Conceptual Issues and Empirical Research

The broad definition of life stress used here—objective or perceived mismatch between environment (opportunities or demands) and self (capacities or needs and/or goals)—yields many directions for operationalization. In the sociological and psychological literature, the most frequent approach has been to use self-reports of troubling environments as an indicator of demands that cannot be readily managed by existing resources (i.e., subjective stress). As discussed in the section "Stress," this is not an unreasonable choice, but it needs to be recognized as one among several possibilities. Further, it has the liability of confounding processes of interpretive appraisal with measures of life stress itself. It will be important for future studies to grapple with this problem both theoretically and empirically, and to consider how our findings may vary with differing approaches to the measurement of stress.

However such mismatch is measured, the key dimensions along which stress seems to be assessed are by role area and by severity or degree. Clearly, other dimensions are both possible and promising. For example, the initial analyses of Lazarus and his colleagues suggest that problems that can be changed may elicit differing coping responses than problems that are (considered) unalterable. Others have suggested that the normatively expectable life course practically mandates certain times and situations of mismatch or stress. To the extent that these are readily anticipated and perceived as temporary phases that may be prerequisites to other desired life experiences, they may be coped with quite differently than persistent, "unnnecessary" annoyances or problems. Even if the coping responses are similar, we may find that their effectiveness varies. Finally, when the meaning, severity, and persistence of problems are themselves difficult to ascertain, the degree of ambiguity about what is being faced may itself influence coping choices, their impact, or both. All of these issues await further research.

Perhaps the most basic recommendation, of course, in matching empirical work to conceptual understandings is to attempt some measure of some dimensions of life stress. The recurrent failure even to assess variations in stress noted here makes it impossible to establish the meaning of reported coping–outcome relationships.

In the assessment of coping, I would suggest that the tripartite categorization of coping possibilities used here—direct action on environment or self, interpretive reappraisals of environmental characteristics or of self, and emotion-managing–releasing–redirecting efforts—may help to clarify and organize the long lists of assorted coping measures extant in empirical research. It also seems important not to build into the measurement of coping a priori assumptions about how these three are related (e.g., that they are mutually exclusive), or how they may affect outcomes (e.g., that direct action is always best, or that interpretive reappraisals are defensive, pathological, and second-rate).

Among outcome measures, I would suggest that cross-sectional correlations with ongoing distress, depression, satisfaction, or well-being need to be supplemented by more long-range assessments. All three of the key outcomes stressed here—emotional distress, problem level, and sense of self—essentially imply longitudinal assessments, not of their absolute level at a single point in time but of their enhancement, stasis, or deterioration over time. How our conclusions may vary with our choice of outcomes and how these outcomes may interrelate with one another are leading questions for the future.

Patterns of Usage

Although the evidence was often thin, there was some suggestion in the studies reviewed here of a malignant spiral in usage correlates. The more severe the problems one faced in a given role, the less likely one was to choose the coping efforts, or to possess the coping resources, that might lessen problems or reduce distress; and the more likely one was to turn to the sorts of efforts, such as retricted expectations, punitive parental discipline, or selective inattention, that if anything worsened distress. The situational correlates found also suggest the same linkage between more problems and worse coping choices: The more negative choices tended to go, for example, with lower prestige jobs and with more and younger children. If subsequent research strengthens this apparent finding, we will need to give sustained attention to the intervention possibilities inherent in such a spiral.

It also appears that the choice of particular coping efforts is influenced by different predictors in different roles. That is, of the situational and demographic correlates examined thus far, conclusions seem to be conditional and role-specific rather than role-invariant. Efforts do not seem to be powerfully linked to one another across roles, and there is little indication that they reflect the workings of some general coping styles or predispositions. The entire question of role specificity, of course, demands further investigation; but the findings reported here suggest that we be quite cautious in generalizing about coping usage patterns.

An almost completely unexplored question about coping usage involves the process or sequence of coping efforts. A few studies (e.g., Alonzo, 1980a, 1980b) have attempted to reconstruct a sequence of coping actions through detailed retrospective questioning, but such efforts are rare. The design of Lazarus's most recent data collection—obtaining closely spaced reports of coping efforts over a year's time from a small (n = 100) and fairly homogenous sample—could be expected to yield at least some individuals who are reporting about their varying (or stable) responses to the same ongoing stress over time. Thus far, however, analyses of these data have involved a resolute disregard for the repeated-measures aspect of their design. Instead, each individual's 4–18 coping reports have been treated as independent data, and analyses have discussed some 1500 "coping episodes" as if there were no dependence among them. Nevertheless, such data hold the promise of yielding information about the sequencing, stability, or change of coping approaches over time.

The question of stability or change over longer periods of time—of presumably stable resources, relatively stable coping styles, or presumably unstable efforts—is also an important unexplored question. Confirmatory factor-analytic measurement models of coping efforts in the Chicago panel data yield moderate intercorrelations (r ranging from around .30 to .45) over a 4-year period. Under what conditions do one's choices shift? Is one more apt to shift away from less effective approaches than from those that are more effective? Do new life contexts, especially as marked by key life events or transitions, push for greater instability of coping choices? As yet we have no information about these matters.

Explorations of Effectiveness

Questions about specificity versus generality, of course, also apply to our conclusions about effectiveness. Under what conditions, we asked initially, are particular coping variables effective? The findings reviewed here point to the probable generality across social role areas of the effectiveness of some coping efforts, notably optimistic comparisons; but such conclusions need to be examined in other data and using other categorizations of stress. Similarly, short- and long-range effectiveness studies may yield different conclusions.

A further important expansion of effectiveness studies involves the recognition that the coping efforts of any single individual do not occur in an interpersonal vacuum. How do the coping efforts of other involved individuals—spouses, children and co-workers are obvious candidates—affect the outcomes of any one person's coping choices? Cook (1982), for example, suggested that the modal coping approaches of bereaved parents are strikingly at odds for husbands and wives: Wives tended toward ventilation of feelings, preoccupation with the dead or dying child, and prolonged conversation about their stress and responses; husbands preferred to withdraw into distracting activities and avoid dwelling on the situation, and avoid the people (most predictably, their wives) who made it difficult to put the loss out of mind. The clash between such approaches, and the extent to which the preferences of either spouse might undermine the efforts of the other, are obvious. Yet the interaction of individual coping efforts, even of a dyad, and the linkages among individual variables and coping resources, styles, and efforts at the level of families or work groups, are essentially untouched topics. (See Reiss, 1981, and Menaghan, 1983c, for some further discussion of this issue.)

Despite this long (and still quite incomplete) detailing of neglected considerations and unanswered questions, knowledge about coping is beginning to accumulate. As future work builds on the initial efforts of the researchers considered here, it seems reasonable to be optimistic about the richness and detail with which we may be able to discuss stress, coping, and outcomes in the future.

REFERENCES

Alonzo, Angelo
    1980a   "Acute illness behavior: A conceptual exploration and specification." So-
             cial Science and Medicine 14A:515–526.
    1980b   "The mobile coronary care unit and the decision to seek medical care
             during acute episodes of coronary artery disease." Medical Care 18:297–
             318.
Andrews, Gavin, Christopher Tennant, Daphne Hewson, and George Vaillant
    1978   "Life event stress, social support, coping style and risk of psychological
             impairment." Journal of Nervous and Mental Disease 166:307–316.
Antonovsky, Aaron
    1979   Health, Stress, and Coping. San Francisco: Jossey-Bass.
Averill, James R.
    1973   "Personal control over aversive stimuli and its relationship to stress." Psy-
             chological Bulletin 80:286–303.
Barofsky, Ivan
    1981   "Issues and approaches to the psychosocial assessment of the cancer pa-
             tient." Pp. 55–65 in Charles K. Prokop and Laurence A. Bradley (eds.),
             Medical Psychology: Contributions to Behavioral Medicine. New York: Ac-
             ademic Press.
Benner, Patricia, Ethel Roskies, and Richard S. Lazarus
    1980   "Stress and coping under extreme conditions." Pp. 219–258 in J. E. Dims-
             dale (ed.), Survivors, Victims, and Perpetrators: Essays on the Nazi Holo-
             caust. Washington, D.C.: Hemisphere.
Berman, William H., and Dennis C. Turk
    1981   "Adaptation to divorce: Problems and coping strategies." Journal of Mar-
             riage and the Family 43:179–189.
Boss, Pauline G.
    1980   "The relationship of psychological father presence, wife's personal
             qualities and wife/family dysfunction in families of missing fathers." Jour-
             nal of Marriage and the Family 42:541–550.

Boss, Pauline G., Hamilton I. McCubbin, and Gary Lester
    1979   "The corporate executive wife's coping patterns in response to routine husband-father absence." Family Process 18:79–86.
Buehler, Cheryl A., and M. Janice Hogan
    1980   "Managerial behavior and stress in families headed by divorced women: A proposed framework." Family Relations 29:525–532.
Colletta, Nancy D., and Carol H. Gregg
    1981   "Adolescent mothers' vulnerability to stress." Journal of Nervous and Mental Disease 169:50–54.
Cook, Judith
    1982   "Adjustment to the death of a child: Gender differences in responses and outcomes in the first years." Doctoral dissertation, Department of Sociology, The Ohio State University.
Coyne, James, Carolyn Aldwin, and Richard Lazarus
    1981   "Depression and coping in stressful episodes." Journal of Abnormal Psychology 90:439–447.
Dimsdale, J. E.
    1979   "The coping behavior of Nazi concentration camp survivors." Pp. 163–204 in J. E. Dimsdale (ed.), Survivors, Victims, and Perpetrators: Essays on the Nazi Holocaust. Washington, D.C.: Hemisphere.
Epstein, S.
    1979   "The stability of behavior: 1. On predicting most of the people much of the time." Journal of Personality and Social Psychology 37:1097–1126.
Eron, Leonard, and Rolf A. Peterson
    1982   "Abnormal behavior: Social approaches." Annual Review of Psychology 33:231–264.
Fletcher, Ben C., and Roy L. Payne
    1980   "Stress and work: A review and theoretical framework, I." Personnel Review 9:19–29.
Folkman, Susan, and Richard S. Lazarus
    1980   "An analysis of coping in a middle-aged community sample." Journal of Health and Social Behavior 21:219–239.
Folkman, Susan, Catherine Schaefer, and Richard S. Lazarus
    1979   "Cognitive processes as mediators of stress and coping." Pp. 265–298 in V. Hamilton and D. M. Warburton (ed.), Human Stress and Cognition: An Information Processing Approach. New York: Wiley.
Frenkel-Brunswick, E.
    1954   "Social research and the problem of values." Journal of Abnormal and Social Psychology 49:466–471.
Frydman, M. I.
    1981   "Social support, life events and psychiatric symptoms: A study of direct, conditional and interaction effects." Social Psychiatry 16:69–78.
George, Linda K.
    1980   Role Transitions in Later Life. Belmont, Calif.: Wadsworth.
Gleser, G. C., and D. Ihilevich
    1969   "An objective instrument for measuring defense mechanisms." Journal of Consulting and Clinical Psychology 33:51–60.
Haan, Norma
    1977   Coping and Defending: Processes of Self-Environment Organization. New York: Academic Press.

Haan, Norma
  1981   "Adolescents and young adults as producers of their development." Pp. 155–182 in R. M. Lerner and W. A. Busch-Rossnagel (eds.), Individuals as Producers of Their Development: A Life Span Perspective. New York: Academic Press.
Hackman, J. R.
  1970   "Tasks and task performance in research on stress." Pp. 202–237 in J. E. McGrath (ed.), Social and Psychological Factors in Stress. New York: Holt, Rinehart & Winston.
Hall, Douglas
  1972   "A model of coping with role conflict: The role behavior of college educated women." Administrative Science Quarterly 17:471–486.
Hansen, Donald S., and Vicky A. Johnson
  1979   "Rethinking family stress theory: Definitional aspects." Pp. 582–603 in W. Burr, R. Hill, F. Nye, and I. Reiss (eds.), Contemporary Theories About the Family. Volume 1. New York: The Free Press.
Harrison, Algea, and Joanne H. Minor
  1978   "Interrole conflict, coping strategies, and satisfaction among black working wives." Journal of Marriage and the Family 40:799–805.
Hirsch, Barton
  1981   "Coping and adaptation in high risk populations: Toward an integrative model." Schizophrenia Bulletin 7:164–172.
Horowitz, Mardi
  1978   "The coping inventory." Informal presentation at meeting on Measurement Issues in Coping Research, University of California at San Francisco.
House, James, S.
  1981   Work Stress and Social Support. Reading, Mass.: Addison-Wesley.
Joffe, Paul, and Murray P. Naditch
  1977   "Paper and pencil measures of coping and defense processes." Pp. 280–297 in Norma Haan, Coping and Defending. New York: Academic Press.
Johnson, J. W., and I. G. Sarason
  1979   "Moderator variables in life stress research." Pp. 151–167 in Irwin G. Sarason and Charles D. Spielberger (eds.), Stress and Anxiety. Volume 6. New York: Hemisphere.
Kandel, D. B.
  1980   "Drug and drinking behavior among youth." Annual Review of Sociology 6:235–285.
Kaplan, Howard B.
  1975   Self-attitudes and Deviant Behavior. Pacific Palisades, Calif.: Goodyear.
  1980   Deviant Behavior in Defense of Self. New York: Academic Press.
Kessler, Ronald and Paul D. Cleary
  1980   "Social class and psychological distress." American Sociological Review 45:463–478.
Klein, David M., and Reuben Hill
  1979   "Determinants of family problem-solving effectiveness." Pp. 493–548 in W. R. Burr, R. Hill, F. Nye, and I. Reiss (eds.), Contemporary Theories about the Family. Volume 1. New York: The Free Press.
Kohn, Melvin, and Carmi Schooler
  1978   "The reciprocal effects of the substantive complexity of work and intellectual flexibility: A longitudinal assessment." American Journal of Sociology 84:24–52.

Lazarus, Richard S.
   1981   "The stress and coping paradigm." Pp. 177–214 in C. Eisdorfer and D.
           Cohen (eds.), Models for Clinical Psychopathology. New York: Spectrum.
Linden, Wolfgang, and Michael Feuerstein
   1981   "Essential hypertension and social coping behavior." Journal of Human
           Stress 7:28–34.
Maynard, Peter, Nancy Maynard, Hamilton I. McCubbin, and David Shao
   1980   "Family life and the police profession: Coping patterns wives employ in
           managing job stress and the family environment." Family Relations
           29:495–502.
McCubbin, Hamilton I.
   1979   "Integrating coping behavior in family stress theory." Journal of Marriage
           and the Family 41:237–244.
McCubbin, Hamilton I., B. Dahl, G. Lester, D. Benson, and M. Robertson
   1976   "Coping repertoires of families adapting to prolonged war-induced separa-
           tion." Journal of Marriage and the Family 38:461–471.
Menaghan, Elizabeth G.
   1982a   "Assessing the impact of family transitions on marital experience." Pp.
           90–108 in Hamilton I. McCubbin, A. Elizabeth Cauble, and Joan M. Patter-
           sons (eds.), Family Stress Coping and Social Support. Springfield, Ill.: Ch
           Thomas.
   1982b   "Measuring coping effectiveness: A panel analysis of marital problems and
           coping efforts." Journal of Health and Social Behavior 23:220–234.
   1983a   "Coping with occupational problems: The limits of individual efforts."
           Unpublished paper, Department of Sociology, The Ohio State University.
   1983b   "Coping with parental problems: Panel assessments of effectiveness." Jour-
           nal of Family Issues 4.
   1983c   "Individual coping efforts and family studies: Conceptual and meth-
           odological issues." Marriage and Family Review 6:113–135.
Miller, Joanne, Carmi Schooler, Melvin L. Kohn, and Karen A. Miller
   1979   "Women and work: The psychological effects of occupational conditions."
           American Journal of Sociology 85:66–94.
Moos, Rudolf
   1977   Coping with Physical Illness. New York: Plenum.
Morris, Larry W., and W. Benjamin Engle
   1981   "Assessing various coping strategies and their effects on test performance
           and anxiety." Journal of Clinical Psychology 37:165–171.
Needle, Richard, Thomas Griffin, and Roger Svendsen
   1981   "Occupational stress: Coping and health problems of teachers." Journal of
           School Health 51:175–181.
Pearlin, L. I., and M. A. Lieberman
   1979   "Social sources of emotional distress." Pp. 217–248 in Roberta Simmons
           (ed.), Research in Community and Mental Health. Volume 1. Greenwich,
           Conn.: JAI Press.
Pearlin, Leonard I., Morton A. Lieberman, Elizabeth G. Menaghan, and Joseph T. Mullan
   1981   "The stress process." Journal of Health and Social Behavior 22:337–356.
Pearlin, Leonard I., and Carmi Schooler
   1978   "The structure of coping." Journal of Health and Social Behavior 19:1–21.
Reiss, David
   1981   The Family's Construction of Reality. Cambridge, Mass.: Harvard Univer-
           sity Press.

Rosenstiel, Anne K., and Susan Roth
    1981   "Relationship between cognitive activity and adjustment in four spinal-cord-injured individuals: A longitudinal investigation." Journal of Human Stress 7 (1):35–43.
Rutter, M.
    1981   "Stress, coping and development: Some issues and some questions." Journal of Child Psychology and Psychiatry and Allied Disciplines 22:323–356.
Schutz, W. C.
    1967   The FIRO Scales Manual. Palo Alto, Calif.: Consulting Psychologists Press.
Selye, Hans
    1956   The Stress of Life. New York: McGraw-Hill.
Shalit, Benjamin
    1977   "Structural ambiguity and limits to coping." Journal of Human Stress 3(4):32–45.
Shanan, Joel, Atara Kaplan De-Nour, and I. Garty
    1976   "Effects of prolonged stress on coping style in terminal renal failure patients." Journal of Human Stress 2(4):19–27.
Stagner, Ross
    1981   "Stress, strain, coping, and defense." Research on Aging 3:3–32.
Stern, Melvin J., and Linda Pascale
    1979   "Psychosocial adaptation to post-myocardial infarction: The spouse's dilemma." Journal of Psychosomatic Research 23:83–87.
Turk, Dennis C.
    1979   "Factors influencing the adaptive process with chronic illness: Implications for intervention," Pp. 291–311 in Irwin G. Sarason and Charles D. Spielberger (eds.), Stress and Anxiety. Volume 6. New York: Hemisphere.
Tyler, Forrest B.
    1978   "Individual psychosocial competence: A personality configuration." Educational and Psychological Measurement 38:309–323.
Vaillant, G. E.
    1976   "Natural history of male psychological health: Vol. 5. The relation of choice of ego mechanisms of defense to adult adjustment." Archives of General Psychiatry 33:535–545.
Vanfossen, Beth E., John I. Spitzer, and Dolores J. Jones
    1981   "Social class and emotional distress (comment on Kessler and Cleary, ASR, June 1980)." American Sociological Review 46:688–692.
Vickers, R. R., Jr., and Linda Hervig
    1981   "Comparison of three psychological defense mechanism questionnaires." Journal of Personality Assessment 45:630–638.
Videka, Lynn M.
    1979   "Psychosocial adaptation in a medical self-help group." Pp. 362–386 in M. A. Lieberman and L. I. Borman (eds.), Self-help Groups for Coping with Crises. San Francisco: Jossey-Bass.
Wampler, Karen, S., and Douglas H. Sprenkle
    1980   "The Minnesota couple communication program: A follow up study." Journal of Marriage and the Family 42:577–584.
Worden, J. William, and Harry J. Sobel
    1978   "Ego strength and psychosocial adaptation to cancer." Psychosomatic Medicine 40:585–592.

PART II

Toward a Theoretical Synthesis

5

Psychological Distress in Sociological Context: Toward a General Theory of Psychosocial Stress*

HOWARD B. KAPLAN

INTRODUCTION

In the following pages I present a conceptual framework for the study of psychosocial stress and attempt to synthesize the many more or less empirically based generalizations regarding this process that have been offered by other investigators. Noteworthy among these are the generalizations reported by the other contributors to this volume that deal with role strain, life events, social support, and coping efforts as they relate to each other and associated phenomena. I will try to decompose the complex meanings associated with each of these four constructs and reexamine the usefulness of conducting research that is guided by one or another of these constructs rather than by consideration of all of them simultaneously.

*This work was supported in part by Research Grant DA-02497 from the National Institute on Drug Abuse.

195

Psychosocial stress is a subcategory of determinants of psychological distress. A more inclusive category of determinants of subjective distress might include those that are not mediated by psychological processes (e.g., gastric acidity or noxious air) and those that are mediated by psychological processes but are not necessarily socially derived, structured, or otherwise influenced (as in some instances of sensory stimulation). It is precisely the socially influenced nature of distress-inducing psychological processes that delineates the class of determinants encompassed by the term *psychosocial stress*.

PSYCHOSOCIAL STRESS

Psychosocial stress refers to the socially derived, conditioned, and situated psychological processes that stimulate any or all of the many manifestations of dysphoric affect falling under the rubric of subjective distress. More specifically, psychosocial stress, in its most proximate influence on psychological distress, reflects the subject's inability to forestall or diminish perception, recall, anticipation, or imagination of disvalued circumstances—those that in reality or fantasy signify great and/or increased distance from desirable (valued) experiential states and, consequently, evoke a need to approximate the valued states. The experience of the unfulfilled need is subjective distress. The disvalued circumstances are the subject's own disvalued attributes and behaviors and the disvalued outcomes of others' individual or collective responses. However, it is the cognitive and affective–evaluative interpretation of circumstances rather than the circumstances themselves that evoke psychological distress.

Mutually Influential Components of Psychosocial Stress

These psychological processes—the affective (the need–value structure), the cognitive (perception, recall, anticipation, imagination), and the behavioral (attributes and responses of the subject and others)—are mutually influential. The need–value system influences the subject's perception of reality and motivates the person to behave in ways that will approximate valued states and/or reduce perception of disvalued states; the subject's behaviors and attributes and the consequences of others' behaviors for the subject stimulate subjective awareness; and subjective awareness of one's own or others' behaviors stimulates the need–value system. Together these mutually influential processes have a direct impact on the experience of subjective distress.

The nature of this mutual influence is shown in Figure 5.1. The need–value system, on the one hand, and the subject's own behaviors and attributes as well as the consequences of others' behaviors for the subject, on the other hand, are pictured as having a direct impact on the subject's cognitive processes. The person's traits or behaviors and the consequences of others' behavior for the subject stimulate the more or less veridical perception, recall, anticipation, or imagination of such traits, behaviors, and consequences. These cognitive responses, however, are conditioned by the meanings that the traits, behaviors, and consequences have for the person's system of values—the symbolic representations of desirable experiential states. The person is more likely to become aware of occurrences if they are relevant to his or her needs and values and is likely to structure cognitions in ways that are dictated by his or her needs and values. These influences are depicted in the figure as unidirectional arrows numbered "1," indicating the early and simultaneous impact of the person's (1) traits, behaviors, and experienced consequences of others' behaviors and (2) need–value system on cognitive responses in the course of the distress-inducing process. In short, the de facto possession of attributes, performance of behaviors, and

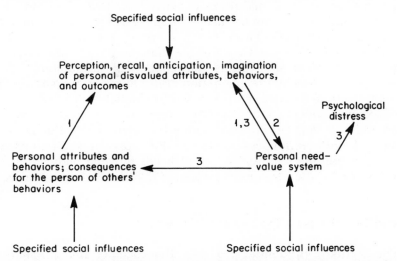

Figure 5.1. Mutual influences among components of psychosocial stress. Numbered arrows reflect the temporal ordering of effects. Lower numbers reflect earlier occurrences. Like-numbered effects indicate simultaneous occurrence.

experience of adverse outcomes of others' actions that, in the context of the need–value system, reflect disvalued states stimulate the subject's *perception* (or other cognitive responses) of having disvalued attributes, performing disvalued behaviors, and being the victim of disvalued consequences of others' actions.

The subject's perception of (or other cognitive responses to) these disvalued states stimulates the person's need to reduce the perceived psychological distance from the valued experiential state (and to increase the perceived distance from undesirable states). This relationship is depicted by the unidirectional arrow numbered "2" in Figure 5.1.

The experience of the unfulfilled need is reflected as more or less severe subjective distress (in any of its possible manifestations, contingent on the nature of the frustrated need), depending on the priority of the violated value and the perceived probability of closing the perceived distance from the valued state. This is pictured in Figure 5.1 as the unidirectional arrow numbered "3" from the need–value system to psychological distress. Simultaneously, the subject's felt need to approximate the valued state motivates him or her to behave in the way that is valued (shown by the unidirectional arrow from the need–value system to personal attributes and behaviors, etc.), and/or to change *perceptions* of disvalued states by distorting perceptions of reality or changing the personal definition of what is valued (reflected in the unidirectional arrow from the need–value system to perception of disvalued circumstances). These last two arrows are numbered "3" in Figure 5.1 to indicate that they are simultaneous with the experience of subjective distress and occur subsequent to stimulation of the need–value system by the perception of disvalued circumstances. The two numbers associated with the unidirectional arrow between the need–value system and cognitive responses indicates that the need–value system (together with objectively given disvalued circumstances) initially influences *perception* of the disvalued circumstances and, following the stimulation of felt needs by such perception, may have a further influence on perception of disvalued circumstances.

Social Influences on Psychosocial Stress

The mutually influential processes that together are intimately involved in the genesis of psychological distress are variously influenced by still other factors. That is, less directly, the frequency, intensity, course, and duration of experiences of psychological distress are a function of those factors that influence: (1) the nature of and changes in the person's need–value system; (2) the frequency and continuity of disvalued circumstances; and (3) the fact of and changes in the subject's perception, recall, anticipation, or imagination of such circumstances. As is suggested in Figure 5.1, these influences are largely social in nature. From a diachronic point of view, personal values, the system of concepts that gives structure to personal awareness, and appropriate behavioral responses are learned in the course of the socialization process. From a synchronic point of view, the perceptual and evaluative significance of a person's behaviors and attributes varies according to the social context. Further, within any given social context the discrete responses of the interacting parties (that is, social behaviors) are the stimuli for the subject's cognitive, evaluative, and further behavioral responses. The understanding of psychosocial stress will be enhanced through the consideration of the social influences on the person's need–value system, cognitive processes, and objectively given circumstances, which together directly impinge on the experience of psychological distress. It is to a consideration of such social influences that the remainder of the chapter is devoted.

THE SOCIAL BASIS OF PSYCHOSOCIAL STRESS

The nature of psychosocial stress is such that the need–value system, the occurrence of circumstances that are disvalued, and the cognitive processing of the disvalued circumstances are in reality all intimately intertwined in the process of stimulating psychological distress. However, because particular social influences may relate to one, all, or some combination of these three sets of phenomena, for purposes of understanding the social basis of psychosocial stress it is useful to draw analytic distinctions between them and to consider the social basis of each in turn.

The Social Basis of the Need–Value System

The order to consider the social basis of the need–value system some consideration will be given first to the nature of the personal need–value system and second to the social basis of the general need for positive self-evaluation and of the more specific values that are the basis for evaluation of self and all else.

The Need–Value System

Values are the symbolic expressions of more or less desirable experiential states. Ordinarily the individual or group will conceive of numerous values that are more or less relevant depending on the situational context. Certain values will be employed to judge particular attributes or behaviors in given situations, and other values will be used for judging other attributes and behaviors in other situations. Values of strength and beauty might be appropriate for judgments about physical characteristics, values of honesty and efficiency might be relevant for judging the performance of one who holds political office, and values of leadership potential and courage might be relevant to the evaluation of an army officer in the field. Very often, however, a person is placed in a situation where different values are relevant but the person can so behave as to approximate one value only at the cost of increasing the distance from another value. That this situation is rarely personally untenable is due to the normal practice of ordering values hierarchically so that in a choice situation one value is judged to take priority over another. For example, it might be more important to act for the public good and be disloyal to a friend than to be loyal to a friend at the cost of the public good. Similarly, it might be more important to have a job that is creative but pays little rather than to have one that pays well but does not permit creativity. The priority assigned to particular values depends, as will be noted later, primarily on the degree of association of the socially derived values with the social processes by which congenitally given needs such as hunger and thirst are satisfied. The totality of the values of a group or an individual organized in terms of such principles as situational specificity and hierarchical priority is a *value system*. The desirable qualities or values in question may be conceptualized as continuous dimensions, and may be approximated in varying degrees. For example, a person may be more or less industrious, or more or less beautiful. Alternatively, the same values may be conceptualized as discrete and mutually exclusive categories. For example, a person is either industrious or lazy, either beautiful or not beautiful. The poles of the continuous dimensions or the discrete and mutually exclusive categories may be thought of in terms of opposite qualities, one of which is defined as desirable, the other as undesirable (for example, beautiful versus ugly, healthy versus diseased, moral versus immoral). Or they may be thought of in terms of the presence or absence of a desirable or undesirable quality (for example, beautiful versus nonbeautiful, healthy versus nonhealthy, moral versus nonmoral).

Values reflect more or less desirable states in the sense that the outcomes of approximating those states are distress reducing and the outcomes of increased distance from the valued state are distress inducing. To the extent that the distress-reducing/inducing consequences are symbolically expressed, values can only be defined in terms of other values (desirable states). To the extent that an identifiable population shares a set of values and orders them in a similar fashion, a consensual value system exists.

Values, as the symbolic expressions of desirable states, are applicable to the perceptions of the behavior of others, the physical environment, imaginary states, and of course to the self. We evaluate the environment as dirty or clean, we evaluate others as good or bad, we evaluate paintings as aesthetically satisfying or not. We judge Camelot to have been a chivalrous environment, and we judge ourselves to be more or less accomplished. The evaluations of anything but the self are not *necessarily* immediately relevant to the achievement of personal values but rather are expressions of what we regard as desirable states for others, the environment, and so on. However, such evaluations may be directly relevant to the achievement of certain personally held values, such as when we feel that it is desirable to judge others in terms of certain moral standards, family background, or other evaluative criteria.

The most inclusive value in the personal hierarchy is the self-judgment of approximating high-priority, personally relevant values. The ability to make such a judgment rests on the self-evaluations of approximating other higher desirable states.

Needs are the reflections of the subjective distress experienced when we perceive, recall, anticipate, or imagine our own distance from a *personally applicable* valued state. As noted earlier, values reflect the judgmental criteria that we use to measure the worth of everything—other people, the behavior of others, the physical environment. Ordinarily, however, relatively little affect is evoked by such value judgments unless—and only to the degree that—the more or less desirable states are perceived as (or, in the case of empathy, *as if*) relevant to our own outcomes, that is, as reflecting or influencing the approximation or distancing of self from personally valued states. For example, since we value intellectual facility, we might disvalue our child's classmate's poor grades but not be very distressed by this circumstance. However, the same poor grades received by our own child would not only be disvalued but would evoke negative affect—perhaps because this circumstance reflects badly on the environmental and genetic basis of the child's intellectual capacity and, therefore, on our own intelligence. Thus, we are less distressed by the perception of violation of closely held values by others than by ourselves unless this reflects badly on ourselves. The more intense experience of (psychosocially based) affect occurs when the value judgments are personally applicable—when circumstances reflect the subject's own approximation to or distance from personally desirable states. The affect that derives from the person's anticipation, recall, perception, or imagination of having disvalued attributes, performing disvalued behaviors, or being the victim of disvalued outcomes of environmental circumstances constitutes the negative self-feelings that make up psychosocially influenced psychological distress. (Self-feelings are evoked by evaluation of one's own attributes behaviors, or outcomes, and are to be distinguished from any feelings that are evoked by evaluation of environmental states or others' traits, behaviors, or outcomes.) The precise form and intensity of the negative self-feelings are a function of the nature of the valued state, the perceived distance from the valued state (and the probability of closing the distance), and the priority of the value in the person's hierarchy of values. Specifically, personally valued states might include the related experiences of being part of a social network, eliciting good opinions from valued others, doing what is expected, and the achievement of occupational aspirations. The perceived frustration of the need to be part of an interpersonal network may be experienced as the self-feeling of loneliness or alienation. The failure to approximate the desire to evoke positive responses from others may be experienced as shame. The inability to satisfy a felt need to meet what a person regards as others' legitimate expectations may be experienced as feelings of guilt. The person's achievement of valued occupational goals may be experienced as the self-feeling of pride.

The most *general* self-feeling, however, is that which is the consequence of perceived proximity or distance to the goal of general positive self-evaluation. The general self-evaluation of approximating valued states is the ultimate value in the hierarchy of values. People need to think of themselves positively—that is, as having valued attributes, performing valued behaviors, and as the object of valued outcomes of social and other environmental processes. The extent to which they evaluate themselves positively in these regards—that is as experiencing attributes, behaviors, and outcomes that reflect high priority values— influences in large measure the more or less intense experience of the general self-feelings that are reflected as self-derogation or self-hate when the self-evaluation is negative, and as self-acceptance or self-love when the self-evaluation is positive. The weights that various perceived values contribute to the overall self-evaluation are a function of the degree of perceived association between the more recently acquired values and earlier congenitally given or acquired values. The nature of these associations is suggested in the next section in the course of considering the social origin of self-evaluation in general and the self-evaluative judgments that contribute more specifically to overall self-evaluation.

The equating of psychological distress with the felt needs or negative self-feelings that are consequences of subjectively perceived distance from high priority, more or less general personally applicable values has been expressed by others in similar terms. Rollo May, for example, notes: "The distinctive quality of human anxiety arises from the fact that man is a valuing animal, who interprets his life and world in terms of symbols and meanings. It is the threat to these values—specifically, to some value that the individual holds essential to his existence as a self-that causes anxiety" (1980:241).

The Social Origin of Self-evaluation and Values

Our self-evaluations as more or less approximating highly valued states and the more specific values that are the basis for these judgments are the normal outcomes of early dependence on adults for physical need satisfaction. Infants associate the presence of adults with the satisfaction of physical needs. As long as all of the adults in an infant's environment are associated with noncontingent need satisfactions the infant will come to value the presence of adults. As the circle of people in the child's world widens the child may note that need satisfaction is associated with certain persons and not others. We may thus come to value the traits and behaviors that are associated with those persons who satisfy our needs and to disvalue the traits and behaviors that are associated with those persons who frustrate (or are irrelevant to) satisfaction of congenital or acquired values. Because the persons who ordinarily facilitate our approximation to desirable states are somewhat variable in this regard, we will associate certain behaviors of caregivers with occasions of approximating values and other behaviors of those who ordinarily minister to our needs with the occasions on which we failed to approximate valued states. These behaviors (which later will be conceptualized as approving or disapproving attitudes), by virtue of their association with other valued responses, come to be valued in their own right. We have come to value the positive and disvalue the negative attitudinal responses of others and the forms in which the attitudes are expressed—physical punishment, disapproving words, failure to reciprocate expectations.

Insofar as the attitudes of others are contingent on our attributes and behaviors as they might be when such attributes or behaviors frustrate achievement of the others' own values (in the most general sense, when they fail to conform to the expectations of others), we come to *value in their own right the attributes and behaviors that were perceived as evoking positive attitudinal responses* and to disvalue those that were perceived as evoking negative attitudinal responses from others. Such behaviors and attributes in the aggregate constitute the range of normative expectations applied by others to ourselves transsituationally or in specific relational context.

Insofar as we are (by definition) moved to achieve these valued states we will come to *value in their own right any behavior patterns, resources, or relationships that have been perceived as instrumental to the achievement of these valued states.*

Knowledge of the responses of others is prerequisite to self-awareness of achieving valued states. Indeed, some of the values are the responses of others. Other of the valued states are known to have been reached by the cues provided by others' responses. That is, we know we are ethical, of good repute, accomplished, or attractive in part because of others' confirmation that we achieve these values. In addition to needing to know others' responses because they are valued in themselves and because they serve as cognitive cues that we have achieved other valued states, it is important to know how others respond in order that we might behave in the future to maximize the achievement of valued states, including evoking positive responses from others. What constitutes values will vary according to our developmental stage and social situational contingencies at any particular time in life. We do not always know, then, what traits or behaviors at any given time will reflect the achievement of personally valued states and/or will evoke rewarding responses from others. Because we are motivated to perceive ourselves as achieving valued states and as the object of positive responses by others, we adopt the perspective of others in his environment and evaluate ourselves from the point of view of the others. We are thus able to imagine if others will respond to us favorably and if particular traits or behaviors in particular situations will reflect valued states, and to vary our behavior so as to maximize the approximation to desirable states. Because we perceive the instrumental value of self-evaluation (from the perspective of others) toward the goals of achieving and knowing we have achieved value states, we come to *value the self-evaluation process* in its own right.

In the course of imagining how the other person responds (or would respond) to us evaluatively, we express attitudes toward ourselves that are symbolic representations of the imagined attitudinal response of the other person and then respond to our own attitudinal expressions as if the other person had actually expressed the attitude. Because we are motivated to evoke positive evaluations from others (in their own right as well as because they signify achieving valued states) we respond to favorable self-evaluations with positive self-feelings and to an unfavorable self-evaluation with distressful negative self-feelings. Our attitudinal responses to ourselves thus become motivationally significant. Through their original association with the imagined attitudes of others, our attitudinal expressions toward ourselves consistently tend to evoke relatively gratifying/distressing emotional experiences. At this point we may be said to have acquired the need to respond to ourselves in terms of positive evaluations and thereby to evoke further gratifying emotional experiences and to avoid responding to ourselves in terms of negative evaluations that would evoke continued experiences of subjective distress. In short, we have come to *value positive self-evaluation* and to disvalue negative self-evaluations, a value that is the normal outcome of the human infant's early dependence on and subsequent interaction with other human beings in the context of stable social relationships.

To this point I have argued that general self-evaluations and the particular values that contribute to overall self-evaluation derive from the dependence on and interaction with other human beings. At a more general level, in addition to overall self-evaluation certain values appear in all societies. As Dodge and Martin (1970:59) have pointed out, the human species survives through collective organization to meet biologically given or acquired psychological and social needs by exploiting its environments. Because almost all of our goals are achieved through participating with other human beings in a structure of social relationships, participation in this network comes to be highly valued in itself. Thus, banishment or enforced silence would be interpreted as a highly disvalued circumstance, as would any other situation that reflected a threat to disruption of social relationships. Other values, however, vary according to the sociocultural matrix and the person's social identities within this matrix. People do not universally value money, courage, or academic achievement. In certain cultures and for certain positions within the social structure, however, the frustration of these values would be highly stressful.

Just as these values and their structure are determined by the stable sociocultural matrix, so will sociocultural change influence these factors by creating new values and a reordering of old consensually defined values. In the process of change, new expectations are imposed on individuals, depending on their various positions in the social position. However, social mobility and developmental processes *within* stable sociocultural structures (particularly in sociocultural systems that define mobility as normative) will also lead to the adoption of new values associated with the new positions adopted in the course of the mobility experience.

A growing empirically based literature illustrates the influence of the social systems in which individuals participate. Among U.S. Navy enlisted men, for example, recent disciplinary problems predicted illness (Rahe, 1974:68). In view of the functional requirements for discipline in the military system it is not surprising that such events were of evaluative significance. In the more inclusive sociocultural system, observations by Scotch (1963) among the Zulus are consistent with the interpretation that the same characteristics and behaviors are differently evaluated in rural tribal as opposed to urban settings, and thus differentially related to the development of hypertension in the two settings.

Different social positions within the same system appear to influence the nature of personal need–value systems. For example, a growing number of studies have suggested that individuals who occupy positions of leadership and responsibility are significantly more likely to manifest higher levels of psychophysiological activation in response to life events that appear to threaten their ability to fulfill leadership responsibilities. Thus, student aviators making their first aircraft carrier landings had higher mean serum cortisol levels and higher levels of urinary excretion of cortisol and 17-OH-CS metabolites than the radar intercept officers in the rear cockpit, who had no flight control and had to rely completely on the pilot's skill (Rubin, 1974). In an earlier study, the only men in a special combat unit in Vietnam anticipating enemy attack that showed elevated 17-OH-CS levels were the two officers and the radio operator (Bourne et al., 1968). Kiritz and Moos (1974) cited reports of (1) higher heart rates in pilots than in copilots, a difference that reversed itself when individuals changed positions; (2) a positive association between responsibility for other individuals and diastolic blood pressure; (3) greater amplitude of gastric contractions in subjects who were able to press a button to avoid the strong auditory stimulus to both members of the pair than in the passive members of the pair; (4) highest levels of 17-OH-CS secretion in aircraft commanders; and (5) sharp increases in heart rate of key NASA (National Aeronautics and Space Administration) personnel when they were suddenly given additional responsibility.

What remains to be accomplished, however, is the systematization of the current empirically based propositions and future specifications about the sociocultural factors influencing the genesis, structure, and content of personal need–value systems.

Nevertheless, we may take it as given that in any society people share values that are more or less applicable to individuals depending on their positions in the social system, and that these values (somewhat variably) are incorporated into the individual's need–value system as more or less personally applicable. I now turn to a consideration of the social influences on the occurrence of *circumstances* that are personally disvalued—that reflect or threaten psychological distance from relatively high priority values that, in turn, contribute to the more inclusive value of overall positive self-evaluation.

The Social Basis of Disvalued Circumstances

In order to understand the psychosocial basis of stress it is necessary to understand not only what the person defines as more or less highly valued states, but also the extent to which the person perceives himself or herself as approximating or being distant from the valued states. That which the individual perceives constitutes the more or less disvalued circumstances. Depending on the nature of the person's need–value system such circumstances might include his or her own traits or behaviors (including self-referent behavior and extensions of the self) and being the object of behaviors by others, individually or collectively considered.

The person is characterized by a complex of interrelated traits and behaviors, including physical aspects (tall, hook-nosed, weighing 150 pounds), behavioral predispositions (aggressive, task-oriented, happy, logical), ascribed or achieved social identities or positions (male, father, Roman Catholic, friend, businessman, motorist, middle class), characteristic role behaviors (father who takes an interest in his children, active member of the church, willing to do anything for a friend), abilities (leadership, musical talent, effectiveness), specific behaviors in specific situations (refusal to follow an employer's instruction), and even the nature of the personal value system that might encompass such desirable states as loyalty, honesty, bodily pleasures, economic success, and professional achievements (after all, we evaluate ourselves in terms of how worthwhile our values are).

A noteworthy subset of personal traits includes symbolic extensions of the self, that is, aspects of the environment including membership groups and physical possessions which we identify as belonging to, or which are identified by others as belonging to, ourselves. Both James (1890) and Cooley (1902) early recognized extensions of the person as influential in self-conception. James referred to the material Me as one part of the self that included the person's body as well as his material possessions and those groups of which he or she is most intimately a part, such as the family; and Cooley's discussion of self-conception referred to "that toward which we have the 'my' attitudes" (1902:40).

A significant subset of personal behaviors consists of responses to self which may reflect valued states. Thus a person may devalue her athletic ability, perceive herself as self-depreciating, and positively evaluate herself because of her ability to depreciate herself (insofar as this self-evaluative behavior approximates other personally held values such as the ability to be "realistic" about one's limitations).

In addition to personal traits and behaviors, our circumstances include what happens to us. We experience life circumstances that are the outcome of individual and collective responses of others. Such outcomes as losing a job, the death of a loved one, loss of money, disapproval by significant others, and, more generally, ongoing failure of others to reciprocate our expectations are clearly value-relevant in the sense that they reflect distance from relatively high-priority desirable states. From one point of view these disvalued circumstances when perceived by the subject become self-disvalued personal attributes. That is, the person perceives himself or herself as a person whom others disapprove, as one who is diminished or alone as a result of the loss of a loved one, as a pauper, or as unemployed or dismissed from a job. For practical purposes, however, the distinction need not be drawn in order to consider the social origin of disvalued circumstances.

To the extent that these attributes, behaviors, and experiences reflect the approximation of personally disvalued states (or being distant from valued ones) and are perceived as such by the subject, he or she will experience subjective distress. The degree of distress associated with the occurrence of disvalued events will depend on priority of the value that is being threatened. Although we may value wealth and a loss of money may constitute a threat to that goal, the degree of distress felt will not be great if the value is fairly low in our hierarchy of values. However, if we strongly identify with wealth as a basis of our self-esteem then even a moderate loss will reflect badly on us and will evoke feelings of self-rejection. Similarly, loss of a loved one will cause distress to the extent that our identity is closely linked with the identity of the loved one that is lost. And the loss of a loved one who is more peripheral to our core being, although regretted, will not be productive of severe and prolonged subjective distress. The extent to which other people's failure to conform to our expectations and to approve of our behavior induces subjective distress depend on the degree of association between these circumstances and our overall self-evaluation. If the failure of others to validate our expectations reflects badly on highly valued social identities, and if the disapproving others are those we admire and with whom we identify, then the degree of felt distress (experienced as self-derogation) will be relatively severe. As other of the contributors to this volume have concluded, the occurrence of disvalued circumstances are distressful by virtue of their implications for overall self-evaluation.

The relevance of the evaluative significance of circumstances for the experience of subjective distress is reflected in a large body of research. An interesting subset of studies reflects a relationship between physiological responses and apparent evaluative significance of social circumstances. Thus, Kaplan (1972) observed that subjects interacting with liked or disliked others were significantly more likely to manifest physiological (galvanic skin) responses, as well as other (particularly socioemotional) responses, than were subjects interacting with neither liked nor disliked social objects. Congruent with these findings are observations of higher subject diastolic blood pressure when the interviewer showed a warm and interactive, as opposed to a neutral and noninteractive, style (Williams et al., 1972), and of significantly greater rises in plasma free fatty acid level where the experimental induction suggested that the task was important rather than unimportant (Back and Bogdonoff, 1964).

To understand the sociogenesis of psychosocial stress, then, we must comprehend the social influences on the occurrence of value-relevant circumstances, particularly on the occurrence of personal traits and behaviors, and—where these may be distinguished from personal attributes—the personal experience of disvalued outcomes of others' responses.

As students of psychosocial stress, we are primarily interested in the social influences on disvalued attributes, behaviors, and other-induced experiences. However, these are understandable only when it is recognized that virtually all personal traits, behaviors, and experiences, valued or disvalued, are socially influenced whether these are considered from a developmental or contemporary point of view. From a developmental perspective the nature of the person's traits and behaviors is profoundly influenced by the responses of significant others in the child's environment who positively or negatively reinforce subject traits and behaviors and with whom the subject identifies more or less strongly (depending on the traits and behaviors of the interacting parties). A child of a particular gender will be rewarded for displaying certain behaviors and characteristics—those displayed by certain role models with which the child will be asked to identify depending on a number of social conditions such as the reward value associated by the subject with traits of the putative role model—but not others. The establishment of an appropriate sex-role identity may be motivated by the need to identify with a model in order to command the attractive goals possessed by the model. Children appear to make the assumption that if they possessed some of the external characteristics of the model they would also possess the desirable psychological properties such as power or love from others (Kagan, 1964).

The stimulus value of the social reinforcement and the nature of the characteristics the child is asked to adopt both presume the operation of social forces that more or less directly influence the child's actual gender-related social role characteristics. The effectiveness of parental reinforcement, for example, depends on the ability of the parent to be in command of rewards and punishments that are meaningful to the child. Such a condition is assured by the early placement and prolonged tenure of the dependent child within the socially defined family unit and by the socially prescribed authority that is a parental prerogative. The actual characteristics that define the gender-related roles are reflected in cultural stereotypes, which in the course of the socialization process induce appropriate sex-related self-descriptions. Thus, "the self-descriptions of men correspond with the male stereotype on such qualities as self-confidence, leadership, independence, ambition, aggression, and ruggedness. For women an analogous correspondence between self-descriptions and the female stereotype is suggested with respect to such attributes as kindness, interest in others, sympathy, sensitivity, and cultural interests" (Wylie, 1979:303). The culturally defined role behaviors associated with a given gender, however, may change over time, and subcultural differentiation has been noted as well (Kagan, 1964).

Looking at a person's traits, behaviors, or experiences from a contemporary perspective, it is clear that the presentation of subject traits and behaviors and the individual or collective responses of others uniformly occur in social context. Society in its nature is "a complex arrangement of social statuses or 'positions' interrelated in lesser social structures through socially defined and sanctioned demands and expectations that incumbents of given statuses are permitted and expected to make upon incumbents of other specified statuses" (Dodge and Martin, 1970:63). At any given time any of a range of statuses or social identities may be applicable to a person. Different people ascribe

different identities to a subject, and in each capacity different expectations of the person are applicable. In short, as this is articulated in
social-interaction theory, the self is seen "as a complex and differentiated construction of many parts. These parts are identities. Thus one's
self may consist in part of an identity as mother, sister, employee,
friend, student, etc., i.e., a set of identities representing one's participation in structured social relationships" (Stryker, 1977:151). Which
identify the person is called upon to accept and conform to in any given
situation is defined by the social context, that is, by the identities of the
other people in the situation. If the identity of the other person in a
particular social context is that of the subject's employer, then the
subject is likely to conceive of himself as an employee and play the role
that is appropriate to this identity. This being the case, how an individual behaves, the attributes she presents to others, and the consequences for the subject of others' responses are normally conditioned
by the self- and other-imposed demands dictated by the social identities and situational context of the interacting parties.

On the understanding that valued as well as disvalued traits, behaviors, and outcomes are socially derived and are conditioned by current
social context, I will phrase the inquiry before us in terms of the social
origins of *disvalued* circumstances.

To the extent that individuals are born with or acquire attributes
(including experiences of disvalued outcomes of others' responses) and
are circumstantially required to perform behaviors that threaten their
basic values or reflect the inability to achieve these values, individuals
will experience a degree of subjective distress. Insofar as the basic
value in question is positive self-evaluation, a history of circumstances
in which individuals come to experience themselves as possessing
highly disvalued attributes and performing disvalued behaviors will
evoke highly distressful self-rejecting feelings.

Because the valuations of traits and behaviors are derived in the
course of the socialization process and are structured by the current
situationally circumscribed social identities of the subject and of those
with whom he or she interacts, it may be assumed that traits and behaviors that are personally disvalued reflect instances of failure to be and
do what the subject and others consensually judge are appropriate
traits or behavior for the subject in the current situation (and, perhaps,
transsituationally). More generally, the failure to be and do what is
appropriate is a disvalued circumstance. Further, to say that the traits
and behaviors are *disvalued* is to presume that the occurrences of the
disvalued circumstances are contrary to the will of the person because,
by definition, people are motivated to distance themselves from disvalued states and to approximate valued states. Thus, in effect, the

occurrence of disvalued traits and attributes reflects instances of *un-motivated deviance*, the subject's unwilling failure to conform to the perception of situationally applicable normative expectations regarding the attributes the subject should possess and the behaviors he or she should perform in specified social situations. To seek the social origins of disvalued attributes and behaviors is, in large measure, to seek the social origins of unmotivated deviance. This is not to say that the personal experience of disvalued circumstances necessarily reflects the de facto failure of the subject to conform to others' judgments regarding situationally appropriate attributes and behavior that are currently applicable to the subject. By the nature of the socialization process, the subject and others will *generally* agree regarding the expectations that are situationally applicable to the subject. However, in the last analysis it is the occurrence of a circumstance that the *subject* defines as a failure to conform to the appropriate expectations of others that is distress inducing.

The occurrence of disvalued circumstances (possession of disvalued attributes, the performance of disvalued behaviors, and/or the experience of adverse consequences of others' individual or collective responses) is a function of four sets of influences: biosocial attributions, situational constraints, inadequate resources, and disvalued responses by others. Each of these is discussed in turn.

Biosocial Attribution

The concept of unmotivated deviance classifies together instances of failure to conform to the normative expectations of specified groups, *where the failure to conform is contrary to the will of the person.* The subject wishes to conform but is unable to do so. Thus, in effect, he or she deviates from the expectations of others. Such unmotivated deviance includes failure to possess *consensually* valued traits. A major source of the inability to display traits within an acceptable range of values is biosocial attribution, the characterization of a subject as possessing a disvalued attribute by virtue of being born with the attribute or having had a particular experience. Independent of or contrary to our wishes, by virtue of being born we find ourselves (1) possessing physical or psychological impairments; (2) characterized in terms of undesirable racial-, ethnic-, religious-, or socioeconomic-related social categories; or (3) falling below acceptable levels of intelligence, physical appearance, strength, or other criteria that form the basis of invidious comparisons. Because along with other group members we have each internalized these values and wish to approximate them, the failure to do so constitutes one class of unmotivated deviance. In addition to the fact of being born, later experiences by definition stigmatize the sub-ject. To have been imprisoned, to have been a patient in a mental hospital, in another age to have been divorced, all constitute enduring disvalued attributes. Whether or not the subject might have been able to control the circumstances leading to imprisonment, hospitalization, or divorce, once the circumstance occurred the subject (contrary to his or her will) is stigmatized. In short, whether by the fact of birth or given social experiences the subject is necessarily disvalued. To be black in a society that values whites, to be foreign born in a society that values native heritage, to be born into the lower classes in a class-conscious society, to be an ex-convict in a law-abiding society is to possess dis-valued attributes due to circumstances that are currently beyond the subject's control. The common element is that what has been done cannot be undone, and given the value system what has been done is disvalued.

Many of these instances of unmotivated deviance are profoundly influenced by such factors as biogenetic dispositions. Thus the proba-bility of being born black, of slight build, of less-than-normal intel-ligence, and broad-nosed will be influenced by such factors. But genet-ic pooling in turn is affected by social conventions regarding social attractiveness and endogamy. The likelihood of being born of a particu-lar social class and ethnic background is a function of such conventions as well. The social influences on stigma that result from later experi-ences is also apparent, consensus dictating the disvalued nature of the past experiences.

Situational Constraints

A second class of circumstances that increase the probability of our failing, contrary to our wishes, to possess valued attributes relates to situational constraints. Two kinds of such constraints are considered here. The first kind relates to inability to identify the appropriate ex-pectations, and the second relates to the inability to fulfill the correctly identified situationally appropriate expectations. The constraints are imposed by the current situation and are therefore to be distinguished from biosocial attributions as explanations of unmotivated deviance that derive from the immutable past. Because the constraints are situa-tionally imposed they are distinguished from personal characteristics, such as inadequacy of resources, which is considered in the following as contributing to the occurrence of involuntary deviance.

Misidentification of Social Expectations. Subjects are increasingly likely to fail to conform to the expectations of others, even under conditions when they are motivated to conform, if they are unable to identify correctly their own social identities and the social positions of those with whom they are interacting in the current situation. Assuming that subjects were properly socialized regarding the roles associated with these identities and otherwise possessed the resources for playing the roles (the contrary case will also be considered), correct identification of the social positions of the interacting parties would be necessary for subjects to behave appropriately. In the absence of correct understanding regarding social identities people cannot know what is expected of them and, therefore, cannot do what is expected of them. A person not knowing the social positions of those with whom he or she is interacting is unable to identify his or her own complementary position and play the role associated with the position. Such circumstances are most likely to arise when the person encounters new sets of interpersonal relationships and where situational cues are vague and/or ambiguous. Members of more mobile segments of our society are more vulnerable to these circumstances.

Conflicting Expectations. A second set of situational constraints against conforming to appropriate (valued) expectations of others relates to the conflicting demands made on subjects at any given time. Although people are motivated to conform to the expectations of all of the other parties with whom they are interacting, the nature of the conflicting expectations are such that they can conform to one set of expectations only at the cost of violating another set. The social system is conceived of as an interlocking set of expectations variously incumbent on individuals depending on their identities and the identities of those with whom they are interacting in particular situations. A person has many such identities (that is, occupies social positions or statuses) in the various subsystems that make up the more inclusive social system. In the nuclear family subsystem a man has numerous identities, such as husband, father, parent, as well as the identities involved in the more inclusive familial system. In the economic subsystem the individual is a consumer, an employee and/or employer, a stockholder. In the political institution, the individual is a voter, a citizen, a member of a political party. In each of these capacities the person is expected to play specific roles (that is, conform to sets of expectations) when interacting with others who have identities within the same or other institutional subsets. A woman who occupies the status of mother in the family subsystem plays one role in relation to her son and a somewhat different role in relation to her daughter within the family system, and in the same capacity (as mother) plays a different role (conforms to other expectations) when interacting with the children's teacher (a social position in the educational subsystem). The possession of identities in the various institutional contexts is assured by the role requirements associated with a particular status that the occupant of the status (1) have identities in other institutions (the mother, in order to fulfill correctly the role obligations associated with that position, is expected to be a consumer in the economic institution and to set a good example for her children in terms of citizenship responsibilities by voting in the context of the political institution) and (2) interact with functionaries in other institutional contexts (as a mother the person is expected to interact with teachers in order to keep abreast of how her children are doing in school).

Because the person may be simultaneously involved in multiple relational contexts (that is, have multiple identities and play more than one role in each capacity in relationship to others who occupy complementary statuses and play complementary roles), the potential exists for the experience of conflicting demands being made on the subject—a situation that frequently arises. Two conditions must be in place for the conflict situation to exist.

First, the *nature of the multiple expectations* that are applicable to the individual at the same time must be such that the satisfactory fulfillment of one precludes the satisfactory fulfillment of others. One cannot be expected to work toward the achievement of worldly goods and to reject them at the same time as would be the case if, *simultaneously*, the person were required to play the role of a businessperson and that of member of a nonmaterialistic religious order. Excluded from consideration are situations where the conflict may be resolved by the availability of increased resources. If, for example, increased economic resources permit the hiring of childcare specialists or homemakers, a woman may be able simultaneously to conform to the work-related expectations of an employer and the requirements of the husband regarding her duty to manage their home. In the absence of such resources, the expectations of husband and employer are not equally likely to be fulfilled. Such situations properly relate to the explanations of involuntary deviance that will be considered in the following section.

Second, for a conflict situation to exist the subject must have an equal emotional investment in fulfilling the various expectations that are incumbent on him or her. The person must perceive the expectations as equally legitimate, and the fulfillment of the expectations must be equally valued. If one expectation is valued more highly than another, the conflict is resolved.

Essentially, two types of situations involving conflicting expectations exist. In the first type the person simultaneously occupies two or
more social positions and in those capacities engages in two or more
social relationships. The roles the person is expected to play (expectations that the subject endorses) in interacting with the other parties in
the context of the two relationships are incompatible. For example, a
person simultaneously is identified as a businessperson and the devout
member of a religious sect. The person is expected by his or her partner
to perform business-related acts that are endorsed by the business community but that the person knows are ethically questionable from the
perspective of the religious sect. The person values business success
and the positive attitudes of the religious fellowship equally. However,
the conflicting expectations ensure that the subject must violate the
expectations of either the business partner or the religious collectivity.

A subcategory of this type takes the form of conflicting role definitions associated with a particular status. For example, a subject occupies the status of husband in relationship to his wife and is expected
by the wife to play an equalitarian role in the relationship, and the
subject is motivated to conform to the wife's expectations. However,
the husband was reared in a family in which the consensus was that the
husband should play an authoritarian role. The subject's parents thus
require that he be an authoritarian husband. The son simultaneously
occupies the status of husband and the status of son. The conflicting
expectations involve how he should behave in the husband role. The
situation is such that he must fail to conform either to the expectations
of the wife or those of his parents with regard to how he plays the role
of husband. Such situations may arise as a result either of social change
in the role definition associated with a particular status or of contemporary subcultural variations in such role definition.

The second type of conflict involves the subject occupying one social
status but simultaneously being called upon to play two or more roles
that make incompatible demands on the subject. The subject is again
engaged in two or more social relationships at the same time. However,
here the multiple relationships stem from multiple roles associated
with one status, rather than from multiple statuses each of which is
defined in terms of its appropriate role. To illustrate this situation, a
mother may be committed to conforming to the expectations of both her
son and her daughter but find that their expectations of her, although
simultaneously applied, cannot be simultaneously fulfilled.

The probability that individuals would be subjected to conflicting
expectations (and therefore would be less likely to perform according
to valued expectations) is a function of a number of interrelated factors.
Generally speaking, the degree to which an individual is subjected to

conflicting expectations is a function of the social rules that (1) preclude simultaneous occupancy of incompatible statuses and/or the requirement of performance in incompatible roles or (2) permit resolution of the incompatibility. The resulting compatibility among multiple statuses is the condition of status integration (Dodge and Martin, 1970). Such social arrangements include the segregation of performance of incompatible roles according to time, place, and person. Such rules would permit business norms to apply in the marketplace during the week and religious norms to apply in church on the Sabbath. Other rules would preclude our interacting with the same people while occupying statuses that make incompatible demands upon those with whom we interact: A man who is promoted from the ranks in the corporate structure to a position of foreman, or in the structure of the armed forces becomes a noncommissioned officer, may find himself in a situation where incompatible expectations are incumbent upon him if he must now change his behavior *toward the same people* from that appropriate to a peer to that appropriate for a superior.

The likelihood of such social arrangements existing at any given time, in turn, is inversely related to (1) the rapid and uneven rates of sociocultural change in diverse social institutional sectors of the more inclusive social system and (2) the resulting complexity and heterogeneity of the social system. These conditions require the person simultaneously to have multiple identities in and interact with representatives of diverse social institutional settings and to be emotionally committed to incompatible role definitions that reflect different stages of the socialization process and the person's diverse subcultural affiliations. Consistent with these conclusions, Mettlin and Woelfel (1974) reported that among rural high-school students stress was positively related to a discrepancy in the expectations of subjects' significant others and to the number of significant others (which presumably would be related to the probability of conflicting expectations). The authors concluded that stress is proportional to the heterogeneity and extensiveness of the communicative network within which the individual is embedded.

In sum, conflicting expectations influence the subject's involuntary failure to conform to others' expectations and thereby influence the experience of distressful self-feelings associated with the perceived failure to achieve valued outcomes.

Inadequate Resources

Whether or not a person will involuntarily fail to possess desirable attributes and to perform desirable behaviors, in effect whether or not the person will display unmotivated deviant responses by failing to meet the expectations that others judge are situationally appropriate for the subject, is in part a function of the inadequacy of the personal and collective resources available to the individual. Adequacy of resources must be considered both in terms of environmental demands and the resources of the person that are available to meet those demands. Any incongruity may be expressed in terms of the demands being too great relative to the resources and/or the resources being inadequate relative to the situational requirements. This viewpoint is well represented among theoretical models of the stress process. In one such model (Warheit, 1979) life events are viewed as passing through adaptive–nonadaptive screens representing the coping resources available to individuals as they attempt to meet the demands imposed on them by the life events. In addition to genetic predisposition, biological constitution, and personality, these screens include culturally transmitted systems of belief that give persons explanations for events and symbolic definitions that attach meaning to events. The screens also include socioenvironmentally given personal resources (socioeconomic statuses, families, interpersonal networks, and secondary organizations). Stress, an altered state of the organism occurring when demands on the person exceed response capabilities, is "a function of the number, frequency, intensity, duration, and priority of the demands viewed in apposition to coping resources" (Warheit, 1979:503).

The social influences on the nature of the socioenvironmental demands and on the adequacy of available resources to meet those expectations are considered in turn.

Socioenvironmental Demands. The nature and level of the expectations incumbent on individuals at any given time is determined by consensual definitions among members of the subject's groups, as well as by more idiosyncratic definitions of those with whom they interact regarding the appropriate attributes they should possess and the appropriate behaviors they should perform given the identities ascribed to the subject, the social relational context, and the more inclusive sociocultural matrix in which these are embedded. Because, as noted earlier, people may be involved in various relational contexts at any given time, different sets of (not necessarily mutually exclusive) demands may be simultaneously applicable to the subject. Because the identities possessed by the person at any particular time in his or her life will change from situation to situation, the demands made on him or her vary. Even where a particular identity is applicable to the person, the demands made on him or her will vary to the extent that the others with whom he or she interacts reflect different subcultural backgrounds, specifically regarding the role definition associated with the identity in question. The variable definitions may reflect cultural heterogeneity or different rates of culture change for different segments of the population. In addition the other person's expectations may reflect idiosyncratic definitions and be deviant from all relevant perspectives.

Over time, as well as at any particular time in people's lives, the demands made on them will change. These changes are associated with (1) changing cultural definitions of role expectations that define particular identities, (2) changing role expectations of the subject by others associated with the others' idiosyncratic experiences, (3) developmentally appropriate changes in identities (and concomitant changes in role definition) over the life course, and (4) other changes in the person's life circumstances that reflect the loss, addition, or redefinition of role expectations applicable to social identities (statuses or positions). Any change in the demands made on individuals effectively changes the availability of resources to meet those changes in the absence of concomitant changes in resources. An increase in demands in the face of constant resources has the effect of decreasing available resources, as a decrease in demands has the effect of increasing the available resources.

The distress-inducing effects of implacable environmental demands has been widely recognized, as in Frank's assertion that the state of demoralization arises when an individual finds that "he cannot meet the demands placed on him by the environment and cannot extricate himself from his predicament" (1973:316). The inability to meet the day-to-day demands of social relationships or the increase in such demands occasioned by life events as noted earlier may be viewed in terms of the appropriately or inappropriately high level of demands or in terms of the inadequacy of the person's resources. Having considered the relevance of level of expectations (environmental demands), the discussion now turns to the availability of resources to meet the expectations.

Adequacy of Resources. Independent of the influence of level of socioenvironmental expectations on the effective availability of resources are the influences of a number of other factors. Before considering these influences, however, the concept of *resources* should be clarified. The term is meant to refer to all circumstances that aid the individual in approximating desirable states and in achieving greater distance from undesirable ones, including the circumstances of genetic dispositions, material possessions, membership groups, social identities, physical characteristics, cognitive patterns, social experiences, perception of environmental demands, and a range of cognitive, affective, and behavioral attributes and response patterns. Excluded from consideration are circumstances that specifically relate to forestalling or reducing the subjective distress ordinarily associated with the failure to meet environmental demands, that is, to approximate valued states and to distance oneself from disvalued ones. Such circumstances will be considered later as influencing the onset and continuity of subject perception of disvalued experiences. These patterns are more like what has often been referred to as *defensive responses*. The circumstances to be considered here as facilitating the meeting of environmental requirements are more appropriately named *adaptive devices* or *coping resources*.

I am making the distinction between the instrumental resources that an individual may use to reach personally and socially valued goals on the one hand, and the strategies employed by the individual to reduce the present and subsequent experience of subjective distress on having failed to achieve these goals (that is, to possess desirable attributes and to perform appropriate behaviors) on the other hand. Personal resources include many of those referred to by Menaghan and Pearlin in earlier chapters: cognitive flexibility, analytic skill, complex conceptual schemata, knowledge (whether based on a broad range of experiences or formal and self-study), a belief in one's ability to master problems, and understanding of the interrelationships among phenomena, motivation to succeed, a facility in influencing others, ability to anticipate the needs of others, the ability to communicate with others, and so on. Also included are awareness of the skills that others in the environment have and the criteria (including material resources) for membership in interpersonal networks that allow one to utilize those resources. Adaptation and coping are facilitated by such traits as the ability to appraise a situation accurately, a tendency to create alternative plans should a primary tactic fail to work, and the ability to anticipate longrange consequences of one's acts. Such traits are discussed by Antonovsky (1979) and are similar to Haan's (1977) characterization of adaptive modes of coping in terms of flexibility, future orientation, and freedom from reality distortion.

A parallel distinction is drawn between the collective resources that are of instrumental value in achieving desirable states (most generally, those goals that contribute to overall positive self-evaluation) and those functions of groups that relate to forestalling or assuaging the distress associated with the failure to achieve valued states (collective patterns of self-justification for failure, provision of emotional support). Again, the latter functions are more appropriately considered later in connection with influences on the onset and continuity of perceived failure to achieve valued states.

The possession of adequate resources is influenced by a number of circumstances. The available literature suggests the following generalizations regarding these mutually influential factors that determine whether the individual (1) will come to possess resources that are necessary to meet environmental demands and (2) will continue to have such resources in the face of changes in the nature of environmental demands and personal resources.

1. *The adequacy of a person's resources are a function of the genetic dispositions, biological constitution, group memberships, and other social identities given to the person at birth.* Not only are these attributes of intrinsic evaluative significance but they also reflect the resources (intelligence, physical hardiness, freedom from pathogenic dispositions) and the likelihood of achieving other adaptive and coping resources that are necessary to meet environmental demands. The likelihood of the achievement of needed resources is a function of (1) the nature of the social groups into which the person is born, (2) the social identities gained from such group memberships, and (3) other socially meaningful attributes possessed by the subject at birth.

Many of the resources developed by the person are the outcomes of interaction in the context of a socially responsive, caregiving group. Thus it is not surprising to learn that less cohesive family environments were found to be associated with developmental delay, speech and language deficits, and behavioral aggression (Fowler, 1980)—traits that impede rather than facilitate the meeting of environmental demands.

In large measure the environmental demands on the subject take the form of role expectations that are associated with particular identities. At birth the subject is assigned a number of such identities by virtue of the structure and characteristics of the family into which the person is born—social identities such as birth order, familial socioeconomic status, and religious affiliation. Other identities are assigned to the subject by virtue of such characteristics, apparent at birth, as gender and race. The early assignment of social identities permits early (informal or formal) instruction to begin regarding the attributes and responses that are the necessary resources for that subject to do what is required throughout the life cycle by virtue of having those social identities. This, of course, presumes the absence of radical social change in these regards during the subject's lifetime. With this proviso, it is concluded that early social identification facilitates the achievement of necessary resources to meet environmental demands.

The social identities (including those based on group memberships) that a person has at birth influence the possession of resources that are more or less effective in facilitating the satisfaction of environmental demands. The identity associated with socioeconomic status is a case in point. Thus, birth into higher socioeconomic strata increase the likelihood of receiving more formal education. Formal education, as Menaghan reminds us elsewhere in this volume, increases the likelihood of cognitive complexity and increases readiness to deal with complexity and novelty, intellectual flexibility, and positive self-perceptions. On the other hand, lower socioeconomic origins are associated with an impoverished learning environment with regard to the acquisition of such resources as cognitive development and language skills (Eron and Peterson, 1982). Billings and Moos (1981) found that more reliance on active attempts to deal with an event and fewer attempts to avoid dealing with the event were associated with less stress. The use of such strategies is more prevalent among the more highly educated and those with more income. Kohn (1976) suggested that the relationship between social class and schizophrenia might be partially accounted for by the influence of lower social class on developing limited and rigid conceptions of social reality that impair resourceful coping with life problems and stresses. Social-class-related differences in coping style were also suggested by findings (Hogarty and Katz, 1971) that lower-class subjects tended to manifest passiveness–dependency, suspicion, and nonparticipation.

2. *Individuals will fail to acquire the skills and experiences necessary for adapting to or coping with the environment as a result of faulty socialization experiences.* Distinct from the variables (such as those just considered) that condition the nature of the socialization experiences are the socialization experiences themselves. These experiences in sum are the patterns of responses that are necessary to fulfill the expectations associated with their various social identities.

Whether or not the individual has the capacity to adapt to value-relevant environmental requirements (thereby forestalling the experience of subjective distress) will depend on the adequacy of his or her socialization experiences with regard to the transmission of specific adaptive patterns for current and anticipated roles, the range of early life experiences provided by socializing agents, the degree of responsibility the subject was assigned in early life roles, and the related induction of such general capacities as autonomy and flexibility. Thus, studies have shown (Forman and Forman, 1981) that children reared in families that supported independence and achievement manifested traits of assertiveness and self-sufficiency, but children reared in families who are actively involved in religious and ethical issues manifested traits of insecurity and guilt. With regard to the general capacity of the individual to adapt to or cope with new requirements of life events, Gutman (1963) attributed the presumed lack of difficulty experienced by middle-class U.S. migrants to the internalization of typical U.S. character traits, including the ability to initiate conversations with strangers and the recognition of the legitimacy of a wide range of behaviors in others. Diversity of experience, as provided by early socialization experience, also appears to be relevant to future coping capacity. At least this conclusion is consistent with the observation (Mann, 1972) that students from families who had made many moves reported less anxiety and placed more value on autonomy and independence than students from nonmobile families.

Adequate socialization with regard to meeting environmental demands is a function of appropriate responses being known to the socializing agent. If such responses are known they can be taught. Consistent with this conclusion are laboratory findings that demonstrated decreased stress (as manifested in physiological responses) as the subjects learned procedures to meet environmental demands. In the context of U.S. Navy underwater demolition team training, Rubin and Rahe (1974) noted that elevated mean serum cortisol coincided with novel experiences about which the men had some anticipatory anxiety, but the levels declined with practice and familiarity. Frankenhaeuser and Rissler (1970) reported an experiment in which subjects were exposed to unpredictable and uncontrollable electric shock; epinephrine output was observed to decrease greatly as the degree of control was varied from a state of helplessness to ability to master a disturbing influence.

To the extent that the environment is characterized by rapid social change, individuals will have less opportunity to learn stable response patterns to known stimuli. They will be, in these circumstances, more exposed to novel stimuli for which stable adaptations are not available. Nor will individuals be willing to teach younger generations specific adaptations if they anticipate that these adaptations will be outdated by the time occasions for their use arises. In like manner cultural heterogeneity (stemming in part from rapid and uneven rates of change) along with a pattern of geographic mobility precludes effective socialization into specific adaptive patterns.

However, as initially novel stimuli (as divorce once was) become more prevalent and in the range of expected events, a common folklore may develop regarding the nature of the demands imposed by the event and how best to meet the demands; such a folklore may be facilitated in its development and dissemination by the mass media.

3. *The adequacy of a person's resources is a direct function of his or her membership in social groupings that make available to the individual resources that are relevant to the approximation to valued states.* Although, as we have noted elsewhere, membership in social groupings may be intrinsically desirable, such groupings also represent collective resources that are more or less available to the individual and are more or less effective in facilitating the fulfillment of environmental demands. The degree to which the resources are available and effective in turn influences the subject's attraction to the group. Consistent with this perspective, Moss (1973) conceived of social relations as information-communicating networks consisting of groupings of communicating and interacting people who transmit a particular configuration of information. People "resonate" with the information in the networks through interaction and communication media. The networks resonate with each other through communication channels that link them. The type of involvement people have with communication networks is based on the degree to which the information utilized is taken from a communication network and the extent to which the information is observed to be accurate and effective by people in their milieus. If individuals find their information taken from the network to be accurate and effective, they feel involvement in the communication network—that is, they identify with the network. If they perceive incongruities between the information they have learned and what they determine to be accurate and effective in the environment, they feel negative involvement with that network—that is, they are alienated from the network. If they do not take their information as a whole from the network but, rather, find their own configuration of information and values accurate and effective in their environments and in that network, they are detached in their involvement with that network—that is, they experience autonomy. Finally, if they do take their information as a whole from the given communication network and observe that what information they have is neither accurate nor effective in that milieu or network, they are uninvolved with that communication network—a noninvolvement characterized as anomie.

Not only does the availability of collective resources facilitate meeting environmental demands but subjects' awareness of this also influences their willingness to undertake adaptive and coping attempts, because they know that in the event of a failure other resources are available.

Although this is not always made clear it should be recognized that among the collective resources of a person are the conforming responses of others to the subject's expectations. The ability of the subject to do what is expected is contingent in part on others reciprocating the subject's expectations. Whether or not the others do so is partly determined by the subject's own behavior (as I will note immediately following) and in part by other influences that will be considered elsewhere in this chapter. In any case, generally, the fulfillment of expectations by others ensures an orderly, predictable environment in which individuals are able to anticipate the outcomes of their own responses and thereby perhaps, meet their own obligations.

The availability of resources is positively related to others' perceptions of subjects' conformity to the expectations of others. Deviant behavior, whether involuntary or purposive, evokes negative sanctions that, in addition to being intrinsically disvalued, may have the effect of depriving people of needed resources that would permit them to achieve other valued states. Subjects may find themselves the objects of negative sanctions of others that effectively deprive them of needed resources even when they conform, in their own minds and from the point of view of group members, to the expectations associated with their own social identity in their current relational contexts. This situation arises from the existence of more or less inclusive and interlocking social systems. This interrelationship among systems makes it possible for a subject to conform successfully to the expectations of his or her membership group in his or her own view and that of other group members, and yet be judged deviant by other groups because the same behavior that was conforming in the socionormative system of the membership group was judged to be deviant from the perspective of the other group's system of normative expectations. To the extent that the other group judges the subject's behavior to be deviant and has the power to do so, it will implement negative sanctions. These negative sanctions will adversely affect the availability of legitimate instrumental resources that are required if the subject is to be able to conform to the expectations of his or her own membership group. In failing to conform to these expectations, against his or her will, the subject by definition manifests unmotivated deviance. Thus, unmotivated deviance may be the indirect result of the attribution of deviance and consequent administration of effective negative sanctions by a non-membership/reference group for behavior by a person who is normative in the context of that person's own membership/reference group.

Not only will deviant behavior evoke responses from others that limit the availability of needed resources but the self-perception of deviant responses may inhibit the subject from feeling free to call upon the group's collective resources when the request might well have been honored.

4. *Adequacy of resources is adversely affected by the subject's past history of (1) failing to display valued attributes and to perform valued behaviors and of (2) being the object of adverse socioenvironmental influences.* Among the major resources possessed by the person are the beliefs the subject holds regarding his or her ability to influence environmental outcomes. Past experiences in which particular responses by the subject are observed to lead to desired outcomes induce what has been termed efficacy expectations, that is, the belief that a person can perform the behavior required to produce an outcome (Bandura, 1977). Related terms referred to in this volume to express such a belief include *self-confidence, mastery,* and *internal locus of control.* Although feelings of self-efficacy may be intrinsically valued, these feelings also reflect instrumental resources because the belief that one can reach desirable states through one's own actions will lead to the search for appropriate resources and goal-oriented action. Objectively available resources will not facilitate goal achievement unless the person believes they exist and is motivated to seek them; and a desired objective is more likely to be met if the person takes action to achieve the goal than if he or she does not (assuming that situational constraints do not preclude successful achievement of valued ends).

On the other hand an individual who is characterized by (1) a history of disvalued life events and (2) the ongoing failure to conform to others' expectations in various relational contexts and to evoke appropriate reciprocal responses from others will develop feelings of impotence—a felt inability to control personal outcomes. The subject's sense of self-efficacy, if it ever existed, erodes, and is replaced by feelings of powerlessness and the expectation of continued adversity regardless of any action the person might take. The cumulative experience of inability to forestall or mitigate adversity is accompanied by loss of motivation to attempt to better one's circumstances. The results of the cumulative experience of adversity have been summarized as *learned helplessness.* Based on the examination of performance and emotional responses to uncontrollable aversive events (Abramson *et al.,* 1978; Miller and Norman, 1979) it has been concluded that learned helplessness arises when failure is attributed to stable causes within the self resulting in self-depreciation, negative affect, low motivation, and generalized expectations for failure.

Consistent with this generalization is a growing body of literature that suggests an association between the inability to control the occurrence of undesirable experiences (or the experience of undesirable events that are beyond one's control), on the one hand, and indices of subjective distress on the other. Such observations are to be expected on two grounds. First, the uncontrollable adverse events are intrinsically undesirable and thus evoke distressful self-feelings. Second, the occurrence of the events signifies the likelihood of being unable to forestall such events in the future. The association of undesirable and/or uncontrollable events with subjective distress specifically suggests that the felt inability to control (that is, to forestall) adverse life events may call into question the individual's feelings of self-efficacy, possibly increasing a sense of helplessness. That is, the exposure to stress represents a situational lowering of self-esteem (Helmreich, 1972) and related feelings of confidence or mastery over the environment. Helmreich (1972) cited a number of observations relevant to this conclusion. Grinker and Spiegel (1945) reported that combat had the effect of inducing a loss of self-confidence regarding personal invulnerability; Wolfenstein (1957) reported a like effect among survivors of natural disasters. Schmideberg (1942) reported that feelings of vulnerability increased among victims of bombing raids. Also consistent with the conclusion is the observation (Johnson and Sarason, 1978) that a person's sense of control obviates any relationship between life events and measures of depression and anxiety. In the absence of feelings of personal control over life events (that is, where individuals are characterized by external locus of control or fatalistic orientations), adverse life events increase the likelihood of depression or anxiety.

5. *Adequacy of resources is adversely affected by changes in life circumstances that increase the environmental demands incumbent on the person relative to existing resources and/or decrease the availability of resources relative to existing life demands.* The changes in the person's life circumstances are in large measure influenced by sociocultural change, passage of the subject through the various stages of the life cycle, and life events resulting from the subject's own behavior or the behaviors of others (in addition to those caused by sociocultural change or signifying movement through the life cycle).

Sociocultural change has both direct and indirect influences on the adequacy of personal resources. More directly, sociocultural change influences both new levels of expectations and the availability of resources. In the case of new expectations, generally sociocultural change introduces novel stimuli into the environment that require adaptive responses but before the adaptive responses are widely disseminated. Redefinition of the female role, which has been called the new feminism (Moulton, 1980), challenges women to meet new expectations prior to the provision of resources (free access to professional training resources, equal employment opportunities) that are necessary to meet those expectations. The growing divorce rate becomes a reality and imposes new expectations on people before the culture provides the adaptive patterns that permit them to meet the expectations. Sociocultural change directly affects the availability of resources, as in the instance of a society-wide economic downturn that deprives people of individual and collective financial resources, and also affects the levels of adaptation required of individuals.

Less directly, sociocultural change may require individuals to respond in ways that increase the probability of a disjunction between environmental demands and necessary resources. Cultural patterns requiring geographical and social mobility are likely to disrupt the normal range of interpersonal patterns and familiar modes of response that individuals employ. Most generally, the individual's repertoires of effective adaptive/coping patterns may become ineffective and maladaptive as social changes create conditions that render existing patterned responses ineffective in meeting the demands newly imposed by others with whom they interact in new regions, communities, or social strata. Geographical mobility, for example, may deprive the person of such resources as language, understanding of customs, and the range of day-to-day response patterns that other people use to achieve their goals or to conform to the normal range of social obligations.

Movement through developmental stages signifies biological change as well as changes in the social identities assigned to the person and in the role definitions associated with the individual's social identities during the various stages of the life cycle. During earlier stages of the life cycle the maturing organization of the nervous system increases the resources available to the person; during late stages the decline in energy and physical dexterity represent a loss of resources. The social identities assigned to the subject at different stages of the life cycle (infant, youth, young adult) and the nature of the social expectations associated with the various identities change as well. More demands are made of older children than younger children; older children tend to experience more life events than younger children (Coddington, 1972). Very old people tend to have fewer demands made on them, perhaps reflected in the fewer events reported by older than by younger men (Ander et al., 1974). Older and married U.S. Navy enlisted men tended to report experiencing events requiring greater readjustment than younger single subjects (Rahe, 1974). However, for employed men between the ages of 30 and 60, Payne (1975) reported that older and married men reported lower magnitudes of life change, perhaps because the middle period of life is more stable than other periods.

Generally the change in demands on the individual is congruent with change in available resources. However, circumstances may arise that create a disjunction between expectations and resources needed to meet those expectations. In early phases of the life cycle, the individual's dependency responses might be appropriate to the expectations of the individuals in the family environment. At later phases of the life cycle, however, these resources are inappropriate to environmental demands for independence. At that stage new demands, which might be beyond the capacity of the individual, are imposed. The passage from elementary to junior high school may involve demands on resources that the individual has yet to acquire, resulting in a disturbed self-image (Simmons et al., 1973). The loss of energy, economic resources, and physical dexterity, and other accompaniments of the aging process, may lead the individual to fail to conform to what the person continues to regard as legitimate expectations. Here, the change is in the diminution of resources in relation to constant expectations due to a lag in the adjustment of expectations to resources.

Among the developmentally linked changes in personal circumstances that have implications for the adequacy of personal resources are *life events*. These events are a subset of a more inclusive set of events that are not necessarily tied to socially recognized stages of the life course but do have implications for the adequacy of the resources possessed by the person relative to environmental demands.

In form, life events are manifested as the acquisition of new social identities (or statuses), the divestment of other social identities, and the redefinition of the roles associated with social positions that the person continues to occupy. The life events are evidenced in the subject's recognition of the changes and/or in the changes in others' attributions to and expectations of the subject. Any event may imply one or more of the formal changes. Death of a wife, for example, implies the loss of the status of husband, the redefinition of the role expectations of the status of father (functions previously performed by the mother must now be performed by the remaining members of the family), and the addition of the status of widower, with its new set of rights and obligations.

Independent of their intrinsic evaluative significance (insofar as the event reflects approximation to or increased distance from desirable or undesirable states), life events have implications for changes in the adequacy of resources available to the person. As noted earlier, the degree of congruence between demands of the environment and the appropriateness of the personal and interpersonal resources of the individual to meet those demands depends on both the range of effective resources that the individual possesses and the level of demands made on the individual. Changes in the individual's life circumstances that either reduce the range of available effective resources or increase the demands made on the subject will decrease the congruence between demands and resources and, thereby, ultimately increase the experience of psychological distress. Various life events may bring about changes in resources and/or environmental demand. With regard to personal and interpersonal resources, completing a course of study or receiving a promotion may increase the sense of confidence in one's own ability; entry into a graduate program may provide the knowledge necessary to adapt to a range of environmental demands; a range of experiences may lead to the acquisition of skills in adjusting to changing circumstances; illness or injury may deprive an individual of strength or stamina; residential mobility may deprive an individual of various helping resources such as advisers or professional services. These or other life events may increase the range of environmental demands on the individual. Receiving a promotion may carry with it demands for higher levels of performance and a new set of obligations; marriage and parenthood involve obligations to provide for other individuals; graduation from school implies obligations to enter the work force; retirement decreases obligation regarding performance, as does hospitalization.

The same events may have complex consequences for changes in resources and environmental demands. An event may either increase or decrease personal and interpersonal resources and may either increase or decrease environmental demands on the individual. Generally, a decrease in personal and interpersonal resources and an increase in environmental demands will be associated ultimately with an increase in psychological distress. When considering the consequences of life events with regard to resources and demands, however, it is necessary to consider the net consequence: A particular event may serve both to increase some resources and decrease others, and to increase some obligations and decrease others. Thus, residential mobility on the one hand provides the kinds of experiences that increase people's knowledge of how to adapt to changing circumstances while at the same time depriving them of habitual responses in solving everyday problems and of the network of others whom they come to depend on to help solve the problems. People learn flexible responses but lose the comfort of the established patterns of where to shop, what doctor to use, neighborhood friends to call on for advice, and so on. The event of a person's child getting married and leaving home, on the one hand, decreases the range of obligations he or she may feel toward the child, but on the other hand may increase the range of obligations imposed on the subject by the spouse.

Considering the effects of life events on both resources and demands, a *single* event may have any of four kinds of net outcomes. The event may result in (1) a net increase in resources and a net increase in environmental demands (as when marriage increases level of social supports but also increases the range of demands made on the individual by the spouse), (2) a net increase in resources and a decrease in environmental demands (as when a child leaves home, thus increasing the availability of material resources while decreasing the range of obligations the subject feels toward the child), (3) a net decrease in resources and a net increase in environmental demands (as when buying a new house results in a decrease in available funds and an increase in a person's range of obligations with regard to keeping the house and grounds in good repair), or (4) a net decrease in resources and a net decrease in environmental demands (as when retirement decreases income and decreases the range of expectations incumbent on an individual).

Just as a single event may influence a net increase or decrease in environmental demands with the result of more or less adequate resources being available to the individual, so will the concentration and conjunction of events at any time influence the adequacy of resources that are available to meet environmental demands. A person may possess adequate resources to meet the demands of evenly spaced events (along with the ongoing demands of social relationships), but the concentration of demanding life events over a brief period may strain the person's previously adequate resources. In related fashion the linkages of the events over a brief period will influence the availability of resources. A person may have adequate resources to meet the demands of even a concentration of life events over a brief time span. However, should these events occur following an event that diminishes the person's resources (as when migration to another cultural region disrupts normal coping/adaptive patterns) then the subject would not have the resources available to meet the environmental demands.

Life events may arise from independent causes or be mutually influential. In any case the effects of various individual events, varying concentrations of events, and different temporal linkages among life events over time, along with the other influences previously considered, result in more or less adequate resources to permit the subject's desired conformity to socioenvironmental expectations.

The focus on instrumental resources may help explain the observation from the life-events literature that, in general, adverse events that are predictable and controllable are experienced as less aversive than stresses that are not controllable (Bootzin and Max, 1980). Perhaps reflecting the former phenomenon, during World War II Londoners who were bombed with considerable frequency showed relatively few anxiety reactions compared to the considerable anxiety and fear experienced in the surrounding country villages where bombing was much less frequent and predictable (Vernon, 1941). An example of the stress-inducing effect of absence of controllability is that during World War II pilots of heavy bombers reported less fear than their gun crews. Fighter pilots experienced the least fear although causalties were higher for fighters (Rachman, 1978).

The significance of predictability and controllability may be in their influence on perceived personal resources for achieving valued and avoiding aversive states. The predictability of an event may permit the individual to garner whatever resources are perceived as necessary to forestall or achieve a future activity, or at least to mitigate the inevitable disvalued experience. In the case of controllability, this characteristic of an event implies that the subject possesses or at least perceives himself or herself as possessing the personal resources to minimize the occurrence of disvalued events. Pilots would have more control over the situation than crew members and fighter pilots would perceive themselves as being better able to avoid attack. In any case, inadequacy of instrumental resources remains a major determinant of the occurrence of disvalued circumstances.

Attention is now focused on the fourth set of influences on the occurrence of disvalued circumstances (in addition to biosocial attribution, situational constraints, and inadequate instrumental resources): disvalued responses by others.

Disvalued Responses by Others

Although other aspects of the environment such as natural events (floods, earthquakes) may have adverse impacts on the individual, the emphasis here is on socially induced adversity—the collective or individual responses of others that frequently constitute the occurrence of personally disvalued outcomes. As noted earlier, disvalued attributes and behaviors are influenced by a number of factors. One of these factors is the failure of others to reciprocate our expectations, circumstances that we perceive as reflecting personally disvalued states. The failure to reciprocate expectations may take any of a number of forms depending on the social relational context. As Pearlin points out else-where in this volume, a spouse may fail to conform to the expectations of the subject in a number of ways including not having the same degree of emotional investment in the relationship as the subject, not sharing the subject's self-image, not performing the instrumental role functions associated with the spouse's social position, and failing to feel and express affection toward the subject. The failure to conform to parental expectations may be reflected in the subject's child's bad be-havior at school, achieving less-than-acceptable grades, failing to show respect to parents, associating with undesirable peers, failing to gain popularity among peers, embarking on a career line that is inappropri-ate to the family socioeconomic position, and rejecting such parental virtues as religious participation, abstinence from misuse of alcohol or other drugs, and hard work. As a consequence the subject perceives himself as the husband of a shrewish wife and the father of incorrigible children, self-perceptions that contribute to the subject's overall self-evaluation as less than worthy.

Disvalued responses of others encompass such diverse responses as disobedience by children, absence of positive responses by others, loss of job, death of a loved one, bizarre behavior by significant others, and ostracism by erstwhile friends. Each of these is interpretable as the failure of others to conform to the subject's expectations of how they will and should respond to the subject and those with whom (or that with which) the subject identifies—expectations relating to patterns of deference, reciprocity of positive affect, continuity of employment, continuing physical presence, patterns of cognitive and affective re-sponse, and acceptance by membership groups.

The failures of others to conform to the subject's expectations, that is, instances of personally disvalued responses by others, may be cate-gorized according to the several causes of these responses. One set of such disvalued behaviors includes purposive negative responses by others that serve as negative sanctions stimulated by the others' percep-tions of the subject's disvalued attributes or behaviors. A second set includes response patterns by others that constitute unintended dis-valued outcomes for the subject. The third set encompasses others' responses that reflect purposive failure to conform to the subject's ex-pectations, that is, responses that stem from deviant dispositions of the others. Each is considered in turn.

Negative Sanctions by Others. Negative sanctions by others reflect the purposive failure to conform to the subject's ordinarily legitimate expectations of the others in response to the others' perception of the subject's failure to be and do what is regarded as appropriate, given the subject's social identity, in the situation. Thus, the loss of respect for and the withholding of affection from the subject by the wife and children in the example just given might reflect negative attitudinal responses to the subject's inability to earn a living if he were laid off from his job—manifestly, a failure of the subject to conform to consensual expectations regarding his roles as husband and father. Similarly, others will negatively sanction gender-inappropriate role behaviors. The intensity of the sanctions (the value associated with the unreciprocated expectations) is a function of the consensual values relating to conformity to gender-appropriate expectations and, less directly, of the social determinants of the consensual evaluative structure.

Others may apply negative sanctions to the subject's ongoing or episodic display of particular attributes or behaviors, in effect punishing him or her for possessing disvalued attributes or behaviors. In addition the others may apply negative sanctions to the person because of the *cumulative* impact of adverse socioenvironmental influences as well as the possession of disvalued attributes and the performance of disvalued behaviors. The person is derogated as a "loser" or as having "hard luck."

Unintended Disvalued Responses. A second set of others' deviant responses stems from biosocial ascriptions, situational constraints, or absence of adequate resources that—contrary or irrelevant to the will of individual or collective others—preclude fulfillment of the subject's expectations. Thus, the expectations of having a "normal" infant, of the continuing presence of a loved one, and of receiving a raise may be thwarted by the fact of congenital deficiencies, accidental death, and social system-wide economic depression. In like manner, in the context of ongoing social relationships the person with whom the subject is interacting may fail to reciprocate the subject's expectations for the same range of reasons that apply to the subject's involuntary deviance. Thus, the person may be involved in status sets or role sets that preclude conformity to the subject's expectations without violation of higher-order values; the person may perceive the other's expectations of him or her as ambiguous; the person may not have the resources available, including those that are biogenetically given, that are prerequisite to the fulfillment of role expectations. As a result of upbringing, a person may be incapable of freely expressing emotion, thus precluding conformity to the expectation of the subject that the other person do so.

Not infrequently the failure of others to conform to the subject's expectations is the simple result of the interacting parties not sharing expectations regarding situationally appropriate behavior. This may occur as a result of subcultural differentiation or of the lag between the performance of newly developmentally appropriate behaviors by one party and the acceptance of the behaviors as appropriate by the other party. The former situation is illustrated by variable subcultural definitions of the appropriate role to be played by a wife. The latter situation is illustrated by the developmentally appropriate changes in children who become more immersed in the peer subculture and attenuate the emotional relationship with parents over time. To the extent that parents continue to expect attention and obedience from the children, and to the extent that this expectation is unrewarded by virtue of their developmentally appropriate physical and emotional distancing from the parents, the parents will perceive the children as failing to conform to their expectations.

Many of the examples of role restructuring cited by Pearlin in this volume may be reinterpreted in terms of changes in the willingness of others with whom people interact to conform to formerly legitimate expectations that the subjects continue to think of as legitimate. In the case of the gradual reversal of roles between parents and children during the aging process, the points at which the children with whom the subject (as parent) interacts in the context of the interpersonal relationships redefine their roles as less subordinate. Consequently, these points of interaction fail to conform to the expectations of the subject and reflect instances of deviant (from the point of view of the subject) responses by the children. It is to be hoped, of course, that over time consensus will be achieved between the parents and children regarding the legitimacy of the restructured roles. However, until that point the individual will continue to feel distressed by the refusal of others to reciprocate what the subject regards as continuing legitimate expectations. It is also possible that the subject will never adapt to the changing expectations although the social order at large regards the change as legitimate. Depending on the emotional investment the individual has in the old identity and role he or she may resist greatly the demand by others that the role be restructured, as when the superordinate parent is expected to relinquish authority over the child and finally, with advancing years, become dependent on the child.

Others' Motivated Deviant Responses. A third category of deviant responses by others encompass instances where the others' responses stem from their own deviant dispositions, as when failure to conform to expectations of the subject in one relationship reflects the others' displacement of anger toward those who rejected him or her in another relational context. Unlike the first category of responses, such behaviors refer to the failure of *members of the subject's membership group* to reciprocate the subject's *appropriate* behavior. Where subjects in their own minds and from the perspective of other group members conform to others' expectations and yet either fail to evoke conformity to their own legitimate expectations or are called on to conform to illegitimate expectations, they will suffer the experience of increased frustration of personal values. This frustration as well as that stemming from the other self-devaluing experiences in the normative structure initiates processes that culminate in deviant dispositions.

The causes of the purposive failure of others in the interpersonal network to conform to the subject's expectations are the same as those leading to the subject's motivated failure to conform. These causes have been outlined elsewhere (Kaplan, 1980, 1982) and will be discussed here in connection with a consideration of determinants of the perception of self-devaluing circumstances. Briefly, the genesis of deviant dispositions is thought to derive from the cumulative experience of self-devaluing experiences in membership groups. Where the experience of self-devaluation is pervasive, the subject loses motivation to conform to, and acquires motivation to deviate from, the total normative structure. Thus the particular motivated deviant response adopted in the hope of reducing self-rejecting feelings reflects the total rejection or avoidance of the membership group's normative system, as when people totally isolate themselves from interpersonal experiences, affiliate with an oppositional subculture, or operate within systems of delusional thinking. However, if a particular subsystem is associated with self-devaluing experiences, the subject loses motivation to conform to, and acquires motivation to deviate from, the normative expectations *of that subsystem*, and in fact adopts available deviant response patterns that offer the promise of net self-enhancing consequences. If the source of self-rejection is the occupational subsystem, the deviant behavior might take the form of leaving the job or of lowered productivity. If the source of self-rejection is the marital relationship, the deviant response (from the perspective of the subsystem) might take the form of divorce or denial of affectional and instrumental reciprocity.

The social influences on deviant responses by others, then, are varied, and include: (1) the others' perception of the subject's deviant response (perceptions that in turn are a function of the subject's actual traits and behaviors and the situations in which they are presented), (2) factors that influence unmotivated deviance by the others (the same factors that were considered as influences on the subject's unmotivated deviance), and (3) factors that influence the genesis of motivated deviance by the others (the same factors that will be considered later as influencing the adoption of deviant adaptations to stress). Regardless of the cause, the continuing failure to receive desirable reciprocal responses in diverse relational contexts (as when experiencing refractory children, an unaffectionate spouse, or inadequate job satisfactions) is akin to what has been referred to as persistent role problems (Pearlin and Schooler, 1978), daily hassles (Lazarus and Cohen, 1977) and major difficulties in living (Brown and Harris, 1978). Episodic occurrences whereby others fail to conform to the subject's expectations (as when the subject is fired or experiences divorce, a child leaves home, or a loved one dies) are generally called stressful life events (Dohrenwend and Dohrenwend, 1974).

Specific instances of deviant responses by others may properly be categorized in one or more of these classes. The failure of children to obey or of the spouse to reciprocate affection may reflect variously the administration of negative sanctions, situational constraints, or their own deviant dispositions. Other instances generally fall into only one category. The death of a loved one (excluding suicide), accidental death, or being laid off from a job will generally fall into the second category of responses—nonmotivated failure to conform to the subject's expectations—although the subject may appear to attribute malevolence to the other (as when the person becomes angry with the deceased for "leaving" or the employee views the low salary level as punitive rather than as a function of impersonal laws of the marketplace).

The various disvalued responses of others are mutually influential. For example, the employer's act of firing the subject (whether because of economic changes or as a result of the subject's inadequate role performance) evokes negative sanctions in the form of disobedience or withholding of affection by other family members.

Together the adverse responses of others, whether due to the subject's own deviant responses, the unmotivated (circumstantially required) responses of others, or the deviant dispositions of the others, are distress inducing insofar as they reflect badly on the achievement of valued states that in turn influence the degree to which the need for overall positive self-evaluation is achieved. Being demoted or fired may reflect badly on people's professional performances, which they value, as the failure of others to reciprocate in any relational context reflects adversely on the ability of subjects to perform adequately in their more or less valued social identities—adequacy being indicated by the ability to elicit appropriate responses from others as well as by the perception of their own role performances. Additional workplace-related deviant responses by others include the inappropriate (as viewed by the subject) expectations by work supervisors of inordinate amounts of work and the failure of employers to provide appropriate rewards including individual recognition, credit for contributions, and material rewards. The failure to receive appropriate rewards indicates that what individuals do is of little value in the system and, indeed, that they are easily replaceable. The material rewards that an individual receives, quite apart from any other intrinsic or instrumental value they might have, is directly stressful insofar as material rewards are interpreted as an indication of the worth of the work and, therefore, of the individual.

The ongoing failure of others to reciprocate legitimate role expectations in a variety of relational contexts calls into question the worth of the subject as an object of reciprocation and the validity of the subject's conforming behavior in a social position in which he or she is emotionally invested. Because we are emotionally invested in our social roles, the failures of others to validate these roles by conforming to the expectation of others we hold in these roles represent intrinsic sources of distress. Proper performance (including the ability to evoke appropriate responses from others) in these roles represents intrinsic criteria for self-acceptance. The degree to which the failure of others to reciprocate expectations is self-devaluing will depend on the degree to which we are emotionally invested in the particular role, that is, the degree to which they contribute to our identity. To the extent that the failure of others to reciprocate our expectations impinges on highly valued roles, such failure will be highly distressful. And ongoing role strains, as reflected in the failure of others to reciprocate expectations, are functions of their relevance to our self-evaluation and self-feelings.

The expression of negative responses by others, independent of their relevance for validation of the subject's prized social roles, reflects psychological distance from intrinsically valued states. In the course of socialization experiences in membership groups, we learn that to be the object of positive attitudes by significant others (to be loved by our parents, to be well liked) is in itself the basis for approving responses from others and self. We learn that to be hated by others is a basis for rejection by others and self-rejection.

These experiences along with others (such as the experience of physical injury, death of a loved one, or a child leaving home) impinge on still other personal values. Physical injury threatens highly valued aspects of the self. The death of a loved one and a child leaving home threaten the valued integrity of membership groups with which we closely identify and, together with other adverse circumstances, call into question our desirable sense of having control over environmental outcomes.

Certain events have a dual significance for our personal values. On the one hand they reflect the failure of others to conform to our expectations of how they should behave toward us. On the other hand they may reflect adverse socioenvironmental impacts on others with whom we identify. The death of a loved one may seem to reflect the failure of a loved one to conform to our expectations of indefinite physical presence of the loved one. In this instance we may feel betrayed by the "deviant behavior" of the other. Alternatively (but not necessarily mutually exclusively) the significance of the death of the loved one may be that a person with whom we identify closely experiences an adverse outcome, with the effect that we feel ourselves diminished by the loss. Either meaning would imply the personal experience of disvalued outcomes.

These last observations call to mind that those we love, the groups we belong to, in general that with which and those with whom we identify, are extensions of the self. Responses by others that have disvalued outcomes for the psychological extensions of the self have disvalued outcomes for us ourselves. An injury to them psychological or otherwise is an injury to us. We suffer for them as we would suffer ourselves. When the athletic team with which we identify or the school that the team represents is the loser in a contest it is our own esteem that suffers. And the extent to which we experience distress is the extent to which we need the success that identification with a winning team would have brought.

In sum, a major source of disvalued experiences consists of the responses of others that reflect adverse outcomes for ourselves. The intensity of the experience of distress consequent on others' responses is a function of the personal priority of the values that appear to be frustrated by such responses, particularly as they appear to frustrate or appease the overall need for positive self-evaluation.

The Social Basis of Perception of Disvalued Circumstances

To this point psychological distress has been explained by the occurrence of circumstances that are disvalued by the subject. However, the presence of psychological distress further presumes that the subjectively disvalued circumstances are perceived, anticipated, recalled, or, indeed, imagined as such. If the person does not become aware of the

(real or fantasized) circumstances that signify to him or her approximation to disvalued states or distance from valued states, the person presumably will not become distressed. If the person does not remain
aware of such circumstances he or she will not experience prolonged
distress. Under what conditions, then, will a person become and remain aware of circumstances that are subjectively interpreted as contrary to his or her relatively high-priority values? The remainder of this
section considers the social influences on the perception of disvalued
experiences.

In general the perception of personally disvalued experiences is a
function of (1) whether or not the personally disvalued circumstances,
in fact, occurred, (2) the nature of the person's system of concepts and
values that attribute cognitive and affective significance to the circumstances, and (3) the person's personal resources that permit changes in
the cognitive and evaluative significance of the circumstances.

Occurrence of Disvalued Circumstances

Current awareness by the individual that he or she currently possesses disvalued attributes and performs disvalued behaviors, fails to
possess valued attributes and to perform valued behaviors, and/or is
the object of disvalued happenings or ongoing responses by others in
the environment is influenced by the actual occurrence of these phenomena. The person, indeed, fails to possess valued attributes and
perform disvalued behaviors, and is in fact the object of disvalued
environmental responses. If any support for this generalization is
needed, the empirical literature includes numerous reports of associations between personal traits or behaviors and isomorphic self-conceiv-
ing responses, although these reports permit very different interpretations regarding the causal relationships among these variables and the
associations reported are far from perfect. Sweet and Thornburg (1971),
for example, reported that black and white 3-, 4-, and 5-year-olds were
able to choose as the picture that looked most like them a picture of the
child of their own sex and race from among a set of pictures of six males
and six females equally divided among black, white, and Oriental categories; school grades have been observed to be correlated with self-
concept of school ability or intelligence (Bachman, 1970; Purkey,
1970). Awareness of certain personal traits and behaviors such as group
membership increases with maturational stage. Thus, Sweet and
Thornburg (1971) provided 3-, 4-, and 5-year-olds with figures of various size asking them to "make" their very own family and to identify
the various members of the family to the examiner. Only 50% of the

subjects included themselves in the family group. However, there was a steady increase with age in the tendency to include the self as part of the family. Generally, in the course of maturation older children are increasingly likely to conceive themselves in terms of inner thoughts and feelings rather than the public and visible aspects of self. Rosenberg (1979), summarizing literature on self-concept, noted that the young children are likely to conceive of themselves in terms of elements of a social exterior (that is, more or less specific components that are easily observed and do not require probing or sophisticated synthesis).

The actual occurrence of disvalued (or, for that matter, valued) circumstances influences self-awareness both directly and indirectly.

Personal Traits or Behavior as Direct Stimuli for Self-perception. The most direct route by which personal traits or behaviors may influence self-referent cognitive responses is by immediately and directly becoming objects of self-awareness. That is, "the person could develop concepts of himself by simply labeling his dominant behavior patterns" (Gergen, 1971:64). A sense of self-efficacy, for example, is said to be derived primarily from personal mastery experiences based on performance accomplishments, particularly where favorable outcomes were perceived to be self-determined, success is achieved with minimal effort, the task mastered was challenging rather than easy, and discernible progress in the face of setbacks was discerned (Bandura, 1977). Or a person may come to identify with a role he or she is required to play. In this regard Gergen, defining identification in terms of the person coming to see himself or herself as actually having the attributes characterizing the role and secondarily as tending to adopt the role behavior for use in situations where the behavior is not strictly required, comments: "In short, the person comes to develop an identity based on the role and to use this identity in his behavior over a wide variety of circumstances" (1971:55).

Whether or not particular circumstances directly stimulate self-perception of experiences will depend upon a number of factors, not the least important of which are the nature of the circumstance and the context in which it is observed. Regarding the *nature* of the circumstance, some traits, behaviors, or occurrences depend on the responses of others (we are aware of our popularity because people express the desire to be in our company). However, we may become aware of some physical talents more directly, without the intervening responses of others. The distribution of such circumstances may be related to social identities such as those based on gender. In this culture, a girl requires feedback from the social environment to influence her awareness of many of the traits associated with her gender-related role (attractiveness, social poise). However, the situation is different for a boy. Many of his important sex-related behaviors are developed while alone. Many such skills involve solitary practice and at the same time permit direct awareness of the skills in question. He does not require the reactions of others in order to become aware of, for example, when he has reached a level of achievement in certain gross motor or mechanical skills. The boy receives from these private activities information that confirms his belief that he is acquiring appropriate masculine traits (Kagan, 1964:152).

The traits or behaviors that are directly perceived may be taken at face value (we might conceive of ourselves exactly in terms of what we observe) or may be interpreted as implying nonobservable characteristics. The delineation of the process whereby we interpret our attributes or responses as implying nonobservable traits or behaviors is the special contribution of self-perception theory. Central to self-perception theory (Bem, 1972) is the statement that individuals come to know their own attitudes, emotions, and other internal states in part by inferring them from observations of their own overt behavior and/or the circumstances in which the behavior occurs; and thus, to the extent that internal cues are weak, ambiguous, or uninterpretable, an individual like an outside observer must rely upon external cues to infer his or her own inner state. To this might be added "or any other nonobservable state" such as a social identity. Thus, while a male's skill with tools might simply influence the self-cognition of being skilled at using tools, it might also be interpreted as an appropriately masculine trait, that is, as a confirmation of a masculine identity. Traits that have no *necessary* connection with social identities permit inferences regarding that class of self-cognitions known as *identifications*, that is, beliefs "that some of the attributes of a model (parents, siblings, relatives, peers, and so on) belong to the self" (Kagan, 1964:146).

The *context* as well as the nature of the circumstances influence the person's self-perception. Not all of the person's traits, behaviors, and experiences are subjectively perceived in any given situation. Those that are perceived tend to be those that are stimulated by environmental cues—either those that imply the *distinctiveness* of, or those that imply the particular *relevance* of, certain traits, behaviors, or experiences. McGuire and Padawer-Singer, applying the distinctiveness theory of selective perception to the spontaneous self-concept, argued that "we notice any aspect (or dimension) of ourselves to the extent that our characteristic on that dimension is peculiar in our social milieu"

(1976:744). For example, a black woman is more likely to become aware of her womanhood when associating with black men and of her blackness when associating with white women. In support of the personal-distinctiveness hypothesis, data were offered indicating that those who were atypically younger or older were more likely to mention their ages spontaneously than those who approximated the class mode as part of their self-description. Foreign-born children were appreciably more likely than native born children to mention their birthplaces. With regard to hair color, eye color, and weight as well, people having unusual characteristics spontaneously mentioned them more than those with more typical characteristics. Additionally, members of the minority sex in any given class were more likely to spontaneously mention their sex in self-descriptions. Elsewhere, McGuire and his associates (McGuire *et al.*, 1978) found support for the general proposition that ethnic identity is salient in children's spontaneous self-concepts to the extent that their ethnic group was in the minority in their social milieu at school.

Other environmental cues stimulate subject awareness of personal traits, behaviors, or experiences because of the relevances of these in the present context. The person is more likely to be aware of a student identity and of accomplishments (or lack thereof) as a student when in a school building and interacting with a teacher than in other social contexts. Other important cues in the social context are the *manifest* expectations that others with whom the subject interacts apply to the subject. The expectations stimulate the awareness of the personal circumstances that signify the person's ability or inability to meet the environmental demands.

Personal Traits or Behaviors as Indirect Influences on Self-referent Cognition. Personal circumstances (in context), in addition to evoking directly self-awareness of the circumstances that occur in reality, are not necessarily perceived by the subject. Frequently the perception must be mediated by the responses of others (including the manifest expectations of others, referred to previously, that serve as contextual cues). The person's traits, behaviors, and experiences stimulate others' recognition of and response to the subject's circumstances depending on the meaning of the person's attributes and responses in the social context and as evaluated against the background of the consensual value system. However, once the others have responded, these responses will influence the subject's self-referent cognition by sensitizing the subject to the personal circumstances that evoked the (presumably meaningful) responses by the others in his or her environment or to the implications of the circumstances. Thus, if people are rewarded or punished for a particular behavior, they are more likely to be aware of having performed the behavior than if they are not.

The responses of others to a person may be more or less directly related to the subjectively recognized attribute or behavioral tendency. More directly, others may communicate to a person that he or she possesses a particular trait or is displaying certain behaviors. Under certain conditions, the subject may interpret (accept as true) the communications of others as indications that he or she does in fact display the precise trait or behavior in question. Less directly, the others' responses may stimulate the subject's inference that he or she possesses a nonobservable attribute, as when self-awareness of being the object of deferential responses by others leads to the self-cognition "therefore I must be a powerful person."

The subject is more likely to become aware of and to conceive of himself or herself in the terms that elicited others' response to the extent that the responses of others are relatively persistent over time and are uniform at any given point in time. If the differential responses are observed on a day-to-day basis and uniformly from diverse significant others the subject is more likely to become aware of the responses than if they are given only occasionally and by some, but not others, of the significant people in his or her environment.

Personal Conceptual and Value Systems

It is apparent that a person is more likely to be aware of personal traits, behaviors, and experiences, and to conceive of himself or herself in these terms, if these personal experiences in fact occur than if they do not. Yet a person does not always become aware of and conceive of objective circumstances. Whether or not a person becomes aware of, and how the person conceives of, personal experiences is conditioned by the person's conceptual and evaluative systems.

Personal Conceptual System. People's cognitive responses to their own attributes, behaviors, and experiences will depend in part on the system of concepts that they characteristically use to structure their environment. The mass of sensory data that impinge on individuals' sensory organs are selectively perceived and organized in accordance with these concepts or symbolic constructs that (1) sensitize the individual to common elements of otherwise heterogenous examples, (2) categorize the diverse instances sharing the common elements, and (3) label the categories in ways that express the common elements of the diverse examples. In theory, the ways in which personal traits, behaviors, or experiences can be categorized are limitless. The ways in which these phenomena *are* categorized, however, are limited by the concepts available to the person. The person attends to certain traits, behaviors, or experiences (or particular aspects of these), rather than others, because of the concepts that are habitually used. Through the use of these concepts the person, in effect, imposes a reality on a mass of otherwise unorganized sensations. Particular activities are classified as, for example, work rather than play, and as exemplars of efficient rather than inefficient behavior. Were the concepts habitually used by the person different, such distinctions might not be drawn. Although people will on occasion offer self-descriptions that are contrary to their conceptualization of and beliefs about themselves for the purpose of eliciting desired responses from others, generally the system of concepts used to structure perceptions of personal traits, behaviors, and experiences are reflected in verbal self-descriptions.

Although intergroup, interindividual, and developmental (Montemayor and Eisen, 1977) variability in systems of concepts used to structure data about self (as well as about the world in general) may be noted, at any given time a person uses a relatively stable and more or less consensual conceptual system to guide selective cognitive structuring of personal attributes, behaviors, or experiences. This universal pattern is consistent with the postulate that universally people *need* to conceptualize themselves. Subjects learn that need satisfaction is contingent on their environment, in particular the responses of others. People also learn that the responses of others are contingent on their own attributes and behavior. Therefore, in order to anticipate how others might respond to their own traits and behaviors they must be able to rehearse the responses of others to their own hypothetical traits or behaviors, an ability which in turn depends on the ability to conceptualize the self in terms of a socially meaningful set of arbitrary symbols. In fact, among the behaviors that evoke responses from others is the use of particular conceptual systems. As part of the socialization process people are taught numerous other social conventions. As in the case of any normative expectation, then, conformity (here in the form of using certain conceptual distinctions) is rewarded, and deviation (here in the form of use of inappropriate conceptual distinctions) is punished. The severity of the appropriate sanctions administered by others will be a function of the socially defined value attached to the conceptual distinction (and this in turn may be associated with the functional value of the conceptual distinction for survival of the social system in its present form).

In addition to being influenced by the *reward value* of using it, the particular conceptual system is influenced to some extent by the *regularities in behavior* displayed by people whether out of a need to conform to expectations associated with particular social identities or for other reasons. Such regularities tend to facilitate symbolic recognition of the pattern in the form of self-referent concepts or, in the words of Markus (1977), self-schemata (the cognitive structures which are used in encoding one's own behavior and for processing information about one's own behavior). Self-schemata represent *"cognitive generalizations about the self, derived from past experience"* that, having been derived, *"organize and guide the processing of self-related behavior contained in the individual's social experiences"* (Markus, 1977:64; italics in original).

Consistent with these assertions, Markus (1977) reported studies relating self-schemata to a number of self-referent cognitive operations. Thus, groups of individuals who thought of themselves as independent tended to endorse more adjectives associated with concepts of independence than did individuals who did not so characterize themselves, required shorter processing time for *me* judgments to words concerned with independence than to other types of words, were able to supply more specific examples of independent behavior, believed they were likely to engage in future independent behavior, and resisted acceptance of information implying that they were not independent. Parallel results were observed for individuals who thought of themselves as dependent people. Those who thought of themselves as neither independents or dependents (i.e., the aschematics) did not differ in processing times for independent and dependent words, had greater difficulty in providing behavioral evidence of independence and dependence, and believed they were as likely to engage in independent as in dependent behavior. Further, they were relatively accepting of information about themselves on this dimension. In short, they did not seem to view themselves along an independence–dependence dimension.

To summarize, then, the influence of personal traits and behaviors on self-referent cognition is contingent on the nature of the system of concepts the person habitually uses to structure the sensations and perceptions evoked by the world in general and by the self in particular. The use of particular concepts, in part motivated by social expectations and the ultimate utility of the conventional conceptual schemes in gaining gratifying responses from others, are in part derived from the subject generalizing from observed regularities in his or her personal attributes and behavior. Once derived, however, the self-referent concepts exercise a great influence on the nature of subsequent self-referent cognition in response to the stimulation of sensory processes by personal traits and behavior.

Personal Evaluative System. Personal awareness and conceptualization of objectively occurring circumstances will be influenced by the affective significance of the circumstances in the context of the person's need–value system. The nature and intensity of the subject's felt needs will influence both the likelihood that subjective traits and behaviors will be perceived and whether or not they will be conceptualized in relatively undistorted form. Individuals are characterized by a relative stable hierarchy of needs that require the achievement of valued attributes and the performance of valued behaviors in order to be assuaged. The needs are hierarchically organized in the sense that situations that theoretically might pose a threat to several of these needs or might be relevant to the satisfaction of several of these needs will be evaluated in terms of their relevance to one rather than to the others of the needs, giving priority to the apparent significance of the situation for needs that are more highly placed in the hierarchy of values. The individual is most likely to be sensitive to the implications of a situation for the threat it poses to a highly placed value or for the promise it has for the achievement of the value if the underlying need is unsatisfied or has recently been exacerbated.

Among the highest-placed values in the hierarchy is the experience of self-approving attitudes. Particularly where the need is unresolved, the individual is most likely to be sensitive to the self-threatening and esteem-giving implications of the behavioral situation. Those attributes of self and behaviors the individual has learned to associate with the threat to the value or the achievement of the value will be viewed as most attractive or to be feared, depending on whether it relates to the achievement of the value (and the diminishment of the felt need) or to the frustration of movement toward the value (and the consequent intensification of the felt need). The need to conceive of ourselves in positive terms in order to evoke positive self-feelings may influence us to recognize that we indeed possess personally and socially valued traits and that we normally perform valued behaviors. Conversely the threat to our self-esteem posed by the recognition of our disvalued attributes or by the lack of valued attributes may lead us to contrary-to-fact perceptions of not possessing the disvalued attributes or of possessing the valued attributes. Thus, a male subject who is in fact highly dependent may come to see himself as independent because he needs to conform to what he accepts as the proper stereotype of his gender-based role. In short, as Wylie pointed out, self-concept theorists argue that "in order to maintain a favorable self-image, persons use selective perception, interpretation, and memory of feedback regarding their characteristics. That is, theorists expect that unfavorable feedback will tend to be distorted, minimized, ignored, or forgotten to some degree, whereas favorable information will be exaggerated and remembered longer or more clearly" (1979:665).

Even otherwise positively valued traits or behaviors may evoke contrary-to-fact self-perceptions if these pose a threat to the individual's overall self-evaluation. Ordinarily, it might be expected that an individual who has a history of success would come to think of himself or herself as being an effective person. However, this implies the expectation of a continuing high level of performance and a consequently greater risk of failure to reach the high standard than if the expectation level were lower. Insofar as the person has a strong need to avoid experiences of failure he or she may distort self-perceptions by thinking of himself or herself as possessing a low level of effectiveness (and, by implication, as one who should not be expected to succeed).

On the other hand traits that are personally and socially disvalued may induce self-awareness of the traits in relatively undistorted form if such awareness is in the service of the self-esteem motive. For example, it has been observed that often people are labeled by others with a negative identity as a result of having been observed to deviate from consensual expectations (Becker, 1963; Kitsuse, 1962; Lemert, 1951; Scheff, 1966). Such negative responses by others may lead directly to negative self-conceptions. Nevertheless, self-awareness and self-conceptualization in terms of the deviant identify might be facilitated by the operation of the self-esteem motive. The need for approval by others and for self-approval may increase the need to conform to the expectations of others. These expectations may be interpreted as including self-conceptualization in terms of the same labels applied to the subject by the significant others whose approval he or she needs. By adopting the same standards of rectitude as the other group members, he or she may hope to gain their approval.

In sum, the likelihood that objectively occurring circumstances will stimulate awareness and the form in which the circumstances will be perceived are, in part, functions of their relevance for the achievement or frustration of relatively highly valued outcomes. A person is more likely to be aware of and admit to consciousness in undistorted form (relative to past cognitive and evaluative standards) those circumstances that are relevant to the approximation of highly valued states. A person is more likely to be sensitive to—but then to exclude from awareness, perceptually distort, or revalue—circumstances that threaten the achievement of high-priority values. The person's success in doing so and the form that attempts to accomplish these ends take are both functions of the person's defensive resources, the third category of determinants of perceptions of disvalued circumstances.

Defensive Resources: Redefining and Reevaluating Disvalued Circumstances

The likelihood that a person, having experienced disvalued circumstances, will become and remain aware of the circumstances and will perceive the circumstances as disvalued, is a function of the more or less effective and socially acceptable resources available to the person that are variously labeled *protective attitudes*, which are defined as "a constellation of related ideas by means of which the individual maintains, enhances, and defends the self" (Washburn, 1962:85), or *controls and defenses*, which "refer to the individual's capacity to define an event filled with negative implications and consequences in such a way that it does not detract from his sense of worthiness, ability, or power" (Coopersmith, 1967:37).

Such self-protective patterns may influence self-perception of disvalued circumstances by excluding them from awareness, or by distorting perception of them. Thus, individuals might not perceive that they possess disvalued attributes or have performed disvalued behaviors or that valued others have expressed negative attitudes toward them, or they might misperceive themselves as having performed valued behaviors. Alternatively, subjects' self-protective resources might permit them to change their evaluations such that they: (1) give higher priority to, or adopt, values that permit them to evaluate their existing attributes and behaviors positively (e.g., the subject happens to be a good athlete, so she defines athletic ability as a more highly valued trait, although she had not previously considered this ability to be quite so valuable); (2) give lower priority to or reject values by which they would necessarily evaluate themselves negatively (e.g., the subject happens to be receiving poor grades at school, so he comes to value good grades less than he had previously valued them); (3) come to value, more positively than previously, groups or individuals whom they perceive as positively evaluating them (e.g., an individual comes to seek out the company of a particular clique of students whose company she did not previously value, because she now perceives that they admire her or probably would if they became acquainted with her); and/or (4) come to value more negatively than previously individuals or groups who are perceived as negatively evaluating them (e.g., an individual may come to reject a group of students at school to whom he had previously been attracted, because he perceives himself as being rejected by them). The effect of these responses is to permit self-perception of valued attributes, behaviors, and experiences.

Any of these patterns might function, then, to preclude or diminish the continuity of self-perceptions of disvalued experiences, and, thereby, the experience of relatively intense and prolonged psychological distress by affecting perception (whether of a subject's own attributes and behaviors or of the attitudes toward the subject expressed by others) or evaluation (whether of a subject's own attributes and behaviors or of the other people who are perceived as expressing attitudes toward the subject).

This category of resources, variously called defensive or self-protective, patterns, is to be distinguished from those resources that have previously been called adaptive or coping patterns. The latter resources relate to the achievement of personally valued environmental demands. The defensive or self-protective mechanisms, on the other hand, relate to the perception by the subject of experiencing valued or disvalued circumstances. As such, these resources are more proximate influences on the experience of more or less intense and prolonged subjective distress.

Differential Effectiveness of Resources. The resources available to individuals are not equally effective in forestalling or limiting their perceptions of disvalued experiences and, therefore, the subjective distress (or its correlates) that derives from the perception of personally disvalued experiences. Using data from self-reported anxiety, pulse rate, and skin resistance measures, Holmes and Houston (1974) reported that the threat of painful shocks increased stress, but that subjects using redefinition (thinking of shocks as interesting new physiological sensations) and isolation (remaining detached and uninvolved) showed smaller increases in stress than subjects who were not told to use these coping strategies. The effectiveness of certain ego defenses is suggested by other physiological observations of 17-OH-CS excretion associated with emotional vulnerability in a study of 30 women hospitalized with breast tumors awaiting biopsy (Katz et al., 1970). Those with the least-effective defenses showed the highest 17-OH-CS elevations, and those who manifested any of several defensive patterns (stoicism–fatalism, prayer and faith, denial with rationalization) manifested both lower secretion rates and higher psychiatric rating scores. Other studies have suggested that ineffective defenses include selective ignoring, resignation, vigilance or sensitization, emotional discharge, and, generally, immature mechanisms. Menaghan (1982) observed that selective ignoring and resignation increased ongoing distress, whereas optimistic comparisons were associated with lower distress. Others have observed that preoperative surgical patients who showed a vigilance rather than an avoidance coping style had the most complicated postoperative recovery (Cohen and Lazarus, 1973) and that a year or more after open-heart surgery patients manifested better morale if their coping style was one of repression rather than sensitization (Brown and Rawlinson, 1976). Billings and Moos (1981) found that, although problem-solving coping is positively related to psychological well-being, emotional discharge or avoidance coping is negatively related. Vaillant (1976) reported that long-term psychological health could be predicted from knowledge of the maturity of ego-defensive coping styles that subjects characteristically used in the face of environmental crises.

It is possible that the literature relating to the association between interpersonal support and psychosocial stress (summarized elsewhere in this volume) may reflect the operation of particular defensive resources that are facilitated by membership in a giving, caring social network. Does membership in a supportive group facilitate optimistic comparisons or shared justifications for failure, for example? Unfortunately, this must remain a matter for speculation at this time.

As suggested by the foregoing studies, the same defensive resource, such as denial, might be variably effective depending on circumstances. Thus, Speisman and associates (Speisman et al., 1964) reported that executives who were high in a disposition to employ denial as a coping device manifested the greatest reduction of stress response on listening to a denial message emphasizing that the stimulus film was staged and the actors suffered no injury. In contrast, a student group that was relatively low in disposition to employ denial showed very little stress reduction in response to the denial message but did show marked reduction to an "intellectualization" message encouraging a detached, analytic attitude toward the events and persons in the stress-inducing film. This study and those reviewed earlier suggest a number of conditions that facilitate or impede the effectiveness of defensive patterns in precluding or limiting over time the perception of self-devaluing circumstances. These conditions relate to the nature of the disvalued circumstance, correlates of the defensive pattern, and situational constraints.

Regarding the nature of the disvalued circumstance, it has been noted that "some of the most persistent strains originate in conditions impervious to coping interventions, thus discouraging individual ameliorative coping efforts" (Pearlin and Schooler, 1978:6). Not all modes of coping mechanisms are equally effective in different role areas: "With relatively impersonal strains, such as those stemming from economic or occupational experiences, the most effective forms of coping involve the manipulation of goals and values in a way which psychologically increases the distance of the individual from the problem. On the other hand, problems arising from the relatively close interpersonal relations of parental and marital roles are best handled by coping mechanisms in which the individual remains committed to and engaged with the relevant others" (Pearlin and Schooler, 1978:18). Consistent with this conclusion, in circumstances where the person could not control the outcome (threat of painful shocks, surgery, breast tumors) mechanisms such as redefinition, denial, isolation, and avoidance were effective. In situations where effective intervention was possible and the disvalued circumstance was ongoing, these techniques had less salutary results. However, the nature of the disvalued circumstance (beyond the characteristic of not being amenable to change) may be more or less amenable to such defensive techniques as perceptual distortion. Although Wylie noted consistency among studies in showing trends toward self-favorability biases concerning evaluative characteristics, this "was least true or not true in the case of reported memories of grade-point averages and more true with respect to characteristics which would be more open to self-favorable distortion" (1979:681).

A second condition for the effectiveness of a defensive resource is that positive affect be associated with (or negative affect not be associated with) the resource in question. Thus a membership group would be effective in facilitating reevaluation only insofar as the group is not the source of the negative sanctions that constitute the disvalued experience. Perhaps because groups that ordinarily provide social resources are the present source of the individual's self-devaluing experiences, the relationship with these groups is increasingly attenuated and the avoidance of these groups is the only practical response. Conversely, the findings reported by Speisman and associates (Speisman et al., 1964) suggested that congruence of the currently used pattern with the normal patterns of usage in *valued* life circumstances may influence effectiveness of the pattern. Where the pattern (intellectualization) was congruent with requirements of a particular, presumably valued role (student) the pattern was effective in reducing distress.

Finally, situational constraints preclude effective use of certain defensive resources, as when crowded housing conditions prevent subjects from avoiding adverse interpersonal transactions. However, where role definitions require solitary work or where physical conditions (noise, physical separation) prevent interpersonal contact, avoidance mechanisms may be effectively used, but the benign use of interpersonal support-related mechanisms is effectively precluded.

Particular patterns of defensive response are associated with different positions in the social structure. To the extent that some specific patterns are more effective than others (where they are not differentially effective for people with particular characteristics), some segments of the population will be better able to forestall or limit self-perceptions of disvalued circumstances. Thus, effective coping modes are disproportionately available to men, the educated, and the affluent (Billings and Moos, 1981; Pearlin and Schooler, 1978).

Deviant Defensive Patterns. At any given time a person may find it necessary to use deviant defensive patterns in order to forestall or limit the perception of highly disvalued personal circumstances. The adoption of deviant response patterns is a function of the past ineffectiveness of normative response patterns in accomplishing these ends. So long as the resources available to the individual are adequate and the perceived demands on the individual are not insurmountable, the stress process can be reflected in a closed-system model whereby the antecedents of psychological distress are self-limiting or are mitigated by the responses of the individual. However, insofar as the occurrence of psychosocial stress overwhelms the resources of the individual that might be used to mitigate the experience of distress, the model must be expanded to an open system in which the individual adopts response patterns that are beyond the normative limits of his or her system.

In this model (Kaplan, 1980, 1982) the pervasive and continuing perception by the subject of highly disvalued circumstancs and consequent subjective distress *associated with membership group experiences* predisposeṣ the person to seek and adopt *deviant* patterns that will facilitate the perceptual avoidance and reevaluation of experiences in order to reduce subjective distress. The avoidance might occur at intrapsychic or interpersonal levels. At the intrapsychic level avoidance of perceiving disvalued experiences might be accomplished by mild to severe distortions of reality. At the interpersonal level deviant acts will attenuate the relationships with group members who were the occasion for the disvalued experiences.

Deviant behaviors also facilitate the devaluation of the standards by which the subjects perceive themselves as being less than worthy. The behaviors may take the form of (1) verbal abuse against normative standards, institutions, and those who represent them or (2) more extreme hostile responses including physical aggression toward both group members and material representations of the normative structure. Devaluation may take the alternate form of severe withdrawal of emotional investment (as in depression) in that which the person has lost, is in danger of losing, or has little hope of attaining. Deviant behaviors simultaneously reflect reevaluation of goals so that previously disvalued deviant social networks are now positively valued because they offer the promise of approving responses for reaching goals that the subject views as more easily attainable than the now-disvalued former goals.

As observed earlier the deviant responses will be focused upon the subsystem or more inclusive system that is subjectively identified with the perceived disvalued circumstances. If the disvalued circumstances were identified with the total normative system then extreme emotional withdrawal, delusional thinking, and/or affiliation with counter-cultures might result. However, if the disvalued circumstances are perceived as involving only one or a few relational systems, then the deviant behaviors may reflect the perceptual restructuring and reevaluation of those systems only. In the context of marriage perceptual avoidance may be accomplished by denial of the spouse's expectations, misperception of need satisfaction, or separation. Reevaluation might be accomplished by emotional withdrawal, placing a greater value on occupational accomplishments, extramarital relationships, and rejection of the concept of marriage.

Whether the source of disvalued circumstances is perceived of as the general system of relationships or as particular subsystems, the deviant patterns must be defined with reference to the expectations of the others in that system. Which specific deviant patterns are adopted is a function of the availability of the specific deviant pattern and the subjective expectation of net self-enhancing consequences of adopting the deviant pattern. *Availability* of the pattern connotes biogenetic disposition to respond in the particular mode (e.g., inherited tendency toward schizophrenia) and characteristic acquired defensive modes with which the deviant pattern is compatible, as well as the visibility of the pattern by virtue of its prevalence and/or obtrusive nature.

To the extent that the deviant patterns facilitate perceptual avoidance and reevaluation of disvalued circumstances and are not accompanied by unanticipated adverse consequences, the intensity and duration of the distress consequent on the earlier disvalued circumstances will be contained. Whether or not the net outcome of the deviant response pattern is positive will be a function of such mutually influencing variables as the nature of the deviant act, societal response to the act, and the person's need–value and adaptive–coping–defensive patterns. For example, a highly visible and highly disvalued act might lead to apprehension and adjudication, with consequences of stigmatization, enforced deviant role enactment, exacerbation of a need to justify the act by its continued performance, isolation from social control, isolation from legitimate opportunities, and exposure to self-enhancing illegitimate patterns. Such an act may be congruent with personal need disposition (such as power) and preferred defensive mechanisms (attack). The deviant pattern thus might become part of the subject's personal and (new) social lifestyle, with gratification coming from conformity to the life-style. Insofar as the new life-style at the same time precludes the experience of the self-devaluing life events characteristic of former membership-group experiences, the likelihood that the deviant pattern will have positive consequences is further increased.

Alternatively, the deviant pattern may have a *low* probability of severe sanctions from membership groups (perhaps because of low visibility), but still may have positive consequences. In this case, the subject may be expected to perform the pattern in response to discrete life events with self-devaluing implications. The frequency of the deviant pattern becomes a function of the frequency of self-devaluing life events and the continuity of a net aggregate of gratifying over punishing consequences of the deviant response.

If the currently preferred deviant pattern has adverse consequences but is still preferable to normative patterns with even greater self-devaluing implications, then continuity of the pattern will persist until the person becomes aware of alternative deviant patterns with self-enhancing potential or of the self-enhancing potential of some aspects of normative response patterns. With regard to the latter, the person is likely to adopt normative response patterns only where they are so discontinuous with the remainder of the normative context as to preclude their subjective association with the same normative context that was, in fact and subjectively, associated with the genesis of highly disvalued circumstances. For example, such discontinuity might occur for adolescents when they mature sufficiently to be exposed to the potential gratifications to be derived from new occupational and familial roles or under conditions of radical social change.

DISCUSSION

In the conceptual framework being considered here psychological distress is the direct reflection of subjective perception of disvalued circumstances and, less directly, is the outcome of the influences on (1)

the person's *need–value system,* (2) the *occurrence of the circumstances* that, from the perspective of the personal need–value system,
are disvalued, and (3) the *perception* of the occurrence of the disvalued
circumstances. In presenting this framework I do not maintain the integrity of the concepts of role strain, life events, coping mechanisms,
and social support. To do so would be dysfunctional. Each of these
constructs encompasses analytically distinct processes that reflect the
person's values, the occurrence of disvalued circumstances, the perception of these, and diverse influences on these phenomena. If the
process of psychosocial stress as it is conceptualized here is to be
understood it is necessary to disaggregate the complex meanings associated with the constructs. To fail to do so will be to mask the diverse
meanings of the constructs for psychosocial stress. Further, unless the
more precise meanings of the constructs are broken down the indices
that are selected to reflect them in empirical research will simultaneously reflect, *but in unknown ways,* these diverse meanings. For
example, membership in a social-support network simultaneously reflects (1) a source of consensual values, (2) an intrinsically valued
attribute and a source of instrumental resources for the achievement of
other valued circumstances, and (3) resources that facilitate the perceptual redefinition and reevaluation of more or less disvalued circumstances. Even if a social-support network is conceived of as encompassing all of these meanings, any observed relationships involving social
support might reflect in fact only one or a few of these meanings.
Which of these were influential would necessarily be a matter of con-
jecture in the absence of their disaggregation and appropriate operationalization. As an example, a particular measure of membership in a
social-support network might be observed to be inversely related to
psychological distress. If this measure, however, is correlated with the
meanings just enumerated, we could not know which if any of these
measures influence psychological distress. Rather than have a single
measure of social support, it would be necessary to have separate measures of shared values among members of a network, emotional attraction to the network, availability of various instrumental resources in
the network, and characteristics of the network that presumably facilitate perceptual avoidance and reevaluation. It could be then determined whether these measures make separate contributions to the explanation of psychological distress in multivariate models.

The implication of the foregoing conceptual framework for empirical
research is that the anticipation of psychological distress must take into
account (1) what the person values, (2) the likelihood of circumstances
occurring that reflect the contravention of the values, and (3) the likeli-

hood that the person will perceive the occurrence of the disvalued circumstances rather than redefine and reevaluate the circumstances. Under the guidance of this framework the investigator is sensitized to the implications of an observed correlate, or the putative influences, of a variable on subjective distress with reference to the relevance of the variable for the person's value system, as a reflection of a disvalued circumstance, or as an influence on the perception of the disvalued circumstances.

When the literature reviewed in the first four chapters of this volume is reexamined it is clear that the individual studies and the conclusions based on these are compatible with the present model. Specifically each of the bodies of literature dealing respectively with role strain, life events, interpersonal support, and coping resources may be reinterpreted with regard to their relevance as reflecting or influencing the nature of the need–value system, the occurrence of disvalued circumstances, and the perception of the occurrence of disvalued circumstances. In several instances this was accomplished in describing the conceptual framework. However, it might be well to review in a very general way how certain of the conclusions from each of the four bodies of literature either manifestly relate or may be reinterpreted as relating to need–value systems, the occurrence of disvalued circumstances, and perceptions of the occurrence of disvalued circumstances.

Role strain occurs in social relational contexts. From a diachronic point of view these contexts are the sources for the person's transsituational or situationally relevant values. The particular social context presently defines the relevance of various evaluative standards. Role strains constitute disvalued occurrences whereby individuals are prevented on an ongoing basis from conforming to what they view as legitimate expectations of themselves by others in the relational context and/or fail to evoke desirable responses from the others with whom they interact. The role strain may result from such situational constraints as role conflict or the absence of adequate adaptive or coping resources with which to meet the role expectations that are applicable in the situation. The absence of resources are in part occasioned by the application of negative sanctions for failure to conform to others' expectations or by other insidious or marked changes in subjects' circumstances over time. The failure to assuage ongoing role strain may lead to perceptual redefinition and reevaluation of role expectations that constitute purposive failure to conform to others' expectations and the consequent increase in the failure of others to conform to subjects' expectations.

Life events, defined as the loss, addition, or redefinition of social

identities, frequently reflect a change in the evaluative standards that
subjects use to judge themselves as others. By changing the expectations incumbent on them, peoples' self-acceptance becomes problematic insofar as the same attributes and behaviors heretofore acceptable
are now unacceptable or unattainable with the same resources. By oc-
casioning changes in evaluative standards, then, the probability of intrinsically disvalued circumstances is increased. This probability is
further increased if the event decreases the resources available to the
individual that were theretofore adequate to achieve valued states. Finally, life events frequently are themselves intrinsically disvalued circumstances. In addition to the roles played by life events in reflecting
or inducing intrinsically disvalued circumstances, these occurrences
may have benign outcomes as well by reflecting intrinsically valued
circumstances or by facilitating the perceptual redefinition and reevaluation of circumstances, so that previous recognition of disvalued
circumstances is now perceived as valued attributes, behaviors, or
outcomes.

As noted earlier, *social-support* networks are ontogenetically a
source of personal values and currently provide the symbolic context
for the applicability of evaluative standards. Memberships in social-
support networks constitute intrinsically valued circumstances and
represent collective adaptive and coping resources that are available for
the achievement of other valued states. However, the emotional and
instrumental significance of the social-support networks renders the
subject highly vulnerable to the occurrence of disvalued circumstances
in the form of negative sanctions administered by the group in response
to the subject's voluntary or involuntary failure to conform to group
expectations. Nevertheless the support network provides opportunities
on an ongoing basis or as a new membership group to redefine perceptually or reevaluate previously perceived disvalued circumstances. The
opportunities may take the form of collective self-justifications for
failure or perceptual avoidance of negative judgments by other membership groups. However, once again, if the disvalued circumstance
reflects contravention of the social-support network's norms, membership in the group will impede perceptual redefinition and reevaluation.

Coping efforts are stimulated by the evaluative significance of environmental stimuli and are oriented toward the attainment of valued
states and increasing the psychological distance from disvalued states.
The occurrences of disvalued circumstances are a function of the lesser
or greater effectiveness of adaptive and coping patterns. In part due to
the effectiveness of various patterns, the use of particular adaptive or
coping resources tends to be intrinsically valued. The history of effec-

tive use of coping and adaptive resources in forestalling disvalued circumstances in turn influences the availability of coping efforts, in particular a sense of self-efficacy. The inability to forestall the occurrence of disvalued circumstances increases the likelihood of using defensive resources that function to forestall perception of the disvalued circumstances by perceptual redefinition and reevaluation of reality.

The reinterpretability of the findings in terms of the present conceptual structure, however, does not in itself justify the framework, although it may decrease resistance to its acceptance. Any justification for this framework lies in its finer specification of the nature of the influences exercised by role strains, life events, social supports, and coping efforts in the genesis, continuity, or exacerbation of psychological distress. The conceptual scheme is in part derived from past research on the social-psychological and sociocultural antecedents of psychological distress and its correlates, but in effect disaggregates the many meanings associated with the traditional concepts that dominate the research on psychosocial stress. It is offered in the hope it will be a more useful, albeit still tentative, framework to facilitate the interrelationship of the existing body of research findings with the results of future efforts and to guide future research toward the goal of correctly specifying the complex relationships that will make up a general theory of psychosocial stress.

REFERENCES

Abramson, L. Y., M. E. P. Seligman, and J. P. Teasdale
    1978   "Learned helplessness in humans: Critique and reformulation." Journal of Abnormal Psychology 87:49–74.
Ander, S., B. Lindstrom, and G. Tibblin
    1974   "Life changes in random samples of middle-aged men." Pp. 121–124 in E. K. E. Gunderson and Richard H. Rahe (eds.), Life Stress and Illness. Springfield, Ill.: Thomas.
Antonovsky, A.
    1979   Health, Stress, and Coping. San Francisco: Jossey Bass.
Bachman, J. G.
    1970   Youth in Transition. Volume 2. The Impact of Family Background and Intelligence on Tenth Grade Boys. Ann Arbor, Mich.: Survey Research Center, Institute for Social Research.
Back, K. W., and M. Bogdonoff
    1964   "Plasma lipid responses to leadership, conformity, and deviation." Pp. 24–42 in P. H. Leiderman and D. Shapiro (eds.), Psychobiological Approaches to Social Behavior. Stanford, Calif.: Stanford University Press.
Bandura, A.
    1977   "Self-efficacy: Toward a unifying theory of behavioral change." Psychological Review 84:191–215.

Becker, H. S.
    1963   Outsiders: Studies in the Sociology of Deviance. New York: Free Press.
Bem, D. J.
    1972   "Self-perception theory." Pp. 1–62 in L. Berkowitz (ed.), Advances in Ex-
            perimental Social Psychology. Volume 6. New York: Academic Press.
Billings, A. G., and R. H. Moos
    1981   "The role of coping responses and social resources in attenuating the stress
            of life events." Journal of Behavioral Medicine 4:139–157.
Bootzin, R. R., and D. Max
    1980   "Learning and Behavioral Theories." Pp. 36–47 in I. L. Kutash and L.
            Schlesinger (eds.), Handbook on Stress and Anxiety. San Francisco: Jossey-
            Bass.
Bourne, P. G., W. M. Coli, and W. E. Datel
    1968   "Affect levels of Special Forces soldiers under threat of attack." Psycholog-
            ical Reports 22:363–366.
Brown, W., and T. Harris
    1978   Social Origins of Depression: A Study of Psychiatric Disorder in Women.
            New York: Free Press.
Brown, J., and M. Rawlinson
    1976   "The morale of patients following open-heart surgery." Journal of Health
            and Social Behavior 17:135–145.
Coddington, R. D.
    1972   "The significance of life events as etiologic factors in the diseases of chil-
            dren: II. A study of a normal population." Journal of Psychosomatic Re-
            search 16(3):205–213.
Cohen, F., and R. S. Lazarus
    1973   "Active coping processes, coping dispositions, and recovery from surgery."
            Psychosomatic Medicine 35:375–389.
Cooley, C. H.
    1902   Human Nature and the Social Order. New York: Scribner.
Coopersmith, S.
    1967   The Antecedents of Self-Esteem. San Francisco: Freeman.
Dodge, D. L., and W. T. Martin
    1970   Social Stress and Chronic Illness. University of Notre Dame, Indiana: Uni-
            versity of Notre Dame Press.
Dohrenwend, B. S., and B. P. Dohrenwend (eds.)
    1974   Stressful Life Events: Their Nature and Effects. New York: Wiley.
Eron, L., and R. A. Peterson
    1982   "Abnormal behavior: Social approaches." Annual Review of Psychology
            33:231–264.
Forman, S., and B. Forman
    1982   "Family environment and its relation to adolescent personality factors."
            Journal of Personality Assessment 45:163–167.
Fowler, P.
    1980   "Family environment and early behavioral development: A structural anal-
            ysis of dependencies." Psychological Reports 47:611–617.
Frank, D.
    1972   Persuasion and Healing. Baltimore: Johns Hopkins University Press.
Frankenhaeuser, M., and A. Rissler
    1970   "Effects of punishment on catecholamine release and efficiency of perfor-
            mance." Psychopharmacologia 17:378–390.

Gergen, K. J.
    1971   The Concept of Self. New York: Holt, Rinehart, & Winston.
Grinker, R. R., and J. P. Spiegel
    1945   Men under Stress. New York: McGraw-Hill.
Gutman, R.
    1963   "Population mobility in the American middle class." Pp. 172–183 in L. J.
            Duhl (ed.), The Urban Condition. New York: Basic Books.
Haan, N.
    1977   Coping and Defending: Processes of Self-Environment Organization. New
            York: Academic Press.
Helmreich, R.
    1972   "Stress, self-esteem, and attitudes." Pp. 33–44 in B. T. King and E. McGin-
            nies (eds.), Attitudes, Conflict, and Social Change. New York: Academic
            Press.
Hogarty, G. E., and M. M. Katz
    1971   "Norms of adjustment and social behavior." Archives of General Psychiatry
            25:470–480.
Holmes, D. S., and B. K. Houston
    1974   "Effectiveness of situation redefinition and affective isolation in coping
            with stress." Journal of Personality and Social Psychology 29:212–218.
James, W.
    1890   Principles of Psychology. Two Volumes. New York: Holt.
Johnson, J. H., and I. G. Sarason
    1978   "Life stress, depression, and anxiety: Internal-external locus of control as a
            moderator variable." Journal of Psychosomatic Research 22:205–208.
Kagan, J.
    1964   "Acquisition and significance of sex typing and sex role identity." Pp.
            137–165 in M. Hoffman and L. Hoffman (eds.), Review of Child Develop-
            ment Research. Volume 1. New York: Russell Sage Foundation.
Kaplan, H. B.
    1972   "Studies in sociophysiology." Pp. 86–97 in E. Gartley Jaco (ed.), Patients,
            Physicians and Illness. New York: Free Press.
Kaplan, H. B.
    1980   Deviant Behavior in Defense of Self. New York: Academic Press.
Kaplan, H. B.
    1982   "Self-attitudes and deviant behavior: New directions for theory and re-
            search." Youth and Society 14:185–211.
Katz, J., H. Weiner, T. Gallagher, and L. Hellman
    1970   "Stress, distress and ego defenses." Archives of General Psychiatry
            23:131–142.
Kiritz, S., and R. Moos
    1974   "Physiological effects of social environments." Psychosomatic Medicine
            36(2):96–114.
Kitsuse, J. I.
    1962   "Societal reaction to deviant behavior: Problems of theory and method."
            Social Problems 9:247–257.
Kohn, M. L.
    1976   "The interaction of social class and other factors in the etiology of schizo-
            phrenia." American Journal of Psychiatry 133:177–180.
Lazarus, R. S., and J. B. Cohen
    1977   "Environmental stress." Pp. 90–121 in I. Altman and J. F. Wohlwill (eds.),

Human Behavior and the Environment: Current Theory and Research. Volume 1. New York: Plenum.

Lemert, E. M.
1951   Social Pathology. New York: McGraw-Hill.

Mann, P.
1972   "Residential mobility as an adaptive experience." Journal of Consulting and Clinical Psychology 39:37–42.

Markus, H.
1977   "Self-schemata and processing information about the self." Journal of Personality and Social Psychology 35:63–78.

May, R.
1980   "Value conflicts and anxiety." Pp. 241–248 in I. L. Kutash and L. B. Schlesinger (eds.), Handbook on Stress and Anxiety. San Francisco: Jossey-Bass.

McGuire, W. J., C. V. McGuire, P. Child, and T. Fujioka
1978   "Salience of ethnicity in the spontaneous self-concept as a function of one's ethnic distinctiveness in the social environment." Journal of Personality and Social Psychology 36:511–520.

McGuire, W. J., and A. Padawer-Singer
1976   "Trait salience in the spontaneous self-concept." Journal of Personality and Social Psychology 33:743–754.

Menaghan, E.
1982   "Measuring coping effectiveness: A panel analysis of marital problems and coping efforts." Journal of Health and Social Behavior 23:220–234.

Mettlin, C., and J. Woelfel
1974   "Interpersonal influence and symptoms of stress." Journal of Health and Social Behavior 15:311–319.

Miller, I. W., III, and W. H. Norman
1979   "Learned helplessness in humans: A review and attribution theory model." Psychological Bulletin 86:93–118.

Montemayor, R., and M. Eisen
1977   "The development of self-conceptions from childhood to adolescence." Developmental Psychology 13:314–319.

Moss, G. E.
1973   Illness, Immunity, and Social Interaction. The Dynamics of Biosocial Resonation. New York: John Wiley.

Moulton, R.
1980   "Anxiety and the new feminism." Pp. 267–284 in I. L. Kutash and L. B. Schlesinger (eds.), Handbook on Stress and Anxiety. San Francisco: Jossey-Bass.

Payne, R. L.
1975   "Recent life changes and the reporting of psychological states." Journal of Psychosomatic Research 19:99–103.

Pearlin, L. I., and C. Schooler
1978   "The structure of coping." Journal of Health and Social Behavior 19:1–21.

Purkey, W. W.
1970   Self-Concept and Academic Achievement. Englewood Cliffs, N.J.: Prentice-Hall.

Rachman, S.
1978   Fear and Courage. San Francisco: Freeman.

Rahe, R. H.
    1974   "Life change and subsequent illness reports." Pp. 58–78 in E. K. E. Gunderson and R. H. Rahe (eds.), Life Stress and Illness. Springfield, Ill.: Thomas.
Rosenberg, M.
    1979   Conceiving the Self. New York: Basic Books.
Rubin, R. T.
    1974   "Biochemical and neuroendocrine responses to severe psychological stress: I. U.S. Navy aviator study, 2. Some general observations." Pp. 227–241 in E. K. E. Gunderson and R. H. Rahe (eds.), Life Stress and Illness. Springfield, Ill.: Thomas.
Rubin, R. T., and R. H. Rahe
    1974   "U.S. Navy underwater demolition team training: Biochemical studies." Pp. 208–226 in E. K. E. Gunderson and R. H. Rahe (eds.), Life Stress and Illness. Springfield, Ill.: Thomas.
Scheff, T.
    1966   Being Mentally Ill: A Sociological Theory. Chicago: Aldine.
Schmideberg, M.
    1942   "Some observations on individual reactions to air raids." International Journal of Psychoanalysis 23:146–176.
Scotch, N.
    1963   "Sociocultural factors in the epidemiology of Zulu hypertension." American Journal of Public Health 53:1205–1213.
Simmons, R. G., F. Rosenberg, and M. Rosenberg
    1973   "Disturbance in the self-image at adolescence." American Sociological Review 38:553–568.
Speisman, J. C., R. S. Lazarus, A. Mordkoff, and L. Davison
    1964   "Experimental reduction of stress based on ego-defense theory." Journal of Abnormal and Social Psychology 68:367–380.
Stryker, S.
    1977   "Developments in 'two social psychologies': Toward an appreciation of mutual relevance." Sociometery 40:145–160.
Sweet, J. R., and K. R. Thornburg
    1971   "Preschoolers' self and social identify within the family structure." Journal of Negro Education 40:22–27.
Vaillant, G. E.
    1976   "Natural history of male psychological health. V: The relation of choice of ego mechanisms of defense to adult adjustment." Archives of General Psychiatry 33:535–545.
Vernon, P.
    1941   "Psychological effects of air raids." Journal of Abnormal and Social Psychology 36:457–476.
Warheit, G. J.
    1979   "Life events, coping, stress, and depressive symptomatology." American Journal of Psychiatry 136:502–507.
Washburn, W. C.
    1962   "Patterns of protective attitudes in relation to differences in self-evaluation and anxiety level among high school students." California Journal of Educational Research 15:84–94.
Williams, R., C. Kimball, and H. Williard
    1972   "The influence of interpersonal interaction on diastolic blood pressure." Psychosomatic Medicine 34:194–198.

Wolfenstein, M.
    1957   Disaster. New York: Free Press.
Wylie, R. C.
    1979   The Self-Concept. Volume 2. Theory and Research on Selected Topics.
              Lincoln: University of Nebraska Press.

PART III

Methodological Issues

6

Methodological Issues in the Study of Psychosocial Stress*

RONALD C. KESSLER

INTRODUCTION

In this chapter I discuss methodological issues in the design and analysis of research on the stress process. As an organizing device, I begin by describing three core questions of interest to stress researchers. Then I critically review the adequacy of four commonly used nonexperimental research designs to answer each of these questions. The final sections of the chapter deal with a number of analytical issues that transcend individual designs.

I have omitted any discussion of conceptualization and measurement of variables. This does not imply that I consider these issues less important than those involving design or analysis. Problems of measurement are so diverse, however, and so closely tied to substantive considera-

*The preparation of this chapter was supported by National Institute of Mental Health Grant MH34479. I would like to thank Duane Alwin, William Mason, Jane McLeod, and Michael Sobel for helpful discussions about various topics considered here.

267

tions that I found it impossible to deal adequately with them in a chapter of this sort. At the same time, several sections of the chapter describe analysis procedures that can be used to build into one's statistical model the possibility of some measurement problems: omitted variables or correlated measurement errors or reciprocal causal influences due to systematic measurement contamination.

It is useful to define some terms at the onset. I follow conventional practice in using the terms *strain* and *stressor* interchangeably to refer to an objective situation that has the potential to provoke psychological reactions in the individuals who find themselves in this situation. The term *stress* refers to these subjectively experienced reactions to an objective strain. A family with little money is exposed to a strain, whereas a family in which there are worries about money experiences a stress. Stresses can be, and typically are, caused by objective strains, but this need not be the case. Indeed, an important part of stress research involves the attempt to understand why the strain–stress relationship is less than perfect.

There are two broad types of strain: discrete events and more enduring situations. As the chapter by Thoits has shown, it is relatively easy to measure events. We know, within the bounds of recall and honesty, for instance, whether a respondent lost his or her job in the year prior to our interview. But it is much more difficult to assess objectively the magnitude of ongoing job-related strains among people who are employed. It is not that respondents hesitate to discuss the conditions of their work but that they have difficulty reporting their situations objectively without allowing subjectively experienced stresses to color their perceptions. As a result of this difficulty, research on the effects of chronic strains has not proceeded nearly as far as research on life events. Therefore, in the major part of this chapter I discuss design and analysis issues appropriate to the study of life events. In the section "Evaluating Causal Priority" I deal with modifications required when working with measures of chronic strain.

Research of the sort considered in this volume is carried out by epidemiologists, behavioral scientists, and clinicians. The concerns of these different researchers vary considerably, from the descriptive interests of epidemiologists to the analytic ones of behavioral scientists to the more practical ones of clinicians. But they share an interest in three research problems: (1) documenting that a particular strain or set of strains causes illness; (2) describing the course of adjustment to a strain known to cause illness; and (3) determining why only some of the people exposed to the strain become ill. Together, these three problems underlie most research that is carried out on the stress process by these groups of scientists.

The first problem is the foundation on which the others are built. In the absence of a demonstration that a particular strain is related to illness onset it is meaningless to ask any more refined questions about vulnerability and adjustment. Although most stress researchers accept it as an article of faith that some strains can lead to illness, it is extremely difficult to document this with epidemiologic data. Small sample sizes of people who experience any one life crisis over a short interval of time and noncomparability between those who do and do not experience crises make it difficult to support causal inferences. A substantial part of the chapter deals with methodological considerations that play a part in the creation and resolution of this problem.

Once evidence is obtained that a life crisis plays a part in causing illness, the process of normal adjustment to that crisis becomes of interest. The intent here is to develop an understanding of typical patterns of response. Most research of this sort follows over time a group of people who have had a life event occur to them and monitors changes in coping strategies, social support, and other variables thought to be important determinants of adjustment, as well as assessments of health and social functioning.

Although the methodological issues associated with this descriptive phase of research are not nearly so formidable as those connected to the problem of demonstrating causality, there are nonetheless some points worth making about design considerations here. In several parts of the chapter these points are discussed in a comparative assessment of different designs.

The most difficult phase of stress research is that associated with the third research problem enumerated earlier: probing the reasons for variation in adjustment to particularly serious life crises. Here we must not only contend with the problems of imputing causality to the event but we must do so while simultaneously considering intervening variables that can modify the effect of the event on illness outcome measures. There are not only issues of causal ambiguity here, but also serious problems of estimation and interpretation. All of these will be discussed.

As noted earlier, many of the methodological problems I am about to review would be resolved if it were possible to conduct experiments in which exposure to a stressful event is randomly assigned. Research of this sort has been done by experimental social psychologists. The stressors found in these laboratory studies are very tame compared to those encountered in the real world—mild electric shocks, noise bursts, or exposure to graphic films that show a medical operation or a circumcision ritual in an aboriginal tribe. Although it is possible to manipulate these experimentally to study subtle connections between strain and stress, it is not at all clear that results obtained with mild stressors of this sort generalize to the more serious life crises that are of interest to applied researchers. As a result of this and other problems of external validity (Silver and Wortman, 1980:280–81), the present use of laboratory experiments is minimal in stress research.

Field experiments are much more common. On occasion, natural variation in exposure to some disaster makes it possible to analyze the impact of a serious life event as if exposure were assigned randomly. These naturally occurring experiments provide the best evidence available to date that life events can, in fact, cause illnesses of various sorts (Dohrenwend and Dohrenwend, 1981). More typically, field experiments vary access to coping resources among victims of a life crisis to compensate for being unable to vary exposure to the crisis itself. The intent here is to test out intervention efforts aimed at ameliorating the health effects of the crisis (Regier and Allen, 1981). When experiments of this sort are successful, they offer definitive evidence about the causal forces that determine adjustment to life crises.

There are several practical problems with intervention experiments. It is hard to construct a significant intervention effort, one that might reasonably be expected to have a health effect for a sizable proportion of the people to whom it is administered. It is hard to maintain the experimental and control groups over a long enough period of time to let the effect of the experimental treatment have a chance to show itself. Only seldom is it possible to maintain a multitude of experimental conditions, so usually only one or two are considered. Because of this, it is usually not possible to pinpoint specific elements of a multifaceted intervention as of critical importance in themselves.

As a result of these problems, field experiments are almost always grounded in a firm foundation of prior nonexperimental research. In the latter, hypotheses are provisionally tested out and intervention plans are refined by a process of successive elimination. Because field experiments are enormously expensive and because it is not possible to manipulate a large number of experimental conditions simultaneously, nonexperimental research is relied on heavily to sift through likely candidates for intervention before a serious attempt at field experimentation is made.

In the discussion that follows I do not address methodological issues in field experiments of this sort. The methodological issues central to that type of research are the subject of a vast literature (e.g., Bennett and Lumsdaine, 1975; Cook and Campbell, 1979), and there is no need to review them here. Instead, I concentrate on the most commonly used nonexperimental research designs. The methodological issues here are quite different from those that are important in experimental research. And they have been much less widely discussed in accessible summary statements.

The next four sections of the chapter discuss, in turn, the four most important nonexperimental research designs in stress research: normal population surveys, surveys of crisis victims, prospective case-control designs, and retrospective case-control designs. In each section I begin with a description of the design and then consider its appropriateness for addressing each of the three major research questions enumerated earlier: documenting causation, describing the course of adjustment, and predicting variation in adjustment. Subsequent sections deal with data-analysis issues that transcend these individual designs.

NORMAL POPULATION SURVEYS

In normal population surveys respondents are asked about the life events that occurred to them in the recent past and about ongoing situations in their lives that might be considered stressful. These measures of strain are correlated with measures of illness to make inferences about the impact of strain on illness. In the presence of a significant association, multivariate statistical model building is used to make inferences about intervening and interacting variables linking strain and illness.

Documenting the Impact of Strain

In cross-sectional surveys, causal inferences are made on the assumption that the people who do not experience the strain under investigation stand as proxies for how the people who are strained would have been if they had not experienced the strain. In this way the difference in the rates of ill health in the strained and unstrained groups is interpreted as the effect of the strain on health. (In the more characteristic case the measure of strain is a continuum rather than a dichotomy, and we test the significance of a correlation rather than a mean difference. The logic is the same in the two cases, so I continue in this example and in those that follow to discuss designs as if dichotomous measures of strain were being considered.)

This sort of inference hinges centrally on the assumption that the comparison groups are equivalent in all respects other than exposure to the strain. If strain occurs randomly, as it does when it is controlled by experimental assignment, results in the cross-sectional survey are identical to those in an experiment.[1] Actually, a somewhat stronger assertion can be made. If we are interested in the influence of strain on some outcome H, then the gross association between strain and H is an unbiased estimate of the strain effect so long as the occurrence of strain is random with respect to all other determinants of H and prior values of H do not influence the probability of strain occurring.

We can see why this assertion holds by referring to the statistical literature on specification bias (Johnston, 1972:168–169). Let us say that strain S is not randomly distributed but is more likely to occur among people who have high scores on some variable C, which along with S is causally related to the health outcome H. Let us assume, further, that the structural equation describing these causal influences for each individual in the population is

$$H = b_1 + b_2 S + b_3 C + e, \tag{1}$$

where e is the disturbance term in the population for the individual. If we know about C and control it in our model, then b_2 can be estimated without bias by regression analysis. This estimate is the same one we would obtain if we had used an experimental design to evaluate the effect.

If, however, C is omitted from the model, we estimate a biased equation in which we have

$$H = b_1' + b_2' S + e', \tag{2}$$

where $e' = b_3 C + e$. The least-squares estimator of b_2' in this equation has the expectation $b_2 + b_3(b_{CS})$, where b_{CS} is the regression of C on S. In substantive terms this means that the effect of S is biased by the proportion of the C effect equal to the correlation between C and S. (In the multivariate case the bias is equal to b_3 times the partial regression of C on S when all other predictors in the model are controlled.) This bias vanishes under either of two conditions: (1) when $b_3 = 0$; or (2) when $b_{CS} = 0$. Therefore, the only cases to consider when thinking about the possibility of specification bias are those in which $b_3 \neq 0$ and $b_{CS} \neq 0$, that is, when an omitted variable is both a cause of H and is

---

[1]Some experiments obtain pretest measures as a way of guaranteeing that the random assignment of subjects to treatments has succeeded in producing equivalent groups of subjects and controls. Because random assignment will almost never produce absolute equivalence, the pretest scores can be used to adjust statistically for initial differences, thereby refining the experimental results. This level of refinement is not possible in cross-sectional surveys, even when the occurrence of the strains under consideration is truly random.

related to S even when other control variables are taken into consideration.

There is no way to demonstrate nonexperimentally that important control variables have not been omitted from a model. The best one can do is to think of all potential sources of bias and control them. This state of affairs is not desirable, but it is the price one must pay when randomization of S is not possible. Only by randomization can we be assured that the correlations between S and other causes of H are governed by the laws of probability. In all other cases some uncertainty in this respect is inevitable.

When longitudinal survey data are available we can narrow this range of uncertainty somewhat by working with lagged values of H. The important feature of this design is that a measure of H is available *before* the event occurs. This measure can be used to approximate a situation in which assignment to the strain is random. This is not as complete as real randomization but, as I show next, it is an improvement on the situation where only cross-sectional controls are available.

To understand this it is important to appreciate that the problem of nonequivalence is really a missing-variable problem, as has been shown earlier. The strategy I am about to describe hinges on this realization and on the fact that the influence of an omitted variable from a prediction equation can sometimes be removed by working with difference scores.[2]

Let us assume that the structural equation governing the relationship under investigation is as in Eq. (1). This is the standard situation of nonequivalence in exposure to S. Let us assume that we have omitted C from our prediction equation, so that we have the situation described in Eq. (2). Then, as shown earlier, the least-squares estimator is biased. By making some relatively plausible assumptions about the structure of relations among these variables it is possible to place bounds on the magnitude of the coefficient of interest with longitudinal data. The key assumption is that the process described in Eq. (1) is constant over the time interval of the panel, so that we can write

$$H_1 = b_1 S_1 + b_2 C_1 + e_1, \tag{3a}$$

$$H_2 = b_1 S_2 + b_2 C_2 + e_2, \tag{3b}$$

where the subscripts associated with H_t, S_t, and C_t refer to time and all variables are expressed as deviations from their means. We can manipulate Eq. (3a) to obtain

$$C_1 = (H_1 - b_1 S_1 - e_1)/b_2. \tag{4}$$

[2]The material in this section is an extension of Kessler and Greenberg (1981:15–18).

If C_t is governed by a first-order autoregressive process, we can also write

$$C_2 = d_1 C_1 + f_2. \tag{5}$$

By substituting the equivalence for C_1 from Eq. (4) into Eq. (5) and then substituting this equivalence for C_2 into Eq. (3b) we obtain

$$H_2 = dH_1 + b_1 S_2 - b_1 dS_1 + bf_2 + e_2 - de_1. \tag{6}$$

This equation cannot be estimated in the form expressed here because e_1 is correlated with H_1. This violates one of the basic assumptions of ordinary least squares regression (OLS). However, we can transform the equation to

$$H_2 - dH_1 = b_1 S_2 - b_1 dS_1 + bf_2 + e_2 - de_1 \tag{7}$$

to circumvent this estimation problem.

Without knowing the value of d it is not possible to estimate this equation. However, by making a series of assumptions about the magnitude of d—from its highest to its lowest possible values—we can obtain a range of estimates for b_1. Because Eq. (7) is linear in the parameters, the range of estimated values of b_1 is monotonic in the range of assumptions about d_1. This means that we need only consider the two extreme values for d_1 in making our evaluation. Because d_1 is the stability parameter for C_t, these extremes are 1 (C_t does not change over time) and 0 (C_t is a random variable) when the variance of C_t remains constant over time.

At the first extreme, Eq. (7) reduces to

$$H_2 - H_1 = b_1(S_2 - S_1) + e^*, \tag{8a}$$

and at the second it reduces to

$$H_2 = b_1 S_2 + e^*, \tag{8b}$$

where $e^* = bf_2 + e_2 - de_1$. The values of b_1 in these two equations are upper and lower bounds on the true value of b_1 in the correctly specified model, which is given by Eq. (1). When either b_2 is close to zero or r_{SC} is close to zero these two bounds will be very similar, in which case their estimates will be close to each other and either can be interpreted. However, when the two estimates diverge considerably we know that omitted variables distort our assessment of the relationship between S and H and that interpretations should be made only with great caution.

Predicting Adjustment

In a model of the relationship between strain and health the parameter associated with the exposure variable estimates the impact of strain on health. This impact coefficient tells us the *average* difference in the health of people who are and are not exposed to the strain. When we study adjustment rather than impact we are no longer interested in this average, but in *variations* around the average. We are interested in why the impact is more pronounced among some people than others. When we find a characteristic that is associated with a lower-than-average impact we say it is a predictor of good adjustment. When we find a characteristic that is associated with a higher-than-average impact we say it is a predictor of poor adjustment.[3]

It is important to recognize that in this definition of adjustment we are not conceptualizing predictors as variables that are significantly associated with the health outcome. Instead, a predictor of adjustment is a variable that is significantly associated with variation in the relationship between strain and the health outcome. Typically a predictor of this sort is operationalized as a statistical interaction in a structural equation model. For example, we might have

$$H = b_1 + b_2S + b_3M + b_4(S \times M) + e, \tag{9}$$

where M is a modifier of the relationship between S and H. This modifying influence is captured in the parameter b_4, which is associated with the product of the two predictors S and M.

Models of this sort are becoming increasingly common in multivariate research on the stress process. As we will see, these modifier models are used not only in normal population surveys but also in case-control studies. Yet there is a good deal of conceptual and methodological disagreement about how models of this sort should be analyzed and interpreted (Blot and Day, 1979; Hamilton, 1979; Hogan et al., 1978; Kupper and Hogan, 1978; Miettinen, 1974). In the remainder of this subsection I review the bases of this disagreement and provide a

---

[3]The term *adjustment* must not be used too casually, especially when working with measures of strain rather than stress. Some people can be less emotionally influenced by a particular strain than others because it is not experienced subjectively as stressful. Only if we are willing to assume that the strain has the same subjective meaning for people who respond differently to it should we interpret differential response as evidence of differential adjustment. In this chapter I use the word *adjustment* with this caveat in mind.

discussion of how substantive researchers can choose a preferred method of working with models like this.[4]

Terminology

A variety of terms have been used to describe the parameters in models that contain modifiers. Before discussing the models themselves it is useful to define a few of these terms.

By a *main effect* I mean an effect that is constant irrespective of the presence or absence of other factors (Cramer and Appelbaum, 1980). In linear models with only first-order terms, all independent variables are assumed to have main effects in this sense of the term.

Many strains do not have main effects because their effects vary depending on characteristics of the individual at risk or of his or her environment. Such effects are typically modeled using interaction terms (Southwood, 1978). A first-order term in a model of this sort is referred to as a *marginal effect*. This is the effect of a factor at a particular value of other factors and/or modifying influences.

The terms used to describe an interaction effect are numerous; *modifier, moderator, buffer* and *vulnerability factor* are the most common of these. When I use any of these terms I mean that the relationship between an event and illness depends on the presence, absence, or level of the modifier.

The term *mediator* is sometimes included in this list (for example, Dohrenwend and Dohrenwend, 1970). I prefer not to use it in this context, though, because there is a much more common and conventional use of the term that means something very different. In this conventional terminology a variable is called a mediator when it is causally intervening between two other variables. When, for example, part of the observed association between variables A and C is brought about by A causing B and B causing C, then B is said to mediate part of the relationship between A and C.

Interpreting Coefficients in Linear Models with Modifier Effects

It might be useful to refer to a concrete example at this point. Let us assume that we are concerned with the impact of life events LE on

---

[4]Substantial parts of the material presented in this subsection appeared originally in Cleary and Kessler (1982).

depression D. If the only independent variable we consider is LE, then we have

$$D = b_0 + b_1 LE, \tag{10}$$

where all variables are expressed at their means. If the model is correctly specified (the effect of LE is not dependent on influences that have been omitted from the model), b_1 is the main effect of life events on depression. What if the impact of life events is conditional? Let us say that the influence of LE on D is modified by the social support SS available to the individual. Then we might have

$$D = b_0 + b_1 LE + b_2 SS + b_3 (LE \times SS), \tag{11}$$

where $LE \times SS$ is a multiplicative interaction between life events and social support.

If social support has only two values (present $= 0$; absent $= 1$), we can rewrite Eq. (10) in terms of conditional values of SS as

$$\text{If} \quad SS = 0, \qquad D = b_0 + b_1 LE. \tag{12a}$$

$$\text{If} \quad SS = 1, \qquad D = (b_0 + b_2) + (b_1 + b_3) LE. \tag{12b}$$

A geometric representation of this model is shown in Figure 6.1. Each of the regression lines in the figure represents the effect of life events on depression at a particular value of social support.

If social support is a continuous variable we have an infinite number of equations, each written at a value of SS as

$$\text{If} \quad SS = i, \qquad D = (b_0 + ib_2) + (b_1 + ib_3) LE. \tag{13}$$

In a situation of this sort the geometric analogue of Figure 6.1 would contain as many regression lines as there are values of SS.

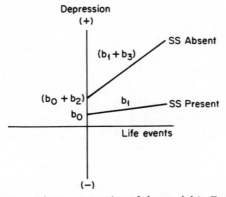

Figure 6.1. A geometric representation of the model in Eqs. (12a) and (12b).

The terms b_1 and b_2 are marginal effects: b_1 is the effect of LE on D among those with a score of zero on the social support scale; b_2 is the difference in the intercepts of LE among those with and without support. The intercept is evaluated at the zero point of the abscissa, which means that it is the effect of SS on D among those with a score of zero on the life-events scale.

I emphasize the important part played by zero points in the interpretation of conditional effects because this is frequently overlooked in practice. The conditional effect is arbitrary when the zero point is arbitrary. By adding or subtracting a constant from one scale, as can be done without loss of generality when that scale is measured at the interval level, it is possible to make the conditional effect of the other variable involved in the interaction significantly positive, significantly negative, or zero (Allison, 1977).

The term b_3 is the modifier effect of SS on the relationship between LE and D. As the decomposition in Eqs. (12a)–(12b) shows, when the modifier is a dichotomy, b_3 is the slope difference between the two subsamples. When the modifier is continuous, as in Eq. (13), b_3 is the average change in the slope across subsamples defined in units of the modifier.

Unlike first-order terms, modifier effects do not depend on the zero points of the two variables making up the interaction. This fact can be grasped intuitively by noting that a modifier is geometrically equivalent to an angle between two regression lines, whereas a conditional effect is the distance between the intersection of these two lines and one of the axes that define the regression plane. A change in the zero point of one variable is equivalent to changing the location of one of these axes. In Figure 6.1, for example, adding a constant to the scale of life events would be equivalent to moving the ordinate to the left. When this happens the distance between the intercepts of the two lines changes, but the angle is unaffected.

It can be shown either algebraically or geometrically that the dependence of conditional effects on the zero points and the independence of modifier effects from these points leads to the following statements about equations like Eq. (11) (Allison, 1977; Cohen, 1978; Southwood, 1978). First, addition or subtraction of a constant from one of the two scales making up a modifier effect will change the conditional effect of the other variable. The metric regression coefficient, the standardized coefficient, and the ratios of these coefficients to their standard errors will all change. Second, addition or subtraction of a constant from one of the scales will not change the metric coefficient of the modifier or the ratio of this coefficient to its standard error. The standardized coefficient will change.

Because first-order effects define the axes in terms of which the angle represented by the modifier effect is evaluated, it is important that these effects be included in an estimation equation even if they are statistically insignificant. It is not appropriate to trim the model of insignificant conditional effects before interpreting the modifier effect. In the absence of both first-order effects, the estimate of the modifier effect will be biased. We can see this in Figure 6.1. If the conditional effect of SS is omitted from the estimation equation we constrain our estimate of b_2 to equal zero and so constrain the two regression lines to cross on the ordinate. If the conditional effect of LE is omitted from the estimation equation we constrain our estimate of b_1 to equal zero and so constrain the regression line in the SS = 0 case not to cross the abscissa. This means that this line is constrained to parallel the LE axis. Either of these constraints changes the angle defined by the intersection of the two regression lines and so systematically distorts the estimate of b_3.

Complications from Nonlinearities in the Marginal Effects

A number of published analyses have used models like that in Eq. (11) to study the modifying influence of some variable or variables on the relationship between life events and psychological distress. Most of these analyses have documented a significant modifying influence.

When an influence such as this is shown, and *before* it is interpreted, it is important to be certain that nonlinearities in the marginal effects are not distorting the magnitude of the estimated modifier. Strong nonlinearities, if they are not explicitly estimated, can give the false appearance that there is a modifier effect when in fact there is none. This can only happen, though, if the life-event index and the modifying variable are significantly correlated with each other.

To understand how this can come about, consider Figure 6.2, which is a scatterplot of a nonlinear relationship between some modifying influence M and distress D. As shown in Eq. (13), when we estimate a multiplicative interaction model in which it is assumed that the marginal effects are linear, we essentially disaggregate this scatterplot into a series of subplots, each one defined for people who have none, one, two, or n events. If we find that the slope of the regression line changes systematically from one of these disaggregated plots to another there is a modifying influence between LE and M.

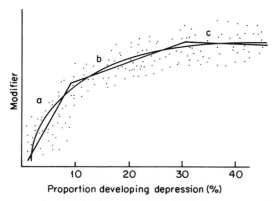

Figure 6.2.   A scatterplot of a nonlinear relationship between a modifier and distress.

This is where the possibility of error arises. If *LE* and *M* are related to each other and if we incorrectly estimate a linear, rather than a quadractic, equation for each of the disaggregated scatterplots, then we will find systematic variation in the slopes even though there is no true modifying influence. The reason for this is that the disaggregated plots will overrepresent certain parts of the scatter. If, for example, people who have no life events generally have very low values of *M*, then the slope of the linear segment a will fit the scatter of their observed *D* scores very nicely. People with one or two life events might have mostly average values of *M* and so the slope of segment b will fit the scatter of their *D* scores. And people who have three or more life events might have, on average, high values of *M*, which means that the slope of segment c will fit their scatter. Together, these good fits give the appearance of a modifying effect when, in reality, they are generated by an underlying nonlinearity in the effect of *M*.

It is easy to guard against this mistake. First, pay attention to the magnitude of the correlation between *LE* and *M*. If this correlation is insubstantial, there is no reason for concern. If, however, the correlatiion is large it becomes possible for an unexamined nonlinearity to manifest itself as an apparent interaction. This possibility can be avoided by including terms to capture this nonlinearity in the prediction equation. For example, we might have

$$D = b_0 + b_1 LE + b_2 M + b_3 LE^2 + b_4 M^2 + b_5 (LE \times M). \qquad (14)$$

As a routine precaution when *LE* and *M* are strongly related, I suggest estimating an equation like this one.

Complications from Nonlinearities in the Modifying Influences

As shown in Eq. (13), there is a linear constraint imposed on the modifying influence in multiplicative models. This constraint is not always plausible. Indeed there are some theoretical formulations that quite explicitly postulate that modifying influences will be nonlinear. Wortman et al. (1976), for example, postulated that people who have a realistic perception about their ability to control events will be best able to cope with events that are difficult to control. This means that the impact of events on distress will be least pronounced when the individual has neither a very high nor very low score on an index of fatalism. A condition of this sort cannot be tested with a multiplicative interaction model.

Although I shall not review extensions of the simple multiplicative modifying model here, there are several different ways to specify a model that takes into consideration the existence of more complex modifying influences such as this one. Many of these models are reviewed by Taylor and Hornung (1979) and by Southwood (1978).

Distinguishing Provoking Agents and Vulnerability Factors

The arbitrary nature of conditional effects is not always appreciated in practice. One example of this is the ongoing debate about whether the absence of social support is in itself capable of provoking depression (Kaplan et al., 1977) or if it only leads to depression by increasing the emotional impact of stressful life events (Cobb, 1976). This debate is about the significance of support's marginal effect. But participants in the debate have not always been sensitive to the fact that this effect can arbitrarily be made significant or insignificant by changing the zero point of the scale measuring stressful experience.

This arbitrariness can be avoided if one of the scales has a true zero point, but this is seldom the case. A common approach intended to approximate this situation is to create dichotomies to represent the presence versus absence of some stress or modifier. But even here the interpretation of marginal effects is unambiguous only if the variables are true dichotomies rather than collapsed continua. One can see this concretely in the work of Brown and Harris (1978b), who used their data to argue that support is related to depression as a modifier but not as a risk factor in its own right. They argued that there are times when only one of the two variables in an interacting pair is capable of bringing about depression in the absence of the other. They called this variable the provoking agent. The other variable, which they called the vulnerability factor, is capable of increasing or decreasing the impact of the provoking agent, but is incapable of bringing about depression in the absence of the provoking agent. They claimed that their data demonstrate that life events and the absence of a confidant interact in this way to produce depression, with life events the provoking agent and absence of a confidant the vulnerability factor. Figure 6.3 presents the data on which this argument is based (Brown and Harris, 1978a:585). I have diagrammed the data differently than Brown and Harris, who reported only the probability of depression in each cell of a four-cell table defined in terms of the presence or absence of a confidant and the presence or absence of a recent stressful life event.

On first examination it is easy to see why they concluded that the absence of support does not directly provoke depression. In the absence of an event there is no meaningful association between having a confidant and being depressed. Both those with and without a confidant have extremely low rates of depression (1% and 3%, respectively). It is only in the presence of a stressful life event that the absence of a confidant increases risk of depression (32% among those without a confidant compared to 10% among those with a confidant).

This is compelling evidence *if* one is willing to assume that exposure to life events and access to a supportive relationship can accurately be described as dichotomies. However, if these dichotomies truncate the real distributions of exposure and access, the analysis might be creating an erroneous view of what really is happening. Let us assume, for example, that the dichotomous measure of events collapses a range of

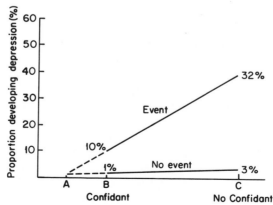

Figure 6.3. A geometric presentation of the Brown and Harris (1978a) data.

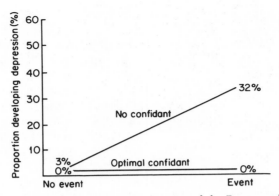

Figure 6.4. An alternative geometric presentation of the Brown and Harris (1978a) data.

values that accurately defines the extent to which an individual is exposed to acute stress. Furthermore, let us assume that access to a confidant is really a continuum rather than a dichotomy and that persons whom Brown and Harris defined as having a confidant actually have an average access score of B in Figure 3, those they defined as lacking a confidant have an average access of C, and that people who have optimal access to a confidant have a score of A. If these assumptions hold, then life events no longer have the central feature of provoking agents: At the highest level of access to a confidant there is no relationship between life events and depression. In fact, if we transpose the ordinate and abscissa, as in Figure 6.4, we might argue that events are nothing more than buffers for the relationship between support and depression. In that transposed diagram we see that events are unrelated to depression in the presence of an extremely strong confidant relationship, whereas absence of a confidant increases risk of depression even in the absence of events.

The point is that an assertion that one variable is a provoking agent and another is a vulnerability factor is meaningful only when we have great confidence in the zero points of our scales. Given the nature of social science data, we are seldom certain that the zero point of a scale is the correct one. Consequently, it is only rarely the case that we can empirically distinguish between a provoking agent and a vulnerability factor. The scales we use in research are, at best, proxies for true levels of support, exposure to events, resources, or vulnerabilities. So when we interpret marginal effects we should think of them as being evaluated at an empirically observed low point on the sample distribution. LaRocco *et al.* (1980), for instance, did this in their analysis of work stress, social support, and health. They assigned the lowest observed point on their support scale the score zero and interpreted conditional effects at an empirical low point rather than at some absolute zero point. It is also possible to carry out sensitivity analyses, to see if conditional effects are significant even at a lower point than the lowest observed point in a sample, by adding some arbitrary constant before estimating the regression equation. In this way the significance of the effect is evaluated at a point below the observed minimum value, thus taking into account the possibility that the population minimum (or the theoretical minimum) might be lower than the minimum value observed in the sample.

Explaining Modifier Effects

So far we have considered how to estimate and interpret a modifier effect. But that is only the beginning, as our earlier discussion made clear. We know, for instance, that lower-class people are more likely than their middle-class counterparts to become depressed when they are exposed to a stressful life event. It is not difficult to collect data and demonstrate that this is true using Eq. (11) or (if in the data set under consideration there is a strong relationship between class and LE) Eq. (14). But how do we go about testing whether one or more hypothesized causal variables that we have measured account for that modifying influence? Let us say that we have a measure of chronic financial strain FS, which we believe explains the interaction between financial loss events and social class. If we hypothesize that this strain *mediates* the interactive influences of class and financial loss events, then we merely have to include FS as a variable in the basic model that uncovered the interaction. We might have

$$D = b_0 + b_1 LE + b_2 SC + b_3 (LE \times SC) + b_4 FS. \qquad (15)$$

If we find that our estimate of b_3 is no longer significant when we control FS then we have evidence that the apparent differential impact of financial loss events on people from different class positions stems from the fact that these events are more likely to bring about financial strains when they are experienced by lower-class than middle-class people.

It is important to recognize that this interpretation does not imply that financial strains totally account for the effect of events on depression. For this to be true, estimates of b_1 as well as of b_3 would have to be insignificant when FS is controlled. Instead, the argument is that the differential effect of these events on the well-being of people in different social classes can be accounted for by differences in the extent to which the events are likely to create financial strains.

An analysis of this sort shows how it is that life events have a more emotionally damaging effect on lower-class people. But there is another, somewhat more complicated, hypothesis: that it is not social class at all, but rather some variable closely related to social class, that accounts for what seems to be a modifying influence of social class. For example, we might believe that social support SS and self-esteem SE *modify* the influence of life events on depression. But we also know that SS and SE are related to social class and we suspect that what appears to be a modifying influence of class actually reflects nothing more than the modifying influences of its correlates SS and SE.

One needs a somewhat more complex model to test this *modification* hypothesis than to test the *mediation* hypothesis, for now we have to include in the prediction equation marginal effects for SS and SE and interactions of each variable with LE along with all the coefficients we would have in a model evaluating the modifying effect of social class. This equation might be

$$D = b_0 + b_1 LE + b_2 SC + b_3 (LE \times SC)$$
$$+ b_4 SS + b_5 SE + b_6 (LE \times SS) + b_7 (LE \times SE). \qquad (16)$$

Our concern is with evaluating the magnitude of b_3 in this equation compared to its value in the equation that omits the marginal and interactive effects of SS and SE. When a previously significant estimate of b_3 is reduced to insignificance by the controls we can say that what seemed to be a modifying influence of social class is, in reality, an influence of SS and/or SE.

In a later section I describe a decomposition strategy that can help us interpret the influences of variables like SS and SE on an interaction such as that between LE and SC. Without an explicit decomposition we cannot discriminate the *mediating* and *modifying* influences of SS and SE. For now, though, I want to mention only two important technical considerations in estimating a model like this one. First, there are no parameters in the terms $SC \times SS$ or $SC \times SE$ in the equation. The reason for this is that we do not hypothesize that the influence of social class on depression *varies as a function of* social support or self-esteem. Instead, we are hypothesizing that the modifying effect of class is *explained by* SS and SE. This hypothesized explanatory effect is estimated in a fashion that is logically identical to any other regression analysis: by including the SS and SE interactions in the prediction equation along with the $LE \times SC$ interaction that we want to explain.

Second, we have included the marginal effects of SS and SE in the equation even though we think that the interactions are the important explanatory terms. We do this for the same reasons described in our discussion of models that contain only one interaction term. These arguments apply equally well to the case of multiple interactions. All variables involved in any of the interactions in a model should be included as marginal terms in that model. This is true also when we estimate higher-order interactions. This means that if we include a three-way interaction $LE \times SC \times SS$ in our model we should also include all three of the two-way interactions embedded in the three-way term—$LE \times SC$, $LE \times SS$, and $SC \times SS$—as well as all one-way marginal terms—LE, SC, and SS.

Alternative Functional Forms

So far I have discussed modifier effects as if they were equivalent algebraically to multiplicative interactions in linear models. When models predicting values on a continuous outcome variable—such as scores on a depression-screening scale—are developed, this is usually the case. When the outcome variable is dichotomous, as many measures of morbidity and mortality are, there is slippage in the equivalence. Alternative models can be developed and only some of these specify that statistical interactions are multiplicative. This variation leads to interpretation problems that do not arise when working with continuous outcomes.

A linear-probability model for a dichotomous outcome can be estimated using generalized least-squares estimation techniques. Both continuous and categorical predictor analogues exist (Grizzle et al., 1969). In models of this sort, the probability of the outcome is estimated by coding the outcome as either present ($p = 1$) or absent ($p = 0$) and fitting a linear model using least-squares procedures. This yields an equation of the following form:

$$p = b_0 + b_1 LE + b_2 SS + b_3 LE \times SS, \tag{17}$$

where p is the probability of the outcome.

Alternative models for describing dichotomous outcomes include discriminant analysis, logistic regression, and probit analysis. Both logistic and probit functions can be estimated with either continuous or categorical independent variables (Swafford, 1980). All of them describe the probability of the outcome as a nonlinear function of the predictors. They differ in the exact functional form and in the estimation techniques used, but they are alike in relating the probability of the outcome to the predictors with a sigmoid curve that does not exceed one or go below zero (Hanushek and Jackson, 1977:187). The most commonly used function in such cases is the logistic distribution. Here the probability of the outcome is

$$p = 1/(1 + e^{-Xb}), \tag{18}$$

where Xb is a matrix product. However, rather than focus on probabilities, this model considers interactions in terms of log-odds. This is done by logging Eq. (18) and then manipulating this logged equation to yield

$$\ln [p/(1 - p)] = b_0 + b_1 LE + b_2 SS + b_3 LE \times SS. \tag{19}$$

The log-odds of the outcome is a linear function of the independent variables. Yet, at the same time, in the scale of probabilities the model is nonlinear and as a consequence the effect of each independent variable on the probability of the outcome is conditional on the values of the other independent variables. This is the most salient characteristic of sigmoid models for purposes of this discussion. The effects of the independent variables on the dependent variable are inherently interactive. That is, it can be shown that the functional form described in Eq. (19) necessarily implies that the effect of one independent variable is conditional on the value of the other independent variable when the model is expressed in terms of probabilities.

The most important implication of this conditional feature for purposes of estimating modifier effects is that the multiplicative effect of the modifier on the probabilities can often be described using only first-order terms in the ratio model. In the example from Brown and Harris described in Figure 6.2, this means that the statistical "interaction" present in the difference model is not a significant interaction in a log–linear model; that is, the presence or absence of the interaction depends on whether we are studying additivity in terms of probabilities or probability ratios. The differential probability of being depressed due to the absence of social support is 2% (3% − 1%) in the absence of life events and 22% (32% − 10%) in the presence of events. These two percentages differ considerably and were interpreted by Brown and Harris as evidence that social support modifies the effect of life events on depression. But the relative risks of being depressed or not in the absence or presence of support are very similar in these two groups: about 3:1 (3%:1% and 32%:10%) in each, so in terms of relative risk there is no modifying effect. This is a critical distinction between linear difference models and ratio models.

This important difference in the conceptualization of modifiers is sometimes overlooked in practice, as evidenced by a controversy between Brown and Harris (1978a) and Tennant and Bebbington (1978) about the importance of social support as a buffer. Using a log–linear model equivalent to Eq. (19), Tennant and Bebbington reanalyzed Brown and Harris's data and found the interaction between LE and SS insignificant. On the basis of this result they disputed Brown and Harris's assertion that support modifies the LE–D relationship. Brown and Harris countered by arguing on intuitive grounds that the difference between the relative probabilities—2 versus 22%—is so large that no statistical test could convince them that a modifying effect is not present.

In their critique of Brown and Harris, Tennant and Bebbington failed to appreciate that they were defining modifier effects in the context of different models. Brown and Harris were making use of a linear probability difference model, but Tennant and Bebbington used a log–linear ratio model.

There are times when the two models will yield consistent results. When the outcome is not highly skewed (the rarer outcome occurs at least 10% of the time) there is an approximately linear relationship between probabilities and sigmoid curves like the logit and probit (Cox, 1970:26–29). Probability and sigmoid models consequently yield similar results in cases of this sort. Even when the outcome is highly skewed the models sometimes lead to similar conclusions. For example, were the probabilities in the Brown and Harris data 1, 3, 10, and 52% there would be no disagreement that a modifying effect exists. The probability differences would be 2 and 42%, and the probability ratios would be 3:1 and 5:1, both comparisons showing the effect of LE on D to be greater when social support is absent than when it is present. But there are many times when the two types of conceptualizations will yield discrepant results. In fact, it is relatively easy to come up with combinations of probabilities that could demonstrate: (1) a modifying effect in the difference model but not in the ratio model, (2) a modifying effect in the ratio model but not in the difference model, or even (3) a positive modifying effect in one model and a negative modifying effect in the other.

There is no way to determine empirically which of the two formulations—difference or ratio—more accurately describes the causal processes at work in observed data. Arguments independent of the data must be marshalled in defense of one formulation over the other. Unfortunately, there is no unanimity about the considerations that are important in making this decision.

One position is that linear probability models should be used because it is natural to measure the extent to which a provoking agent produces an outcome in terms of probabilities (Rothman, 1974, 1978). It can also be argued that a linear probability model breaks down at the margins, because usually the influence of a provoking agent on an individual who has an otherwise extremely high probability of the outcome will be less than on an individual who has a lower base-line probability (Hanushek and Jackson, 1977:183). Because of this, linear probability models run into technical estimation problems when the skew is high. Specification errors become heteroskedastic and predicted probabilities for individual cases can lie outside the bounds 0 to 1.

These problems as well as the substantive appeal of a function that asymptotes at the values of 0 and 1 have led to the widespread use of sigmoid models. They require a greater change in the provoking agent to cause equal marginal probability shifts in the outcome as the baseline probability becomes more extreme. Furthermore, predicted probabilities in sigmoid models are constrained to lie within the 0–1 range, so they are superior to linear probability models when the outcome skew is extreme. When the skew is not extreme, as noted earlier, the models yield very similar results. So there is no reason to avoid sigmoid models even in this case.

I endorse this preference for sigmoid models to study the determinants of a dichotomous outcome. At the same time, though, I am seldom willing to accept unconditionally the existence or nonexistence of an interaction in a sigmoid model when a linear probability model yields a discrepant result. This uneasiness about accepting either model as the definitive basis for assessing interactions is one I share with others (e.g., Cleary and Kessler, 1982; Walter and Holford, 1978).

One solution to this uncertainty is to accept the more parsimonious formulation, the one requiring the fewer parameters to describe the data, as the "preferred" model (Greenland, 1979). This is an expedient solution but an atheoretical one that masks conceptual uncertainty with a technical decision rule. In the absence of a good substantive reason to choose one formulation over the other I prefer to accept discrepant results as evidence of uncertainty in the existence of a modifying influence rather than try to mask it with ad hoc resolutions.

The only truly adequate way to determine the correct model when the two formulations yield discrepant results is to appeal to one's theory about the processes that generate the causal link between the risk factor under investigation and the outcome. If there is no basis in theory to assert what the appropriate formulation of this causal link is, then uncertainty about the existence of a modifier effect, and indeed about what is meant by a modifier effect, is a necessary result.

SURVEYS OF CRISIS VICTIMS

A major limitation of normal population surveys is that only a small fraction of people experience any one life event in a short interval of time. This makes it impossible to study the effects of specific events. Instead, summary measures of overall exposure to many different types of events are created. We know that these summary measures are significantly correlated with measures of psychological distress and physiological symptoms in normal population samples (see the chapter by Thoits). And we know that several characteristics of individuals and their social world modify the relationship between these summary measures of life events and measures of ill health. Social support and coping strategies are among the most important of these (see the chapters by Turner and by Menaghan). However, as long as our measures of life events are aggregated in this way it is impossible to develop specific models of adjustment. As a result, researchers who have been concerned with particular types of strain or with sophisticated models of adjustment have turned away from normal population surveys to more focused investigations of people who have experienced particularly traumatic life crises.

The most common research design employed by the latter group of researchers is a survey confined to victims of one particular crisis. I will refer to this as the case-only design. (The designation *only* is used to distinguish designs of this sort from case-control designs, which are discussed next.)

A major problem in studies of this sort is obtaining a representative sample of people who have experienced the crisis. Conventional population-sampling methods can be used to screen for respondents with the desired characteristics, but this is very expensive when the event is as rare as many crises are. Network-sampling methods can be used to reduce this cost considerably if informants selected by probability-sampling procedures are willing and able to report the names of people in their social networks who have the desired characteristics. However, informants often do not know about some crises, like rape, that have occured even to people very close to them. And when they are aware of the crises they might be hesitant to disclose the identity of the person who experienced it.

As a result of these problems almost all case-only surveys have relied on samples drawn by means other than normal population screening. This has been a source of great concern about the generalizability of research findings, especially when there is reason to believe that the people who are in the sample have some self-selection characteristics that differentiate them from people who are not part of the sample. Studies of rape victims, for example, usually rely on women who have contacted the police (Burgess and Holmstrom, 1979). It is very likely that these women are different in important ways from women who failed to report the crime. Studies of marital separation pose a similar problem; they usually focus on men and women who have obtained a legal separation (Bloom et al., 1978) and leave unexamined people who dissolve their marriages without the benefit of a legal agreement.

Fortunately, there are times when one can inexpensively obtain representative samples of people who have experienced some life events of interest. Widows, for example, can be found by sampling death certificates (Lopata, 1979). Unemployed workers can be found through unemployment insurance rolls (Liem et al., 1982). These opportunities are more the exception than the rule, but they should be exploited whenever possible. In their absence the researcher is faced either with a very expensive screening operation or with the prospect of obtaining a sample that is biased in some unknown way.

Documenting the Impact of Strain

Documenting the impact of strain on health is seldom a central concern in case-only studies. There is some evidence that the number of health problems found among those who have experienced a life crisis are substantially higher than expected in the normal populations, yet this is almost never the subject of systematic attention. This is not necessarily bad. In fact, it seems somewhat pedantic to document in any great detail an effect of this sort. For instance, one study reported that 89% of widows suffer from crying spells 1 month after bereavement (Clayton and Darvish, 1979). It is clear that this is a much greater percentage than we would expect to find in the normal population. Indeed, there would be no reason to conduct a survey of crisis victims if there were no prior evidence that the crisis had some adverse health impact worth studying.

Nonetheless, it is worth noting that a case-only design is incapable of documenting that the strain under investigation has effects of this sort.

This documentation requires a comparison group of people who have not been exposed to the event.

Describing the Course of Adjustment

A major purpose of case-only studies is to describe the process of adjustment to strain over time. This is done in different ways depending on the type of design on which the analysis is based. There are two basic approaches here. The first is the cohort design, where a sample of people who have recently experienced a crisis are followed over time. The second is the synthetic cohort design, where the sample is usually cross-secitonal rather than longitudinal and is made up of people who experienced the crisis at some time in the past, but not necessarily the recent past.

In both of these designs the researcher is interested in the developmental course of adjustment to the crisis. In a cohort study this is done by observing how victims change over time. In a synthetic cohort study it is done by interpreting cross-sectional differences in the adjustment of people to whom the event happened at different times as if they represented snapshots of the changes that occurred over time in a single cohort.

A good example of a synthetic approximation to a true cohort can be found in the work of Blanchard et al. (1976), who conducted a cross-sectional survey of widows in which respondents were asked to report the frequency with which they experienced 20 symptoms of depression. The authors were able to show that substantially fewer of these symptoms were found among widows who had lost their spouses a long time before the interview than among those whose bereavement was more recent. Those symptoms associated with time since the loss were mostly somatic reactions—crying, sleep disturbance, and appetite loss. Another set of symptoms was not associated with time since the loss. These included psychological reactions like depressed mood, feelings of hopelessness, and suicidal thoughts.

As noted earlier, designs of these two sorts are used commonly to describe the "normal" (in the statistical sense of that word) course of adjustment to life crisis. Research on the existence of stages of adjustment falls into this class of studies. Here an attempt is made to demonstrate that people who adjust most adequately to a particular crisis pass through a predictable set of stages, in each of which a different emotional issue is salient. The best known of these stage theories is that of Kubler-Ross (1969), who described five stages of adjustment among the terminally ill: denial, anger, bargaining, depression, and acceptance. But there are a great many other stage theories that focus on different crises (Silver and Wortman, 1980: 300–305).

Synthetic cohort studies are typically used to generate hypotheses about stages, but because they do not include multiple time-point interviews with the same people they do not demonstrate that any given individual passes through a series of stages. They can only show that *aggregate* trends exist in the emotional issues that arise as time passes after the crisis has occurred (or, in the case of some enduring crises like terminal illness, after the crisis has begun). True cohort studies are more typically used to demonstrate that particular individuals pass through stages.

Each of these two designs has a major limitation when it comes to describing the course of adjustment. In the synthetic cohort study, one problem is that individual level change is never observed. It is only inferred. I mentioned earlier that the Blanchard *et al.* study of widows found that whose who had been widowed longest reported a higher proportion of psychological than somatic symptoms of distress; those widowed for the shortest amount of time reported the reverse pattern. But does this mean that widows change from an early period of mostly somatic reactions to a later one of mostly psychological ones? Does it mean that some widows never develop somatic symptoms whereas others have them for only a brief time? Or does it mean that the proportion of widows who have early psychological symptoms that subsequently change into somatic symptoms is much smaller than the proportion who have early somatic symptoms that change into psychological ones? There is no way to discriminate these various possibilities with synthetic cohort data.

Another problem with synthetic cohort studies is that the validity of aggregate inferences hinges on the assumption that there is no cohort effect in the process of adjustment—that the process of adjustment is the same among people who experience the event at different times in the past. If this assumption is incorrect and people in different cohorts actually adjust in different ways, synthetic cohort estimates of adjustment will be biased.

A true cohort study resolves this last problem by focusing on a single cohort: people who have experienced the crisis at roughly the same time. It also has the advantage of allowing the study of how individuals change over time rather than making it necessary to guess about individuals from aggregate trend data. In these respects, then, the true cohort design is superior to the synthetic cohort design. However, a true cohort study is open to one very important and pervasive source of bias: history. Inferences about the adjustment process will be biased when a change in symptoms over time is due to some historic event or cyclic pattern of influence that occurs between measurement periods. For instance, we know that many types of mental health problems, like depressed mood and suicide, vary seasonally (Kessler and Stipp, forthcoming). As a result, assessment of emotional adjustment in a cohort of crisis victims will almost surely be biased if these assessments are made at intervals of a few months.

There are two ways to guard against a history effect of this sort. One is to compare the results of a synthetic cohort analysis with those of a true cohort study. When the results conform it is almost surely the case that both cohort and history effects are absent. (It is possible that both are present and counterbalancing, but this is much less likely.) An illustration can be found in the work of Clayton and Darvish (1979), who replicated the work of Blanchard in a cohort study of widowed men and women. Widows were interviewed 1 month after the death of their spouses and then a year later. A comparison of mental health symptoms showed clearly that somatic complaints decreased over time while psychological ones remained elevated, which is in perfect conformity with the synthetic cohort results of Blanchard et al.

The second way to guard against history effects is to include a normal population control group along with the sample of victims in the longitudinal design. History effects should influence the controls as well as the victims, so a comparison of the two groups allows an assessment of health outcomes net of history. This design, known as a prospective case-control design, is discussed next. But first we need to say something about the possibility of using case-only studies to make inferences about the predictors of adjustment.

Predicting Adjustment

So far I have discussed case-only studies as ways of describing the course of adjustment to a crisis. But the true cohort design is also used to study the predictors of adjustment. This type of research correlates individual-level change in health with characteristics of the individual known as of the first time of measurement. There are several reasons for doing research of this sort. For one, clinicians find it useful to have early markers that help pinpoint people who are likely to have difficulties in adjustment. Bereavement studies, for example, show quite consistently that lower-class widows are more likely than their middle-class counterparts to have problems adjusting to the death of their spouses (Clayton and Darvish, 1979). Furthermore, theoretically sensitive attempts to predict adjustment can give us clues about how to intervene in these high-risk groups. For example, analysis of social class differences in adjustment to bereavement shows that passive coping styles and attempts to avoid social interaction characterize the response styles of working class widows. These, in turn, make it difficult to build bridges between their old and their new lives.

These prediction analyses do not require a control sample because they are intended to provide information that is relevant to clinicians who work only with victims of crisis. However, this design is not a very powerful way of investigating the predictors of *adjustment* as opposed to *outcome*. By outcome I mean the emotional functioning of the person who has experienced a life crisis. By adjustment I mean something a bit more specific: the person's response to the crisis as displayed in the difference between his or her emotional functioning and the functioning we could have expected had the crisis not occurred.

A concrete illustration will be useful here. Let us assume that we are studying a sample of people who have been permanently paralyzed by a spinal cord injury, and that we are concerned with the emotional effects of this tragedy. We know from the research of Bracken and Bernstein (1980) that social class position is not significantly related to psychological distress 1 year after the injury. Yet I would argue that we cannot say on the basis of this that social class is not related to adjustment. The reason is that we know from epidemiologic survey data that there is a significant negative relationship between social class and psychological distress in the normal population. And because these victims are presumably a random sample from that population we would expect, in the absence of this tragedy in their lives, that social class would be significantly related to their distress as well. The fact that we do not find this relationship among them suggests, then, that there is some difference in the class–distress relationship before and after their accidents. This, in turn, can be interpreted as evidence of a relationship between class and *adjustment* even though there is no relationship between class and short-term emotional *outcome*. In fact, I suggest that the most likely interpretation of these data is that the lower the social class, the better the emotional adjustment to the tragedy. A higher rate of emotional distress among lower- than middle-class people prior to the event was erased after it occurred, which means that the *change* in distress must have been more pronounced among those in the middle than in the lower class.

If the researcher is interested in studying emotional *outcomes* in a sample of people who are at high risk for mental health problems due to a life crisis, then there is no need to include a normal population control gorup in the longitudinal analysis of outcome. An analysis of victims will yield a perfectly acceptable assessment of those who are more or less likely to develop health problems. The important point to note, though, is that only some of these problems will be due to the crisis. For example, as I noted earlier, lower-class widows are much more likely than their middle-class counterparts to develop a health problem in the year after their husband's death. This does not mean, though, that the probability of developing a health problem *as a result* of bereavement is highest in the lower class. It might be that lower-class women are more likely to develop health problems *due to* that loss, but we also know that lower-class women are more likely to develop health problems *in general*. Or, to take another example, we might find that age is associated with ill health after job layoff. But this does not necessarily mean that older people are more likely to develop health problems *as a result* of layoffs. It might simply be that older people have more health problems, whether they are laid off or not. When the discrimination of these different types of causal influences is important, case-only designs are inadequate and we must turn to case-control designs.

PROSPECTIVE CASE-CONTROL STUDIES

Surveys that compare crisis victims with a sample of people who have not experienced the crisis are known as prospective case-control studies. They are prospective in that they focus on the health effects of the crisis that appear some time after it has occurred. It is instructive to note that this design is a variant on the normal population survey design, where the sample is stratified on the recent occurrence of a particular life event. This means that the prospective case-control design has all the features of a cross-sectional normal population survey, with the exception that the limited number of crisis victims found in the latter is increased by stratified oversampling.

It is important to note that the analogue here is with a cross-sectional normal population survey, not a longitudinal one. The reason for this is that stratification in the prospective case-control design occurs after victims have experienced the event being studied. In the longitudinal normal population survey, by comparison, health is assessed before the event occurs. As a result of this difference it is considerably easier to make causal inferences in longitudinal normal population surveys than in longitudinal surveys of victims and controls, just as it is easier to make such inferences in longitudinal than in cross-sectional normal population surveys.

If we bear in mind this equivalence between the prospective case-control design and the cross-sectional normal population design, it is relatively easy to understand the research questions that can and cannot be answered with surveys of crisis victims and normal population controls.

Documenting the Impact of Strain

The appropriate way to address this research question is to use membership in the two samples as a predictor variable of the health outcome in a multivariate model that controls for all other determinants of the outcome that are exogenously related to the probability of having experienced the crisis. In other words, we have the same situation as described in Eq. (1) for the cross-sectional normal population survey, with the same potential for bias when important control variables are omitted from the prediction equation.

There is no approximation in these case-control designs to the sort of sensitivity analysis presented earlier in Eqs. (3)–(8), where we used longitudinal data to place bounds on the true effect of strain. This is true even if, as is often the case, the design calls for repeated interviewing of cases and controls over time. The reason for this, as noted earlier, is that all waves of interviewing take place after the crisis has occurred. In terms of the logic of data analysis these additional waves do not help us resolve the omitted variable problem because they do not yield information about the functioning of cases prior to the onset of the crisis.

One might ask, at this point, why collect data over time in case-control studies if they are not helpful in resolving this problem of causal priority? The answer is that longitudinal data can be used in a sophisticated cohort analysis of cases and controls to study the course of adjustment to crisis. This is the next topic.

Describing the Course of Adjustment

I described earlier how history effects can bias inferences about the course of adjustment in true cohort studies. And I mentioned that one way to combat this problem is to work with longitudinal case-control

data. The appropriate strategy is to replicate an analysis of crisis impact, as discussed in the last subsection, across the successive time
points of the longitudinal data collection. A comparison of the coefficients linking S to the outcome at these different time points is the best
estimate of how adjustment progresses over time.

This strategy is not commonly used in investigations of adjustment.
The standard approach is to present case-control mean differences in
the outcome variables at the different time points of the longitudinal
investigation (e.g., Burgess and Holmstrom, 1979), which is equivalent
to the strategy I recommend here without any control variables. (This
can be seen by noting that the slope of an outcome on a dummy predictor variable defining membership in the case or control sample is algebraically equivalent to the difference between the two groups in
mean levels of the outcome.) If it is assumed that there are no omitted
variables in the structural equation model defining the impact of the
event on health, then the two approaches are equivalent. But, as noted
earlier, we can seldom have this much confidence that the life event
occurred entirely at random with respect to the background characteristics of its victims. So, in general, it is preferable to monitor the
process of adjustment with a series of structural equation models rather
than with a series of mean difference calculations.

There are actually two different ways to carry out the necessary com-
putation of the case-control difference. The first is the way I have described in the last paragraph—to estimate a series of cross-sectional
structural equation models in which membership in the case or control
samples is used as a predictor of the outcome. The second is to estimate
two separate through-time models, one each for the case and control
samples. Both approaches include control variables.

These two approaches are equivalent because they both compare the
difference between two differences, which is a symmetric operation. In
the first approach, the difference $H_{11} - H_{21}$ is compared with the
difference $H_{12} - H_{22}$, where H_{ij} is the mean level of the health outcome
in sample i at time j. This is a comparison over time of cross-sec-
tional/between-group differences. In the second approach, the difference $H_{11} - H_{12}$ is compared to the difference $H_{21} - H_{22}$. This is a
between-group comparison of over-time/within-group changes. In both
cases we have the same overall result. That is,

$$(H_{11} - H_{21}) - (H_{12} - H_{22}) = (H_{11} + H_{22}) - (H_{21} + H_{12})$$
$$= (H_{11} - H_{12}) - (H_{21} - H_{22}). \quad (20)$$

Similar difference calculations can be made for the time intervals 2–3,
3–4, and so on.

To demonstrate how we can embed these comparisons in a single structural equation model, I use the cross-sectional/between-group difference parametrization to write equations for $H_{1_t} - H_{2_t}$ at times $t = 1, 2$.

$$H_{i_1} = b_1 + b_2 S + b_3 C, \tag{21a}$$

$$H_{i_2} = b_4 + b_5 S + b_6 C, \tag{21b}$$

where S is a dummy variable for membership in the case or control samples and C is a control variable. In each of these equations the parameter associated with S can be interpreted as the mean cross-sectional/between-group difference in H_i standardized on C. That is,

$$b_2 = H_{11} - H_{21}, \tag{22a}$$

$$b_5 = H_{12} - H_{22}. \tag{22b}$$

By subtracting Eq. (21b) from (21a) we obtain

$$\begin{aligned} H_{i_1} - H_{i_2} &= (b_1 + b_4) + (b_2 - b_5)S + (b_3 - b_6)C \\ &= b_1{}^* + b_2{}^* S + b_3{}^* C. \end{aligned} \tag{23}$$

The parameter $b_2{}^*$ gives us the desired contrast because

$$b_2{}^* = b_2 - b_5 = (H_{11} - H_{21}) - (H_{12} - H_{22}). \tag{24}$$

If our estimate of this parameter has a confidence interval that includes 0, there is no significant evidence of adjustment over the time interval 1–2. If the estimate is significantly negative, on the other hand, there is evidence that rates of ill health have decreased more in the victim sample than in the control sample.

Predicting Adjustment

Because the prospective case-control design is logically similar to the cross-sectional normal population design, the same considerations about conceptualizing predictors of adjustment apply in the former as in the latter. Nothing more needs to be said about this conceptualization, as it has been discussed fully in the earlier review of the normal population survey design. There is one special issue that arises in case-control designs more frequently than in normal population surveys, though, that was not touched on in my earlier discussion. There are times when the predictors of interest are variables that can only be measured in the sample of people who have experienced the life crisis. For instance, we might want to know if initial emotional reactions after the crisis are associated with long-term adjustment. Or we might want to know if a particular coping strategy is associated with subsequent adjustment. How can we study these predictors when they are only measured for victims and not controls? Put another way, how can we study interactions when the predictor is not measured in one of the two comparison groups?[5]

There are two answers to this question, one technical and the other conceptual. The technical answer is that one can include within-group predictors in an interaction model. We can think of the situation as a degenerate form of a modifier model, where some predictors are measured in both samples M_1 and others are only measured in the case sample M_2. In standard notation we can write

$$H_t = b_1 + b_2 M_1 + b_3 M_2 + b_4 S + b_5 M_1 S + b_6 C. \qquad (25)$$

The only difference between this model and the standard modifier model is that there is no interaction between M_2 and S. This term is omitted because M_2 has no observed values in the $S = 0$ sample. By assigning all people in this sample a score of 0 on M_2 we can disaggregate Eq. (25) into the following within-group equations:

If $\ S = 1$ (the case sample), $\begin{aligned} H_t &= (b_1 + b_4) + (b_2 + b_5)M_1 \\ &\quad + b_3 M_2 + b_6 C. \end{aligned} \qquad (26a)$

If $\ S = 0$ (the control sample), $H_t = b_1 + b_2 M_1 + b_6 C. \qquad (26b)$

There is one nonobvious point here that bears mentioning. If we assign any nonzero value of M_2 to the $S = 0$ sample we can still decompose Eq. (25), because M_2 does not vary in this sample, and the product $b_3 M_2$ consequently goes into the intercept. The coefficients b_2 and b_6 are estimated without bias, the coefficient of multiple determination is unaffected, and the standard errors of b_2 and b_6 are the same as in Eq. (25). However, there is one parameter that is influenced by this choice: the standard error of b_3. We can see this by noting that

$$\text{var}(b_3) = \text{var}(e_t) / \sum (M_2 - \overline{M}_2)^2, \qquad (27)$$

---

[5]This situation should not be confused with one in which the outcome variable is not measured in one of the two comparison groups. This latter situation is often referred to as a problem of "censored" data and has been studied extensively by econometricians as a special case of selection bias. By defining a joint model of the regression equation to be estimated in the censored sample and an equation to describe when the dependent variable will be observed, estimation procedures have been developed to correct for this bias (Heckman, 1979; Olsen, 1980). There has been at least one attempt to apply these procedures to prospective case-control data (Glass et al., 1982). However, since the missing data here are associated with a *predictor* variable rather than an *outcome* variable, these procedures are not appropriate.

where we sum the denominator over all respondents, both cases and controls. The imputed value of M_2 enters into both terms in the denominator.

It seems obvious that we would like to obtain a standard error of b_3 that applies only to the $S = 1$ sample, but there is no way to do this in Eq. (25) unless the imputed value of M_2 is selected so that it will produce a value for Eq. (27) that is identical to the value it would have in the $S = 1$ sample. It is possible to select a value of M_2 in this way by solving Eq. (27) for the imputed value but this is a tedious operation that can be side-stepped by estimating Eqs. (26a)–(26b) directly in a two-group LISREL analysis (Joreskog and Sorbom, 1979). Here it is possible to impose between-group equality constraints on b_3 and b_6 while still obtaining within-group standard errors.[6]

Now we get to the conceptual part of the issue—how to interpret b_3 once it is estimated. I argued earlier that any variable that is not evaluated as an explicit interaction must be considered a predictor of *adjustment*. But what of M_2 in our current example? Surely we want to interpret it, and variables like it, as predictors of adjustment. But can we do so legitimately? Can we, for instance, say that strong reliance on social support networks during the first months of bereavement is associated with good emotional adjustment? Or should we make the somewhat weaker claim that this style of coping is associated with good mental health outcome? In coming to a resolution between these two alternatives it is important to bear in mind that the stronger of the two holds that social support ameliorates the distress that would otherwise have resulted from the loved one's death, and the weaker assertion implies that social support is important for reasons that might not be directly linked to this event.

Resolution of this interpretive decision will, of course, vary as a function of the theoretical assumptions we are willing to make. I believe that, in general, it is wisest to interpret associations of this sort as predictors of outcome rather than adjustment. In coming to this conclusion I am persuaded by the fact that even though coping responses cannot be measured in a control sample, it is almost surely the case that these responses are associated with coping predispositions that are as much characteristics of people who have not had a crisis as they are of crisis victims. To interpret coping responses as predictors of adjustment, rather than of outcome, it is necessary to assume that predisposi-

---

[6]The only constraint in this approach is that the imputed value of M_2 must be zero, because otherwise the estimate of b_1 will be incorrect. The estimated value of b_1 will differ from the correct value by $-b_3 M_2$ when $M_2 \neq 0$.

tions of this sort either do not exist or that they play no part in the well-being of people who are not currently in crisis situations. Neither of these assumptions strikes me as plausible. (In some special cases it might be possible to make an argument that a predisposition of this sort does not exist and so interpret the within-subgroup association as evidence of adjustment. Such a case, for example, could be associated with the social support provided by a physician to a family in which one member has a major acute illness. Access to this resource will vary from one family to the next as a function of the luck of assignment to one rather than another physician (when this assignment is random, as in a clinic population). It is plausible to assume that there is no equivalent to this resource in the control sample. So the association between physician support and the health outcome can be interpreted as evidence of adjustment. In a similar fashion, intervention experiments in crisis samples yield evidence about factors that influence adjustment, not merely outcome, so long as the resources being considered are assigned randomly to people in the crisis intervention sample.)

We are on the firmest ground when we use measures of coping response to interpret predictors of adjustment. For instance, in a study of adjustment to having a heart attack we might estimate a model like that in Eq. (25), where M_1 is a predictor that is measured in both the case and control samples and M_2 is measured only among cases. From what is known about adjustment to a heart attack it is not implausible to assume that M_1 measures education and that having a good education is associated with positive mental health adjustment. If we want to understand how education has this effect we can introduce a series of measures like M_2 as intervening variables, with the goal of explaining away the gross effect of education. In this way we might find that the highly educated actively seek out information about what they can and cannot do physically, set realistic goals for their physical recovery, and have a comparatively easy time regaining a feeling of renewed competence because their occupations do not require a great deal of physical activity (Croog and Levine, 1977). These results can all be interpreted as ways in which education fosters good adjustment to a heart attack because the explicit inclusion of education as a predictor of health in both case and control samples effectively controls the coping predispositions that are associated with educational attainment. By building up a series of specifications like these we can construct an argument for the importance of particular coping responses as determinants of adjustment even though we are unable to measure explicitly the predispositions that generate them.

RETROSPECTIVE CASE-CONTROL STUDIES

In retrospective case-control studies we are interested in a rare outcome like the onset of schizophrenia. In a normal population survey it is most unlikely that we would discover a large enough number of respondents with this outcome to allow a powerful analysis of its determinants. In the retrospective design this difficulty is solved by comparing a sample of people who have recently developed the disease to a control sample. We then work backward in time to uncover differentiating characteristics that might have played a part in causing the illness.

In one sense this design is not very different from the cross-sectional normal population survey, where respondents are asked about the events that occurred to them in the recent past. In fact, the logical considerations about our ability to assess impact, describe the course of adjustment, and study the predictors of adjustment are exactly the same here as in the cross-sectional population survey design (just as they are in the prospective case-control design). There are important differences in the designs, though, when we turn to issues of estimation.

Odds-Ratio Models

In the normal population survey we can use retrospective reports about exposure to calculate the conditional probabilities of the health outcome, given variation in exposure to strain. This is not possible in the retrospective case-control design. The latter stratifies on the outcome variable and so makes it impossible to make inferences about population proportions. And this, in turn, makes it inappropriate to use conventional linear structural equation models in the estimation of impact and adjustment.

This is a difficult point to grasp in the abstract, so I will use an example. Let us assume that the population association between exposure to an event and subsequent disease onset is as follows:

Subsequent disease onset	Exposure to an event	
	Yes	No
Yes	a	c
No	b	d

Then the probability of disease onset can be written

$$\text{event} = \text{yes}, \quad P_d = a/(a + b); \tag{28a}$$

$$\text{event} = \text{no}, \quad P_d = c/(c + d). \tag{28b}$$

And the slope of disease on exposure to an event (b_{de}) is

$$b_{de} = a/(a + b) - c/(c + d). \tag{28c}$$

In a probability sample this slope can be estimated without difficulty. This is true also in a prospective case-control design, where we sample cells a + b (event) and cells c + d (no event) with different fractions, because

$$w_1 a/(w_1 a + w_1 b) = a/(a + b), \tag{29a}$$

$$w_2 c/(w_2 c + w_2 d) = c/(c + d). \tag{29b}$$

The situation is different in a retrospective case-control design. Here we sample cells a + c (disease) and cells b + d (no disease) with different fractions. These sampling fractions no longer drop out in forming probability ratios. That is,

$$w_1 a/(w_1 a + w_2 b) \neq a/(a + b), \tag{30a}$$

$$w_1 c/(w_1 c + w_2 d) \neq c/(c + d). \tag{30b}$$

Indeed, in the absence of knowledge about the precise values of w_1 and w_2 it is impossible to obtain an unbiased estimate of b_{de} from retrospective case-control data.

This dependence of model parameters on sampling fractions is a characteristic of linear probability models. It does not exist when we shift to a model that works with odds ratios. The odds on disease in the population of people who have been exposed to a life event is a/b whereas the comparable odds in the unexposed sample is c/d. The relative odds, or odds ratio, of the two groups is

$$(a/b)/(c/d) = ad/bc. \tag{31}$$

In the retrospective case-control sample, we can estimate this odds ratio without bias. That is,

$$w_1 a w_2 d/w_1 b w_2 c = w_1 w_2(ad)/w_1 w_2(bc) = ad/bc. \tag{32}$$

As a result of this equivalence, analysis of retrospective case-control data is conventionally carried out with statistical models that use the odds ratio as the outcome (Fienberg, 1977:105–107). The most commonly used model with this feature is the logit model, which is one of the models I discussed in the section "Alternative Functional Forms," on strategies for interpreting modifier effects in models with dichotomous outcomes. As noted there, when the population distribution of the disease is in the range .1–.9, the linear probability distribution and the logistic distribution are in reasonably close agreement (Cox, 1970:26–29). When the probability of disease is very small, on the other hand, the odds ratio closely approximates the relative risk of disease in the exposed and unexposed groups. The latter is the ratio of the probabilities a/(a + b) and c/(c + d). This ratio is much more interesting than the probability difference when the disease is rare (Schlesselman, 1982:32–33).

As I noted in the earlier section on estimation and interpretation of modifier effects, the way in which predictors of adjustment are conceptualized is somewhat different in a logit model than in a linear probability model. However, this is a difference in functional form, not in logic. Consequently, all of the conceptual issues about assessing impact and predicting adjustment in cross-sctional population surveys and prospective case-control studies apply as well to retrospective case-control designs. There is no need to repeat these here.

Hazard Models

One feature of retrospective case-control data that is not typically shared with data obtained from the other designs considered earlier is that the health outcome is discrete and dated. By this I mean that the outcome can be considered either present or absent in a qualitative sense (as compared to measures that rate ill health or emotional distress on a scale ranging from high to low) and can be said to have begun at a relatively well-defined point in time. The second of these characteristics is not inherent in the retrospective design, but is a necessary condition in practice to guarantee that the retrospectively reported predictor variables occurred prior to the onset of the illness. In the absense of information that this is so, one runs the risk of confounding causes with results of the illness.

As noted, the standard approach to analyzing data like these is to estimate a logit model where membership in one of the two samples is treated as the outcome variable. Predictors consist of some combination of variables that characterize the respondent's ongoing life situation (chronic strains and resources, personality characteristics, and features of sociodemographic status) and ones that are less characteristic (life events). The latter are typically assessed for some well-defined period of time prior to illness onset, usually 1 year (Brown and Harris, 1978b). This means that the time-dependent part of the predictor set is confined to some prespecified period. The prediction of the outcome is consequently a prediction of the hazard of becoming ill within a specific period after exposure to an acute strain.

When a conventional logit approach is used to make this prediction, a good deal of information is lost because there are a series of more refined outcomes embedded in the dichotomous outcome of whether illness onset occurred within a year after an event that tell us whether onset occurred within 1 month, 2 months, and so on. The amount of lost information depends on how accurately illness onset and the occurrence of prior life events can be dated. In typical studies this can be done within a month. So my discussion of appropriate analysis methods is confined to this situation.

A good deal of work has been done to develop methods to analyze dated outcomes of this sort (Elandt-Johnson and Johnson, 1980; Gross and Clark, 1975; Kalbfleisch and Prentice, 1980). Special applications of these methods to retrospective case-control designs have also been developed (Prentice and Breslow, 1978). The basic parameter in these models is a variable that describes the occurrence or nonoccurrence of the illness outcome over a small time interval. This variable is commonly called a *hazard rate*, which can be written as

$$HR = f(t)/[1 - F(t)], \tag{33}$$

where $f(t)$ is the probability density function of a random variable T denoting the uncensored time of illness onset (an unobserved variable), and $F(t)$ is the cumulative distribution function of T. By uncensored time of onset I mean the time that onset would be observed for each case had we not arbitrarily confined information about precipitating life events to some cutoff period of time. In practice, it is necessary to truncate data on events in this way, both because we know that events occurring more than a year in the past seldom influence illness onset significantly (Paykel, 1978) and because the accuracy of retrospective event reporting and dating declines markedly as we go farther back in time.

In this general case, HR is the instantaneous probability that illness onset occurs at time t, given that it has not already occurred. In the discrete time case that we consider, there is a special variant on this general hazard rate, known as the *discrete-time hazard rate*, which can be written as

$$P_{HR} = \Pr(t_i = t, \text{ given that } t_i \geq t). \tag{34}$$

Here the hazard rate is the conditional probability that illness onset occurs at time i, given that it has not already occurred.

Estimation proceeds by specifying how this hazard rate depends on the explanatory variables and then using appropriate estimation routines to derive the parameters of the model as specified. The most commonly used specification is the logistic regression model. Here the discrete-time hazard rate is treated as a dichotomous outcome that is a logistic function of the predictors. In practice, this means that the same sort of estimation procedure is used for a hazard model as in a more conventional retrospective case-control model. This might seem to be a somewhat surprising result, given that I began this discussion by calling into question the appropriateness of the conventional approach, but the problem with the latter is that it inefficiently uses data and not that it is based on a faulty estimation procedure.

The main refinement of the discrete-time hazard model over the conventional approach is that each time point for each individual is treated as a separate unit of analysis. Let us assume that we are interested in the effect of precipitating life events, dated by month of occurrence, in the year prior to illness onset and that we interview a sample of n_1 cases and n_2 controls about the monthly occurrence of events in the 2 years prior to interview. (We assume that the interview takes place near the time of illness onset for the cases.) We then consider the sample to consist of $12(n_1 + n_2)$ monthly observations, in each of which information is available about the monthly occurrence of events in the past year. In $11(n_1) + 12(n_2)$ of these observations, the outcome variable is coded 0 (illness onset did not occur in that month), and in the remaining n_1 observations the outcome variable is coded 1 (illness onset did occur in that month).[7]

This shifting of the ratio of onset to no-onset observations from n_1/n_2 to $n_1/(11n_1 + 12n_2)$ regains the information that is lost in conventional case-control analysis schemes by letting us examine not only the odds-ratio of cases to controls with and without events but also the ratio

---

[7]Discrete-time hazard models can also be estimated with prospective survey or case-control data if illness onset can be dated. However, in this case the expression for the time-specific observations becomes more complex. There are still 12 (n_2) monthly observations on respondents who have not had the illness, but there are fewer observations on respondents who have. Among the latter, monthly observations are included up to and including the month of illness onset. Later observations are discarded. If the probability of onset in month i among respondents who sometime in the year have an onset is defined as p_i, then the number of monthly observations among these respondents is $(12 - 11p_1 - 10p_2 - \cdots - 1p_{11})n_1$.

among cases of illness onset at different times after the occurrence of a particular event. It might seem illegitimate to inflate the sample size by 12, on the assumption that test statistics will be made artificially high. But Allison (1982) has shown that this is not the case. If we begin with a model that is specified in terms of discrete-time hazard rates rather than in terms of a logit that does not differentiate time of onset by month, the estimation procedure described here yields the correct parameters for the corresponding model. It is possible to obtain the same estimates in the framework of an $n_1 + n_2$ analysis, but the estimation procedures are much more complex than those needed when we work with the same data in a $12(n_1 + n_2)$ framework.

This discrete-time, single-outcome hazard model is only one special case of a much broader range of models. In the most general case we can consider instantaneous hazard rates (when precipitating life events are dated with sufficient precision that we are willing to call the dating exact) that vary as a function of time to predict a number of different outcomes (competing risks) or a succession of onsets, remissions, and relapses of a single outcome, with a series of predictor variables that can themselves change over time. The methodology for models of this sort is developing rapidly and interested readers should consult several review papers that describe the most important of these developments and directions of current work (Allison, 1982; Flinn and Heckman, 1982; Tuma, 1982).

EVALUATING CAUSAL PRIORITY

In the models considered up to this point I have implicitly assumed that the causal order among the variables was recursive and that this order was known. In practice there are several issues of causal priority that are more complicated than this treatment assumed. For instance, concern has been expressed that some life events might be effects rather than causes of psychological distress. There is also a good deal of interest in knowing the causal order between distress and the intervening variables in models of the stress process—chronic strains, social resources, personality characteristics and coping strategies or styles. It is extremely difficult to measure some of these intervening constructs objectively, so most measures rely on the introspection of respondents. The respondents' level of distress might color these perceptions and so yield measures with artificially strong relationships with the outcome variable.

These concerns about causal priority have led to the increasing use of panel data in both normal population surveys and prospective case-control studies. It is not necessary to discuss the obvious advantages of having data collected from the same individuals at multiple time points. Most of these are well known. And methods for analyzing data of this sort have been developed (Kessler and Greenberg, 1981). I say something about these methods in the section "Estimating Selectivity Bias in Life Events Analyses." But now I want to deal with a limitation of panel data. For many of the causal priority problems that face students of the stress process panel data are not the cure-all they have been advertised to be. Indeed, I believe that most analyses of the stress process based on two-wave panel data can also be carried out with cross-sectional data. And I believe that many of the causal order problems faced by the analyst who works with cross-sectional data are not resolved merely by obtaining panel data. In this section I review the major problems of causal order, discuss the limitations of panel data as a means of solving these problems, and then describe other strategies.

It has frequently been said that it is not possible to make causal inferences from correlations calculated cross sectionally. I believe that this is incorrect. If for example, we find that there is a cross-sectional relationship between the unemployment rate and the probability that an individual in a community survey is depressed, we would probably be willing to impute some causal meaning to that relationship. We might disagree about the mechanism at work, but would agree that causality flows from the economy to the individual's distress rather than the other way around. I doubt that we would feel more secure in this imputation of causality if the unemployment rate were measured a month before the individual's depression instead of during the same month. Longitudinal data, then, would not be particularly helpful for assessing causality in this situation. (Longitudinal data would be useful for studying the time lag between aggregate economic changes and the appearance of its effects in individual psychopathology. But that is a different matter from the imputation of causality.)

The reason for our comfort in imputing causality in this case stems from the fact that we are willing to assume that causality is in one direction only. We cannot conceive of an individual's depression having any meaningful influence on the unemployment rate of the town in which he or she lives. The situation becomes more complex when we believe that causality might be reciprocal. Here there are times when panel data can be useful. Eaton's (1978) reanalysis of the New Haven panel is a case in point. His concern was with the possibility that some life events might be results of distress rather than their causes. To evaluate this possibility he used the overtime feature of the panel to estimate the effect of life events at time 1 on distress at time 2, controlling distress at time 1. He then estimated the effect of distress at time 1 on life events at 2, controlling life events at time 1. By controlling the initial values of the outcome variables in these two equations, Eaton effectively studied change in the outcomes and so was able to infer causality by temporal priority. He discovered that although initial life events were associated with changes in distress there was no statistically significant relationship between initial distress and change in life events. This is powerful support for the assertion that distress does not influence subsequent exposure to the events contained in this particular life-events inventory.

The power of this demonstration comes from our willingness to assume that causal influences flow in one direction here because the data are collected over time even though we are not willing to make this assumption about the very same variables measured at a point in time. This feature of panel data—that they allow us to make assumptions about causal influences with which we feel comfortable—is their central benefit for purposes of causal analysis.

The situation is less clear-cut when we are considering chronic role strains rather than life events. Indeed, when we are trying to separate the reciprocal influences between chronic strains and distress it is not at all clear that panel data are of any assistance. Let us consider the situation of job strains. Most people have held their jobs for a number of years and so the conditions of their jobs, relative to the job conditions of people in other occupations, have remained relatively constant over this period. How, then, can we hope to disentangle the reciprocal influences between perceptions of strain and distress with panel data? Are we in a better situation knowing that a change in perceived job strain is related to a change in depression than knowing that there is a cross-sectional relationship between the two? I think not. Nor is there any particular reason to believe that the respondent's initial level of job strain will be associated with change in depression. Because the objective conditions of a job are relatively constant over a period of several years the influence of these chronic conditions on the respondent's well-being will be in equilibrium, and so will not bring about any change in distress over time. The strategy Eaton used in his analysis of life events, then, breaks down in the analysis of chronic strains. Furthermore, even if we do find some meaningful change in perceived job strain over the period of a panel it is likely that the time 2 value of this strain is the more appropriate predictor of time 2 distress. There is no reason to think that the level of chronic role strain experienced at the beginning of a time interval influences change in distress. It is more likely that *change* in the chronic strain influences *change* in distress.

When we begin considering correlations between changes in two variables we are back to the same situation of causal ambiguity that we have when we consider cross-sectional relationships. We can no more interpret this association in terms of one-way causation than we can a cross-sectional relationship. This problem, to my mind, is the central reason that work on chronic strain has not progressed nearly as far as work on the effects of life events. Life events became popular to study at least in part because problems of causal priority could be resolved by fiat. When we find a relationship between the death of a loved one and depression we are usually willing to assume that the depression is caused by bereavement rather than the other way around. It is much more difficult when we study chronic strains. A typical index of job strain, for instance, might be made up of several yes-or-no responses to questions like "people at work act toward me as if I had no feelings." Responses to such questions could reflect psychological distress as much as objective conditions of the workplace.

This same problem applies to other important variables in models of the stress process: social resources, personality characteristics, and coping strategies and styles. They are all difficult to measure objectively and there is usually a suspicion that indexes created to measure them are contaminated by the respondent's emotional state. In the next subsection I describe a strategy for overcoming this problem.

A Generalized Approach to the Assessment of Reciprocal Causation

It is a mistake to tackle the problem of confounding between an index of chronic strain (or social resources or personality characteristics or coping strategies and styles) and distress by thinking of it merely as a measurement problem that can be corrected by coming up with better items to include in an index. Item analysis is important, of course, but it will almost never be possible by this means alone to remove the suspicion of reciprocal causation between measures of chronic strain and distress.

An alternative and more feasible strategy is to combine good index construction with explicit use of structural equation models of the reciprocal influences between measures of strain and distress. This can be done by taking an instrumental variable approach to the problem of reciprocal causation. By an instrumental variable I mean a predictor

variable that can be assumed to influence the outcome variable of ultimate interest (in this case a symptom-screening scale) only through the
intervening influence of the variable which we feel is involved in the
reciprocal relationship with this outcome variable (in this case the
contaminated role-strain scale). When we have an instrument of this
sort, and when we feel confident that its influence is mediated by the
intervening variable, it is possible to estimate the relative magnitudes
of the reciprocal influences between the intervening variable and the
outcome.

A rigorous discussion of instrumental variable techniques can be
found in any standard econometrics text (e.g., Johnston, 1972, Chapter
9). Here I shall do no more than give an intuitive presentation. Let us
assume that we have a measure of job strain that contains some contamination due to the respondent's distress. Presumably there is also an
element of reality in this measure. When a respondent is asked how
much responsibility he or she is given, how much noise or dirt there is
in the workplace, or how frequently he or she has to learn new things,
the answers almost surely have some relationship to real variations in
these job conditions. The trick is to separate this real component from
the selectively perceived component.

The instrumental variable approach begins by obtaining relatively
objective, even if incomplete, measures of at least some of these strains.
In the case of job strain we could do this with Dictionary of Occupational Titles (DOT) aggregated codes (Roos and Treiman, 1980). These
allow us to code each respondent's occupation (as long as that occupation is precisely enough defined to be assigned a unique three-digit
census code) into a series of DOT dimensions. The latter are the standard occupational descriptions used by the Department of Labor to
characterize jobs in the U.S. labor force. These dimensions are coded by
Department of Labor employees whose job it is to go into workplaces
and observe exactly what people with different jobs titles do during a
typical day. Dimensions exist for the amount of dirty work, the amount
of heavy work, the substantive complexity of the work, the amount of
supervision, and so on.

Once these measures are obtained we can estimate a simultaneous
equation system of the sort diagrammed in Figure 6.5. Here we assume
that the objective DOT measures have some influence on the respondent's perceived job strain, that the latter has an influence on the
individual's distress, and that this distress influences the perception of
job strain. If we have only one objective measure of strain this model
will be just-identified, which means that we can estimate all the parameters in the model but we cannot evaluate how well the assumptions

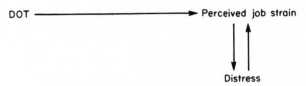

Figure 6.5. An instrumental variable model of the reciprocal relationships between perceived job strain and distress.

conform with the observed data. With multiple objective measures of strain, like those available with the DOT scales, it is possible both to estimate the parameters and to evaluate the model assumptions. We can also carry out a sensitivity analysis, which is an evaluation of how much the critical parameters of the model—estimates of the reciprocal influences between perceived strain and distress—vary when we modify the assumptions about the objective strain effects in various ways. This is an important final step to take in an analysis of this sort, for the parameter estimates obtained in this way can be quite sensitive to the identification assumptions used to estimate the model. It is important to determine empirically the range of values critical model parameters take on when these assumptions are varied.

An equivalent procedure is to use instruments that are assumed to influence perceived job strain only through their intervening influence on distress. There are a great many variables that could be used in this way, such as measures of stressful life events that have no implications for work overload. The death of a loved one, for instance, probably does not have any direct effect on the objective conditions in the work environment. To the extent that events of this sort predict job strain, then, they probably do so because they influence the individual's level of distress, which in turn influences perceived job strain.

The availability of instruments that influence distress but do not directly influence role strains is terribly important, because some role strains lack the sort of objective strain indicators mentioned earlier as valid instruments for a job-strain analysis. It is difficult, for instance, to think of a way to measure objectively marital role strain in a survey. But we can easily think of variables that influence distress but do not influence marital role strain other than through the strain placed on the marriage by the fact that one marital partner is suffering from a high level of distress.

Although an approach of this sort has not, to my knowledge, been used in previous analyses of the relationship between role strain and distress, an intuitive analysis containing the essentials of the approach has been presented by Pearlin et al. (1981), who were interested in

whether feelings of self-esteem mediate the relationship between income-loss events and depression. In doing this they were sensitive to
the possibility that low self-esteem might be as much a result as a
determinant of depression. They evaluated this possibility by turning
to a completely different type of life event, the death of a loved one.
They reasoned that although job loss probably has some negative influence on self-esteem and through this on depression, no such intervening influence is likely in the relationship between bereavement and
depression. If self-esteem is truly an intervening variable, according to
this reasoning, it should be unrelated to bereavement even though the
latter is related to depression. When this was investigated empirically
Pearlin discovered that his guess was correct: Although the recent
death of a loved one was related to change in depression, it was not
related to change in self-esteem. On the basis of this demonstration
Pearlin proceeded with his analysis of income-loss events under the
assumption that self-esteem was functioning primarily as an intervening variable between events and depression.

Although it was not described in this way, nor was a model ever
parametrized and rigorously estimated using the method of instrumental variables, Pearlin was arguing intuitively in a fashion that is identical to the logic of an instrumental variable analysis. He was assuming,
implicitly, that bereavement events do not directly cause self-esteem
loss and that to the extent that they are related to the latter it is because
the death of a loved one causes depression, which in turn reduces self-
esteem. By demonstrating that the relationship between death of a
loved one and self-esteem was insignificant, then, Pearlin called into
question the assumption that depression significantly influences self-
esteem.

One will not always be as lucky as Pearlin was in finding that there is
absolutely no significant reciprocity between the intervening and outcome variables. If the goal of the analysis is to do no more than estimate
the magnitude of the reciprocal effects, as it might in an assessment of
the relative importance of social causation and selection (e.g., Wheaton, 1978), then there is no difficulty. As long as we can come up with a
plausible instrument we can estimate the parameters of interest. However, when this is only a beginning step—as in Pearlin's analysis,
where he wanted to go on to use his measure of self-esteem as a modifier of the events–depression relationship—then the situation becomes
more complex. In this latter case it becomes necessary to purge the
variable of the contamination due to the reciprocal influence of the
distress scale. This can be done by using the objective indicators of
strain to construct a *predicted* measure of perceived strain based on the

objective measures. This predicted component can be taken as a proxy measure for the part of perceived strain that is independent of biases introduced by the influence of distress on perceptions of strain. In subsequent analyses this proxy measure is substituted for the original measure of perceived strain.

One might wonder why the measure of perceived strain is needed at all if we end up using a composite made up of the objective strain measures. There are two answers to this question. First, if preliminary analysis shows that there is no significant reciprocity between perceived strain and distress, as was true in the Pearlin *et al.* analysis, then it is better to work with one global measure of perceived strain than with a grab bag of separate objective strain scales. The overall scale of perceived strain represents a composite of all the strains a person experiences in his or her role. This is generally more comprehensive than the set of objective strain measures that can be obtained about that role.

Second, even if preliminary analysis shows that there is a significant reciprocity, we still have no way of knowing how best to combine the various measures of objective strain into an overall measure of perceived role strain. If we regress the distress scale on the set of objective measures and use the regression weights to create a composite, we run the risk of absorbing some part of the relationship between exposure to strain and resources or vulnerabilities into the composite weights. This would defeat the purpose of searching for modifying influences once the composite is created (Dohrenwend, 1980). It is preferable to base the composite construction on a regression of the perceived strain on the objective measures. By constructing the proxy measure of objective strain in this way the confounding of composite weights with resources or vulnerabilities is avoided.

The use of instrumental variables is the best available strategy for dealing with the problem of reciprocal causation between two variables of interest. It has several limitations that should make us cautious in its use, but there is really no viable alternative if we are faced with a complex situation of the sort described here: We cannot be sure that the strain will change enough over time to allow the use of panel data, and there is a strong possibility that the perceptual reports that make up the strain measure are in part influenced by the individual's emotional well-being. I will discuss the limitations of the approach but will first attempt to tie together some of my earlier assertions by making a heretofore overlooked connection between the method of instrumental variables and the use of cross-lagged panel analysis.

When panel data are available a common strategy is to use the lagged values of the two reciprocally related variables as instruments: That is, we can assume that X_1 influences X_2 but not Y_2, that Y_1 influences Y_2 but not X_2, and that X_2 and Y_2 reciprocally influence each other (where X_t and Y_t are two variables measured at times $t = 1, 2$). If X_t and Y_t change meaningfully over time and the model assumptions are correct this is a perfectly reasonable approach. Furthermore, when X_t and Y_t are highly stable this specification yields results that are close to those we would obtain by estimating the more traditional cross-lagged model used in the Eaton analysis described earlier, where X_1 and Y_1 are assumed to influence X_2 and Y_2 (Hannan and Tuma, 1979).

There are two problems with the use of lagged values as instruments. One is that the approach breaks down when there is no change in the variables over time, as might occur when one of the variables is a measure of chronic strain or a long-term personality characteristic. When there is some slight change, the approach will yield a solution, but the parameter estimates will be very unstable, and firm conclusions about statistical significance will be difficult to draw. Second, there is always the danger that the instrument is impure because of serial correlation in the variable over time. This is a technical problem in estimation that leads to bias. An informative discussion of this problem would take us too far afield, so I shall not attempt it here. The interested reader is referred to Kessler and Greenberg (1981) for a discussion of serial correlation in panel models.

Because of these two problems, it is generally preferable not to use panel data to solve the problem of finding an instrument. If at all possible, even when panel data are available, it is best to work with theoretically defensible instruments other than the time 1 values of the dependent variables. The instruments might be measured at time 1 if panel data are available, but could just as well be measured at time 2. The time of measurement is less important than the analyst's ability to argue plausibly that the instruments are truly related in a causal fashion to one and only one of the two variables whose reciprocal influences are being estimated.

This discussion would be incomplete without a brief discussion of limitations. The first and most important of these has been mentioned already: that the method of instrumental variables is highly sensitive to the identification assumptions used to estimate the simultaneous equation system. If we incorrectly assume that a particular variable is a valid instrument when it actually has a direct causal influence on both variables in the reciprocally related pair, parameter estimates will be biased, perhaps badly so. This makes it important to work whenever possible with multiple instruments in each of the two estimation equations and to carry out a complete sensitivity analysis.

The creation of proxy measures for purposes of more detailed modification analysis also has limitations. First, there are times when it will be difficult to obtain objective measures of the concept under consideration. This will be true even when it has been possible to estimate the simultaneous equation system that contains the reciprocity between strain and distress, because the latter can be estimated with an instrument that causes distress but not strain. Second, even when objective indicators exist, the procedure will not be efficient unless these indicators are strongly related to the strain index. If they are only weakly linked to strain, the proxy measure will be a highly attenuated indicator of objective strain. Its use in multivariate models will produce parameters that are descriptively accurate, but these will have large standard errors and so significant relationships will have a low likelihood of being detected.

Novices at the use of this method commonly fail to appreciate the seriousness of these limitations and so proceed by making use of variables that are only weakly defended as valid instruments. When this is done the results are of little or no practical use. In situations of this sort a rigorous sensitivity analysis almost always shows that the range of values critical parameters can take on when assumptions about the instruments are varied is so large as to be useless. For instance, by using a maximum-likelihood approach to linear modeling that allows constraints to be imposed on some parameters, we can investigate the changes in the reciprocal effects between X and Y when we modify the typical assumption that the instrument has absolutely no effect on one of these two variables to allow the effect to be .10, .05, $-.05$, or $-.10$. It is not uncommon to find across this range of assumptions that the reciprocal effects between X and Y vary in sign and in significance. I emphasize this point because one has to realize that there are times when plausible instruments are unavailable. When this is the case and when one or both of the variables in the XY pair is so highly stable over time that a panel approach cannot be taken, it is not possible to separate the reciprocal influences between these two variables.

Estimating Selectivity Bias in Life-Events Analyses

There has been a great deal of discussion about contamination of life-event inventories because of reciprocal relationships between some events and distress. Brown (1974) describes two ways in which this might happen. The first is by measurement contamination, a process whereby people who are depressed or anxious at the time of interview will "recall" more life events than will people who are not suffering from these emotional problems. This differential recall could be due to a greater sensitivity to recent events. Or it might be due to a desire to justify one's distress to an interviewer by pointing out how truly terrible life has been lately.

A second source of possible contamination is a more direct one. An individual's emotional state may causally influence the life events to which he or she is exposed. It is obvious that marital disruption, for example, could be influenced by the partners' abilities to get along. Job loss could be due to the deterioration of an individual's work performance caused by an emotional problem. It may be sufficient to note that investigators who have pondered this problem in detail suggest that as many as half the life events found in standard inventories are potentially biased in this way (Hudgens, 1974).

Brown (1974) has suggested a measurement strategy to sidestep this problem: discarding from the event inventory any event that could possibly be influenced by the respondent's present or past level of emotional functioning. In this way, even though the power of the summary event measure is lessened by reducing the number of events on which it is based, we are assured that the association between events and distress is due to a causal influence of events on distress rather than the reverse. This is a useful strategy and, indeed, Brown has demonstrated that a significant association between this refined battery and a measure of depression can be detected (Brown and Harris, 1978b). However, the strategy is unnecessarily restrictive. There is no real need to discard the events that we think might be contaminated in this way, especially if we are willing to work with an overall index of events that adds up different kinds of events into one summary score. A variety of methods exist to include the potentially contaminated events in the analysis by building a model with explicit assumptions about how the contamination operates.

This explicit modeling of contamination provides two advantages that are not found in Brown's approach. The first is that his method discards a great many events that may be important determinants of emotional functioning. Divorce, for example, is one of the most commonly experienced life crises, one that can have a devastating emotional effect on the people who experience it. Yet, because it may be the result of one or both partner's previous psychological difficulties, it has to be discarded from a purified life-events inventory. It would be desirable to retain such events while adjusting for the possible contamination of effect coefficients, in order to investigate the full power of life events in a normal population.

Second, although Brown's method does yield an uncontaminated measure of life-event effects, it tells us nothing about the magnitude of contamination in the events that were discarded from his list. It might be that we find that these potentially contaminated events are not contaminated at all. Without developing an explicit model to estimate the magnitude of the contamination, this possibility will never be discovered.

There are several ways to model the reciprocal relationships between events and distress. One has made use of panel data to estimate the reciprocal influences between events and distress with time-lagged analysis. Eaton (1978), for example, did this in his previously described reanalysis of the New Haven panel data. As noted earlier, Eaton used time 1 life events to predict time 2 distress, controlling on time 1 distress, and he used time 1 distress to predict time 2 life events, controlling on time 1 events. This standard two-wave cross-lagged model is only one of several variants on two-wave panel analysis that might apply to a particular situation (Augustyniak et al., forthcoming; Greenberg and Kessler, 1983), but it is a particularly plausible one in this case. By controlling the time 1 values of the dependent variables in his two prediction equations, Eaton effectively converted his dependent variables into measures of change (Kessler and Greenberg, 1981), and so was able to estimate the influences of the time 1 predictors on change in the outcomes over the course of the panel. The influence of life events on change in distress was estimated while controlling statistically the influence of initial distress on change in life events.

Thoits (1981) has proposed a variant on this model that combines the Brown and Eaton strategies. She was particularly concerned with contamination of the event inventory because of the inclusion of physical illness. Many of the psychological distress screening scales contain psychophysiological items, and Thoits speculated that these might be symptoms of physical health problems rather than the psychological effects of life crises. To test this possibility she estimated a panel model like Eaton's; she included separate measures of health-related life events (onset of chronic illness, major illness or accident, etc.) and nonhealth-related events between times 1 and 2 as predictors of time 2 distress, controlling time 1 distress. She found that only the health-related events significantly predicted distress in her sample. On the basis of this demonstration Thoits concluded that operational confounding of health-related items in both the independent and dependent variable scales created an upward bias in the estimate of life-event effects.

As innovative and intriguing as this model is, I do not recommend it as a general approach to the investigation of confounding. The reason is that it potentially underestimates the influence of nonhealth-related events. This is so because health-related events might intervene between nonhealth-related events and the distress scale. For example, the death of a spouse can precipitate a psychosomatic illness that is reported as a life event. If this health-related event is controlled when we assess the influence of conjugal bereavement on distress, we might find that bereavement has no net effect once the illness is controlled, but it would be a mistake to conclude from this that nonhealth-related events have no influence on emotional functioning.

We could evaluate this potential difficulty in Thoit's approach by estimating the impact of nonhealth-related events on health-related ones before estimating the joint influences of both event types on distress. In this way we could compute the indirect effect of nonhealth-related events on distress through health-related events. With this refinement, the Thoits strategy is a very useful one for studying the simultaneous presence of reciprocal causation between distress and some events, along with conceptual confounding of the scales due to the presence of similar items in the measures of the predictor and the outcome.

All of the strategies I have discussed so far require panel data. However, it is not always necessary to have data collected over time to separate reciprocal influences, as I have discussed earlier in my review of instrumental variable techniques. If we can obtain valid instruments, it is possible to estimate the joint influences between events and distress just as effectively as in panel analysis (with the exception that the true time lag between cause and effect might be better modeled with data collected over time). There are several instruments that would work here. One is the distress score of respondents' siblings or other close relatives. There is reason to think that these will be significantly associated with the respondent's impairment because of common childhood socialization experiences and genetic makeup. But there is no reason to think that siblings' impairment will be associated with the life events to which respondents are exposed other than through the intervening link of respondents' impairment. It might, then, be more reasonable to use the funds that would otherwise be invested in multiple time-point interviews and obtain interviews with close relatives.[8]

---

[8]This is not to say that panel data are not useful for other purposes. I merely want to point out that the problem of attributing causal order can be resolved as successfully in other ways. When there is substantive reason to think that the time lag of the causal influence is short relative to the time interval in the panel, it will be necessary to estimate reciprocal cross-sectional relationships whether panel data are available or not.

An even more useful instrument is the subscale of life events known not to be influenced by mental illness. This subscale could be used as an instrument on the assumption that it causes "events," where the latter are defined as the overall life-events scale, but does not cause mental illness other than through the intermediary of events. This allows reciprocal relationships between events and mental illness to be estimated.

The model assumes that each event (or unit on the weighted events scale) influences mental illness in the same way, with the same effect. This is an assumption made implicitly in creating any scale that adds up more than one piece of information into a larger whole. The model also assumes that despite this common pattern of influence there is a reciprocal influence of mental illness on a subset of the events in this scale. This means that we could write two structural equations:

$$H = b_0 + b_1 LE_i + b_1 LE_j, \tag{35a}$$

$$LE_i = d_0 + d_1 H, \tag{35b}$$

where LE_i is reciprocally related to H and LE_j is not caused by H.

Notice that I have assumed that the effects of LE_i and LE_j on H are the same (b_1). The only difference is that one of the life-events measures is made up of contaminated events, events that occur more frequently to people at some values of H than others, whereas the other group of life events is not influenced by H. This set of equations can be estimated simultaneously in a maximum-likelihood approach that allows equality constraints to be imposed on some of the coefficients (Joreskog and Sorbom, 1979).

DECOMPOSING MODIFIER EFFECTS

Estimation equations that contain nonlinearities and several different interaction terms are extremely difficult to interpret because the coefficients in these models generally consist either of uninterpretable lower-order terms or of interactions that can be interpreted only in terms of relative, rather than absolute, influences. There are ways of making interpretation easier, though, by using two different sorts of decomposition strategies. The first of these is the *decomposition of mean differences*. Here we begin with two subgroups (e.g., men and women), a series of predictor variables (e.g., a life-events inventory, a measure of social support, an interaction between life events and social support), and perhaps some control variables. The purpose of the decomposition is to determine the relative importance of these various predictors in accounting for the observed difference in the outcome variable between the two subgroups. This approach can be generalized to multiple subgroups—like the married, separated, widowed, divorced, and never-married—by carrying out separate pairwise contrasts for each combination of two subgroups in the total set.

For a continuous variable decomposition, a different strategy must be used. This is the *decomposition of total effects*. Here we begin with a multivariate model that contains any number of predictor variables consisting of marginal effects and modifier effects. Nonlinear as well as linear terms can be included. The purpose of the decomposition is to trace the variety of intervening mechanisms that create an overall relationship between any one predictor and the outcome measure. There can be as many decompositions as there are predictor variables, and the decomposition can be done whether the predictor is a continuous variable or a dichotomy.

In the following section I describe the algebra of these two decomposition strategies and discuss instances when each of them can provide insight into the dynamics of the stress process.

The Decomposition of Mean Differences

This technique works best when there are two groups, such as men and women or blacks and whites, whose average levels of some health outcome we want to compare. In a situation of this sort we usually believe that the between-group difference in this average is due to some combination of three influences: (1) differences in the characteristic levels of variables we have measured that can cause the health outcome, (2) differences in the impact of these causal variables, and (3) differences due to variables other than those we have measured. A situation of this sort can be estimated with the same sort of interaction model described earlier in Eq. (9), but in this instance we have a dummy variable for group memberhsip (like a dummy variable D coded 1 for men and 0 for women), one or more measures of strain, and interactions between the dummy and each of these causal variables. In the simplest case this would yield an equation like

$$H = b_0 + b_1 D + b_2 S + b_3 (D \times S), \tag{36}$$

where all variables are exposed at their means.

The decomposition of mean differences is a procedure that allows us to calculate the importance of these three components. It does this by simple algebraic manipulation, the first step of which is to decompose the pooled equation into two separate subsample-specific equations. The decomposition for Eq. (36) is

$$H_m = (b_0 + b_1) + (b_2 + b_3)S_m, \tag{37a}$$

$$H_f = b_0 + b_2 S_f, \tag{37b}$$

where both equations are expressed in terms of mean values and the two subsamples of D are defined as m and f. In the discussion following, we shall assume that D = sex, m = male, and f = female.

If we subtract Eq. (37b) from Eq. (37a), we can express the mean sex difference in distress as follows:

$$H_m - H_f = (S_m - S_f)b_2 + (b_3)S_f + (b_3)(S_m - S_f) + b_0 \tag{38a}$$

$$= (S_m - S_f)b_f + (b_m - b_f)S_f + (b_m - b_f)(S_m - S_f)$$

$$+ (a_m - a_f), \tag{38b}$$

where b_m and b_f are the slopes of H on S in the sex-specific equations and a_m and a_f are the intercepts in these two equations.

There are four terms in each equation. Together they add up to the observed mean sex difference in H. The first component tells us how much of this difference is due to a difference in the mean levels of stress experienced by men and women (exposure component). The second component tells us how much of the sex difference in H is due to the fact that the impact of S on H differs by sex (impact component). The third component is referred to in the literature as an *interaction* component (Winsborough and Dickinson, 1971) because it captures the influence of simultaneous variation in exposure and impact. This component is not to be interpreted in substantive terms because it is an arbitrary function of the overlap between the exposure and impact components. Two approaches can be used to deal with it. One is simply to ignore it when interpreting the two more interesting substantive components (Kessler, 1979). The other is to divide it into two equal parts that are added into the exposure and impact components. When this latter approach is taken, the two substantive components can be interpreted as if they were calculated by comparing women to the average S and b scores for men and women combined rather than to the scores for men (Iams and Thornton, 1975). Finally, the fourth component tells us how much of the mean sex difference in H is unrelated to differences in either exposure or the impact of S between men and women (residual component).

The decomposition can be generalized to the case of multiple predictors by using the following general expression:

$$H_i - H_j = \sum (b_{ik} - b_{jk})M_{jk} + \sum (M_{ik} - M_{jk})b_{jk}$$

$$+ \sum (b_{ik} - b_{jk})(M_{ik} - M_{jk}) + (a_i - a_j), \qquad (39)$$

where i and j are two subgroups being contrasted on H, k is the number of predictor variables in each of the two subgroup equations, b_{ik} is the slope of H on the kth predictor in the ith subgroup, and M_{jk} is the mean of the kth predictor in the jth subgroup. A complete decomposition of the k predictors yields $3k + 1$ terms. These can be aggregated into the four main terms in the decomposition by summing each of the first three terms in Eq. (39) across the k predictors. Alternatively, all $3k + 1$ terms can be presented along with the four summary terms. Significance tests for the $3k + 1$ terms as well as for the four summary components have been derived by Sobel (1979).

The predictors in Eq. (39) can include nonlinear and nonadditive variables. Impact components for such terms reflect the fact that the nonlinear or nonadditive influences differ across the two subgroups. Exposure components reflect the fact that the proportion of cases at critical points on the nonlinear or nonadditive distributions differs across the two subgroups.

A word of caution regarding this first type of decomposition is in order. The problem of arbitrary zero points described in the discussion of modifier effects arises in the decomposition of mean differences as well because the interpretation of the exposure component is actually nothing more than an intuitive way of interpreting one of the marginal effects in an equation that contains a modifier. To see this concretely, we can ask what would happen to the values of the components in Eq. (39) if we subtracted a constant C from S. This is the type of transformation that would change the zero point of the stress scale but would not influence unstandardized regression coefficients or R^2. This transformation would have an important effect on the decomposition. The new component values would be

$$H_i - H_j = \sum (b_{ik} - b_{jk})(M_{jk} - C) + \sum (M_{ik} - M_{jk}) b_{jk}$$

$$+ \sum (b_{ik} - b_{jk})(M_{ik} - M_{jk}) + (a_i - a_j)C. \qquad (40)$$

The exposure and interaction components are identical to those in Eq. (39), but the relative magnitudes of the impact and residual components have changed. This is because the impact component is contingent on the definition of the zero point of the scale. The effect of differential impact is calculated by assuming that the two regression lines have the same intercept *at the zero point of the scale* and then determining the distance between the regression lines at the mean value of the independent variable. Thus, the size of the impact component can be manipulated to be arbitrarily large or small by adding or subtracting a constant from the independent variable.[9]

The Decomposition of Total Effects

When an outcome variable H is regressed on a zero–one dummy variable that indicates membership in one of two subgroups, the unstandardized zero-order regression coefficient is identical to the mean subgroup difference in H. As a result, the decomposition of the mean difference in H is equivalent to a decomposition of the total association between the dummy variable and H. This equivalence is useful to bear in mind when we begin to consider variables that cannot be expressed as dichotomies. Another sort of decomposition can be used here, the decomposition of the total association between the variable and H.

The best way to understand this sort of decomposition is to begin with a structural equation model like that in Figure 6.6. This model is described by three structural equations:

$$X = b_0 + b_1 S + b_2 D + e_x, \tag{41a}$$

$$C = d_0 + d_1 S + d_2 D + d_3 X + e_c, \tag{41b}$$

$$P = f_0 + f_1 S + f_2 D + f_3 X + f_4 C + e_p. \tag{41c}$$

Each of these equations can be multiplied through by one of its predictor variables and expectations taken to obtain an equation that expresses the covariance between the outcome variable and the predictor as a sum of products between structural parameters and covariances. If we multiplied Eq. (41a) by D and took expectations we would have

$$DX = b_1 DS + b_2 DD, \tag{42}$$

where DX is the covariance between D and X, DS is the covariance between D and S, and DD is the variance of D.

This is the basic form of a decomposition of a total association, ex-

[9]An analogous situation occurs when one of the predictor scales is reflected. Rather than use a scale of social support, for instance, a scale of social isolation could be created by subtracting the support scale from some constant. This reflection changes both the zero point of the scale and the signs of the slopes. By factoring -1 from each term in the four transformed products in this decomposition we obtain a result that is identical to Eq. (40). Thus the effect of reflecting the scale is similar to the effect of changing the zero point by adding or subtracting a constant.

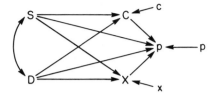

Figure 6.6. A hypothetical model to illustrate the decomposition of total effects.

pressed in terms of covariances. It is not a very intuitive expression, though, so it is seldom used. Two other expressions are much more common. The first is obtained by dividing through the covariance equation by the variance of the predictor. This yields a decomposition of the zero-order slope of the outcome on the predictor. Dividing Eq. (42) by the variance of D, for instance, results in

$$b_{XD} = b_1(b_{SD}) + b_2. \tag{43}$$

The general form taken by all decompositions of this sort is

$$b_{OP} = \sum_i b_{Oi}b_{iP}, \tag{44}$$

where b_{OP} is the zero-order slope of the outcome O on a particular predictor P, b_{Oi} is the partial regression of O on some arbitrary predictor i (where i could equal P) in an equation containing K predictors (where i goes from 1 to K), and b_{iP} is the zero-order slope of i on P.

A second approach is to standardize the covariance equation to obtain a decomposition of the zero-order correlation between the outcome and the predictor. Under this transformation, Eq. (43) becomes

$$r_{XD} = b_1{}^*r_{SD} + b_2{}^*, \tag{45}$$

where $b_i{}^*$ is the standardization of b_i. The general form taken by all decompositions of this sort is

$$r_{OP} = \sum_i b_i{}^*(r_{iP}), \tag{46}$$

where r_{iP} is the zero-order correlation between P and i (Alwin and Hauser, 1975).

We see from Eqs. (44) and (46) that there are at least as many terms in the decomposition as there are predictors in the structural equation. It is possible, though, to have a good many more terms than this. For instance, we could express the relationship between S and P in terms of the following standardized components,

$$r_{SP} = f_1{}^* + f_2{}^*r_{DS} + f_3{}^*r_{XS} + f_4{}^*r_{CS}, \tag{47a}$$

where there is one component for every predictor in Eq. (41c). However, we could also decompose r_{CS} through Eq. (41b) and substitute the three components in this decomposition into the fourth term in Eq. (47a) to yield

$$r_{SP} = f_1{}^* + f_4{}^*d_1{}^* + (f_2{}^* + f_4{}^*d_2{}^*)r_{DS} + (f_3{}^* + f_4{}^*d_3{}^*)r_{XS}.$$
(47b)

We could similarly decompose r_{XS} through Eq. (41a) and substitute the two components in this decomposition into the last term in Eq. (47b). With this step the decomposition of r_{SP} would be complete, by which I mean that the total correlation between S and P is decomposed into a sum of products involving only structural parameters ($b_i{}^*$, $d_j{}^*$, and $f_k{}^*$) and exogenous correlations (r_{SD}). This complete decomposition is

$$r_{SP} = f_1{}^* + f_4{}^*d_1{}^* + f_3{}^*b_1{}^* + f_4{}^*d_3{}^*b_1{}^*$$
$$+ (f_2{}^* + f_4{}^*d_2{}^* + f_3{}^*b_2{}^* + f_4{}^*d_3{}^*b_2{}^*)r_{DS}.$$
(47c)

Although there can be a great many components in any one decomposition, there are only four types of effects described by them: direct, indirect, spurious, and unanalyzed effects. A *direct effect* is the influence of a predictor on the outcome net of the influences of all other predictors in the model. It corresponds to the amount of change in the outcome that would be associated with a unit change in the predictor with all other predictors held constant. In Eq. (47c), $f_1{}^*$ is the direct effect on S on P. An *indirect effect* is the influence of a predictor on the outcome through the intervening variables in the model that are caused by the predictor and, in turn, cause the outcome. In Eq. (47c), $f_4{}^*d_1{}^*$ is an indirect effect of S on P through C. There are two other indirect effects in this particular decomposition. In general, there are as many indirect effects as there are intervening paths between the predictor and the outcome. An *unanalyzed effect* is one that is due to an exogenous association between the predictor and some other variable in the structural equation. In Eq. (47c), the last term is the unanalyzed effect; because the exogenous relationship between D and S is part of the product. A *spurious effect*, finally, is the influence of a common cause on both the predictor and the outcome. There is no spurious component in the SP association because S is not determined by any other variable in the model. But the total associations between intervening variables and the outcome have spurious components through their common causes. For example, with the exception of a direct effect, $f_3{}^*$, and an indirect effect through C, $f_4{}^*d_3{}^*$, the remainder of the association between X and P is spurious through the influences of D and S on X and P.

When one is working with a complex model, a decomposition of this sort can help interpret results. This is especially true when there are modifying variables in the model, for in a situation of this sort it becomes difficult to interpret parameters in a simple way. For example, variable X in Eqs. (41a)–(41c) might be equal to the product of S and D. In this situation we can think of S as a strain, D as a specifier of the SP relationship (a special case of which is a dummy variable defining subgroups like men and women), X as the multiplicative interaction of S and D, and C as a control variable. The direct effect of S on P is then equal to $f_1{}^* + f_3{}^* b_1{}^*$—the direct effect of S and its indirect effect through X. To understand why this is the direct effect, it is useful to note that the partial derivative of P with respect to S in Eq. (41c) equals $f_1 + f_3 D$ (under the assumption that $X = D \times S$). This is the amount of change in P that would result from a unit change in S with all other predictors held constant (Stolzenberg, 1980). But notice that it is impossible for *all* other predictors to be constant when S changes by one unit; X, the product of S and D, must change. From Eq. (41a) we see that the change in X equals b_1. Consequently, a typical unit change in S will change P by $f_1 + f_3 b_1$. This is the unstandardized expression of the direct effect given by the first two terms in Eq. (47c).[10]

The indirect effect of S through the intervening variable C can be calculated by using the chain rule for partial derivatives, which expresses the indirect effect as the product of two derivatives, dP/dC and dC/dS. Using Eqs. (41c) and (41a), respectively, the indirect effect is $(f_4) \times (d_1 + d_3 S)$, again noting that $X = D \times S$. Substituting b_1 for S in this expression by using the same sort of reasoning as in the last paragraph, we obtain $f_4 d_1 + f_4 d_3 b_1$, which is the unstandardized expression of the third and fourth terms in Eq. (44c).[11]

[10] The direct effect of S is f_1 when $D = O$ and it increases by f_3 for each unit change in D. At the sample mean it is consequently $f_1 + f_3 \bar{D}$. As the means of all variables are 0 in the standardized case, the direct effect of S here is f_1^* at the sample mean. With the cautions noted above about the necessity of having a defensible zero point, it is clear that this component by itself has no important substantive meaning. In the unstandardized solution, though, the analyst might want to interpret the term f_1 as that part of the influence of S on P that is due to the effect on respondents who lack any modifying resources whatever (that is, whose score on $D = 0$). The term $f_3 b_1$ can then be interpreted as the part of the influence of S on P due to the average variation in the modifying resources available to members of the sample. In the special case where D is a dichotomy, f_2 is equivalent to the residual component in the two-group decomposition of mean differences—the fourth component in Eqs. (35a)–(35b). One can see this by noting that the partial regression of P on D is equal to the difference in the intercepts of the within-group equations, as demonstrated in Eqs. (11)–(12).

[11] In the special case where D is a dichotomy, the unanalyzed effect of D on P through its exogenous association with S is equivalent to the exposure component in the two-group decomposition of mean differences—the first component in Eqs. (35a)–(35b). In

It is more difficult to specify precise expressions for the spurious and unanalyzed effects. Because neither effect is associated with a net change in the outcome variable, differentiation of the structural equations cannot be used to calculate the expressions easily. Instead, one has to derive expressions like that in Eq. (44c) empirically. Parameter estimates from the structural equation models can then be substituted to compute the overall value of each unanalyzed or spurious component. In practice, this is seldom done because the researcher's main interest is in the direct and indirect effects. A conventional procedure is to subtract the sum of these components from the total association to obtain a summary measure of all the spurious and unanalyzed effects together. Significance tests for these components are discussed by Stolzenberg (1980) and Sobel (1982).

CONCLUSIONS

In this chapter I have described the advantages and disadvantages of four nonexperimental research designs: normal population surveys, case-only studies, prospective case-control studies, and retrospective case-control studies. Each of these four has been considered in relation to three research questions that commonly form the basis of research on the relationship between stress and health. These three involve documenting a causal impact of strain, describing the course of adjustment to crisis, and analyzing predictors of adjustment.

Choosing among Designs

The choice among these designs hinges on a variety of theoretical and practical considerations. Perhaps the simplest of these is whether the researcher is fundamentally concerned with studying the range of health outcomes that can result from one particular strain, the variety of risk factors that are associated with one particular illness outcome,

---

the unstandardized case, the expression for the unanalyzed effect is $f_1(b_{SD})$, and the expression for the exposure component is $b_1 (S_2 - S_1)$, where b_1 is the slope of P on S in the group defined by $D = 0$ and $S_2 - S_1$ is the mean difference in S in the two groups defined by $D = 1$ and $D = 0$, respectively. To show that these two expressions are equivalent we merely need to note that f_1, the partial regression of P on S, is equal to the slope of P on S in the subgroup defined by $D = 0$, as demonstrated in Eqs. (11)–(12) and that b_{SD} is equal to the difference in mean levels of S in the two groups defined by D.

or the overall relationship between a number of different strains and a
heterogeneous group of illness outcomes.

In the first of these situations, the appropriate strategy is to use either
a case-only or a prospective case-control design, depending on the
research questions of primary interest. In exploratory research it can be
useful as a first step to work with a combined synthetic and true cohort
case-only design by sampling a cross section of crisis victims and following them over time. When there has been no previous research on
the developmental course of adjustment to the life crisis under consideration, the data obtained from an exploratory study of this sort can be
valuable. In most other cases, a prospective case-control design is superior. This is especially true when the primary research focus is on the
predictors of adjustment. In this situation it becomes mandatory to
obtain information from controls as well as from cases.

When the life event under consideration is relatively common it
might seem preferable to conduct a normal population survey rather
than a prospective case-control study. In one sense this is a good strategy because it solves the problem of finding cases by sampling them
from the population to which results will be generalized. However, it is
an inefficient procedure from the perspective of statistical power, especially when the proportion of cases is much less than 25% of the total
sample. To understand why this is so it is necessary to realize that the
power of a statistical test for a fixed sample size of cases does not
increase meaningfully after the number of controls is about three times
as large as the number of cases (Schlesselman, 1982:145–149). This
means, for instance, that a comparison of the mean difference on some
outcome variable between a sample of 100 cases and 300 controls is
almost as powerful as one based on 100 cases and 3000 controls. The
reason for this can be seen by noting that the variance of a mean difference in two independent samples is

$$\text{var}(\overline{X}_2 - \overline{X}_1) = s_1^2/n_1 + s_2^2/n_2, \tag{48}$$

where s_i^2 is the sample variance of X in sample $i = 1, 2$. As n_2 (the size
of the control sample) becomes very large relative to n_1 (the size of the
case sample), the first term in this equation comes to dominate the total
expression. In the extreme case where n_2 is very large, the second term
becomes essentially zero and the variance approaches the value of the
first term. When this happens, the power of the test will not increase
(the standard error will not decrease) if n_2 is made larger still. Empirical results show that this occurs when the sample of controls becomes
about three times as large as the sample of cases.

Because of this result it makes little sense to sample more than three controls for every case. In a case-control design one can guarantee that this will not be done by establishing at the outset a case-control sampling ratio. In the normal population survey, though, this sort of stratification is seldom carried out. As a result, there are usually many more controls than cases. If the main purpose of the survey is to focus on the effect of one particular type of life event, most of these controls are unnecessary. A case-control design, then, is preferable in that it avoids the collection of these unnecessary interviews.

When the strain to be studied is better described as a continuum of severity than as qualitatively present or absent, a normal population survey becomes much more attractive. A situation of this sort exists in research on the relationship between job strain and health (French et al., 1982). Most workers report at least some job strain, so it makes little sense to conceptualize this type of strain in anything other than continuous terms. As a result, it is difficult to use a case-control strategy, although it is still possible to do so by sampling workers in a small number of occupations that are known to have different amounts of job strain.

When a rare health outcome is of more interest than any particular strain or set of strains, the only feasible strategy is to use the retrospective case-control design. When the outcome is less rare, a normal population survey can be superior. In the normal population survey we obtain information about conditional probabilities of disease onset in the presence or absence of precipitating strains. As noted earlier, this information is lost in retrospective case-control studies. Furthermore, when the normal population survey is administered over time in a longitudinal panel, we are better able to deal with control variables, even those that have not been measured explicitly. This advantage stems from the fact that health can be assessed prior to the occurrence of precipitating events in longitudinal normal population surveys, whereas it is only assessed after the events in case-control studies.

The decision whether to use a retrospective case-control or normal population design in a situation of this sort hinges on the frequency with which the illness outcome appears in the normal population. Information about this is usually available prior to data collection. When considering which design to use, this information should be employed to make explicit calculations of statistical power in the alternative designs (Cohen, 1977). These calculations require the researcher to specify in advance the sort of causal models that will be estimated with the data, the sample size, and the proportion of respondents who will be characterized by the illness. With these values fixed it is possible to calculate the precision with which a statistical parameter of a fixed size can be discriminated from a random component. When these calculations show that a normal population survey of a feasible size is powerful enough to detect effects that are considered substantively significant, we have empirical evidence that the health outcome is not rare in the sense that term was used in the previous paragraph. On the basis of the considerations stated there, the normal population design should be preferred over the retrospective case-control design. When the calculations show that statistical power is too low to detect meaningful effects in the normal population survey, the case-control design is preferred.

When the analyst is more concerned with developing a broad picture of the distribution of strain and illness in the normal population than with any particular strain or illness outcome, the normal population survey design is superior to case-only or case-control designs. And for most purposes a longitudinal survey is preferable to a cross-sectional one. This is especially true when the analysis of life events is a central interest because longitudinal data collection allows the illness outcomes to be measured before events occur. This, in turn, allows unambiguous imputation of causal meaning to the association between events and subsequent change in illness. The situation is more complex for chronic strains, as noted earlier. But even here it does no harm to have data collected over time. In some cases, when the measures of chronic strain change over time, it might even be possible to make some progress in separating the reciprocal effects between stress and health by using lagged measures of the strains as instrumental variables.

Selecting an Analysis Strategy

Once a research design is selected and research questions are framed, there should be little difficulty in selecting the appropriate analysis strategy. The bulk of the chapter has been devoted to a description of the most appropriate strategies for each combination of design and research question. There is no need to summarize these here. It is worth noting, though, that I have glossed over at least two important analysis issues that invariably confront the researcher. The first of these involves problems of conceptualization and measurement. The second involves technical problems that arise when we try to estimate a complex multistage model of the sort typically found in theories of the stress process. I ignored these problems earlier because I wished to focus my discussion on the logic of data analysis rather than on its practicalities. Furthermore, each of these issues is sufficiently complex that a discussion as long as this chapter would be required to do it justice. In this closing section I shall not attempt to begin anything that ambitious, but I shall indicate briefly some sources where the interested reader might find discussions of this sort.

Measurement

As I noted at the beginning of this chapter, the conceptualization of variables is not properly a subject that can be addressed on a narrow methodological level. It is an aspect of theory. Theory and method intersect on the question of validity—whether the variable that one uses in research is really measuring the theoretical construct that one wants to measure. There are no pat answers to this question and I can offer no advice on methodological strategies that make the task of constructing valid measures any less difficult than it is. Methodology proper only comes in when we move beyond this question to the issue of reliability—the extent to which the variable is sensitive to small variations in true values of the underlying construct. It is to this issue that I confine my remarks about measurement.

During the 1970s there was an enormous growth of interest in measurement models. In large part this interest was stimulated by the development of full-information maximum-likelihood methods for the estimation of complex structural equation models that contain both true score equations (those that specify causal relationships among unmeasured variables) and measurement equations (those that specify causal relationships linking observed variables to unmeasured ones). Nontechnical discussions of these methods are readily available (Bentler, 1980; Joreskog and Sorbom, 1979). Furthermore, recent evidence suggests that the likelihood ratio chi-square statistic on which evaluation of these models is based performs well even when the sample is very small (Gwewke and Singleton, 1980), a result that will surely lead to increased use of these models in data sets that previously were considered too thin to warrant their use.

By using these methods it is possible to estimate the sort of causal models I described as appropriate for normal population, case-only, and prospective case-control designs while simultaneously adjusting for unreliability of measurement. Examples of these models can be found in Pearlin et al. (1981) and Elder and Liker (1982). There has also been a good deal of work to develop limited-information and partial-likelihood extensions that can be estimated with weaker assumptions about the form of the data or with incomplete data (e.g., Dempster et al., 1977).

Methods are less well developed for the sort of causal models I described as appropriate for retrospective case-control designs. In large part this is true because the types of variables that have been analyzed to date with models of this sort are well measured—concrete life events and predictors consisting of mostly sociodemographic variables. So there has been no important need to develop extensions that include the possibility of measurement error. However, when all variables in the model can be discretized, logit models can be expressed as log–linear models for contingency tables (Fienberg, 1977:77–90). In this special case one can use latent class formulations of measurement error to derive a true score model (Clogg, 1980).

Estimating Complex Models

As the chapter by Kaplan makes perfectly clear, theories about the stress process are terribly complex—indeed, a good deal more complex than the models that can realistically be estimated empirically. Because of this, most empirical research focuses on only a part of the overall process at once. This is unfortunate, because information about the processual features of the interplay between strain and illness require more comprehensive models (Pearlin et al., 1981).

The major impediment to developing comprehensive models is that multistage models with the many variables that would be required to indicate all the major components of the stress process are unwieldy. This is true in two ways. First, models that contain a great many predictor variables typically yield small and unstable parameter estimates for the individual variables, especially when sets of highly interrelated predictors are included in the prediction equation. This is because the partial effects of individual variables, when all other predictors in the model are controlled, are extremely small. Second, even when causal effects can be estimated precisely, it is difficult to interpret them when there are a great many predictors in the model, each of them contributing in only a small way to the outcome. The sort of decomposition strategies I described earlier become hopelessly complex here, as indirect effects multiply into a mind-boggling array of separately insignificant compound paths of influence.

As of this writing, there has been no readily available solution to these problems. But work on the estimation of block models has made it possible to estimate and interpret models that are much more complex than those that we have worked with up until now. A block model is one in which parameters describing relationships among groups of variables rather than among individual variables are generated. A two-group version, known as a canonical correlation model, has been available for some time (Johnston, 1972:331–334). With the advent of new latent variable structural equation systems it has become possible to generalize the logic from a two-group to an n-group case.

When the analyst is working with a causal model that can be described by one structural equation, it is possible to use block-modeling approaches developed and described by Coleman (1976) or Igra (1979). In these approaches, summary expressions for the overall influences of different groups of predictor variables on a single outcome are developed. In this way, the problem of unstable partial effects of individual variables is resolved by adding them together into theoretically more meaningful composites. The way in which variables are added together is arbitrary in these approaches because they are operationally nothing more than different ways of combining a large number of small-effect coefficients into a smaller number of larger coefficients. This arbitrariness can be overcome when there are multiple outcome variables or multiple stages in the model (as in Figure 6.6). In a situation of this sort the hypothesis, inherent in the creation of blocks, that the relative impact of variables in the block is constant across a range of outcomes can be tested. When this hypothesis cannot be rejected there is an empirical basis for deciding that the variables do, in fact, form a stable block of causal influence. However, the Coleman and Igra approaches are incapable of estimating complex models of this sort.

Marsden (1982a) has developed an approach that is capable of estimating these more complex models. Although it is more expensive and difficult to use than the Coleman and Igra procedures (and so should not be used when there is only a single-outcome variable because, in this case, it has no advantage over the earlier approaches), it allows the researcher to verify empirically if the theoretical blocks of variables specified in his or her model do, in fact, operate as a stable block of causal influence. Marsden has also developed a method that allows total block effects to be decomposed in the same way I earlier described the decomposition of total variable effects.

Interaction terms in these block models are treated in the same way as any other predictors. It is possible to form an entire block that consists of interaction terms. Alternatively, the interaction between two variables in a block can be conceptualized as another variable in that same block. More recently, Marsden (1982b) has developed an extension of his method that allows for the estimation of a single term that defines the interaction between a pair of blocks as well as terms for interactions between a block and individual variables in another block. This is a much more plausible conceptualization than those possible in earlier approaches because here a model in which one block consists of strains, another consists of coping resources, and a third consists of interactions between strains and resources can be estimated. The way is now clear to begin developing comprehensive models of the stress process by conceptualizing blocks in this fashion and by basing analyses on data collected by means of appropriate research designs.

REFERENCES

Allison, P. D.
    1977   "Testing for interaction in multiple regression." American Journal of Sociology 83:144–53.
    1982   "Discrete-time methods for the analysis of event histories." Pp. 61–98 in Samuel Leinhardt (ed.), Sociological Methodology 1982. San Francisco: Jossey-Bass.
Alwin, D. F., and R. M. Hauser
    1975   "The decomposition of effects in path analysis." American Sociological Review 40:37–47.
Augustyniak, S., G. J. Duncan, and J. K. Liker
    Forth-   "Income dynamics and self-conceptions: Linking theory and method in
    coming   models of change." In Glen Elder (ed.), Life Course Dynamics from 1968–1980. New York: Plenum.
Bennett, C. A., and A. A. Lumsdaine (eds.)
    1975   Evaluation and Experiment. New York: Academic Press.
Bentler, P. M.
    1980   "Multivariate analysis with latent variables: Causal modeling." Pp. 419–455 in Annual Review of Psychology. Palo Alto, Calif.: Annual Reviews.
Blanchard, C. G., E. B. Blanchard, and J. V. Becker
    1976   "The young widow: Depressive symptomatology throughout the grief process." Psychiatry 39:394–399.
Bloom, B., S. Asher, and S. White
    1978   "Marital disruption as a stressor: A review and analysis." Psychological Bulletin 85:867–894.
Blot, W. J., and N. E. Day
    1979   "Synergism and interaction: Are they equivalent?" American Journal of Epidemiology 110:99–100.
Bracken, M. B., and M. Bernstein
    1980   "Adaptation to and coping with disability one year after spinal cord injury: An epidemiological study." Social Psychiatry 15:33–41.
Brown, George W.
    1974   "Meaning, measurement, and stress of life events." Pp. 217–243 in Barbara Snell Dohrenwend and Bruce P. Dohrenwend (eds.), Stressful Life Events: Their Nature and Effects. New York: Wiley.
Brown, George W., and Tirril Harris
    1978a   "Social Origins of depression: A Reply." Psychological Medicine 8:577–588.

1978b   Social Origins of Depression: A Study of Psychiatric Disorder in Women. New York: The Free Press.

Burgess, A. W., and L. L. Holmstrom
1979   "Adaptive strategies and recovery from rape." American Journal of Psychiatry 136:1278–1282.

Clayton, P. J., and H. S. Darvish
1979   "Course of depressive symptoms following the stress of bereavement." Pp. 121–136 in James E. Barrett (ed.), Stress and Mental Disorder. New Haven: Raven.

Cleary, Paul D., and Ronald C. Kessler
1982   "The estimation and interpretation of modifier effects." Journal of Health and Social Behavior 23:159–169.

Clogg, Clifford C.
1980   "New developments in latent structure analysis." Pp. 215–248 in David M. Jackson and Edgar F. Borgatta (eds.), Factor Analysis and Measurement in Sociological Research. Beverly Hills, Calif.: Sage.

Cobb, S.
1976   "Social support as a moderator of life stress." Psychosomatic Medicine 38:300–314.

Cohen, Jacob
1977   Statistical Power Analysis for the Behavioral Sciences. Revised Edition. New York: Academic Press.
1978   "Partialed products are interactions; partialed powers are curved components." Psychological Bulletin 85:858–866.

Coleman, James S.
1976   "Regression analysis for the comparison of school and home effects." Social Science Research 5:1–20.

Cook, Thomas D., and Donald T. Campbell
1979   Quasi-Experimentation: Design and Analysis Issues for Field Settings. Chicago: Rand McNally.

Cox, D. R.
1970   The Analysis of Binary Data. London: Methuen.

Cramer, E. M., and M. I. Appelbaum
1980   "Nonorthogonal analysis of variance—Once again." Psychological Bulletin 87:51–57.

Croog, Sydney H., and Sol Levine
1977   The Heart Patient Recovers. New York: Human Sciences Press.

Dempster, A. P., N. M. Laird, and D. B. Rubin
1977   "Maximum likelihood with incomplete data via the EM algorithm." With discussion. Journal of the Royal Statistical Society 140:1–38.

Dohrenwend, B. S.
1980   "The conflict between statistical and theoretical significance (Comment on Ross and Mirowsky)." Journal of Health and Social Behavior 21:291–293.

Dohrenwend, B. S., and B. P. Dohrenwend
1970   "Class and race as status related sources of stress." Pp. 111–140 in Sol Levine and Norman A. Scotch (eds.), Social Stress. Chicago: Aldine.

Dohrenwend, B. S., and B. P. Dohrenwend (eds.)
1981   Stressful Life Events and Their Contexts. New York: Prodist.

Eaton, W. W.
    1978   "Life events, social supports, and psychiatric symptoms: A re-analysis of
            the New Haven data." Journal of Health and social Behavior 19:230–234.
Elandt-Johnson, R. C., and N. L. Johnson
    1980   Survival Models and Data Analysis. New York: Wiley.
Elder, Glen H., Jr., and Jeffrey K. Liker
    1982   "Hard times in women's lives: Historical influences across forty years."
            American Journal of Sociology 88:241–269.
Fienberg, Stephen E.
    1977   The Analysis of Cross-Classified Categorical Data. Cambridge, Mass.: MIT
            Press.
Flinn, Christopher J., and James J. Heckman
    1982   "New methods for analysing individual event histories." Pp. 99–140 in
            Samuel Leinhardt (ed.), Sociological Methodology 1982. San Francisco:
            Jossey-Bass.
French, John R. P., Jr., Robert D. Caplan, and R. Van Harrison
    1982   The Mechanisms of Job Stress and Strain. New York: Wiley.
Glass, Jennifer, Sara McLanahan, and Aage Sorensen
    1982   "The effects of selection bias in studies of the consequences of divorce."
            Paper presented at the Annual Meetings of the American Sociological Asso-
            ciation, San Francisco, 1982.
Greenberg, D. F., and R. C. Kessler
    1983   "Model specification in dynamic analyses of crime deterrence." Pp. 15–32
            in John Hagen (ed.), Deterrence Reconsidered: Methodological Innovations.
            Beverly Hills, Calif.: Sage.
Greenland, S.
    1979   "Limitations of the logistic analysis of epidemiologic data." American Jour-
            nal of Epidemiology 110:693–698.
Grizzle, J. E., C. F. Starmer, and G. C. Koch
    1969   "Analysis of categorical data by linear models." Biometrics 25:489–504.
Gross, A. J., and V. A. Clark
    1975   Survival Distributions: Reliability Applications in the Biomedical Sci-
            ences. New York: Wiley.
Gwewke, J. F., and K. J. Singleton
    1980   "Interpreting the likelihood ratio statistic in factor models when sample
            size is small." Journal of the American Statistical Association 75:133–137.
Hamilton, M. A.
    1979   "Choosing the parameter for a 2 × 2 table or a 2 × 2 × 2 table analysis."
            American Journal of Epidemiology 109:362–375.
Hannan, M. T., and N. B. Tuma
    1979   "Methods for temporal analysis." Pp. 303–328 in Annual Review of Sociol-
            ogy. Palo Alto, Calif.: Annual Reviews.
Hanushek, Eric A., and John E. Jackson
    1977   Statistical Methods for Social Scientists. New York: Academic Press.
Heckman, James J.
    1979   "Sample selection bias as a specification error." Econometrica 47:153–161.
Hogan, M. D., L. L. Kupper, B. M. Most, and J. K. Haseman
    1978   "Alternatives to Rothman's approach for assessing synergism (or antago-
            nism) in cohort studies." American Journal of Epidemiology 108:60–67.

Hudgens, Richard W.
   1974   "Personal catastrophe and depression: A consideration of the subject with respect to medically ill adolescents, and a requiem for retrospective life-event studies." Pp. 119–134 in Barbara Snell Dohrenwend and Bruce P. Dohrenwend (eds.), Stressful Life Events: Their Nature and Effects. New York: Wiley.
Iams, M., and A. Thornton
   1975   "Decomposition of differences: A cautionary note." Sociological Methods and Research 3:341–352.
Igra, A.
   1979   "On forming variable set composites to summarize a block recursive model." Social Science Research 8:253–264.
Johnston, J. J.
   1972   Econometric Methods. Second Edition. New York: McGraw-Hill.
Joreskog, K. G., and D. Sorbom
   1979   Advances in factor analysis and structural equation models. Boston: Abt Books.
Kaplan, B. H., J. C. Cassel, and S. Gore
   1977   "Social support and health." Medical Care 25:47–58.
Kalbfleisch, J. D., and R. L. Prentice
   1980   The Statistical Analysis of Failure Time Data. New York: Wiley.
Kessler, R. C.
   1979   "Stress, social status and psychological distress." Journal of Health and Social Behavior 20:259–272.
Kessler, R. C., and D. F. Greenberg
   1981   Linear Panel Analysis: Quantitative Models of Change. New York: Academic Press.
Kessler, R. C., and H. Stipp
   Forth-   "The impact of fictional television suicide stories on U.S. fatalities." American Journal of Sociology.
   coming
Kubler-Ross, E.
   1969   On Death and Dying. New York: Macmillan.
Kupper, L. L., and D. Hogan
   1978   "Interaction in epidemiologic studies." American Journal of Epidemiology 108:447–453.
LaRocco, J. M., J. S. House, and J. R. P. French, Jr.
   1980   "Social support, occupational stress, and health." Journal of Health and Social Behavior 21:202–218.
Liem, Ramsay, Thomas Atkinson, and Joan Liem
   1982   "Family and personal costs of unemployment." Paper presented at the National Conference on Social Stress Research, University of New Hampshire, Durham, 1982.
Lopata, Helena Z.
   1979   Women as Widows: Support Systems. New York: Elsevier.
Marsden, Peter V.
   1982a   "A note on block variables in multiequation models." Social Science Research 11:127–140.
   1982b   "On interaction effects involving block variables." Paper presented at the annual meetings of the American Sociological Association, San Francisco, 1982.

Miettinen, O.
    1974   "Confounding and effect-modification." American Journal of Epidemiol-
              ogy 100:350–353.
Olsen, Randall J.
    1980   "A least squares correction for selectivity bias." Econometrica 48:1815–
              1820.
Paykel, E. S.
    1978   "Contribution of life events to causation of psychiatric illness" Psychologi-
              cal Medicine 8:245–253.
Pearlin, L. I., M. A. Lieberman, E. G. Menaghan, and J. T. Mullen
    1981   "The stress process." Journal of Health and Social Behavior 22:337–356.
Prentice, R. L., and N. E. Breslow
    1978   "Retrospective studies and failure time models." Biometrika 65:153–158.
Regier, Darrel A., and Gordon Allen
    1981   Risk Factor Research in the Major Mental Disorders: Proceedings of a Con-
              ference, April 3–4, 1980. Washington, D.C.: National Institute of Mental
              Health.
Roos, P. A., and D. J. Treiman
    1980   "DOT scales for the 1970 census classification." Pp. 336–389 in Ann R.
              Miller, Donald J. Treiman, Pamela S. Cain, and Patricia A. Roos (eds.),
              Work, Jobs and Occupations: A Critical Review of the Dictionary of Oc-
              cupational Titles. Washington, D.C.: National Academy Press.
Rothman, K. J.
    1974   "Synergy and antagonism in cause-effect relationships." American Journal
              of Epidemiology 99:385–388.
    1978   "Occam's razor pares the choice among statistical models." American Jour-
              nal of Epidemiology 108:347–349.
Schlesselman, James J.
    1982   Case-Control Studies: Design, Conduct, Analysis. New York: Oxford Uni-
              versity Press.
Silver, R. L., and C. B. Wortman
    1980   "Coping with undesirable life events." Pp. 279–375 in J. Garber and M. E.
              P. Seligman (eds.), Human Helplessness. New York: Acadmic Press.
Sobel, Michael E.
    1979   "Components of a difference between two means: Some statistical tests."
              Working Paper 79–1, Center for Demography and Ecology, University of
              Wisconsin—Madison.
    1982   "Asymptomatic confidence intervals for indirect effects in structural equa-
              tion models." Pp. 290–312 in Samuel Leinhardt (ed.), Sociological Meth-
              odology 1982. San Francisco: Jossey-Bass.
Southwood, K. E.
    1978   "Substantive theory and statistical interaction: Five models." American
              Journal of Sociology 83:1154–1203.
Stolzenberg, Ross M.
    1980   "The measurement and decomposition of causal effects in nonlinear and
              nonadditive models." Pp. 459–488 in Karl F. Schuessler (ed.), Sociological
              Methodology 1980. San Francisco: Jossey-Bass.
Swafford, M.
    1980   "Three parametric techniques for contingency table analysis: A nontechni-
              cal commentary." American Sociological Review 45:664–690.

Taylor, H. F., and C. A. Hornung
     1979   "On a general model for social and cognitive consistency." Sociological
              Methods and Research 7:259–287.
Tennant, C., and P. Bebbington
     1978   "The social causation of depression: A critique of the work of Brown and
              his colleagues." Psychological Medicine 8:565–575.
Thoits, Peggy A.
     1981   "Undesirable life events and psychophysiological distress: A problem of
              operational confounding." American Sociological Review 46:97–109.
Tuma, Nancy Brandon
     1982   "Nonparametric and partially parametric approaches to event-history anal-
              ysis." Pp. 1–60 in Samuel Leinhardt (ed.), Sociological Methodology 1982.
              San Francisco: Jossey-Bass.
Walter, S. D., and T. R. Holford
     1978   "Additive, multiplicative, and other models for disease rates." American
              Journal of Epidemiology 108:341–349.
Wheaton, B.
     1978   "The sociogenesis of psychological disorder: Reexamining the causal is-
              sues with longitudinal data." American Sociological Review 43:383–403.
Winsborough, H. H., and Peter Dickinson
     1971   Components of Negro-White Income Differences. Proceedings of the Social
              Statistics Section. Washington: American Statistical Association.
Wortman, C. B., L. Panciera, L. Shusterman, and J. Hibscher
     1976   "Attributions of causality and reactions to uncontrollable outcomes." Jour-
              nal of Experimental Social Psychology 12:301–316.

Index